Lonely Planet Publications
Melbourne | Oakland | London | Paris

Becky Ohlsen

Seattle

The Top Five

1 Ferry across Puget Sound
Explore the most gorgeous islands in the country on a day trip (p192)

2 Gas Works Park
Great skating, cycling, picnics or hanging out with the locals (p85)

3 Space Needle
Oh, come on, you know you want to see the view from up here! (p63)

4 Pike Place Market
Fresh local produce and Seattle's most colorful citizenry (p55)

5 Pioneer Square
The heart of Seattle is filled with history, restaurants and cafés (p48)

Contents

Published by Lonely Planet Publications Pty Ltd
ABN 36 005 607 983

Australia Head Office, Locked Bag 1, Footscray,
Victoria 3011, ☎ 03 8379 8000, fax 03 8379 8111,
talk2us@lonelyplanet.com.au

USA 150 Linden St, Oakland, CA 94607,
☎ 510 893 8555, toll free 800 275 8555,
fax 510 893 8572, info@lonelyplanet.com

UK 72–82 Rosebery Ave, Clerkenwell, London,
EC1R 4RW, ☎ 020 7841 9000, fax 020 7841 9001,
go@lonelyplanet.co.uk

France 1 rue du Dahomey, 75011 Paris,
☎ 01 55 25 33 00, fax 01 55 25 33 01,
bip@lonelyplanet.fr, www.lonelyplanet.fr

The Author

BECKY OHLSEN

Becky grew up in a microscopic village in the Colorado Rockies, but she has resided in the Pacific Northwest long enough to have moss behind her ears. She's made the three-hour trip from her cloud-covered lair in Portland to Seattle frequently enough that her car can drive itself there now. When not daydreaming over sailboats in Seattle marinas, thrashing fellow newspaper scribes at pinball, scoping the goods at Ohlsen's Scandinavian Foods in Ballard or hiding in a creaky corner of Elliott Bay Books, Becky writes and copy edits for various publications in the Pacific Northwest.

PHOTOGRAPHER
LAWRENCE WORCESTER

After growing up in London through his "pub discovery" years, Lawrence swore off dull and dreary weather forever. However, years spent living in Santa Barbara, California; Manoa Valley, Hawaii; Daytona Beach, Florida; and Yellowstone National Park – as well as years spent traveling in the tropics – grew tiresome, so Lawrence knew it was time to move to Seattle.

Advantages to photographing Seattle off-season? You can sleep in and still catch the sunrise, and you get bellowing fishermen and waterfront dining to yourself. When the sun comes out it's interesting and low on the horizon. The gods must not only be crazy, but occasionally smiling on photographers – every time Lawrence hopped on the ferry into town, the clouds parted and the chorus of singing angels commenced.

Introducing Seattle

Ah, Seattle – glittering jewel on the Sound, or city of grunge? Old-school frontier town, or high-tech headquarters? A collection of villages, or the economic center of the Northwest? Yes, yes and yes: Seattle is all of these things and more. It's a destination as complex and contradictory as it is easygoing.

Head out in a kayak on Lake Union at sunset, breathe in the fresh Northwest air, dock by a lakeside tavern and know you've really earned your beer. Do your grocery shopping in the buzzing hive of mini-transactions that is the famous Pike Place Market, then enjoy a picnic in a park. Slip away on a ferry and cycle around an island in Puget Sound while the rain lashes your face. This is the life, up here in the far northwest corner of the USA.

The snow-capped Olympic mountains rise out of the west across the deep blue waters of Puget Sound, as ships and ferries wind through scattered, green-clad islands. South and east of the city are the massive peaks of the Cascade volcanoes, with Mt Rainier, known in Seattle simply as 'the mountain,' taking up half the horizon. Lakes Union and Washington connect to Puget Sound; water seems to flow around the city in every direction.

The largest city in Washington, Seattle is the core of the USA's Pacific Northwest. Its busy port connects the rest of the nation with the Pacific Rim, and its success as a trade and manufacturing center, mixed with its beautiful, big-as-all-outdoors setting, makes it one of the fastest growing cities in the USA. Young people especially find their way to this seaport, in search of a city that offers economic opportunity, easy access to recreation and forward-looking politics and culture. In short, if you're looking for lifestyle, Seattle has it in spades.

Seattle almost single-handedly made coffee a national obsession. But considering they spend their waking life jacked up on caffeine, the locals are a mellow and laid-back lot. Fitness and outdoor recreation come naturally here, and whether you're climbing mountains or cycling through downtown traffic, there's a healthy respect for the outdoors you don't find in most big US cities. Yeah, sure it rains. OK, it rains a lot. But throw on the proper gear and readjust your attitude, and the rain becomes refreshing.

While many of Seattle's big-ticket attractions – the market, Pioneer Square, the Waterfront – are downtown, Seattle's outlying neighborhoods are distinct enclaves, getting more defined as time goes on. Fremont revels in its quirkiness, Wallingford embraces the solid virtues of an old-fashioned neighborhood, Ballard raises a pint to anyone who will listen and Capitol Hill lovingly embraces any and all forms of sexual orientation. Conversations in the University District cover the gamut from Aldo Leopold's environmental philosophies to where to get a good tattoo. Queen Anne is just so damn good-looking, and Seattle Center keeps a carnival-like atmosphere all year long. Dim sum doesn't get any better than in the International District, and the Central District serves up the best fried chicken this side of the bayou. West Seattle, jutting its shiny nose into the sound, and the neighborhoods along Lake Washington take full advantage of their natural paradise.

These are fine times for the Pacific Northwest's Emerald City. Sure, problems turn up – most noticeably, urban sprawl and traffic snarls caused by the rapid influx of people moving here. But perhaps the best part of Seattle is its contradictions. As much as everyone hates the traffic and the flood of newcomers, longtime residents are gratified that the rest of the world has finally noticed that the good life *is* Seattle.

Lowdown

Population 571,900.
Time zone Pacific Standard Time.
3-star room downtown $200.
Coffee $1.
Grande caffe latte at Torrefazione Italia $3.
Bus fare between downtown sites Free.
Parking ticket $25.
Bottle of water $1.50.
Essential drink Pint of Ballard Bitter for $3.50.
Breakfast 'Jammer' (biscuit) from Grand Central Baking $1.55.

BECKY'S TOP SEATTLE DAY

First things first: a nice, big cup of strong Seattle coffee, preferably accompanied by donuts from the huge new **Top Pot** (p110) next to the Monorail tracks. Then a stroll through the produce stands at **Pike Place Market** (p55), followed by a walk downtown for a leisurely inspection of the shelves at **Elliott Bay Books** (p168). For lunch, a hot turkey sandwich at **Bakeman's** (p110) and some **Pioneer Square** (p48) people-watching. Afterwards it's back up to Belltown to peek into the **Roq la Rue** gallery (p61), take a thrashing from several decades' worth of pinball technology at **Shorty's** (p147), console myself with a beer and, if that works, either see who's playing at the **Crocodile Café** (p61) or cruise out to **Capitol Hill** (p75) or **Ballard** (p86) for further nightlife exploration. If it doesn't, I might just slink off to the **Alibi Room** (p135) and pout at the lovely view of the lights on the water.

Essential Seattle

- **Pike Place Market** (p55) – lose yourself in the labyrinth of market stalls.
- **Pioneer Square** (p48) – dine and dance in the turn-of-the-century heart of town.
- **International District** (p52) – partake of Seattle's Asian heritage with a dim sum lunch.
- **Experience Music Project** (p63) – get experienced at the over-the-top tribute to rock in architect Frank O Gehry's astounding building.
- **Crocodile Café** (p61) – spend an evening in the famous club that helped spawn the band Nirvana – it's still going strong.

City Life

City Life

SEATTLE TODAY

Seattle seems to be emerging from an awkward adolescent stage, marked by growing pains surrounding the rise of grunge and Microsoft and the attention that came from constantly being lauded as one of the country's 'most livable' cities. Now that the national spotlight has dimmed a bit, the callow youth is shaping up to be a sleek sophisticate. Seattle has embraced the spoils of its success in the past few years – fancy new restaurants have cropped up all over the place, the nightlife scene has gone seriously upscale, brand-new condominiums dot former slums. Locals are more likely to strut through Capitol Hill or in Dolce & Gabbana than slouch around in a red flannel shirt.

Hot Conversation Topics

Everyone's talking about politics, war, US foreign policy, the role of the media – Seattleites are a progressive and politically active bunch. In bars and coffee shops, you'll also hear young hipsters talking about their neighborhoods having been 'ruined,' either by an influx of yuppies (Fremont) or an increase in crime (Capitol Hill). There's always chatter about the latest schemes of Paul Allen, and about Microsoft's neverending anti-trust issues. Mostly, though, it's the Seahawks and the Mariners, Mariners, Mariners.

At the same time, the bloom is decidedly off the dot-com rose, and the general US economic downturn of recent years has hit particularly hard in the Pacific Northwest. People are feeling the crunch from the departure of Boeing and its constant layoffs, as well as from cuts in the high-tech industry. So just as Seattleites' tastes have grown toward sophistication, their means have begun to seem rather limited.

An example of how this plays out can be found on restaurant menus: many of Seattle's finer establishments, anxious not to lose customers or sacrifice quality but aware that their former extravagance will no longer go over, have started offering scaled-down, more affordable but still fabulously gourmet bistro or bar menus. It's a compromise, but more than that, it's one way Seattle is settling in to its latest incarnation as a city that's growing up.

CITY CALENDAR

Most travelers choose to visit Seattle in the summer and fall, when the weather is pleasant and rainfall less frequent – the city receives 65% of its precipitation from November to March. September and October are often glorious months, as the Indian summer brings warm days and cool nights. The weather deteriorates after October and can be downright miserable in the dark, drizzly days of December, January and February. Come spring, the rain still drops, but skies lighten and temperatures slowly rise.

If your itinerary brings you to Seattle in winter, all is not lost. Hotel prices drop dramatically and many cultural events, including the symphony, opera and theater, are most active during winter months. Skiers can take advantage of great Northwestern skiing at nearby Snoqualmie Pass and Stevens Pass ski areas.

It's worth noting that Seattle can be very busy in summer and some of the popular sights and ferry trips can get oppressively overcrowded. Off-season travel has its advantages, even if it does mean you'll have to carry an umbrella.

JANUARY
CHINESE NEW YEAR
☎ 206-382-1197

Beginning at the end of January or the start of February and lasting for two weeks, the year's first big ethnic festival is held in the International District; you can call the Chinatown/International District Business Improvement Association for information.

The first day of the new year festival is celebrated with parades, firecrackers, fireworks and plenty of food.

FEBRUARY
FAT TUESDAY
Held the day before Ash Wednesday (usually in early February) the Pioneer Square district embraces its somewhat rowdy reputation on Mardi Gras, when the area convulses with celebration. Music and revelry in bars and restaurants are the main events, although the annual Spam-Carving Contest lends a special Seattle touch.

VALENTINE'S DAY
Held on the 14th. There are lots of theories about why St Valentine is associated with romance, but this is the day to celebrate with a loved one – or a prospective loved one. Most bars, restaurants and hotels have special deals around Valentine's day; check the local papers.

MARCH
ST PATRICK'S DAY
On the 17th the patron saint of Ireland is honored by all those who feel the Irish in their blood, and by those who want to feel Irish beer in their blood. Everyone wears green (otherwise you can get pinched). Irish bars, like Kells, serve green beer and even bars that haven't an Irish trinket in sight get swamped. There's a parade from City Hall to Westlake Center along 4th Ave.

APRIL
CHERRY BLOSSOM & JAPANESE CULTURAL FESTIVAL
☎ 206-684-7200
A celebration of Japanese heritage with performances of music, dance and drama; usually held in early April at the Seattle Center.

MAY
CINCO DE MAYO
The 5th is the day the Mexicans wiped out the French Army in 1862. Now it's the day all Americans get to eat lots of Mexican food and drink margaritas. Seattle celebrates with an annual parade and exhibitions of Hispanic artwork.

OPENING DAY OF YACHT SEASON
Held the first Saturday in May at various locations on Lakes Washington and Union, this Seattle original starts with a blessing of the fleet; it features scull racing and a boat parade through the canals.

SEATTLE INTERNATIONAL CHILDREN'S FESTIVAL
☎ 206-684-7346
Held at Seattle Center in mid-May, this cultural extravaganza includes a wide variety of performances and activities for kids.

NORTHWEST FOLKLIFE FESTIVAL
☎ 206-684-7300; admission free
This festival takes over Seattle Center during Memorial Day weekend. More than 5000 performers and artists from over 100 countries present music, dance, crafts, food and activities.

SEATTLE INTERNATIONAL FILM FESTIVAL
☎ 206-464-5830; www.seattlefilm.com/siff
Held in May and June, this festival brings nearly a month's worth of international film premieres to Seattle. Screenings take place at several theaters.

Public Holidays

National public holidays are celebrated throughout the USA. On public holidays banks, schools and government offices (including post offices) are closed and public transportation follows a Sunday schedule. Plan ahead if you're traveling during many public holidays – flights are full, highways are jammed and on Christmas and Thanksgiving, many grocery stores and restaurants close for the day.

New Year's Day January 1

Martin Luther King Jr Day Third Monday in January

Presidents' Day Third Monday in February

Easter Sunday Falls in March or April

Memorial Day Last Monday in May

Independence Day (Fourth of July) July 4

Labor Day First Monday in September

Columbus Day Second Monday in October

Veterans' Day November 11

Thanksgiving Day Fourth Thursday in November

Christmas Day December 25

Top Five Quirky Seattle Festivals

- **Bumbershoot** (below) – a cultural buffet of music, theater, artwork and poetry on 25 stages.
- **Fremont Fair** (below) – celebrate one of Seattle's quirkiest corners.
- **Winterfest** (p11) – a celebration of all that's cold, furry and white.
- **Trolloween** (in Fremont on Halloween; p82) – just in case regular Halloween isn't weird enough for you.
- **Fat Tuesday** (p9) – a chance to get rowdy and show us your...Spam.

JUNE

FREMONT FAIR
☎ 206-633-4409; www.fremontfair.com
Off-kilter Fremont is just the place you'd want to be for a street fair. The fair features live music, entertainment, food and crafts and is held adjacent to the ship canal usually in mid-June.

FREEDOM DAY CELEBRATION
Seattle's lesbian- and gay-pride event is usually held the last Sunday in June on Capitol Hill. The parade begins along Broadway and continues to Volunteer Park, where there are speeches, music and a rally.

SUMMER NIGHTS AT THE PIER
☎ 206-628-0888
During summer months, outdoor concerts by nationally known music acts are presented by Summer Nights at the Pier. Open-air performances are held on Piers 63–64. Call Ticketmaster for tickets and concert schedule.

JULY

BITE OF SEATTLE
☎ 206-232-2982; www.biteofseattle.com
This culinary celebration is held at Seattle Center, usually the second weekend in July. For a single entry fee, guests can sample foods from dozens of Seattle-area chefs and taste local beers and wines. The evening ends with live music.

SEAFAIR
☎ 206-728-0123; www.seafair.com
Held for three weeks in late July and August, Seafair is an extravagant civic celebration that began as a hydroplane race on Lake Washington. Old families in Seattle jealously maintain their moorages on Lake Washington in order to have the best possible views of these roaring jet boats. Today, however, all manner of festivities extend across all of Seattle and

stretch the event to three weeks. Events include a torchlight parade, an airshow, lots of music, a carnival and even the arrival of the naval fleet. Lodging is in short supply in Seattle on Seafair weekends, so plan accordingly. Unless you want to watch the hydroplane races avoid Seattle on the first weekend in August and don't plan to cross the I-90 or Hwy 520 bridges while the races are in progress (they're closed).

SEPTEMBER

BUMBERSHOOT
☎ 206-281-8111; www.bumbershoot.com
Seattle's biggest arts and cultural event takes over Seattle Center on Labor Day weekend. Hundreds of musicians, artists, theater troupes and writers come from all over the country to perform on the festival's two dozen stages. It's hard not to find something you like. There's also a crafts street fair and lots of good food from local vendors.

NORTHWEST AIDS WALK
☎ 206-329-6923; www.nwaids.org
This incredibly festive and friendly event, held the second weekend in September, grows every year. The 10km or 5km walk starts and finishes at Seattle Center.

WESTERN WASHINGTON FAIR
Mid-September, Puget Sound remembers its agricultural underpinnings at this fair held in Puyallup, south of Seattle. The fair offers a bewildering array of livestock and agricultural displays, a carnival, a home and garden show and live entertainment.

OCTOBER

SEATTLE LESBIAN & GAY FILM FESTIVAL
☎ 206-323-4274; www.seattlequeerfilm.com
Held in the third week of October, this film festival plays at various theaters around town.

NORTHWEST BOOKFEST

www.nwbookfest.org

This annual event, held in the city, draws authors and readers from the Northwest and beyond for panel discussions, readings and a trade show.

HALLOWEEN

On the 31st, kids and adults dress up in scary costumes. In the safer neighborhoods you're likely to see children out 'trick-or-treating' door-to-door for candy. The gay and lesbian bars are especially wild places on Halloween, and Fremont has its own version of the festival, Trolloween (named after the Fremont Troll). It features a candlelight procession of costumed locals on Halloween night, followed by a public dance.

DECEMBER
WINTERFEST

☎ 206-684-7200; www.seattlecenter.com

Seattle Center holds a month-long celebration of holiday traditions from around the globe, starting with Winter Worldfest, a massive concert and dance performance, and continuing with exhibits, dances, concerts and ice skating.

NEW YEAR'S EVE

The place to be on the 31st is Seattle Center, where festivities are focused on the Space Needle. Most people celebrate by dressing up and drinking champagne, or staying home and watching it all on TV. The following day people stay home to nurse their hangovers and watch college football.

CULTURE

Until the 1970s or so, Seattle was a nondescript, midsize city peopled by frontier-stock families with progressive but hardly avant-garde ideas. Then, in the space of one generation, Puget Sound's population more than doubled. The city's collective confidence grew and things started to change.

In the '80s, with the advent of underground music and the hissing sounds of espresso machines, Seattle's locally born idealists, artists and writers began staying home to make their mark instead of heading elsewhere. In fact, they were drawing similar souls from around the country. Seattle seemed like an undiscovered gold mine, and cultural prospectors started mining it in droves.

Still Life Café, Fremont (p84)

Once a town whose economics depended almost solely on Boeing's manufacturing plant, Seattle's financial outlook changed dramatically when high-tech companies, led by Microsoft, realized the brimming pot of gold at the end of the rainbow was right here. The influx of technologically trained Californians and other out-of-state immigrants, who brought with them pop-culture instincts and media savvy, added significantly to the artistic brew.

IDENTITY

Seattleites almost seem to enjoy feeling conflicted. An easygoing bunch, they nevertheless can be driven to violence over principles (witness the December 1999 anti-World Trade Organization riots). Civic leaders constantly struggle to find the next big thing that will put Seattle 'on the map' – but at the same time the city tends to shy away from ambition and fame (ask anyone about grunge and you'll get a horrified shudder). The city's two largest public figures, Bill Gates and Paul Allen, both undeniably ambitious and indisputably successful, are seen simultaneously as points of civic pride and shameless capitalists who are totally alien to the prevailing Seattle culture.

It all starts to make sense when you remember that Seattle loves two things above all else: coffee and beer. Drink enough of both of these clashing beverages at once, and you'll come away with a much better understanding of this complicated city.

Seattle's estimated 2003 population was 571,900, making it the 24th largest city in the US. Seattle's population doesn't reflect the size of the city, whose greater area stretches from Tacoma north to Everett, and from the Kitsap Peninsula east to the Cascades. With a population of 3.5 million, the greater Seattle metro area is the 13th largest in the nation.

According to the most recent US census (2000), Seattle's ethnicity is predominantly white (70.1% of the population). Asian Americans are the largest minority group, representing 13.1% of the population. African Americans comprise 8.4%. Hispanics (5.3%) and Native Americans (1%) are also represented.

Streetcar, Alaskan Way (p207)

Chief Seattle & the Duwamish

'The earth does not belong to human beings; human beings belong to the earth. This we know. All things are connected like the blood that unites one family. All things are connected. Whatever befalls the earth befalls the sons and daughters of the earth.'

These words, part of a speech by Seattle's namesake, Chief Sealth (anglicized to 'Seattle') of the Duwamish tribe, would become a cornerstone in the New Age, environmental-preservation philosophy that is almost the default belief in the Pacific Northwest. In many ways, the interactions between white settlers and the natives who lived on the land for thousands of years before they arrived have been ugly, conflicted, rife with violence and unfairness. But if the people who settled in the Pacific Northwest have absorbed anything from the pre-existing Indian cultures, it's a sense of reverence for nature and the surrounding wilderness – even though that reverence is frequently ineffective and often comes across as hypocritical in light of history.

'How can you buy or sell the sky, the warmth of the land?,' Chief Seattle continued in his most famous speech, delivered at a gathering of natives and white settlers, which included territorial governor Isaac Stevens, who was attempting to purchase Puget Sound land from the area's native inhabitants. This 1855 address is considered one of the masterpieces of Native American oratory, although the standard text of the speech was penned 30 years later from notes by a literary-minded surgeon who attended the event. 'This idea is strange to us. If we do not own the freshness of the air and the sparkle of the water, how can you buy them? Every part of this earth is sacred to my people. Every shining pine needle, every sandy shore, every mist in the dark woods, every clearing and humming insect is holy in the memory and experience of my people...'

The Seattle area was originally the homeland of the Duwamish tribe, whose culture was deeply linked to the salmon that made seasonal runs on the Green and Duwamish Rivers. A peaceful tribe, the Duwamish initially welcomed members of the Denny party when they arrived in 1851. The white settlers received permission from the Duwamish to build their first structures on the site of a summer camp that the area's native inhabitants called Duwamps – the name that the settlers applied to their little town as well.

Chief Seattle (1786–1866) urged peaceful coexistence between the people of his tribe and the whites, and he encouraged the Duwamish to work side by side with the settlers building houses, cutting trees and laying out streets. Relations with other tribes along Puget Sound were not as good. To address growing hostilities, the US government drew up a treaty in 1854 granting area tribes $150,000 in goods and 2600 acres of reservation land in return for vacating 2 million acres of prime real estate in western Washington, including the present-day Seattle area. Distrust and anger soon broke out, and in 1855 warfare erupted between the natives and white settlers.

Chief Seattle persuaded the Duwamish not to become involved in the conflict, but the settlement at Duwamps was besieged by a group of hostile Indians, forcing the settlers to take shelter in the town's small stockade. A visiting navy sloop, the *Decatur,* fired its cannons into the forest above the little town to frighten the Indians away. In retaliation, the Indians burned and looted nearly all of the settlements on Puget Sound.

In the end, the settlers prevailed and one of the Indian rebel leaders, Leschi, was captured, tried and hanged for murder.

The Duwamish were moved to the Port Madison Reservation in 1856, despite their peaceable history. In part to recognize Chief Seattle's aid and pacifist efforts, the settlers renamed their town in the chief's honor. Apparently Chief Seattle was not exactly pleased with the honor: According to Duwamish beliefs, if someone utters a dead person's name, the soul of the deceased is denied everlasting peace.

The city's cultural demographics echo its history. Seattle's first settlers were mostly white colonialists who migrated west from towns along the US eastern seaboard. Later, Scandinavians came to work in the Ballard sawmill and used their seagoing skills to fish in Puget Sound.

During WWII, the demand for airplane manufacturing and shipbuilding brought tens of thousands of new workers to the region, especially African Americans. But today only 52,000 African Americans live in the Seattle area and the population is mostly focused on the Central District. Hispanics have been slow to move to Seattle, unlike other West Coast cities.

The largest group of Native Americans in urban Seattle continues to be the Duwamish, the tribe that originally lived on the shores of Elliott Bay. The Duwamish were given a land grant on the Kitsap Peninsula, but many have returned to their rightful homeland in present-day Seattle. Other Native Americans representing tribes throughout Washington have moved to Seattle for economic opportunity and education.

Though Seattle's population grew 10% between 1990 and 2000, the city is still racially segregated, with most whites and minorities residing in distinct neighborhoods. The segregation is

Bill Gates: Sugar Daddy?

What does it mean when Bill Gates, the richest man on earth, says on national television that poverty is a 'failure of capitalism'? The co-founder of Microsoft, William Gates III, born October 28, 1955, has publicly pledged to give away 95 percent of his wealth – $46 billion as of September 2003. And he seems to be following through, having shown a sincere interest in global health issues. The Bill & Melinda Gates Foundation has given $638.9 million to date for global HIV/AIDS and TB health programs (combined). However pervasive the Windows operating system may be, the man behind it seems more interested in leaving a different kind of legacy.

Gates grew up in Seattle's upper-class Laurelhurst neighborhood and began developing software at the age of 13. In college at Harvard, he hung out in the computer lab and whipped up programming language for the world's first microcomputer. Eventually he dropped out of Harvard and hooked up with his buddy Paul Allen; the two went on to develop DOS, then the Windows operating systems.

At age 37, Gates became the second-richest man in the USA and, soon after, the richest man in the world, with a fortune estimated at $48 billion. From Luther Burbank Park on the northeast corner of Mercer Island, you can see his mansion across the lake if you know where to look. But you'd better get a glimpse while you can – he might just give it away.

particularly acute for African Americans, and bouts of class-tinged violence have erupted over everything from funding for schools to race discrimination in the workplace. The migration of a highly educated, generally white workforce to Seattle hasn't helped. Racial prejudices remain an unspoken undercurrent.

Seattle is a young city. Nearly 38% of its population is between the ages of 25 and 44. Young people poured into the city in droves in the late '90s, finding not only new music, fashion and attitude, but also very high-paying jobs. Though it's tougher than it once was, software engineers right out of college can still land jobs with salaries nearing six figures. This is most apparent when you see a guy in sneakers and a university sweatshirt dialing into his palm pilot to check on the NASDAQ. At a bar, you may be very surprised to find that the shabbily dressed, green-haired woman standing next to you is actually a software developer at Microsoft.

Seattle ranks second only to San Francisco for the smallest percentage of children in a large city. This is attributed to the influx of young professionals, who are waiting longer to start families and whose high earning capacity has helped drive Seattle housing prices up; families are now migrating to the suburbs in order to find affordable homes.

Despite its issues of cultural segregation and growth, Seattle remains a casual and laid-back city. Seattleites are friendly and unpretentious and, despite the rain, cherish their city's outdoorsy way of life.

LIFESTYLE

In keeping with the city's contradictory nature, the typical Seattle lifestyle is decidedly casual on the outside but serious when it counts. People here, famously, will stand and wait several minutes rather than cross a street against the light; this was originally due to a harsh jaywalking law, but now it's just habit. Working life seems similarly laidback. Suits are less common than khakis, even in the business district; most

Satisfaction Records, U District (p174)

Body Art & Accessories

The practices of tattooing and body piercing exploded in popularity nationwide in the late 1980s, and Seattle is still one of the leaders in this trend. If you feel inclined to join in or add to your collection of body embellishments while you're here, there are plenty of places throughout the city that would be happy to oblige you.

Before you go under the needles, however, you should check out the establishment carefully. Make sure it is licensed, that all equipment is autoclaved and that the general environment of the shop is clean. You never want to make hasty decisions when it comes to tattoos, and you should know that most reputable parlors won't tattoo if you're drunk. Think about your preferred design and research the artists and their work. Don't be shy about consulting with an artist; if you aren't satisfied or don't like the vibe, go somewhere else. Finally, if you're wondering about tattoo removal, you shouldn't get one in the first place; the technology of tattoo removal is expensive, painful and not very effective.

Most tattoo prices vary according to the color, location and difficulty of the design, though for most of the following businesses, rates average about $100 to $120 an hour, with a minimum cost of $35 to $50. Piercings generally run $30 per hole for things like eyebrows and cheeks, and you'll need to choose jewelry, which typically runs $15 and up. The more intimate the body part, the more you're going to pay (possibly in more ways than one!).

Most shops are in Capitol Hill, Pike Place Market and the U District. The following list includes those with the best reputation among young Seattle hipsters.

Anchor Tattoo This immaculate operation has two stores, one in **Ballard** (Map p248; ☎ 206-784-4051; 5317 Ballard Ave NW; ☽ noon-8pm Sun-Thu, noon-10pm Fri-Sat) and one in the **U District** (Map pp244-5; ☎ 206-524-6466; 5006 University Way NE; ☽ noon-8pm). It does a variety of tattoos but no piercings.

Mind's Eye Tattoo (Map pp244-5; ☎ 206-522-7954; 5206 University Way NE; ☽ 1-9pm Mon-Sat, noon-6pm Sun) At this U District shop, co-owner Reverend Eric Eye performs a variety of services, such as weddings, baptisms and funerals – and tattoos. Open since 1992, this was the first tattoo shop in the U District and remains the most reputable. It does not do piercings.

Rudy's Barber Shop (Map pp242-3; ☎ 206-329-3008; 614 E Pine St; ☽ 9am-9pm Mon-Sat, 11am-5pm Sun) Wildly popular with gay men and hipsters for both piercings and tattoos, Rudy's on the Pike-Pine Corridor on Capitol Hill started the trend of the rock-and-roll barber shop.

Vyvyn Tattoos (Map pp238-9; ☎ 206-622-1535; 1516 Western Ave, in Pike Place Market; ☽ 11am-7pm) One of the foremost modern female tattoo artists, Vyvyn Lazonga has earned nationwide recognition. Call ahead to book a tattoo appointment.

people fall into that particularly Northwest fashion niche of jeans, hiking boots and polar fleece (thanks, REI). But the fact that they're wearing sneakers and denim shouldn't fool anyone into thinking Seattleites aren't pulling long hours at intense, high-stress jobs. A quick stroll through the Microsoft campus will put that suspicion to rest. In high-tech jobs in the Northwest, people tend to burn out within a few years.

If they work hard, they play hard too. Everyone in Seattle seems to go out all the time, even if only for an after-work happy hour. Bars are more crowded on Friday and Saturday nights but never really empty. Seattle loves its microbrews – almost as much as it loves its coffee. A visitor could be forgiven for wondering just who all these people *are* who are sitting in coffee shops for hours in the middle of a workday. The answer? They could be dot-com casualties, self-employed business consultants, students, writers – whatever they are, they all seem to have laptops with WiFi capability.

FOOD

Two things are particularly noteworthy when it comes to food in Seattle. The first is Northwest cuisine's reliance on the best of what the region produces – seafood so fresh it squirms, fat berries freshly plucked, mushrooms dug out of the rich soil, cornucopias of fruits and vegetables. Using these ingredients in a way that flatters, not disguises, them is the essence of Northwest cuisine.

The second notable thing about eating in Seattle is the blessed abundance of vegan and vegetarian restaurants. Here, strict vegetarians will not find themselves in that familiar situation

Savage Lovin' in Seattle

Born in Chicago in 1964, Dan Savage migrated to Seattle in 1990 and worked as a reporter for Seattle's the *Stranger* from its inception in 1991; he has since become its editor. The weekly paper is Seattle's outlet for political outrage, its medium for critiquing everything from city planning to music and arts. Dan started writing Savage Love – a sex advice column whose frank language and 'taboo' subject matter pushed the limits like no other before it – as a comical and nudging way of waking Seattle up to its sexuality, be it homosexual or heterosexual. By 1993 the column was roaring into syndication and started appearing in newspapers all over the USA and Canada. Dan's popularity as a controversial and confrontational tell-all from both sides of the sexual-orientation fence grew, and soon he had a regular spot on National Public Radio, was getting booked for public appearances and getting more 'feedback' mail than he could possibly read.

Though he says Savage Love started as a joke, Dan asserts that growing up gay in a primarily heterosexual world makes you think about sexuality and gender in ways other kids don't. 'When sex is what makes you different, you think about it more,' he says. 'In fact, that's the price of admission for gay people – thinking about gender and sexuality.' Savage Love brought previously hushed straight and gay sex issues into the wide open; Dan's explicit advice sent shock waves through a world still blushing and tittering over Dr Ruth. Savage Love draws criticism from outraged readers, who accuse Dan of intentionally invoking shock value, but Savage Love isn't that menacing or deliberate. Instead, it's just one guy's way of taking the taboo out of sex and homosexuality. Dan's take is that being gay or being sexually active shouldn't make you have to shut up.

But Dan's not all sex and dirty talk. Along with his partner Terry (whom he met at Seattle's Re-Bar in the early 1990s), he is a parent. After a long and extensive adoption process, Terry and Dan finally adopted a boy, DJ, in 1998. Savage tells the story in his book *The Kid: What Happened After My Boyfriend and I Decided to Get Pregnant*. Now, like any other parent, Dan balances a relationship, a child and his work. While Terry stays home with DJ, Dan commutes to work every day on the ferry from his home on a Puget Sound island. He has expanded his repertoire significantly, writing frequently about politics and the larger social scheme with the kind of political-is-personal attitude that harks back to the days of Tom Wolfe-style New Journalism.

What does Dan have to say about Seattle's gay scene? 'There's nothing self-conscious about it, it just is,' he says. Nongay Seattle's open and generally accepting attitude toward homosexuality keeps the gay scene open and generally accepting of nongays. You'll find every member of the sexual gamut in a lesbian venue, for example, women are welcome at gay male bars and so on. 'This is a great town to be gay in, mostly because the straight people are so remarkable,' says Dan. 'Gay people remade straight people, and straight people allowed themselves to be remade.'

of looking at a four-page menu and settling, in despair, on the house salad. Chefs in Seattle can be incredibly inventive when dreaming up vegetarian options that satisfy even carnivores, the kind of dishes that you might not even notice are veggie because the meat is simply not missed. Of course, Seattle also loves a good steak – but it's nice to know that vegetarians have a vast number of options and won't be stuck nibbling carrot sticks and baked tofu to survive their visit.

Check out the Eating chapter (p105) for a full run-down on places to eat in Seattle.

FASHION

Once upon a time, Seattle ruled the freak-fashion world. Even as late as the early '90s, youth culture was marked by bizarre, usually homemade, always parent-upsetting fashion creations that expressed...*something,* whether it was angst, sexuality, gloom or simple frustration. Then came grunge, the fashion that ate itself. It's odd to imagine an aesthetic so absent of effort would be so easily and instantly co-opted by the mainstream, but it was – very soon after Nirvana hit it big, major fashion designers were dressing catwalk models in ripped clothes, longjohns and unwashed hair. It's almost no wonder Seattle has opted for more of a Banana Republic–Nordstrom brand of chic over anything new that might call attention to itself.

Still, it's fairly easy to find pierced, dyed and tattooed specimens here, mostly in Capitol Hill, Belltown and the U District. The young and hip will dress to the nines to go out on the town – whether that means satin and heels, plaid zippered bondage pants or a perfectly aged, faded-black vintage Aerosmith T-shirt. But, for the most part, Seattle's day-to-day fashion seems to have lost its edge and softened, preferring the comfortable and practical over the weird, funky or runway-ready. Go to the Shopping chapter (p165) for more.

MEDIA

Seattle's major daily newspapers are the morning *Seattle Post-Intelligencer* (usually called the *PI*) and the afternoon *Seattle Times*. They run under a joint-operating agreement, meaning the advertising and business sections cooperate while the editorial elements of the papers compete; it's been contested in a spate of lawsuits recently, and the future of Seattle as a two-newspaper town is uncertain.

Seattle has a lively alternative publishing scene, led by one of the best alt-weeklies in the nation, the *Stranger*. Started by former midwesterner Tim Keck, it's a valuable source for an irreverent take on politics, underground culture, film and music information and is a great guide to the clubs. It's edited by 'Savage Love' columnist Dan Savage, see opposite.

The *Seattle Gay News,* referred to mostly as *SGN,* covers the gay and lesbian scene. The *Seattle Weekly* is the baby-boom generation's alternative news; it has full listings of arts and entertainment and investigative pieces exposing city hall's bad guys.

The University of Washington's news-oriented National Public Radio (NPR) affiliate is heard on KUOW at 94.9 FM (which also carries the BBC World Service). See the Directory chapter (p203) for a list of Seattle's favorite commercial radio stations.

LANGUAGE

English is by far the dominant language of Seattle, but many foreign tongues can be heard floating in the air. In the International District you'll hear a wide mix of Asian languages – these include Japanese, Chinese, Korean, Vietnamese and Laotian, to name a few. In Ballard, it's more common to hear Scandinavian languages spoken on the streets. Throughout town you'll hear little bits of Spanish and Portuguese mixed in with Slavic languages.

ECONOMY & COSTS

More so than many US cities, Seattle has been dependent on a modest number of extremely large companies for much of its economic history. While the economy has certainly diversified since the days when Boeing was the only major concern in town, a handful of large corporations still accounts for a significant portion of the local economy. Even though Boeing is still a major employer, high-tech jobs represent the other pillar of the Seattle economy, and both have taken a significant hit during the recent nation-wide economic slump. Microsoft, now the world's largest software manufacturer for personal computers, employs only 22,000 people at its growing 'campus' in Redmond on the Eastside, but its presence alone has encouraged many of the other high-tech firms – Amazon.com, Adobe, and RealNetworks for example – to call Seattle home.

The Port of Seattle is another big employer. Seattle ranks as the third-largest port on the US West Coast in total tonnage. Washington is the nation's fifth-largest exporting state, and one in four jobs depends to some degree on international trade. The University of Washington employs a large number of people, as do

How Much?

- **Taxi** from the airport to Pike Place Market $35
- **Adult ticket up the Space Needle** $12.50
- **King salmon** at the Flying Fish, Belltown $18.25
- **Super burrito** from Bimbo's Bitchin' Burrito Kitchen $7
- **Dorm bed** at the HI hostel $24
- **Happy-hour drinks** at the Noc Noc $1
- **Ticket to Theater Sports** improv competition at the Market Theater $10
- **Adult admission to the Egyptian Cinema** $9
- **Live music cover** on Saturday night at the Crocodile café $8-10

area hospitals and city and county governments. The federal government employs some 200,000 people, largely in the five military bases that ring Puget Sound. Biotechnology is also a key player in the Seattle economy.

The average visitor can expect to spend about $200 to $300 a day in Seattle, with the bulk of that money going towards accommodation; obviously travelers staying in a youth hostel or a budget hotel will spend substantially less. Most museums have free days or free afternoons; check individual reviews in the Neighborhoods chapter for details. Also, if you're planning to see all the major sights, consider buying a CityPass (p42), which gets you in free to several of Seattle's major attractions.

GOVERNMENT & POLITICS

Seattle is governed by a mayor and a nine-person city council. All city council members are elected on an at-large basis, meaning they are not assigned to a specific council district (this may soon change; efforts to move to a district system have begun to gather force). Although city posts are nonpartisan, politics in Seattle dependably veers to the left-leaning side of the Democratic Party. Greg Nickels was elected mayor in 2001.

Seattle's spectacular economic and population growth during the '90s altered the city's political landscape in ways that still cause problems. Partly due to the explosive growth of Microsoft – and the sudden young millionaires its stock options created – Seattle faced outrageous real estate bidding wars and a glut of traffic.

Transportation is still one of the city's thorniest issues. With the Puget Sound area's population growing fast, the transportation infrastructure simply isn't holding up. Traffic jams are often horrendous, due partly to topography but also to the lack of effective planning for public transport. Voters continually swing back and forth in support of funding light-rail commuter trains, but inevitably a glitch rears its ugly, and often political, head, keeping the construction at bay. Repeatedly voters have approved feasibility studies for expanding the World's Fair Monorail; this idea finally won official approval in 2003 and looks like a go, but whether it will solve the worst of the gridlock problems remains to be seen.

The skyrocketing cost of housing in Seattle is also a major political and social concern. Seattle is playing catch-up with urban growth and land-use planning; the city's rapid growth, especially on the Eastside, has turned thousands of acres of farmland into anonymous tract developments, and the suburbs are rolling up to the foothills of the Cascades. In the Bellevue suburb of Medina, where Bill Gates built his 48,000-sq-ft mansion, a limit is now enforced on how many 'mega houses' are allowed.

Another political concern stemming from the city's growth is how to preserve the city's livability. Voters imposed a cap on building height in the early 1990s, seeking to prevent the downtown area from turning into an increasingly sterile enclave of towering business complexes. However, as high-tech towns across the country are realizing, when you've got a lot of people with a lot of money to spend, you have to keep building to accommodate them all.

Present in all of these issues are two contradictory themes: the first preserves the environment, the community and civic virtue, while the other takes pride in building bigger and better, going beyond the backwater Seattle of yesteryear. The odd thing is that these polar themes are not as evident in the polls as they are, to varying degrees, in each citizen.

ENVIRONMENT

Environmental issues in many ways dominate life in the Pacific Northwest. Seattle was founded on resource-extractive industries; the city's first major employer was a sawmill, and the ability to export the area's wealth in timber was key in the city's development. Fishing Puget Sound and the area's rivers for salmon was also a major source of employment, especially for immigrant workers from Japan and Scandinavia. Today, endangered fish runs, especially of seagoing salmon, top the list of environmental concerns. While

jet manufacturing and software dominate Seattle's present economy, the older resource-based industries continue to be an active feature of the city's economic and political landscape.

THE LAND

Seattle sits right alongside the Cascadia Subduction Zone, one of the earth's most active seismic regions. Beneath the Strait of Juan de Fuca, two tectonic plates – the North American Plate and the Juan de Fuca Plate – struggle against each other, grinding away as the North American Plate slides underneath, causing pressure to build and the earth to rumble. The most recent of these rumblings happened on February 28, 2001, when an earthquake measuring 6.8 on the Richter scale rocked the Seattle area. The quake caused one death, rang up more than $2 billion in damages and caused some dramatic geological change. The earthquake narrowed the Duwamish River by a few inches, shifted Seattle about a fifth of an inch to the south-southwest and pushed the Eastside about a third of an inch further east.

A snapshot of this area taken 60 million years ago would show a vista of jumbled offshore islands, low coastal mountains and marine marshlands invaded by the shallow Pacific. Plants and animals thrived in the tropical climate, which extended inland unobstructed by mountains. Coastal sediments and offshore islands started wedging together, forming today's Olympic Range and setting the stage for three intense periods of volcanic activity, which would utterly change the face of the region. The line of volcanoes that shot up as the Cascade Range caused enormous explosions of lava, ash and mud. The region's most recent volcanic activity drew worldwide attention in 1980 when Mt St Helens, just 150 miles south of Seattle, blew her top, killing 55 people and spreading ash through five states and three Canadian provinces. Volcanic activity continues in the region.

The land on which Seattle now stands was once dense forest, and the waters of Puget Sound and the freshwater lakes that surround the city once teemed with wildlife. While metropolitan Seattle hardly accounts for a natural ecosystem, you don't have to go far from the center of the city to find vestiges of the wild Pacific Northwest.

GREEN SEATTLE

In keeping with its 'green' reputation, Seattle has one of the most comprehensive curbside recycling programs in the USA. Depending on where Seattleites live, their recycling is picked up either weekly or monthly; the cost is included in the price of regular garbage collection. Recycling here is easy; as such, you won't find anyone chucking a tin can or ditching a plastic bottle. Coffee drinkers basically boycott styrofoam, and don't be surprised if somebody scolds you for littering.

Even if you're just visiting and don't have access to curbside recycling, it's easy to find a place to recycle the cans, bottles and papers that accumulate as you travel. Most public areas and food courts will have separate recycling bins for various kinds of products.

Other contentious environmental issues that get locals' ire up include the history and continued practice of logging in old-growth forests; the fate of endangered salmon; and the much-publicized protection of the endangered spotted owl and its natural habitat.

Arts

Arts

Seattle is the cultural center of the Pacific Northwest. Always known as a city of readers (with more bookstores per capita than any other US city), it is increasingly home to a stable of internationally recognized writers. Musically, it has become a hotbed of cutting-edge bands and clubs. The city's visual arts are also dynamic, as its cultural strands – from Native American and Asian to contemporary American – meet and transfuse on canvas, in glass and in sculpture. For more information on venues for the arts, see the Entertainment chapter (p129).

MUSIC
ROCK & ALTERNATIVE

Pioneering Northwest rock bands like the Kingsmen, the Sonics and Seattle's own legendary Jimi Hendrix helped define rock 'n' roll in the '60s. Local groups like Heart and the Steve Miller Band made it big in the '70s. Blues musician Robert Cray and saxophonist Kenny G gained notoriety during the '80s. The media represented none of these artists as being Seattle musicians per say. Not until the city's grunge boom in the '90s did the rest of the world turn to Seattle as the origin of a unique sound.

Grunge is best described as a guitar- and angst-driven derivative of the punk rock scene, but calmer. Grunge grew out of garage rock, where dudes with nothing else to do jammed in their garages because, before grunge, there were few places to rock out in Seattle. These days, there's still a very active local rock scene, though it no longer has the cohesive sound that marked most of the important bands during the grunge years. The core of what's ultra-hip in Northwest music these days has moved slightly south, to Olympia, home of riot grrls, indie-rock and renowned music scribe Greil Marcus' favorite band, Sleater-Kinney. Nobody in Seattle seems very upset about seeing the music-industry spotlight move somewhere else for a change. Still, music fans in Seattle continue to support local bands; there's a new or established group playing somewhere in the city virtually every night of the week.

Grunge Then & Now

'You trendy grunge people suck!' Scribbled with black marker onto the white T-shirt of an anonymous girl at a rock show, this declaration, captured in a now-emblematic photo by Northwest documentarian Alice Wheeler, became an epitaph of sorts for the music scene that had put Seattle on the national media radar.

The photo was taken in 1993; by then, the good years were over. Nirvana's Kurt Cobain would be dead the following year of a self-inflicted gunshot wound. 'Grunge' and 'alt-rock' had been packaged by major labels and corporate radio stations into slick, homogenous, easily marketed slices of pseudo-counterculture, safe enough to be sold in Wal-Mart stores. T-shirts emblazoned with the word 'Loser' – produced by Seattle independent record label Sub Pop, which put out Nirvana's *Bleach* album and launched most of the major grunge bands – were being worn with pride by frat boys who would never really understand what the term meant. Pop culture magazines from Spin to Vogue were leaping on the grunge bandwagon, drooling over bands who bore the Official Grunge seal of approval (Nirvana, Pearl Jam, Screaming Trees, Soundgarden) while ignoring other Seattle musicians doing equally interesting things – Bikini Kill, Sir Mix-A-Lot, Young Fresh Fellows.

Meanwhile, Seattle cut its hair, folded up its plaid flannel shirts and pawned its Superfuzz distortion pedals. By the time everyone else realized the city had sparked a major creative force that would shape rock music for years to come, the people who started it all had grown bored, disgusted or disillusioned and moved on. But the mainstream popularity of the grunge movement, difficult as it often was for Seattleites to handle, had a vital impact on the cultural life of the city. It left in its wake a bunch of new clubs, and it drew musicians and music fans to the city from all over. Many of these people have since started their own bands, and the scene continues, albeit without the questionable benefit of working under the glare of the national media spotlight.

CLASSICAL

Seattle offers a full array of classical music, including well-respected professional symphony and opera companies. The Seattle Symphony is regarded as a major regional orchestra and its downtown performance hall, the **Benaroya Concert Hall** (p46), is as gorgeous as it is acoustically exquisite. The Northwest Chamber Orchestra is the Northwest's only orchestra that focuses on period chamber music; the group performs at various venues throughout the city.

The Seattle Opera is another major cultural focus in Seattle. For a regional company it isn't afraid to tackle weighty or nontraditional works; productions of Philip Glass and a summer *Wagner's Ring* cycle have given opera lovers a lot to mull over. However, the company is perhaps most noted for its unconventional stagings of the traditional repertoire. The Seattle Men's Chorus, a 180-member gay chorus, delights audiences with its 30 concerts each year.

For more information see Opera, Classical Music & Dance, p152.

Seattle Grunge Primer

If you managed to miss the whole 'grunge' thing and aren't quite sure what kind of music it is, how it sounds, or just what the big fuss was all about, here is a shortlist of five representative albums to act as a sort of Cliff's Notes guide to the genre. Just be aware that if you go to a record store in Seattle and walk up to the checkout counter with this selection in your hands, the clerk will almost certainly laugh at you.

- *Superfuzz Bigmuff* (Sub Pop), Mudhoney – released in 1988, the catchy debut single, 'Touch Me I'm Sick,' became an instant grunge classic.
- *Bleach* (Sub Pop), Nirvana – the sizzling precursor to *that* album.
- *Nevermind* (Geffen), Nirvana – grunge anthem 'Smells Like Teen Spirit' may have been named after a deodorant, but it still rocks even by today's standards.
- *Ten* (Epic), Pearl Jam – for the definitive Pearl Jam sound listen to the awe-inspiring 'Alive'
- *Badmotorfinger* (A&M), Soundgarden – the metal side of grunge.

JAZZ & BLUES

A lot of Seattle residents aren't aware that their city had a thriving jazz and blues scene back in the day. There were raging clubs all along Jackson St in Pioneer Square in the 1930s and '40s, and the young (*too* young, actually, but scrappy and talented enough to get away with

Seattle Art Museum (p47)

it) Quincy Jones and his pal Ray Charles would hustle their way into all the clubs and play as much as they could. Nothing of that caliber exists in Seattle anymore, but you can still hear some good jazz and blues, both in Pioneer Square clubs like the **Central Saloon** (p133) and at places like **Tula's** (p133) and **Dimitriou's Jazz Alley** (p133).

Top Five Books

- *Heavier than Heaven,* Charles Cross (2001) – editor of the defunct music zine the *Rocket,* Cross uses his nearly unrestricted access to paint a moving portrait of Nirvana's Kurt Cobain.
- *Indian Killer,* Sherman Alexie (1996) – in Alexie's most controversial book, a series of scalping murders of white men threatens to destroy the Indian community.
- *Waxwings,* Jonathan Raban (2003) – elegant travel writer Raban illuminates Seattle's recent high-tech boom in a novel that tells the parallel stories of two immigrants.
- *The Terrible Girls,* Rebecca Brown (1992) – one of Seattle's most prominent writers dissects the complicated hearts of women in this experimental collection of short stories about lesbian relationships.
- *Another Roadside Attraction,* Tom Robbins (1971) – a mainstay of the Pacific Northwest counterculture, Robbins' wacky word carnival imagines Jesus alongside a flea circus at a pit stop.

LITERATURE

The pioneers of early Seattle had city building on their minds, and didn't exactly fill libraries with weighty tomes. Nonetheless, some of the city's first settlers took time to record chronicles. In 1888 Arthur Denny, one of the founders of Seattle, wrote *Pioneer Days on Puget Sound* (1908); James Swan wrote *The Northwest Coast* (1869) and *Indians of Cape Flattery* (1870) during the 1850s. *The Canoe and the Saddle* (1863) by Theodore Winthrop recounts a young man's trip across Washington on his way to Seattle in 1853.

One of the most prolific Seattle writers in the early 20th century was Archie Binns. Of his many novels, *The Land is Bright* (1939), the story of an Oregon Trail family, is still read today. A socio-economic chronicle of Seattle, *The Northwest Gateway* (1941) provides a good, if dated, introduction to Seattle's attitudes toward itself. Meanwhile, Murray Morgan's *Skid Road: An Informal Portrait of Seattle* (1951) enables the quirky characters of pioneer Seattle to come to life.

In the 1960s and '70s, western Washington attracted a number of counterculture writers. The most famous of these is Tom Robbins, whose books, including *Another Roadside Attraction* (1971) and *Even Cowgirls Get the Blues* (1976), became the scripture of a generation. Poet Theodore Roethke taught for years at the University of Washington, and with Washington native Richard Hugo (p77) he cast a profound influence over Northwest poetry.

Raymond Carver, the poet and short story master whose books include *Will You Please Be Quiet Please* (1976) and *Where I'm Calling From* (1988), lived near Seattle on the Olympic Peninsula. Carver's stark and grim vision of working-class angst has profoundly affected other young writers of his time. Carver's wife, Tess Gallagher, is also a novelist and poet whose books include *At the Owl Woman Saloon* (1997).

Ivan Doig writes of his move to Seattle in *The Sea Runners* (1982). In *Winter Brothers* (1980), Doig examines the diaries of early Washington writer James Swan, who lived among the Makah Indians on the northern tip of the Olympic Peninsula. Noted travel writer Jonathan Raban, who lived in Seattle for years, then left only to return recently, has written such books as *Coasting* (1987), *Hunting Mister Heartbreak* (1990) and *Badlands* (1996). His latest, *Waxwings* (2003), is a fictionalized account of two families of Seattle immigrants. Annie Dillard, essayist and novelist, wrote about the Northwest in *The Living* (1992).

Sherman Alexie (see opposite) writes from a Native American perspective. His short-story collection *The Lone Ranger and Tonto Fistfight in Heaven* (1993) was among the first works of popular fiction to discuss reservation life; in 1996, he published to great critical acclaim *Indian Killer*, a chilling tale of ritual murder set in Seattle. David Guterson writes about the Puget Sound area and the internment of Japanese Americans during WWII in *Snow Falling on Cedars* (1994).

The misty environs of western Washington is a fecund habitat for mystery writers. Dashiell Hammett once lived in Seattle, while noted writers JA Jance, Earl Emerson and Frederick D Huebner currently make the Northwest home.

Local historian Bill Speidel, he of the famous Underground Tour, has written a couple of enthusiastic histories about Seattle's early characters, such as *Doc Maynard: The Man who Invented Seattle* (1978) and *Sons of the Profits* (1967). In *Stepping Westward* (1991), Sallie Tisdale tells her story of growing up in the Northwest, with insights into the region's culture. Timothy Egan's *The Good Rain* (1990) is an insightful discussion of the Northwest and its people by the local *New York Times* correspondent. Seattle preacher Robert Fulghum made it big as an inspirational writer with *All I Really Need to Know I Learned in Kindergarten* (1988). And more recently, Fred Moody, former managing editor of the *Seattle Weekly*, synthesized the city's complex history and uncomfortable relationship with its own gradual success in his engaging history-memoir, *Seattle and the Demons of Ambition: A Love Story* (2003).

Local music critic Charles Cross caused a sensation with *Heavier than Heaven* (2001), his intimate, moving biography of Nirvana's Kurt Cobain. And fearless grunge photographer

Sherman Alexie

Sherman Alexie is a 6ft 2in Spokane-Coeur d'Alene Indian with an even-larger-than-life sense of humor and an unshakeable but hard-earned confidence. He grew up on the Spokane Indian Reservation in Wellpinit, Washington. Born hydrocephalic, he wasn't expected to live; at six months of age he had brain surgery, and doctors expected he would either die or be mentally handicapped.

What happened was the exact opposite. Alexie became an unstoppable reader and, in his 30s, a celebrated writer. Named one of Granta's '20 Best American Novelists Under the Age of 40,' he has won masses of critical acclaim for his novels, short stories and poetry. Recently he's been writing screenplays; he wrote the screenplay for fellow Native American director Chris Eyre's fantastic *Smoke Signals,* and he wrote and directed *The Business of Fancydancing* (p29).

Alexie's readings are the stuff of legend; no one should miss a chance to attend one. Not one for dry recitals of static texts, Alexie memorizes whatever piece he plans to read, then performs it dramatically, much to the crowd's delight. One of the fascinating things about his public speaking appearances is that, although there's a lot of buried anger in what he says, he is also outrageously funny, which means he can, for example, throw a bunch of scathing lines about crazy, clueless white people to an audience full of white people and they eat it up.

Alexie dismisses the idea that his comic presentation might distract listeners from the serious aspects of his work. 'Did Richard Pryor let people off the hook?' he asks. 'Did Lenny Bruce? I'd argue the reverse: I think the reason liberals have so little power is because we're so earnest, and the reason the conservatives kick our asses is because they're funny... Give me a right-wing redneck over a vegan anytime! Give me Rush Limbaugh over an Earth First-er any night of the week.'

Politics are integral to Alexie's life and work; whether he likes it or not, he's been saddled with the role of Official Native American Spokesman. You get the idea that sometimes he likes it, and sometimes he doesn't at all. 'I'm just who I am,' he says. 'I'm an individual. If anything I hope what I do gets *everybody* to question authority, to be eccentric, to get rowdy, to create art, to follow their dreams. In the end all I hope is that I've celebrated eccentricity.'

Alexie's first short story collection, *The Lone Ranger and Tonto Fistfight in Heaven,* was published in 1993. In the decade since then, he says, the cultural milieu of Seattle has seen some changes. 'There's a lot more white-collar Indians. There's now what you would call a Native American elite. It's a very visible Indian elite. Because Seattle's so white, we stand out more.'

On the other hand, he says, day-to-day racism is seldom a problem – at least within city limits. 'In Seattle it mostly amounts to getting looked at, not even that, necessarily. This is a liberal city. I deal with very little overt racism. Once you get outside the Seattle boundaries, that changes. In Seattle you deal with institutional racism. Outside of Seattle you deal with people who might have a gun,' he deadpans.

As for Seattle's literary scene, it continues to thrive. 'It's the only place in the world, I think, where writers are superstars. I get recognized *every day.*' When he went to the Department of Motor Vehicles to renew his driver's license, he says, they called out his name and he ended up signing autographs. 'I don't think the same thing would happen in Manhattan's DMV.' If anything, he says, the city's literary bent has intensified. There are a lot of young people getting involved in readings and events, and there are cultural resources like the Richard Hugo House (p77).

'If you love books and want to be in a book town and want to go to a reading every night of the week,' Alexie says, 'you can.'

Charles Peterson, with cooperation from musicians including Mudhoney's Steve Turner and Pearl Jam's Eddie Vedder, has published a great book of photos from the heydays of grunge, named after the Mudhoney song *Touch Me I'm Sick* (2003).

A peculiar phenomenon is the number of cartoonists who live in the Seattle area. Lynda Barry (*Ernie Pook's Comeek, Cruddy*) and Matt Groening (creator of *The Simpsons*) were students together at Olympia's Evergreen State College. Gary Larson, whose *Far Side* animal antics have netted international fame and great fortune, lives in Seattle. Loads of underground comic book artists live here, too, including the legendary Peter Bagge (*Hate*), Jim Woodring and Roberta Gregory. Fantagraphics, a major and influential publisher of underground comics and graphic novels, is also based in Seattle.

> ## Top Five Museums
> - Henry Art Gallery (p79)
> - Seattle Art Museum (p47)
> - Burke Museum (p79)
> - Frye Art Museum (p48)
> - Experience Music Project (p63)

VISUAL ARTS

Seattle is the center of Washington's art and gallery scene. In addition to its high quality art galleries, a number of exhibition spaces are devoted to contemporary Native American carvings and paintings. Seattle is also home to the **Seattle Art Museum** (p47), where the collection of native artifacts and folk art is particularly impressive. A considerable Asian art collection is located at the **Seattle Asian Art Museum** (p78) in Volunteer Park. More experimental and conceptual art is displayed at the University of Washington's **Henry Art Gallery** (p79).

A specialty of the Puget Sound area is glassblowing, led by a group of inventive and influential artisans known as the Pilchuck School. The most famous of these is Dale Chihuly (p28), whose work is on display at the Benaroya Concert Hall and in a number of galleries.

Pushing the envelope of contemporary art is the specialty of several younger galleries around town, notably Belltown's **Roq la Rue** (p61), the **Center on Contemporary Art** (p77) and **Consolidated Works** (Map pp240-1; ☎ 206-381-3218; 500 Boren Ave N). These unconventional spaces display provocative, boundary-distorting artwork of all kinds, usually by unknown or underground artists. They also regularly host rock shows, theatrical performances and film screenings. Check the local weeklies for listings.

> ## Top Five Galleries
> - **Roq la Rue** (p61) – a very Belltown gallery, where the openings feel like rock shows packed with scenesters.
> - **Center on Contemporary Art** (p77) – a major force in the Seattle art scene, this artist-run collective makes a point of putting on high-energy, slightly wacky shows.
> - **Consolidated Works** – former *Stranger* theater editor Matthew Richter's space hosts an eclectic mix of art, lectures, film screenings and performance.
> - **Suyama Space** (Map pp238-9; ☎ 206-256-0809; 2324 2nd Ave) – tucked inside the offices of architect George Suyama, this space has the calm feel of a secret oasis.
> - **Greg Kucera Gallery** (Map pp236-7; ☎ 206-624-0770; 212 3rd Ave S) – a high-roller who seems unafraid of taking risks, Kucera hosts big names – cult filmmaker John Waters, for example – as well as supporting unknowns in his large gallery. You mustn't miss the outdoor sculpture loft.

PUBLIC ART

Seattle is also known for its interesting and plentiful public art. A King County ordinance, established in 1973, stipulates that one percent of all municipal capital-improvement project funds be set aside for public art. The 'one percent for art' clause, which other cities across the nation have also adopted, has given Seattle an extensive collection of artworks ranging from monumental sculpture and landscape design to individualized sewer hole covers.

Totem Poles of the Northwest Coast

Totem poles are found along the Northwest Pacific Coast, roughly between northern Washington State and Alaska. Carved from a single cedar log by the Haida, Tlingit, Tsimshian and Kwakiutl tribes (Puget Sound tribes typically did not carve totems), totem poles identify a household's lineage in the same way a family crest might identify a group or clan in Europe, although the totem pole is more of a historical pictograph depicting the entire ancestry. Like a family crest, totem poles carry a sense of prestige and prosperity.

Totems serve a variety of functions: freestanding poles welcome visitors to a waterfront or village; a memorial pole is often erected outside a deceased chief's home; mortuary poles are implanted with a box of the honored individual's decomposed remains. Incorporated into the design of a house, totem poles also appear as house posts and front doors. Shame poles, carved with upside-down figures denoting social or ritual transgressions, were temporary fixtures and are found only in museums today. Traditional poles vary greatly in height, though rarely exceed 60ft. Modern poles can be much taller – the world's tallest totem pole at Alert Bay in British Columbia is 173ft.

Despite the saying 'low man on the totem pole,' the most important figures are usually at eye level; figures at the bottom usually have an integral, grounding function that supports the rest of the pole. Figures can represent individuals, spirits, births, deaths, catastrophes or legends.

Unless you're an expert, it's not so easy to identify what's what on a totem. Here are a few rules of thumb: birds are always identified with a pronounced beak – ravens have a straight, mid-size beak; eagles have a short, sharp, down-turned beak; hawks have a short, down-turned beak that curls inward. Bears usually have large, square teeth, while beavers have sharp incisors and a cross-stitched tail. A few animals appear as if viewed from overhead. For example, killer whales' fins protrude outward from the poles as if their heads face downward. Long-snouted wolves also face downward, as do frogs. Pointy-headed sharks (or dogfish), with grimacing mouths full of sharp teeth, face upward, as do humpback whales.

Though totem symbols are usually interconnected and complex, these animals possess certain undeniable characteristics:

beaver – industriousness, wisdom and determined independence
black bear – a protector, guardian and spiritual link between humans and animals
eagle – intelligence and power
frog – adaptability; ability to live in both natural and supernatural worlds
hummingbird – love, beauty and unity with nature
killer whale – dignity and strength; often a reincarnated spirit of a great chief
raven – mischievousness and cunning; the perennial trickster
salmon – dependable sustenance, longevity and perseverance; a powerful symbol
shark – ominous, fierce and solitary
thunderbird – strong, supernatural; the wisdom of proud ancestors

Fremont (p81) is a good place to start looking for examples of off-beat or inspired public art in Seattle. Fremont boasts, among other things, the *Waiting for the Interurban* sculpture, a community centerpiece often decorated with politically pointed costumes and trappings.

All of the county's public artwork is commissioned through a public process. A panel of artists and project and city planners gets together to choose an artist out of thousands of applicants. Keep your eyes open and your art radar on high; you'll find public art throughout Seattle, in the metro bus tunnels, in public parks, on building walls and embedded in the sidewalks.

CINEMA & TV

Seattle has come a long way as a movie mecca since the days when Elvis starred in the 1963 film *It Happened at the World's Fair,* a chestnut of civic boosterism. Films with Seattle as their backdrop include the 1930s *Tugboat Annie; Cinderella Liberty* (1974), a steamy romance with James Caan and Marsha Mason; and *The Parallax View* (1974) with Warren Beatty. Jessica Lange's movie *Frances,* about the horrible fate of outspoken local actor Frances Farmer (she was jailed on questionable pretenses, then institutionalized for

Glassmaster Dale Chihuly

This modern master of glassmaking – claimed by *Fine Art* magazine to be to glass what Steven Spielberg is to film, a statement that can be taken in any number of ways – was born in Tacoma in 1941. After an education in design and fine arts, Chihuly won a Fulbright scholarship to study the art of glassmaking on the island of Murano, the renowned glassmaking center near Venice.

Chihuly returned to the Seattle area in 1971 to found the Pilchuck Glass School; this studio is credited with transforming glass – previously used mostly for utilitarian or decorative purposes – into a medium of transcendent artistic expression. Chihuly's blown-glass sculptures defy the everyday experience of glass: infused with lush color, sensual textures and a physicality that is at once massive and delicate, these pieces extend the very notion of 'glassness' into new realms of recognition.

The Seattle area is home to a number of Chihuly installations, and many local art galleries display his works (as well as the works of other glass artists – Seattle is a hotbed of glass artistry). Get a sense of Chihuly's craft in the 2nd-floor atrium of City Center Mall, which contains several glass sculptures.

Anyone serious about Chihuly's work should make the trip down to Tacoma to see his massive installation in the Union Station Federal Courthouse, smaller works at the **Tacoma Art Museum** (☎ 253-272-4258) and, most importantly, Tacoma's new **Museum of Glass** (☎ 253-396-1768; 1801 E Dock St; adult/child/senior $10/4/8; ☉ 10am-5pm Tue-Sat, noon-5pm Sun, 10am-8pm Thu summer), with its strikingly slanted tower called the Hot Shop Amphitheater. Chihuly also created the Bridge of Glass walkway connecting the museum building with Union Station.

Chihuly lives and works at his 25,000-sq-ft studio on Lake Union, called the Boathouse. A car accident left him blind in one eye (he wears a trademark eye patch); ever since, he has lacked the necessary depth perception to continue solo glassblowing. He now oversees a team of glassblowers who perform the principal construction of his works.

Today, Chihuly's art is represented in more than 125 museums around the world. Some of his recent major works include the Chandeliers series (1992), the Chihuly Over Venice project (1995) and set designs for the Seattle Opera's *Pelléas et Melisande* (1993).

---

years and eventually lobotomized), was shot here in 1981. Debra Winger's hit *Black Widow* (1986) shows many scenes shot at the University of Washington.

John Cusack starred in *Say Anything* (1989), Michelle Pfeiffer and Jeff Bridges did it up in *The Fabulous Baker Boys* (1989), and Sly Stallone and Antonio Banderas flopped in *Assassins* (1995), all partly filmed in and around Seattle. Recently, horror hit *The Ring* and J.Lo vehicle *Enough* both had a few scenes shot in Seattle and on local ferries.

Perhaps the two most famous Seattle movies happened when the city was at the peak of its cultural cachet: *Singles* (1992), with Campbell Scott, Kyra Sedgwick, Matt Dillon and Bridget Fonda, captured the Seattle vibe. (Incidentally, both *Singles* and *Say Anything* were directed by Cameron Crowe, who is married to Seattle rock band Heart's Nancy Wilson.) But no film shot in Seattle garnered as much attention as *Sleepless in Seattle*, the 1993 blockbuster starring Tom Hanks, Meg Ryan and, perhaps more importantly, Seattle's Lake Union houseboats.

Sherman Alexie, having brought mainstream national attention to the city as a literary center, has expanded into the realm of filmmaking as well. *Smoke Signals* (1998), which Alexie wrote based on one of his short stories, starred Adam Beach and was directed by Chris Eyre; an entirely Native American effort, it was a huge success.

Asian motif in 5th Avenue Theater (p150)

For his followup, *The Business of Fancydancing* (2002), Alexie both wrote the screenplay and directed the film.

Some interesting documentaries have also been produced here. *Dragon: The Bruce Lee Story* follows the career of the onetime Seattle resident. *Hype!* (1996) is a documentary about the explosion of underground music in the Northwest and the resulting fallout, with lots of interviews and great live-music footage. On the other end of the spectrum is the always-controversial English rabble-rouser Nick Broomfield's 1998 film *Kurt & Courtney*, which delves without restraint into the troubled lives of Seattle's king and queen of rock.

Television's *Northern Exposure,* filmed in nearby Roslyn, Washington, and *Frasier* have both done a lot to create Seattle's current reputation as a hip and youthful place to live. The creepy, darker side of the Northwest was captured in the moody *Twin Peaks: Fire Walk With Me.* And let's not forget, of course, MTV's *The Real World: Seattle.*

THEATER

Seattle has one of the most dynamic theater scenes in the country; there are apparently more equity theaters in Seattle than anywhere in the US except New York City. This abundance of venues provides the city with a range of classical and modern dramatic theater.

In addition to quality professional theater, the city offers a wide array of amateur and special-interest troupes, including both gay and lesbian theater groups, puppet theaters, children's theater troupes, cabarets and plenty of alternative theaters staging fringe plays by local playwrights.

DANCE

Seattle is home to the nationally noted Pacific Northwest Ballet, which blushes at its acclaim as one of the nation's five best ballet companies. Seattle is a springboard for dancers. The modern dance pioneer Merce Cunningham was born and raised in nearby Centralia and was trained at Cornish College in Seattle. Choreographer Mark Morris, known for his fusion of classical and modern dance, is native to Seattle and has worked everywhere from small opera houses to Broadway and now works mostly in Europe. New York–based avant-garde dancer Trisha Brown is originally from Aberdeen, Washington, and classical ballet choreographer Robert Joffrey hails from Seattle.

The World Dance Series at the University of Washington's Meany Theater brings talent from all over the world, and smaller dance groups, such as On the Boards, which performs at the **Behnke Center for Contemporary Performance** (☎ 206-217-9888), bring an exciting edge to the city's dance scene.

ARCHITECTURE

Seattle is as notable for what is missing as for what remains, architecturally. Seattle's Great Fire of 1889 ravaged the old wooden storefronts of downtown, which were replaced by the stone and brick structures around the city's old center in Pioneer Square. Architect Elmer Fisher is responsible for more than 50 buildings erected immediately after the fire. Any Victorian places that escaped the Great Fire did not escape the Denny Regrade (1899–1912), which flattened a steep residential hill in order to make room for more downtown commercial properties.

Seattle's next big building phase came in the early decades of the 20th century. The beaux arts and art deco hospitals that fill the skyline on First and Beacon Hills are good examples of the civic buildings of that era. Smith Tower (p51), near Pioneer Square, was built in 1914, and with 42 stories it was for many years the tallest building in the world outside of New York City. The campanile-like tower of white terra-cotta brick is still one of the city's beauties. Also during this time, Capitol and Queen Anne Hills filled with homes of the popular Georgian, Federal, English and Arts and Crafts styles.

More recent additions to the downtown skyline include the West Coast's tallest building, the Bank of America Building (formerly the Columbia Seafirst Center), a monolith with no other distinction than its 76-story shadow. Six others rise higher than 50 stories; only the Washington Mutual Building, with its plaidlike facade and turquoise glass, makes a pleasant impression.

As the architectural icon of Seattle, no other modern structure comes close to the Space Needle (p63). Built for the 1962 World's Fair, its sleek but whimsical design has aged amazingly well. The newest and most controversial addition to Seattle architecture is the Frank O Gehry–designed Experience Music Project (p63), whose curvy metallic design caused quite a commotion.

Walrus detail on Arctic Building (p46)

Top Five Notable Buildings

- Space Needle (p63)
- Experience Music Project (p63)
- Smith Tower (p51)
- Benaroya Concert Hall (p46)
- Arctic Building (p46)

History

History

THE RECENT PAST

Seattle's history is equal parts self-deprecation and grappling for a position of international relevance. First there were its laid-back origins as 'New York Pretty-Soon.' Later, in the 1950s and '60s, came the wild anti-boosterism of newspaper columnist Emmett Watson (who wrote things like 'Have a nice day – somewhere else' and 'Our suicide rate is one of the highest in the nation. But we can be No 1!'). More recently, there was the nationwide glamorization of the anti-glamour grunge movement, the repercussions of which can still be felt. And there was the city's naive excitement at being selected to host the 1999 World Trade Organization (WTO) conference and its shock at the resulting fall out. Seattle always seems to have an uncomfortable relationship with the success it has struggled to achieve.

MICROSOFT

The biggest story in Seattle's recent history, of course, is the business behemoth of Microsoft. Springing onto the scene in the mid-1970s and '80s, it was a force that would change Seattle forever. After tinkering around with a little notion called BASIC (a programming language for the world's first microcomputer), local boy Bill Gates joined up with his childhood chum Paul Allen to start Microsoft in 1975. Though the software giant, located in Redmond across Lake Washington, doesn't have quite the total control over Seattle economy that Boeing once had, it is increasingly hard to find someone who isn't a contractor, caterer or car dealer for the Microsoft crowd. Microsoft also attracted other high-tech companies to the area, making the city particularly vulnerable to the high-tech slump that hit the country during its recent economic crisis.

Microsoft's heyday hit something of a capitalist brick wall in the late 1990s, when the federal government began a very long and politically hot suit against Microsoft. The Justice Department accused the company of monopolistic practices and alleged that it used – and abused – its prodigious market power to prevent any competition from getting in its way.

Top Five Seattle History Books

- *Divided Destiny: A History of Japanese Americans in Seattle,* David A Takami (2003) – originally created to accompany an exhibition at the Wing Luke Asian Museum, this richly illustrated book documents 100-plus years of Seattle's Japanese American community.
- *The Good Rain,* Timothy Egan (1991) – the *New York Times* correspondent sheds light on the Northwest and its inhabitants.
- *Seattle and the Demons of Ambition: A Love Story,* Fred Moody (2003) – a former *Seattle Weekly* editor, Moody puts a personal spin on Seattle's complex economic, political and cultural history.
- *Sons of the Profits,* Bill Speidel (1967) – Underground Tour founder Speidel, whose book *Doc Maynard: The Man who Invented Seattle* is also recommended, takes on some of pioneer Seattle's more eccentric characters.
- *Stepping Westward,* Sallie Tisdale (1992) – in this critical memoir, Tisdale casts a keen eye on the often contentious relationship between humans and nature in the Pacific Northwest.

TIMELINE	1792	1804–06	1843–1860
	British Captain George Vancouver sails the Straits of Juan de Fuca and Georgia.	Lewis and Clark Expedition.	53,000 settlers migrate across the 2000-mile long Oregon Trail.

Microsoft's reputation for bullying other players on the technological playfield was deemed, by the most capitalist nation on earth, to be legally unfair.

In April 2000, Judge Thomas Penfield Jackson ruled that Microsoft had violated antitrust laws by 'engaging in predatory tactics that discourage technological competition.' The judge ruled that Microsoft needed to divest the company. Microsoft launched a barrage of seemingly never-ending appeals, which have resulted in various settlements with the federal government and several states. Up next, Microsoft faces antitrust probes from Europe in what promises to be a complex, continuing struggle.

Through the 1990s, Internet start-up companies – often financed by the young, affluent millionaires that Microsoft's early days spawned – sprouted like weeds and attracted a younger, more educated population than Seattle had ever seen. It seemed too good to be true and, in fact, it turned out that way. The 'dot-com' fiasco was the economic equivalent of a candy bar, providing a major rush followed by a depressing crash. You can still see disappointed dot-commers daydreaming over their laptops in coffee shops, seemingly stunned that their plush jobs at productless companies whose offices felt like clubhouses came to an end.

As significant as any industry-related changes they've wrought is what Gates and Allen are doing with the money Microsoft has earned them. Their spending, whether on philanthropic ventures, showpieces like the **Experience Music Project** (p63), or real estate in volatile areas like **South Lake Union** (p66), is shaping the physical and cultural landscape of the city.

BOEING

For years, Boeing singlehandedly ruled Seattle industry. After WWII, the manufacturer diversified its product line and began to develop civilian aircraft. In 1954, Boeing announced the 707, and the response was immediate and overwhelming. The world found itself at the beginning of an era of mass air travel, and Boeing produced the jets that led this revolution in transportation. By 1960, when the population of Seattle topped 1 million, one in 10 people worked for Boeing, and one in four people worked jobs directly affected by Boeing.

Boing, Boing Boeing

Just a few days after Seattle was rattled by a mighty earthquake, the city received a blow that rocked it even more. Boeing head honcho Phil Condit announced in March 2001 that the world's largest airplane manufacturer, the company as synonymous with Seattle as rain, was blowing town. Boeing, he said, would relocate at least 50% of its headquarter staff to bigger and brighter digs in Chicago in September 2001. Seattleites were stunned, and amid the cries of surprise and panic, you could almost hear founder Bill Boeing rolling over in his grave. Boeing's move is as major as Disney leaving Disney World.

While jets still account for about 60% of Boeing's sales, the headquarters shift is part of Boeing's plan to diversify its corporate interests. Condit's reasoning? You can't be the life of the party if you don't mingle, or if you stay stuck in the northwest corner of the room. CEOs of the world's largest airplane manufacturer, it seems, are sick of flying.

Seattleites didn't buy it. When Seattle became more popular to other companies, it became a headache for Boeing. Competition for skilled workers grew fierce, and the antagonistic relationship the company already had with its union workers only intensified. Though Boeing's 80,000 plant workers are staying put for now, everyone worries that the headquarters' move is just the first in a series of big steps to relocate the company entirely.

Since its departure, Boeing has also had to lay off even more of its Northwest work force; the company has taken a beating (at least enough to justify waves of downsizing) in the economic slump that swept the US – and especially the Northwest – during the early 2000s. Only time will tell just how much of a toll Boeing's departure will take. In the meantime, Seattle's economy will lean even harder on high-tech and biotech industries.

1845	1846	1851	1854
First US settlement in Washington established at Tumwater.	US and Britain agree to the present US–Canadian border.	Arthur Denny party settles in Puget Sound and is welcomed by the Duwamish people.	US treaty grants 2600 acres of reservation in return for two million acres of prime real estate.

But the fortunes of Boeing weren't always to soar. A combination of overstretched capital (due to cost overruns in the development of the 747) and a cut in defense spending led to a severe financial crisis in the early 1970s. Boeing was forced to cut its work force by two-thirds; in one year, nearly 60,000 Seattleites lost their jobs. The local economy went into a tailspin for a number of years.

Looking back, that episode seems like grim foreshadowing. In the 1980s, increased defense spending brought vigor back to aircraft production lines, and expanding trade relations with China and other Pacific Rim nations brought business to Boeing too. But the company's announcement in March 2001 to relocate its headquarters to Chicago, followed by massive layoffs in several stages, left Seattleites stunned and more than a little concerned about what the future would hold. Things were beginning to look up in early 2004, as Boeing announced it would build the major new 7E7 plane in Everett, Washington and promised that its new business strategy would avoid its previous pattern of massive hirings followed by large-scale layoffs.

FROM THE BEGINNING

For a major US city, Seattle's civic history begins very late in the chronicle of the nation. While the rest of the country had established firm roots, most of today's Seattle was covered in deep forest that was perennially drenched in rain. Though native groups lived here since before the recognized dawn of time, colonialist settlement didn't reach Puget Sound until 1851.

NATIVE PEOPLES OF PUGET SOUND

When the accumulated ice of the great polar glaciers of the Pleistocene Epoch lowered sea levels throughout the world, the ancestors of American Indians migrated from Siberia to Alaska via a land bridge across the Bering Strait. By this reckoning, the present tribes of Puget Sound arrived here 11,000 or 12,000 years ago, before the glaciers receded.

Unlike the Plains Indians living further inland, who were primarily nomadic hunter-gatherers, the first inhabitants of the Pacific Northwest were intimately tied to the rivers, lakes and sea. The tribe living on the site of today's Seattle was called the Duwamish. They and other tribal groups along Puget Sound – notably the Suquamish, Coast Salish and Chinook – depended on catching salmon, cod and shellfish. On land, they hunted deer and elk, more for their protective hides than for their flesh. Though each group had its own dialect, coastal natives communicated through a language called Lushootseed, which natives today struggle to keep from extinction.

Totem pole, University of Washington State Burke Museum (p79)

1855	1883	1885	1886
Warfare erupts between tribes and white settlers; Chief Sealth delivers his masterful address.	Northern Pacific Railroad links Portland to Chicago.	Anti-Chinese Congress established.	Anti-Chinese riots take place.

Summer and fall were dedicated to harvesting the bounty of the sea and forest. Food was stored in massive quantities to carry the tribes through the long winter months, when the most important ancient legends and ceremonies were handed down to the younger generations. In terms of artistic, religious and cultural forms, the Northwest coastal Indians reached a pinnacle of sophistication unmatched by most Native American groups. Ornately carved cedar canoes served as transportation, and extensive trading networks evolved between the permanent settlements that stretched up and down the coast and along the river valleys.

Extended family groups lived in cedar longhouses, which were constructed over a central pitlike living area. The social structure in these self-sustaining villages was quite stratified, with wealth and power held by an aristocratic class of chiefs. Social and religious rituals were dominated by a strict clan system. Wealth was measured in goods such as blankets, salmon and fish oil; these items were consumed and to some degree redistributed in ceremonial feasts in which great honor accrued to the person who gave away valued items.

Puget Sound natives evolved complex cultural, social, and economic structures, which the invasion of Euro-American settlers in the mid-1800s almost erased. Today tribes struggle for survival, respect and renewal.

EARLY EXPLORATION

Puget Sound and the Pacific Northwest in general were among the last areas of the Americas to be explored by Europeans. In fact, almost 300 years passed between the arrival of white explorers in America and their 'discovery' of Puget Sound.

The first white expedition to explore the Puget Sound area came in 1792, when the British sea captain George Vancouver sailed through the inland waterways of the Straits of Juan de Fuca and Georgia. In the same year, the USA entered the competition to claim the Northwest when Captain Robert Gray reached the mouth of the Columbia River.

The major reason for European and American eagerness to claim this forested and well-watered corner of the map was its immense wealth in furs. The region's waterways were especially rich in beavers and otters, the pelts of which were a highly valued commodity in Europe and Asia and thus an important article of trade.

None of these exploration or trade expeditions, however, led directly to a pioneer settlement or even a permanent trading post. This development awaited the arrival of the powerful fur-trading companies, especially the British Hudson's Bay Company (HBC). From its toehold at Fort Vancouver, the HBC – and hence Britain – had control over all trade in the Pacific Northwest. The Puget Sound area was linked to the fur-trading fort by the Cowlitz River, a short portage from the sound's southern shores. Because of its strict code of conduct and protocol, the company had legal authority over the area's few whites, mostly French Canadian and Scottish trappers. The HBC also policed trade relationships between the whites and the region's native inhabitants.

The first US settlers straggled overland to the Pacific Northwest in the 1830s on the rough tracks that would become the Oregon Trail. The HBC chief factor, Dr John McLoughlin, sought to restrict American settlement to the region south of the Columbia River, in Oregon. In doing so, he kept the prime land along Puget Sound from settlement. McLoughlin sensed that one day the USA and Britain would divide the territory; if US settlement could be limited to the area south of the Columbia, then Britain would have a stronger claim to the land north of the river. It worked: when the settlers in Oregon voted in 1843 to become a US territory, present-day Washington remained in British hands.

American settlers continued rolling into the Pacific Northwest. Between 1843 and 1860 some 53,000 settlers migrated across the 2000-mile-long Oregon Trail. As they pushed northward into land controlled largely by the HBC, boundary disputes between the USA

1887	1889	1893	1897
Northern Pacific builds shipyards in Tacoma.	The Great Fire sweeps through the city.	Northern Pacific reaches Seattle from Portland; city is a terminus for the Great Northern Railroad.	Klondike Gold Rush sparked by ship *Portland*.

Lighthouse, Alki Point (below)

and Britain became increasingly antagonistic. The popular slogan of the 1844 US presidential campaign was 'Fifty-four Forty or Fight,' which urged US citizens to occupy territory in the Northwest up to the present Alaskan border, including all of Washington state and British Columbia. Finally, in 1846, the British and the Americans agreed to the present US-Canadian border along the 49th parallel.

'NEW YORK PRETTY SOON'

Arthur and David Denny were native New Yorkers who in 1851 led a group of settlers across the Oregon Trail with the intention of settling in the Willamette Valley. On the way, they heard stories of good land and deep water ports along Puget Sound. When the Denny party arrived in Portland in the fall, they decided to keep going north. The settlers staked claims on Alki Point, in present-day West Seattle. The group named their encampment Alki-New York (the Chinookan word *Alki* means 'pretty soon' or 'by and by'). After a winter of wind and rain, the group determined that their fledgling city needed a deeper harbor and moved the settlement to the mudflats across Elliott Bay. The colony was renamed Seattle for the Duwamish chief Sealth (pronounced *see*-aalth, with a guttural 'th' being made up of a hard 't' and an 'h' that's almost a lisp off the end of the word), who was the friend of an early merchant (p13).

The attitudes of Seattle's first settlers established it as a progressive, budding community. Traversing the Oregon Trail was an arduous and costly adventure. The Pacific Northwest was not settled by penniless wanderers, but earnest young men and women, mostly in their twenties, who had the wherewithal to make the six-month trip and were determined to establish farms, businesses and communities.

late 1890s	1899–1912	1900	1903
Seattle's small businesses make quick fortunes.	Regrading of Denny Hill.	Height of the gold rush; Seattle's population has doubled since 1890.	Seattle becomes the terminus for Milwaukee Rd.

BIRTH OF THE CITY

Still, early Seattle was hardly a boomtown. The heart of the young city beat is the area now known as Pioneer Square. Although there was a small but deep harbor at this point in Elliott Bay, much of the land immediately to the south was mudflats, ideal for oysters but not much else. The land to the north and east was steep and forested. The early settlers (whose names now ring as a compendium of street names and landmarks: Denny, Yesler, Bell, Boren) quickly cleared the land and established a sawmill, schools, churches and other civic institutions. From the start, the people who settled Seattle never doubted that they were founding a great city. The original homesteads were quickly platted into city streets, and trade, not farming or lumbering, became the goal of the little settlement.

Since it was a frontier town, the majority of Seattle's male settlers were bachelors. One of the town's founders (and sole professor at the newly established university), Asa Mercer, went back to the East Coast with the express purpose of inducing young unmarried women to venture to Seattle. Fifty-seven women made the journey and married into the frontier stock, in the process establishing a more civilized tone in the city.

Seattle's early economic growth came from shipping logs to San Francisco, a city booming with gold wealth. At the time, loggers had to go no further than the bluffs above town, now First and Capitol Hills, to find hundreds of acres of old-growth fir forest. As the sawmill was located on the waterfront, the logs had to be transported down the steep hillside. A skid road was developed on which horses and mules pulled the logs down a chute of ever-present mud. This skid road later became Yesler Way, the prototype of the term 'skid road' – or skid row.

THE BATTLE FOR RAILROADS

The Northwest's first rail link was the Northern Pacific Railroad, which linked Portland to Chicago in 1883. The young towns of Puget Sound – Seattle, Tacoma, Port Townsend and Bellingham – believed their dreams of becoming major trade centers depended on luring a national rail line to link them to the East. Land speculators especially profited when railroads like the Northern Pacific and the Great Northern came shopping for a Puget Sound terminus. Seattle lost out to Tacoma when the Northern Pacific built its shipyards there, but it later became the terminus for the Great Northern Railroad and the Milwaukee Road.

ANTI-CHINESE RIOTS OF 1886

Because of the region's many railroad and mining companies and Seattle's position on the Pacific Rim, a large number of Chinese immigrants settled in the city. The fact that Asian laborers worked at jobs that most white Americans shunned didn't prevent the perception that these 'foreign' workers were taking jobs away from 'real Americans,' and, then as now, it didn't prevent episodes of ugly racism.

As anti-Chinese sentiment grew in outlying communities around the Pacific Northwest, more and more Chinese moved to Seattle, where the multitude of employment opportunities offered them continued security and led to a sense of community. The area south of Yesler Way was considered Chinatown, where most of the new arrivals made their homes; today it has a more varied population, including 'Little Saigon,' and is known as the International District.

The first recorded clash between the Chinese minority and white settlers came in 1885, when a Chinese immigrant was knifed to death. That year, a group called the Anti-Chinese Congress established, by more or less mob assent, a date by which all the Chinese would be forced to leave the Puget Sound area. A majority of the Chinese, between 750 and 1000 workers, left the area. However, about 500 Chinese continued to live and work

1910	1914	1916	1927
Seattle's population reaches a quarter million: the pre-eminent city of the Pacific Northwest.	Opening of the Panama Canal.	William Boeing designs and produces pontoon biplane.	Boeing Air Transport operates first commercial flight between Chicago and San Francisco.

in Seattle, which rankled the Anti-Chinese Congress. In February 1886, a mob entered Chinatown and attempted to forcibly remove the remaining Chinese, driving them onto ships. State and city officials tried to mediate, but violence erupted. Five people were shot; one white protester died from his wounds. Federal troops were called in to restore order. The Chinese population plummeted, especially in light of court rulings that barred Chinese men from sending for their wives in China. This restriction was a result of the Chinese Exclusion Act, which was finally repealed in 1943 when China became a US ally during WWII.

THE GREAT FIRE & THE REGRADING OF SEATTLE

Frontier Seattle was a thrown-together village of wooden storefronts, log homes and lumber mills. Tidewater lapped against present-day 1st Ave S, and many of the buildings and the streets that led to them were on stilts. No part of the original downtown was more than 4ft above the bay at high tide, and the streets were frequently a quagmire.

On June 6, 1889, a fire started in a store basement on 1st Ave and quickly spread across the young city: the boardwalks provided an unstoppable conduit for the flames. By the end of the day, 30 blocks of the city had burned, gutting the core of downtown.

What might have seemed a catastrophe was in fact a blessing, as the city rebuilt immediately with handsome structures of brick, steel and stone. This time, however, the streets were regraded, and ravines and inlets filled in. This raised the new city about a dozen feet above the old; in some areas the regrading simply meant building on top of older ground-level buildings and streets.

A Town Underground

Want to delve into underground Seattle – literally? Local historian Bill Speidel's **Underground Tour** (p43) will take you there. Leaving daily from Doc Maynard's Public House, the slightly cheesy but entertaining tour prowls the streets beneath the streets of Pioneer Square, evoking the past by digging down to the olden days.

While there's not actually much to *see* on the tour except dirty passageways and decayed plumbing from the 1890s, the story of why there is an underground in the first place is pretty interesting. Despite its prime location on Elliott Bay, early Seattle wasn't exactly conducive to urban development. The area lacked an ideal foundation upon which to build; the land was either hilly and steep or shallow and wet. Many of the storefronts in the Pioneer Square area were built upon soggy tideflats and actually dropped below sea level at high tide. When it rained hard (and it rained hard a lot), the streets bloated into a muddy soup, sewage backed up at high tide and things got pretty messy. As you can imagine, the smell wasn't so great either.

When an apprentice woodworker accidentally let a boiling pot of glue spill over onto a pile of wood chips in a shop on 1st Ave and Madison St, he did Seattle a great favor. It was June 6, 1889, and the ensuing flames swept up the town's wooden houses and storefronts faster than a pioneer could swig a pint of beer. The Great Fire gutted the city and gave city planners a chance to lift the town out of its waterlogged foundation. They decided to regrade the streets first. Great piles of dirt were propped up with retaining walls, and streets were raised up to 12ft higher than they originally were. People had to cross deep trenches to get from one side of the street to another. Buildings were constructed around the notion that the first floor or two would eventually be buried when the city got around to filling in the trenches. Storefronts from the old ramshackle town that were once at street level effectively became basements and, later, passageways for the Underground Tour.

Tours are first-come, first-served, so plan to arrive a half-hour early in the busy summer months. They leave from **Doc Maynard's Public House** (Map pp236-7; ☎ 206-682-4646; 608 1st Ave) roughly every 30 minutes between 11am and 5pm; tickets an adult/child/senior cost $10/5/8. You can see bits of the underground by yourself in the Pioneer Square Antique Mall in the Pioneer Building and on the bottom floor of the Grand Central Arcade.

1954	1960	1962	1973
Boeing announces the 707.	The population of Seattle tops one million; one in 10 people work for Boeing.	World's Fair in Seattle takes place.	'One percent for art' rule established

The sense of transformation inspired by the Great Fire also fueled another great rebuilding project. One of Seattle's original seven hills, Denny Hill, rose out of Elliott Bay just north of Pine St. Its very steep face limited commercial traffic, though some hotels and private homes were perched on the hilltop. City engineers determined that if Seattle's growth was to continue, Denny Hill had to go. Between 1899 and 1912, the hill was sluiced into Elliott Bay. Twenty million gallons of water were pumped daily from Lake Union, sprayed onto the rock and soil. Under great pressure, the water liquefied the clay and dislodged the rock, all of which was sluiced into flumes. Existing homes were simply undercut and then burned.

KLONDIKE GOLD RUSH

Seattle's first real boom came when the ship *Portland* docked at the waterfront in 1897 with its now-famous cargo: two tons of gold newly gleaned from northern Yukon gold fields. The news spread quickly across the USA; within weeks, thousands of fortune seekers from all over the world converged on Seattle, the last stop before heading north. That summer and autumn, 74 ships left Seattle bound for Skagway, Alaska, and on to the goldfields in Dawson City, Yukon.

In all, more than 40,000 prospectors passed through Seattle. The Canadian government demanded that prospectors bring a year's worth of supplies, so they wouldn't freeze or starve to death midway. Outfitting the miners became big business in Seattle. The town became the banking center for the fortunes made in the Yukon. Bars, brothels, theaters and honky-tonks in Pioneer Square blossomed.

Many of Seattle's shopkeepers, tavern owners and restaurateurs made quick fortunes in the late 1890s – far more so than most of the prospectors. Many who did make fortunes in Alaska chose to stay in the Northwest, settling in the thriving port city on Puget Sound.

Seattle grew quickly. The Klondike Gold Rush provided great wealth, and the railroads brought in a steady stream of immigrants, mostly from Eastern Europe and Scandinavia. Seattle controlled most of the shipping trade with Alaska and increasingly with nations of the Pacific Rim. Company-controlled communities like Ballard sprang up, populated almost exclusively with Scandinavians who worked in massive sawmills. A new influx of Asian immigrants, this time from Japan, began streaming into Seattle, establishing fishing fleets and vegetable farms.

At the height of the gold rush in 1900, Seattle's population reached 80,000 – doubling the population figures from the 1890 census. By 1910, Seattle's population jumped to a quarter million. Seattle had become the preeminent city of the Pacific Northwest.

THE WAR YEARS

Seattle's boom continued through WWI, when Northwest lumber was in great demand; the opening of the Panama Canal brought increased trade to Pacific ports, which were free from wartime threats. Shipyards opened along Puget Sound, bringing the shipbuilding industry close to the forests of the Northwest.

One of the significant events in Seattle history occurred in 1916 when William Boeing, a pioneer aviator, designed and produced a pontoon biplane. Boeing went on to establish an airline, Boeing Air Transport (later United Airlines). But it was WWII that really started the engines at Boeing; the factory received contracts to produce the B-17 and B-29 bombers, which led in the US air war against Axis nations. Huge defense contracts began to flow into Boeing and by extension into Seattle, fueling more rapid growth and prosperity.

1975	1980	early 1990s	1990s
Bill Gates and Paul Allen start Microsoft.	Mt St Helens blows her top, killing 55 people and spreading ash through five states.	Grunge music and coffee infuse the cultural scene.	Computer businesses attract a young, affluent, educated crowd to Seattle.

WWII brought other, less positive, developments to Seattle. About 7000 Japanese residents in Seattle and the nearby areas were forcibly removed from their jobs and homes; they were sent to the nearby 'relocation center,' or internment camp, in Puyallup, then on to another camp in Idaho where they were detained under prison conditions for the duration of the war. This greatly depleted the Japanese community, which to this point had built a thriving existence farming and fishing in Puget Sound. In all, an estimated 110,000 Japanese across the country, two-thirds of whom were US citizens, were sent to internment camps. Upon their release, many of them declined to return to the homes they'd been forced to abandon.

Meanwhile, the boom in aircraft manufacturing and shipbuilding brought tens of thousands of new workers to the region. Because of Boeing and the shipyards at Bremerton, Puget Sound became a highly defended area, which led to the building of several military facilities in the region. These bases also brought in thousands of new residents. By the end of the war, Seattle had grown to nearly half a million people.

1994	late 1990s	1999	2000
Kurt Cobain, lead singer of influential band Nirvana, dies.	Government begins suit against Microsoft.	World Trade Organization riots.	'Antitrust' ruling against Microsoft.

Neighborhoods

Neighborhoods

Seattleites talk about *everything* in terms of neighborhoods. Though the city is in fact very compact, talking to locals might give you the impression that, say, Capitol Hill and Fremont are *days* apart. And it's true that each neighborhood has its own distinct feel, most likely because of the disconnected terrain: before bridges and ferries made it easy to navigate the canal and lakes, most people just stayed close to home, resulting in the outlying neighborhoods being pretty isolated. Today, though, it's easy to get around the city and well worth the effort to explore the areas beyond the downtown core.

Of course, you wouldn't want to neglect downtown, but the city's cheeky, quirky, youthful culture really blossoms in some of its outlying neighborhoods. You haven't fully experienced Seattle unless you spend part of a day in one of these islands of counterculture, whether it's exploring Capitol Hill – at once flamboyant and edgy – or Ballard, the sleepy Scandinavian village turned hipster hangout. Seattle's excellent public transit system (Map p250) makes it quick and easy to get almost anywhere from downtown.

The sites and destinations in this chapter are arranged by neighborhood, beginning with downtown, which sits on a long isthmus between Lake Washington and Elliott Bay. North of Seattle's downtown area is another freshwater lake, Lake Union. The lakes are linked to the Puget Sound by the canals and locks of the Lake Washington Ship Canal. Although Seattle is a major Pacific port, the ocean is 125 miles away, which seems a little confusing because there's water everywhere. It's a good idea to look at a map to get an understanding of how all the bodies of water connect, and trace the long route that ships must sail from Seattle to the open seas.

The downtown area butts up against Elliott Bay and encompasses the financial and shopping areas, First Hill, Pioneer Square, Pike Place Market, the Waterfront and Belltown. Seattle Center, with many of Seattle's cultural and sports facilities and attractions, including the Space Needle, is just north of downtown. West of Seattle Center is funky Lower Queen Anne, which is connected to Upper Queen Anne by Seattle's steepest hill. East of Seattle Center is gritty Capitol Hill, the city's gay quarter and hub of youthful urban culture. The Central District, Madison Valley, Madison Park and Madrona are residential neighborhoods on the east side of the Seattle peninsula as it slopes down to Lake Washington.

Lake Union and the Lake Washington Ship Canal divide the city into northern and southern halves. The northern neighborhoods include the U District, named for the University of Washington campus, Wallingford, Fremont and Ballard. Each of these areas has a lively commercial center filled with restaurants, shops and bars. Just north of Fremont and Wallingford is Green Lake, the focal point of a large park area that also contains the city zoo.

To the west of Seattle, across Elliott Bay, is another peninsula, appropriately named West Seattle. This is where the original pioneer settlers founded Seattle.

It's worth noting that four bridges (besides the freeway bridges) cross the ship canal. The University and Montlake Bridges connect neighborhoods south of the canal with the U District. West of Lake Union, the Fremont Bridge crosses from Queen Anne to Fremont. The westernmost, Ballard Bridge, links the neighborhood of Magnolia, west of Queen Anne, with Ballard.

CityPass

If you're going to be in Seattle for a while and plan on seeing its premiere attractions, you might want to consider buying a CityPass. Good for nine days, the pass gets you entry into the Space Needle, Pacific Science Center, Seattle Aquarium, Argosy Cruises' Seattle Harbor Tour, the Museum of Flight and the Woodland Park Zoo. You wind up saving 50% on admission costs and you never have to stand in line. A CityPass costs $42/29 for an adult/child aged four to 13. You can buy one at whichever of the six venues you visit first or online at http://citypass.net.

ITINERARIES

One Day

Crack your day wide open with a visit to **Pike Place Market** (p55); the bellows of the fishmongers will be your alarm clock. Grab coffee and a pastry to go, then explore historic **Pioneer Square** (p48) and the totem poles in **Occidental Park** (p50). Don't miss the chance to duck into **Elliott Bay Book Company** (p50), Seattle's best bookstore. Lunch at the café downstairs, or follow your nose to a tasty meal in the **International District** (p52). That night, catch a **Mariners** (p154) or **Seahawks** (p155) game, and stop by the **Pyramid Ale House** (p135) for a quintessential Northwest brewpub experience. If sports aren't your bag, spend the evening barhopping in **Belltown** (p60) instead.

Three Days

Follow the one-day itinerary, then start the next morning with a francophilic breakfast at **Le Pichet** (p114). Take the Monorail over to Seattle Center for a close-up view of the **Space Needle** (p63); if it's a clear day, ride up and check out the stellar views. Explore the **Pacific Science Center** (p63), then duck into the Experience Music Project's **Liquid Lounge** (p138) for happy hour (both good options for keeping the kids happy). If you have the time and energy, hit the shops at **Westlake Center** (p47) on the Monorail's return trip. Spend day three in an outlying neighborhood or two. You might start with breakfast at **Beth's** (p123) and a stroll around **Green Lake** (p85), then peruse funky **Fremont** (p81) and grab lunch at **Still Life** (p84); later, head to well-preserved historic Ballard for dinner at the **Old Town Ale House** (p125) and live music at the **Tractor Tavern** (p133) or the **Sunset Tavern** (p132).

One Week

Follow the three-day itinerary, then, the next morning, catch a ferry to **Bainbridge Island** (p192) and breathe in the salt air. Enjoy a tasting at the **Bainbridge Island Winery** (p192) before your return trip. In the evening, don your best duds and head to **Capitol Hill** (p75) to strut through the chic bar scene. A full week gives you time to plan an excursion; try the **Hoh River Rain Forest** (p202) or majestic **Mt Rainier** (p196). You should also spend a day exploring the **U District** (p78) and its centerpiece, the eminently walkable **University of Washington** (p80), then rent a bicycle and ride along the nearby **Burke-Gilman Trail** (p102) – or rent a kayak and paddle off into the sunset.

ORGANIZED TOURS

ARGOSY CRUISES SEATTLE HARBOR TOUR Map pp238-9

☎ 206-623-1445, 800-642-7816;www.argosycruises .com; adult/child $16/7; departs from Pier 55

One of the major operators, Argosy has a number of different tours departing daily year-round from Pier 55. Its popular Seattle Harbor Tour is a one-hour narrated tour of Elliott Bay, the Waterfront and the Port of Seattle. It also offers tours of the Hiram M Chittenden locks, speedboat cruises and a fine-dining cruise.

BILL SPEIDEL'S UNDERGROUND TOUR Map pp236-7

☎ 206-682-4646; 608 1st Ave; adult/child/senior $10/5/8; ☼ 11am-5pm, schedule varies

Speidel was a local historian (he wrote the book *Sons of the Profits*) who relished stories of Seattle's sordid past – the good old days of hard-drinking politicians and hard-working 'seamstresses,' as the bordello girls were called. This famous 'underground' tour, though it might get a little corny at times, delivers the goods on historic Seattle as a rough and rowdy industrial town (p38). Starting at Doc Maynard's Public House and wandering through the tunnels and sidewalks hidden beneath the streets of Pioneer Square, the tour is massively popular, especially in prime tourist season. No reservations are accepted, so try to arrive half an hour early if you want to be sure you get in.

CHINATOWN DISCOVERY TOURS

☎ 425-885-3085; www.seattlechinatowntour.com; adult $14.95-39.95, child $9.95-22.95

This tour group leads travelers through the International District with stops at historic sites, a fortune-cookie factory and various shops. Options include a daytime tour with a dim-sum lunch and an evening tour with an eight-course banquet. Reservations are required; call ahead.

For Children

Kids will enjoy accompanying their parents on many of the activities described in this book, but a few places are keyed specifically to the short-pants set. Here are some of the best:

- **Alki Beach** (p93) In West Seattle.
- **Burke Museum** (p79) In the U District.
- **Children's Museum** (p63) In the Seattle Center.
- **Children's Park** (p54) In the International District.
- **Experience Music Project** (p63) In the Seattle Center.
- **Odyssey Maritime Discovery Center** (p59), **Seattle Aquarium** (p59) and **Imax Theater** (p60) On the Waterfront.
- **Pacific Science Center** (p63) In the Seattle Center.

GRAY LINE OF SEATTLE CITY SIGHTS TOUR Map pp234-5

☎ 206-626-5208, 800-426-7532; www.graylineofseattle.com; 800 Convention Place; adult/child $29/14.50; ☽ 9am Mar-Oct

Gray Line has a whole catalog of Seattle-area bus tours, but its City Sights Tour is recommended as a quick-hit rundown of the city's highlights in a 20-passenger coach. Gray Line also offers multiday package tours to the San Juan Islands and Victoria, BC. All trips depart from the Gray Line ticket desk at the convention center at 800 Convention Place.

SAILING IN SEATTLE SUNSET CRUISE

Map pp240-1

☎ 206-289-0094; www.sailing-in-seattle.com; 2040 Westlake Ave; up to 6 people $225

Sailing in Seattle offers 2½-hour sunset sails around Lake Union on the 33ft *Whoodat* every evening. There's also a Puget Sound Day Cruise that includes a trip through the Hiram M Chittenden Locks and lasts from eight to 10 hours. Trips meet on Lake Union at Sailing in Seattle's dock behind the China Harbor Restaurant on Westlake Ave.

SEATTLE ARCHITECTURAL FOUNDATION Map pp234-5

☎ 206-667-9186; www.seattlearchitectural.org/viewpoints; 1333 5th Ave, Suite 300; tours $12-20

Viewpoints Walking Tours is a series of theme tours that study historic architecture in downtown Seattle and surrounding neighborhoods. The tours, available mid-May through October,

sell out quickly – be sure to call well in advance; lunch is not included.

SEATTLE TROLLEY TOURS Map pp234-5

☎ 206-626-5208; information centers at 1500 6th Ave & 800 Convention Pl; adult/child $15/7; ☽ every 30min May 1–Oct 15

The trolley tour provides visitors with a great form of flexible downtown transportation. Visitors are encouraged to get on and off these motorized trolley cars at leisure; tickets are good for the full day of operation – and keep your ticket, because the second day is free. The 11 stops, indicated by bright-yellow sandwich boards, are dotted throughout the city, including downtown, the Space Needle, Pike Place Market, Pioneer Square, the International District, Safeco Field, Seattle Art Museum and various points along the Waterfront.

SEE SEATTLE WALKING TOURS

Map pp240-1

☎ 425-226-7641; www.see-seattle.com; per person $20; ☽ 10am Mon-Sat

See Seattle runs a variety of theme tours, from public-art walks to scavenger hunts. While reservations aren't required for the walking tour, which start at the Westlake Center, they are recommended.

TILLICUM VILLAGE TOURS Map pp238-9

☎ 206-933-8600, 800-426-1205; www.tillicumvillage.com; adult/child/senior $65/25/59

From Pier 55, take a trip to Blake Island, the birthplace of Seattle's namesake **Chief Sealth**. The four-hour trip includes a salmon bake, a native dance and a movie at an old Duwamish Indian village.

Westlake Plaza, Downtown (p45)

Street Smarts

Seattle street addresses are really confusing, and few people go to the trouble to figure out how the system fits together. Instead, people use neighborhoods to indicate where things are found. For instance, '10th Ave on Queen Anne' indicates which 10th Ave is being referred to; likewise '1st Ave in Wallingford' directs one to that particular 1st Ave. So it's important to arrive at a working knowledge of Seattle's neighborhoods. With so many numbering systems at odds with each other, it's the only way to easily make sense of the city.

Basically, downtown is in the middle of the hourglass part of Seattle; Pioneer Square is to the south of it. Capitol Hill lies to the northeast, and the Central District/Madrona area to the east. The U District is just north of Capitol Hill, across Lake Washington. Belltown, Seattle Center and Queen Anne are to the slight northwest of downtown. Fremont, Wallingford and Green Lake are almost straight north, across Lake Union, and Ballard is off to the seemingly distant northwest. But keep in mind the outlying neighborhoods are all much closer than they seem to be.

Because of Seattle's topographic stew of bays, islands, hills and peninsulas, nothing as sensible as a standard street grid system fits the city. Instead, Seattle's street system is an amalgam of several separate grids that sometimes overlap each other, leading to maximum confusion. That said, it's fairly easy to get a working understanding of the numbering system and the way all the areas of the city fit together.

Generally speaking, avenues run north and south, and streets run east and west. Yesler Way near Pioneer Square is the zero street for numbering addresses on downtown avenues; Western Ave is the zero street for addresses on streets. Usually Seattle's avenues have a directional suffix (6th Ave S), while its streets have directional prefixes (S Charles St); however, downtown streets and avenues have no directional affixes.

Seattle addresses with a West affix are in the Queen Anne and Magnolia neighborhoods, directly northwest of downtown. A swathe of streets and avenues cutting north from Lake Union, taking in parts of Fremont, Wallingford, Green Lake and the eastern part of Queen Anne, take a simple North prefix (avenues with a North suffix, however, are north of downtown near Seattle Center). Loosely speaking, streets and avenues with a Northeast affix are east of I-5 and north of Lake Union in an area that takes in the University of Washington. To add to the confusion, many of the streets and avenues in this area are numbered. Streets and avenues with a Northwest affix are north of the shipping canal in and around Ballard. Addresses with a Southwest affix are in West Seattle. Streets and avenues south of Yesler Way are labeled South. Up on Capitol Hill, watch for the East affix on streets and avenues.

DOWNTOWN & FIRST HILL

Eating p108; Shopping p167; Sleeping p178

Downtown Seattle is a bit of an anomaly. Instead of being the beating heart of the city, it's a fairly quiet, functional business district between Seattle's twin hearts, Pike Place Market and Pioneer Square. What most people mean by 'downtown' is the collection of office buildings, hotels and retail shops between 2nd and 7th Aves. It's best to visit downtown on a weekday, when throngs of people are working and shopping in the area. At night and on weekends, this part of town feels rather desolate.

Flanked to the south by Pioneer Square and to the north by Belltown (also called the Denny Regrade), today's city center is bordered to the east by First Hill, where Seattle's pioneer elite built elaborate mansions with views of downtown and Elliott Bay. The jungle of high-rises teetering on Seattle's steep streets makes downtown look very imposing when viewed from a distance. The city seems especially daunting on the incoming ferry ride from Puget Sound or at the first glimpse of the city from I-5. The actual core, however, is quite compact. No part of downtown is more than a brisk 20-minute walk from another, and the multiple transit options make it easy to get around.

Orientation

The area is bounded by Virginia Ave and Denny Way to the north, Yesler to the south, I-5 to the east and 2nd Ave to the west. This area contains the vast majority of the city's major hotels, shopping venues and soaring business towers. It's easy to further divide this lengthy strip into two separate sections: the lively retail core to the north and the contemporary business district to the south.

Seattle's retail heaven extends from the corner of 5th Ave and Pike St two or three blocks in all directions. A block north, on 5th Ave at Pine St, is the flagship store of Nordstrom, the national clothing retailer that got its start in Seattle. Just to the west of Nordstrom is Westlake Center, the veritable pumping heart of the retail district.

Across Pine St, a pedestrian plaza called Westlake Park is a popular people-watching haven and a great place to plop down on a bench and eat lunch or sip coffee on sunny days. Skateboarders and bike messengers careen through crowds of trench-coat-clad professionals and shoppers teetering under the weight of their bags. Buskers pipe out songs, entrepreneurs hawk T-shirts, and preachers bellow fire and brimstone. Don't miss artist Robert Maki's water sculpture, which you can walk through without getting wet.

The entire retail area seems to be in a perpetual state of demolition and reconstruction. As the area's older hotels and redbrick warehouses fall to the wrecking ball, new shopping and parking structures go up in a feverish attempt to sustain the growing number of consumers who throng to this area to ogle and buy; see the Shopping chapter, p167.

Seattle's modern business district is south of the retail core, along 3rd, 4th and 5th Aves. Rather dull modern office towers dominate this area; however, some of the older art deco and terra-cotta–fronted buildings are charming – it's worth following the 'Downtown Architecture' tour (p99) for a closer look.

If you're trying to keep track of the street names in downtown Seattle, here's a handy mnemonic device: from Yesler Way up to Stewart, the streets proceed in alphabetic pairs – Jefferson and James, Cherry and Columbia, Marion and Madison, Spring and Seneca, University and Union, Pike and Pine. The tool for remembering the order is the old saw, learned by Seattle schoolchildren for years, that Jesus Christ Made Seattle Under Protest.

It's also worth remembering that Seattle has some *very* steep streets, a consideration for both drivers and pedestrians. In fact, if you're going to spend a significant chunk of time downtown, leave the car at home or parked in one of the outlying neighborhoods. Abrupt uphills, one-way streets and expensive parking make driving downtown a little hectic, especially when you consider that all buses in the downtown core are free.

Transportation

Bus Practically every bus in Seattle goes through downtown; see the Downtown Metro Transit map (p250) and under Transportation in the Directory chapter (p205). Downtown is in the Ride Free Area.

Monorail The terminus is inside Westlake Center, at 4th Ave & Pine St; a Metro Transit information booth is also here.

Parking Metered street parking and some paid lots (but they're very expensive).

1001 FOURTH AVE PLAZA Map pp234-5

Built in 1969, this was one of the city's first real skyscrapers. At the time, 1001 Fourth Ave Plaza was a darling of the architectural world, though nowadays the 50-story bronze block looks incredibly dated. Locals nicknamed it 'the box that the Space Needle came in.' In the plaza outside is the **Three Piece Sculpture: Vertebrae**, a sculpture by Henry Moore – a result of Seattle's 'one percent for art' clause.

ARCTIC BUILDING Map pp234-5

700 3rd Ave at Cherry St

The Arctic Building, completed in 1917, is unique for its intricate terra-cotta ornamentation and 25 walrus heads peeking off the building's exterior. Though the walruses' tusks were originally authentic ivory, an earthquake in the 1940s shook a few of them loose to the ground. To protect passersby from being skewered by falling tusks, the ivory was replaced with epoxy.

BENAROYA CONCERT HALL Map p234-5

☎ 206-215-9494; 200 University St

With a hefty bill of almost $120 million in construction costs, it's no wonder the Benaroya Concert Hall, Seattle Symphony's primary venue, oozes luxury. From the minute you step into the glass-enclosed lobby of the performance hall you're overwhelmed with views of Elliott Bay; on sunny days you might be lucky enough to see the snowy peaks of the Olympic Range far in the distance. Even if you're not attending the symphony, you can walk through the foyer and marvel at the 20ft-long chandeliers, specially created by Tacoma glassmaker Dale Chihuly.

COLUMBIA SEAFIRST CENTER Map pp234-5
4th Ave & Columbia St; observation deck $5;
☯ 8:30am-4:30pm Mon-Fri
Locals call this striking structure the 'Darth Vader' building. Catch a breathtaking view from the observation deck on the 73rd of its 76 floors.

SEATTLE ART MUSEUM Map pp234-5
SAM; ☎ 206-654-3100; 100 University St at 1st Ave; adult/senior & student/child/member $7/5/free/free;
☯ 10am-5pm Tue-Sun, 10am-9pm Thu
The Seattle Art Museum's collection focuses on Asian, African and Native American folk and tribal art. Especially good are the displays of masks, canoes and totems from Northwest coastal tribes. The permanent collection has a small but representational selection of paintings by European and American modern masters, but a rather thin and disappointing display of works by contemporary artists. Contemporary standouts include several Joseph Cornell boxes on the top floor and work by Harlem Renaissance painter Jacob Lawrence, who spent his last 30 years in Seattle. Traveling shows are found in the Special Exhibits gallery and are often outstanding; films and lectures take place in the 300-seat auditorium.

The building itself, a postmodern structure faced in limestone and ornamented terra-cotta, makes the most of its hillside location; the spacious galleries step down the slope and are linked by immense staircases. This Robert Venturi–designed building has proven to be controversial, however, as only a third of its 145,000 sq feet is actually devoted to usable exhibition space. Jonathan Borofsky's four-story action sculpture, Hammering Man, waves tools at the museum's front door. The museum is planning to expand its downtown building and build an 8-acre outdoor sculpture park at the foot of Broad St, next to Myrtle Edwards Park.

SAM admission is free on the first Thursday of every month; it's a good idea to save your ticket, as it's also valid at the Seattle Asian Art Museum in Volunteer Park (p78) within a week of purchase.

SEATTLE TOWER Map pp234-5
1218 3rd Ave
Formerly the Northern Life Tower, this 26-story art deco skyscraper, built in 1928, was designed to reflect the mountains of the Pacific Northwest. The brickwork on the exterior blends from dark at the bottom to light on top the same way mountains appear to do. Check out the 18-karat-gold relief map in the lobby.

TIMES SQUARE BUILDING Map pp234-5
Olive Way & Stewart St
This terra-cotta and granite structure, guarded by eagles perched on the roof, was designed by the Paris-trained architect Carl Gould (who also did the Seattle Asian Art Museum and the UW's Suzzallo Library). It housed the *Seattle Times* from 1916 to 1931.

WASHINGTON STATE CONVENTION & TRADE CENTER Map pp234-5
☎ 206-447-5000; 7th Ave & Pike St (main entrance)
It's hard to miss this gigantic complex decked out with ballrooms, meeting rooms, space for exhibitions and a **visitors' center** (☎ 206-461-5840; 800 Convention Pl; ☯ 9am-5pm Mon-Fri). An arched-glass bridge spans Pike St between 7th and 8th Aves.

WESTLAKE CENTER Map pp234-5
4th Ave & Pine St
This shopping center is the veritable pumping heart of the retail district. One of the Rowse Company developments found in practically every sizable US city (notably Atlanta's Peach Tree Plaza, Boston's Faneuil Hall and Portland's Pioneer Place), Westlake Center is filled with national boutique chains and has a top-floor food court. This is also where the **Monorail** (p207) stops and starts on its 1.2-mile trip to and from Seattle Center. The once-futuristic people-mover makes its 90-second run every 10 minutes daily (tickets $1.50).

Neighborhoods – Downtown & First Hill

FIRST HILL

First Hill, with its commanding position directly to the east and above downtown, became the foremost status neighborhood for early Seattleites. Throughout the area you'll still find traces of the early glory, including a few magnificent old mansions and some excellent examples of early Seattle architecture. But most mansions of the once mighty have long since been torn down and replaced by hospitals. Known as 'Pill Hill,' First Hill is home to three major hospitals. With the accompanying research and support facilities, it can seem indeed that everything up here is related to the medical industry.

Orientation

To reach First Hill, catch bus No 2 on the west side of 3rd Ave downtown and get off at the Swedish Medical Center. First Hill is out of the Ride Free Area, however, so be prepared to pay up if you take the bus. On foot it's a short walk uphill from downtown. From Westlake Center, head over to University St and walk uphill through Freeway Park or, if you're in the business district, walk straight up Madison St to Terry Ave, and you'll be at the Sorrento Hotel.

FRYE ART MUSEUM Map pp234-5
☎ 206-622-9250; 704 Terry Ave; admission free; ⊗ 10am-5pm Tue-Sat, noon-5pm Sun, 10am-9pm Thu
This small museum on First Hill preserves the collection of Charles and Emma Frye. The Fryes collected more than 1000 paintings, mostly 19th- and early-20th-century European and American pieces, and a few Alaskan and Russian artworks. If this inspires a stifled yawn, think again. Since its 1997 expansion, the Frye has gained a hipness that was lacking before; music performances, poetry readings and interesting rotating exhibits, from traveling painters to local printmakers, now make the museum a worthwhile stop.

SORRENTO HOTEL Map pp234-5
900 Madison St
This grand working hotel on First Hill is a fine example of Italian Renaissance architecture.

Built in 1909 by a Seattle clothing merchant, the Sorrento was one of the first hotels designed to absorb the crowds of prospectors journeying through town on their way to Alaska in search of gold; see p180 for more information on the hotel.

STIMSON-GREEN MANSION Map pp234-5
☎ 206-624-0474; 1204 Minor Ave; ⊗ by appointment only
One of the first homes on First Hill, the baronial Stimson-Green Mansion is an English Tudor-style mansion completed in 1901 by lumber and real-estate developer CD Stimson. Built from brick, stucco and wood, this stately home is now owned by Stimson's granddaughter. The interior rooms are decorated to reflect the different design styles popular at the turn of the 20th century. Today the mansion is used for private catered events.

PIONEER SQUARE

Eating p110; Shopping p168; Sleeping p181

Browsing the Pioneer Square Historic District is rather like visiting a movie set of early-20th-century Seattle, except that the food and the shopping are better. This is the birthplace of Seattle, and the redbrick district of historic buildings and totem-lined plazas is still a real crossroads of the modern city.

Seattle's first townsite at Pioneer Square is an enclave of handsome old buildings and shaded squares. The area is also full of restaurants and cafés and some of the best nonchain-store shopping in the city, with great bookstores, antique markets, art galleries and gift shops. Even die-hard antishoppers should stop at a couple of the old storefronts. The **Grand Central Arcade** (214 1st Ave S between S Washington & S Main Sts) has a good bakery-café, plenty of tables, a cozy fire and staircases leading to the underground shopping arcade. You can walk straight through here to Occidental Park (p50). At night,

Top Five Pioneer Square

- **Doc Maynard's Public House** (p50) Old-world charm and history.
- **Elliott Bay Book Company** (p50) Biblio-worship.
- **Il Terrazzo Carmine** (p110) First-class dining.
- **Occidental Park** (p50) Totem poles and a great atmosphere.
- **Zeitgeist** (p149) Drink a latte, feel like a local.

Pioneer Square pubs and clubs kick up an energetic party scene that offers quantity, if not quality (p148).

In the early days of Seattle, Pioneer Square was a haphazard settlement made up of wooden storefronts, log homes and lumber mills. The Great Fire of 1889 leveled 30 blocks – the original town – but the city rapidly rebounded: almost all of the buildings that now stand in the Pioneer Square area were constructed between 1890 and 1905. As many as 50 of these structures were designed by one architect, Elmer Fisher. As part of this massive rebuilding project, city planners took the dramatic step of regrading Denny Hill, one of Seattle's original seven steep hills that rose sharply out of Elliott Bay. This raised the new city about a dozen feet above the original settlement. Back in the good old days, the underground tunnels that remained were used as opium dens and speakeasies (p43).

Many post-fire buildings were built in the grand Romanesque Revival style already popular in Boston and Chicago, which displayed wealth and prosperity to the pioneers. Plus, no-one wanted to see the town go up in flames again and, let's face it, brick, stone and steel are a lot less likely to burn.

Pioneer Square fell on hard times for years – amazingly, there were plans to level the area in the late 1960s to make room for parking lots and office buildings. Eventually, bank loans, cheap rents and Historic Register status brought in businesses, art galleries, antique shops and interior-design stores. These days, many Pioneer Square restaurants play up the frontier image while serving notably good food. Pioneer Square is also a major center for live music and nightlife.

Perhaps mirroring its early days when this was a rough-and-tumble frontier town, Pioneer Square still sees some rowdiness; there's often a juxtaposition of drunken tourists and Seattle's homeless hanging around the bar scene. Though the ruckus may seem a little unnerving, especially at night, there's little danger beyond the occasional incident.

Orientation

The Pioneer Square area is bounded roughly by Cherry and S King Sts to the north and south, and 1st and 3rd Aves S to the west and east. The main street in the area is 1st Ave S. The area is most easily reached by walking or by bus (it's in the Ride Free Area). Join the crowds and wander down the avenue, past upscale stores, art galleries, trendy cafés and homeless missions.

If you're in the bus tunnel, get off at Pioneer Square. From the exit, Pioneer Square is immediately downhill. You can also take any of the aboveground buses that run along 1st Ave. For something more touristy and historic, take the Waterfront Streetcar from any of its stops along the Waterfront, which will put you smack bang in the heart of Occidental Square.

If walking from Pike Place Market (about 10 minutes), take either Alaskan Way south along the Waterfront, or 1st Ave to pass by Seattle Art Museum's *Hammering Man* sculpture and some unusual shops.

From Occidental Park you can catch the Waterfront Streetcar east to the International District or west to the Waterfront. The fare costs $1.25 during peak hours (6am to 9am and 3pm to 6pm) and $1 at other times.

Transportation

Bus Pioneer Square is in the Ride Free Area. There's a Pioneer Square stop in the bus tunnel and several aboveground buses also run along 1st Ave.

Streetcar The Waterfront Streetcar takes you right to Occidental Square.

Parking It's difficult to find parking. There are limited lots (including one at the Seattle Art Museum) but they're pricey.

DOC MAYNARD'S PUBLIC HOUSE
Map pp236-7

☎ 206-682-4646; 610 1st Ave S

This atmospheric pub transports you back to the old days of pioneer Seattle. It's named after Doc Maynard, one of the city's founding fathers and quite a character. An Ohio native, Maynard was divorced when he arrived in the city and was out for a good time; he was vivacious and generous and he liked his liquor. This combination led him to give away cash or land to almost anyone with a promising idea, and he died essentially landless and broke (the rather revealing epitaph on his second wife, Catherine's, tombstone reads, 'She did what she could'). The gorgeous carved bar here was shipped over from Chicago.

ELLIOTT BAY BOOK COMPANY Map pp236-7
☎ 206-624-6600; 101 S Main St; ☽ 9:30am-11pm Mon-Sat, 11am-6pm Sun

Seattle's premier bookstore and literary gathering place and the original home of the Globe Hotel, built in 1890. The place is made for browsing, with its high ceilings, peculiar multilevel bookshelves and funny niches and corners. Downstairs is a snug little café (p110).

GRAND CENTRAL ARCADE Map pp236-7
☎ 206-623-7417; 214 1st Ave S

This lovely meeting point was originally Squire's Opera House, erected in 1879 by Watson Squire, who became one of Washington's first senators after it achieved statehood. When the Opera House burned down, it was rebuilt as the Squire-Latimer Building and later became the Grand Central Hotel. The hotel died during the Depression, but it underwent a major restoration in the 1970s and now contains two floors of shops, including the excellent Grand Central Baking Co.

KING STREET STATION Map pp236-7
303 S Jackson St

The old Great Northern Railroad depot is now in use as an Amtrak station. This jewel of a train station – built in 1906 by Reed & Stem, who also designed New York City's Grand Central Station – has been blighted since the 1960s by a horrible ceiling-lowering revamp, but the fabulous old Italianate plasterwork and detailing are still there. The old depot's stately brick tower has long been an integral (though now dwarfed) piece of the downtown skyline. Renovation of the building will be dramatic; the latest plan is to incorporate the new King

Street plans into a 'super station' along the expanded Monorail track. Regardless, don't expect this area to be free of cranes and cement trucks till 2006 or so.

KLONDIKE GOLD RUSH NATIONAL PARK Map pp236-7
☎ 206-553-7220; 117 S Main St; admission free; ☽ 9am-5pm

In an early example of Seattle civic boosters clamoring to put the city 'on the map,' the Seattle *Post-Intelligencer* trumpeted the news that a ship full of gold had arrived in town on July 17, 1897. Masses of gold-fevered unfortunates swarmed the city on their way to the Klondike River area in the Yukon Territory, and local merchants made a killing. Seattle's seminal position as the outfitting and transportation hub for the Alaskan and Yukon Gold Rush is recognized at Klondike Gold Rush National Park, one of the USA's few indoor national historical parks. It's easy to miss, but worth seeking out. Exhibits, photos and news clippings document the era and give an idea of how much gear, food and true grit were necessary to stake a claim in the Klondike. Gold panning is demonstrated by park rangers, and you can sit down and view a slide presentation about the gold rush.

OCCIDENTAL PARK Map pp236-7
Btwn S Washington & S Main Sts, just off 1st Ave S

Notable in this cobblestone plaza are the **totem poles** carved by Duane Pasco, a nationally respected Chinookan carver and artist from Poulsbo on the Kitsap Peninsula. The totems depict the welcoming spirit of Kwakiutl, a totem bear, the tall Sun and Raven and a man riding on the tail of a whale. For more on the art and purpose of totem poles, see p27.

Also eye-catching is the **Firefighters' Memorial**, featuring life-size bronze sculptures of firefighters in action. Engraved on the granite slabs surrounding the sculpture are the names of Seattle firefighters who have been killed in the line of duty since the department's inception after the Great Fire. The artist is Hai Ying Wu, a University of Washington graduate.

OCCIDENTAL SQUARE Map pp236-7
S Main & S Jackson Sts

Occidental Square, with its cobblestone plaza flanked by unusually handsome Victorian buildings, is one of the nicest places in this area. Visit **Glass House Studio** (☎ 206-682-9939; 311 Occidental Ave S) to see local artists' impressive works of blown, cast and lamp-worked glass. If you need a shot of caffeine or a chance to catch your breath, detour to the original location of **Torrefazione Italia** (320 Occidental Ave S) – you'll love its real Italian faience cups. Coffee junkies, poets or anyone wearing black will want to make the pilgrimage to **Zeitgeist** (p149; S Jackson St & 2nd Ave S). This groovy coffeehouse is a local haunt of artists and architects. Along S Jackson St you'll find an excellent concentration of antique stores and some of the city's most prestigious galleries.

PIONEER BUILDING Map pp236-7
606 1st Ave S
Built in 1891, this magnificent structure facing Pioneer Square Park is one of the finest Victorian buildings left in Seattle; many mining companies had offices here during the Klondike Gold Rush years. It was designed by Elmer Fisher, whose fingerprints are all over Pioneer Square. Resting on the site of Henry Yesler's original home, the building now houses, in part, Doc Maynard's Public House (p50), a handsome old bar and restaurant, and the ticket office for Bill Speidel's Underground Tour (p43). Be sure to catch a glimpse of the Italian marble in the lobby.

PIONEER SQUARE PARK Map pp236-7
Cherry St & 1st Ave S
The original Pioneer Square is a cobblestone triangular plaza where Henry Yesler's sawmill cut the giant trees that marked Seattle's first industry. Known officially as Pioneer Square Park, the plaza features a bust of **Chief Seattle** (Sealth, in the original language), an ornate pergola and a totem pole. Some wayward early Seattleites, so the story goes, stole the totem from the Tlingit natives in southeastern Alaska in 1890. An arsonist lit the pole aflame in 1938, burning it to the ground. When asked if they could carve a replacement pole, the Tlingit took the money offered, thanking the city for payment of the first totem, and said it would cost $5000 to carve another one. The city coughed up the money and the Tlingit obliged with the pole you see today.

The decorative pergola was built in the early 1900s to serve as an entryway to an underground lavatory and to shelter those waiting for the cable car that went up and down Yesler Way. The reportedly elaborate restroom eventually closed due to serious plumbing problems at high tide. In January 2001, the pergola was leveled by a wayward truck; it has been restored and was put back where it belongs in 2002, looking good as new.

SAFECO FIELD Map pp236-7
general information ☎ 206-346-4241, **ticket information** ☎ 206-622-4487; 1250 1st Ave S; adult/child $7/3; 1hr tours ⏰ 10:30am, 12:20pm & 2:30pm on nongame days Apr-Oct; 12:30 & 2:30pm Tue-Sun Nov-Mar
The Mariners' $517 million ballpark, Safeco Field, opened in July 1999. The stadium, with its retractable roof, 47,000 seats and real grass, was funded in part by taxpayers and tourists; more than half the money came from taxes on food sold in King County restaurants and bars and from taxes on rental cars. Money also came from profits on scratch-lottery tickets. The Mariners coughed up most of the difference. The stadium's unique design means it commands fantastic views of the surrounding mountains, downtown and Puget Sound. There's no 2:30pm tour on game days and no tours if the game is before 6pm.

SEAHAWKS STADIUM Map pp236-7
800 Occidental Ave S
The late, mostly unlamented Kingdome, long Seattle's biggest eyesore, was once the sports stadium that served as home field for the city's professional baseball and football franchises. Then it was imploded spectacularly in 2000 and replaced by the 72,000-seat Seahawks Stadium. Seattle's soccer team, the Sounders, also play here; the Mariners now play at Safeco Field.

SMITH TOWER Map pp236-7
☎ 206-622-4004; 506 2nd Ave S at Yesler Way; observation deck adult/senior & student $5/3; ⏰ 10am-4pm May-Oct
You can't miss Seattle's first skyscraper. For half a century after its construction in 1914, the 42-story Smith Tower was well known as the tallest building west of Chicago. The distinctive tower was erected by LC Smith, a man who built his fortune on typewriters (Smith-Corona) and guns (Smith & Wesson). Smith died during the building's construction, so he never got to see the beauty that still bears his name. Walk into the onyx- and marble-paneled lobby, step aboard one of the brass-and-copper manually operated elevators and let it whisk you up to the 35th-floor observation deck for a great view of Seattle's Waterfront.

WATERFALL PARK Map pp236-7

Cnr S Main St & 2nd Ave S

This unusual park is an urban oasis commemorating workers of the United Parcel Service (UPS), which began in a basement at this location in 1907. The artificial 22ft waterfall that flows in this tiny open-air courtyard is flanked by tables and flowering plants. This is a perfect spot to eat a brown-bag lunch or to rest weary feet.

YESLER WAY Map pp236-7

Seattle claims its Yesler Way was the coining ground for the term 'skid road' – logs would 'skid' down the road linking a logging area above town to Henry Yesler's mill. With the decline of the area, the street became a haven for homeless people. Soon the nickname 'skid road' or 'skid row' was being used for equally destitute areas around the country, sort of the opposite to 'easy street.'

As for Arthur Yesler himself, local historians paint him as an ambitious business zealot who clashed frequently with the wild-and-woolly Doc Maynard. These two men, who by all accounts were equally stubborn, both owned part of the land that would eventually become Pioneer Square. This resulted in a highly symbolic grid clash, in which Yesler's section of the Square had streets running parallel to the river, while Maynard's came crashing in at a north–south angle. Yesler maintained, not unreasonably, that Doc was drunk when he submitted his portion of the plans.

INTERNATIONAL DISTRICT

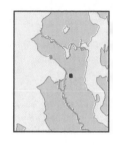

Eating p111; Shopping p169

East of Pioneer Square is the International District, Seattle's Chinatown, where Asian groceries and restaurants line the streets. The updated moniker reflects both a controversial wave of political correctness and the gradual diversification of the area. The Chinese were among the first settlers in Seattle in the late 1800s (the original Chinatown was around 2nd Ave and Washington St), followed by Japanese, Filipinos, Vietnamese, Laotians and others. Later immigrants settled just to the east of present-day Chinatown in an area known as Little Saigon.

Although 'International District' seems a pretty useful term for this mix of races and cultures, it is in fact a relatively recent and controversial moniker, fashioned at the start of political correctness in the early 1970s. The Chinese grew resentful of the term when the renaming left 'Chinatown' a seemingly dirty word, but other Asian groups welcomed representation. Scuffles about who the neighborhood belongs to continue as they have throughout the area's history. Many Seattleites still refer to the area as Chinatown or simply 'the ID.'

Asian immigrants had an important presence in Seattle pretty much from the beginning. The muscle behind this early Asian settlement was the Wa Chong Company, labor contractors who brought in Chinese workers for timber, mining and railroad jobs in the 1860s and 1870s. After the anti-Chinese riots of 1886 (p37), the population of Chinatown dropped from an estimated 1500 to about 500; large numbers of Chinese immigrants didn't start coming back to the area until after the Great Fire of 1889. At that point, Chinatown shifted to where it is now, around the King St and Jackson St area.

Immigrants from Japan settled the area in the later 1800s and remained the largest minority group until WWII. 'Japantown' was just to the north of Chinatown; the Japanese population at one point was about 6000. From the 1920s to '40s, this was a very bustling place, thriving with Asian markets and other businesses that were built and patronized by the country's highest concentration of Japanese and Chinese Americans. African Americans and Filipinos also moved in around this time, but the area remained a veritable Japantown, with Japanese newspapers, schools, banks and restaurants.

The neighborhood took another massive hit during WWII, when all inhabitants of Japanese descent were forcibly moved out and interned at labor camps in the US interior (p40). The once-bustling shops were boarded up. When released, few of those who had been in the internment camps chose to return here to their old homes; those who did return, including the Moriguchis who founded the Uwajimaya store, made quite an impact on the future development of the neighborhood.

When I-5 pushed through the heart of the district, destroying many blocks of housing, the area became even more blighted, its identity even more divided. The arrival of Vietnamese immigrants in the 1970s and '80s, and more recently, an influx of immigrants from Hong Kong and mainland China, have breathed new life into the city's Asian community.

The recent renovation of Union Station, new sports stadiums and nearby office and condo developments sprouting up like weeds around the International District have left neighborhood activists fearing homogeneity in a district already rife with boundary issues. Will the condos win out over low-income housing? Will they fill up with yuppies and open the door to more coffee shops, 24-hour gyms and the Gap? Throughout the USA, major cities boast Chinatowns, Japantowns and other neighborhoods that embody a specific ethnicity. In Seattle, it's all crowded into one small neighborhood whose boundaries are threatened every time a land-use application shows up at City Hall.

Meanwhile, district activists strive to keep the area vital by stressing anti-crime measures and maintaining a strong community voice in housing and commercial development.

Top Five International District

- **Dim Sum** (p111) Chicken feet for breakfast!
- **Hau Hau Market** (see below) Vienamese groceries.
- **Hing Hay Park** (p54) A tranquil retreat.
- **Uwajimaya** (p54) A Japanese food and gift emporium.
- **Wing Luke Asian Museum** (p54) Sobering, illuminating history.

Orientation

The International District has its own exit from the underground bus tunnel; take any bus southbound to this stop, the last in the tunnel. The International District is also the last (or the first) stop on the Waterfront Streetcar route. The best way to get here on foot is to walk east up S Jackson St from Occidental Square.

The center of the district is between 5th and 7th Aves S and S Weller and S Jackson Sts. While this is definitely a Chinatown, it is nowhere near as large or as authentic as those you'll find in San Francisco or Vancouver, BC. Only a few of the old markets and herbal-remedy shops remain, and if you look up, you can see a couple of Hong Kong–style balconies protruding rather oddly from the faces of old redbrick storefronts and apartment buildings. But it's still a lively area, and if you're looking for Asian cuisine, you've come to the right place.

Under I-5 along S Jackson St, the pace changes considerably as you enter the International District's Vietnamese and Laotian areas. This is a genuine lived-in neighborhood; nothing in it panders to tourists. The center of this area is a series of strip malls at 12th Ave S at S Jackson St, where you'll find all manner of Vietnamese businesses including barbershops, real-estate offices, dentists and a profusion of markets and restaurants.

Transportation

Bus Any southbound bus stops here; it's the last stop in the tunnel.
Streetcar The International District is the southernmost stop on the Waterfront Streetcar route.

DANNY WOO INTERNATIONAL DISTRICT COMMUNITY GARDENS
Map pp236-7
Walk up S Main St from 6th Ave S
The Danny Woo International District Community Gardens are a 1.5-acre plot reserved for about 120 older and low-income International District residents, who grow a profusion of vegetables and fruit trees. Visitors can wander along the gravel paths and admire both the tidy gardens and the Seattle skyline and good views of Elliott Bay. Unfortunately, while you take in the view you'll have about 17 lanes of I-5 traffic right at your back.

HAU HAU MARKET
☎ 206-329-1688; 412 12th Ave S
Modern and bustling, the Hau Hau market is the Vietnamese equivalent of Uwajimaya down the hill, where you can get cheap produce, specialty meats such as pork ears and chicken feet, fireworks, and Asian gifts and knickknacks.

Seafood restaurant, International District

HING HAY PARK Map pp236-7
Maynard Ave S & King St
If you need a tranquil spot to rest while wandering the ID, Hing Hay Park lends a little green to the otherwise austere district. The traditional Chinese pavilion was a gift from the people of Taipei.

INTERNATIONAL CHILDREN'S PARK
Map pp236-7
S Lane St & 7th Ave
If the kids aren't up for exploring the Asian markets or sitting still for a dim sum brunch, bring them here to work off some energy playing on the bronze dragon sculpture, designed by George Tsutakawa.

PACIFIC HERB & GROCERY Map pp236-7
☎ 206-340-6411; 610 S Weller St, btwn 6th & Maynard Aves S
A good place to get a sense of Chinatown is along S Weller St. Apart from the many restaurants, there's Pacific Herb & Grocery, where the herbal-medicine specialists can tell you all about the uses of different roots, bones, flowers and teas. The shop next door is a great place to buy tofu at low prices – you can even watch them make it on the premises.

UWAJIMAYA Map pp236-7
☎ 206-624-6248; 600 5th Ave S; ⏱ 9am-10pm
This store is the centerpiece of the ID. Founded by Fujimatsu Moriguchi, one of the few Japanese to return here from the WWII internment camps, this large department and grocery store – a cornerstone of Seattle's Asian community – has everything from fresh fish and exotic fruits and vegetables to cooking utensils, and you'll come face-to-face with those dim sum ingredients you've always wondered about. The current location is a brand-new 'community' that includes living quarters and occupies a whole block. There's a food court in addition to the grocery store. It's a great place to browse. Upstairs from Uwajimaya, the giant **Kinokuniya** bookstore has an excellent collection of books about Asia and by Asian writers.

UNION STATION Map pp236-7
401 S Jackson St
Another landmark that benefited from restoration fever is Union Station, the old Union Pacific Railroad depot (1911). Until 1999 , it had been unoccupied since 1971, when the last train chugged out of the station. The restoration project included the preservation of the original tile floors, clocks and windows. More than 90 years of build-up was hand-scrubbed off the exterior brick. The Great Hall, half the size of a football field, remains an impressive space.

VIET HOA Map pp236-7
7th Ave S at S Jackson St
The Viet Hoa market has a greengrocer in one building and a fish and meat market in the other. Both display foods and cuts of meat you may have never seen before. The big tank of live turtles at the door and the buckets of fish that look like they're one splash away from coming back to life assure you that this market carries only the freshest ingredients.

WING LUKE ASIAN MUSEUM Map pp236-7
☎ 206-623-5124; 407 7th Ave S; adult/child/student $2.50/75¢/1.50; ⏱ 11am-4:30pm Tue-Fri, noon-4pm Sat & Sun
This Pan-Asian museum is devoted to Asian and Pacific American culture, history and art. Named after the first Asian elected official in the continental US, the museum examines the often difficult and violent meeting of Asian and Western cultures in Seattle. Particularly fascinating are the photos and displays on the Chinese settlement in the 1880s and the retelling of Japanese American internment during WWII.

PIKE PLACE MARKET & THE WATERFRONT

Eating p112; Shopping p169; Sleeping p181

These two neighborhoods are perhaps Seattle's most visited areas. They're divided by the Alaskan Way Viaduct, but linked by several corridors and stairways, and it's easy to visit both in the same day. The best bet is to hit the market early in the morning, relax in a waterfront park at midday, then stroll the shops along the boardwalk in the afternoon and watch the sun set over Elliott Bay while you munch a seafood dinner.

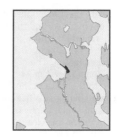

PIKE PLACE MARKET

Pike Place Market is one of Seattle's most popular tourist attractions, noted as much for its exuberant theatricality as for its vastly appealing fish and vegetable market. The lively, always bustling market fills daily with the bounty of local farms, rivers and the sea. Add in arts and crafts, loads of restaurants and cafés and buskers and other performers, and you'll discover why this mazelike market is Seattle at its irrepressible best. It sees about 40,000 visitors a day, and a good portion of them are locals out shopping for fresh fish and produce.

The market features some of the most boisterous fishmongers in the world, whose daredevil antics with salmon merge gymnastics, theater and cuisine. Despite the tourist-tickling showiness, the market maintains a down-home authenticity; real people work and buy here. A tip: don't eat before you go. This is one of the hotbeds of Seattle noshing and dining. You can get everything from a freshly grown Washington apple to a pot sticker, or even a seven-course French meal. Some of Seattle's favorite watering holes are also tucked into unlikely corners of the market buildings – for more details, see the Eating (p112) and Entertainment (p134) chapters.

Pike Place Market is the oldest continuously operating market in the nation. It was established in 1907 to give local farmers a place to sell their fruit and vegetables and bypass the middleman. Soon, the greengrocers made room for fishmongers, bakers, ethnic groceries, butchers, cheese sellers and purveyors of the rest of the Northwest's agricultural bounty. The market wasn't exactly architecturally robust – it's always been a throw-together series of sheds and stalls, haphazardly designed for utility – and was by no means an intentional tourist attraction. That came later.

An enthusiastic agricultural community spawned the market's heyday in the 1930s. Many of the first farmers were immigrants, a fact the market celebrates with annual themes acknowledging the contributions of various ethnic groups; past years have featured Japanese Americans, Italian Americans and Sephardic Jews.

Busking in the Market

Ever dream of ditching your stressful day job and making it on your own talents? Well, if you can sing a tune, play an instrument or be somehow entertaining, you can become a Pike Place Market busker. (Don't knock it – this is how Jewel got her start.) If it seems like the performers in the market are unusually well behaved and strategically placed, well, they are. Notice the red music note painted on the floor beneath a performer's feet – that's an official market Performer Location, and you can't busk anywhere else. The number painted in the middle of the music note indicates the number of musicians allowed to play at that location at any one time, be it a one-man show or a four-piece band. Wannabe market buskers must fill out an application and get a $15 permit from the market **Preservation & Development Authority** (PDA; ☎ 206-682-7452), whose office is behind the Main Arcade. The permit is good for an entire year (don't worry, you'll make lots more than that in an hour on any summer's day). To fill out an application, stop by the market office, located down the stairs just south of the Market Clock, from 8am to 4:30pm Monday to Friday.

By the 1960s sales at the market were suffering from suburbanization, the growth of supermarkets and the move away from local, small-scale market gardening. Vast tracts of agricultural land were disappearing, replaced by such ventures as the Northgate Mall and the Sea-Tac airport. The internment of Japanese American farmers during WWII had also taken its toll. The entire area became a bowery for the destitute and a center for prostitution and peep shows.

In the wake of the 1962 World's Fair, plans were drawn up to bulldoze the market and build high-rise office and apartment buildings on this piece of prime downtown real estate. Fortunately, public outcry prompted a voter's initiative to save the market. Subsequently, the space was cleaned up and restructured, and it has become once again the undeniable heart and soul of downtown; some 10 million people mill through the market each year. Thanks to the unique management of the market, social services programs and low-income housing mixed with the market commerce, the market has maintained its gritty edge. These initiatives have prevented the area from ever sliding too far upscale. A market law denies chain stores or franchises from opening up shop and ensures all businesses are locally owned. The one exception is, of course, Starbucks, which gets away with its market location because it marks the coffee giant's first (it opened in 1971).

Helpful Market Facts

Summer weekends and Friday afternoons at the market can be a lesson in mob dynamics; avoid visiting during these times unless you enjoy being stuck in human gridlock next to a stack of fresh crabs. The best bet for enjoying this wonderful market is to go on a weekday morning.

Market stalls are open from 8am to 6pm. Most of the market remains open for access to restaurants and bars late into the night.

The Main Arcade has restrooms on the lower level, although they're less gender-segregated than one might like, and the stall doors are skimpy. Several of the restaurants within the market also have restrooms (though usually for customers only).

Parking is both limited and expensive in the area, with the exception of a couple of parking structures immediately below the market on Western Ave. To find them from 1st Ave, turn west (downhill) on Lenora St, then south (left) on Western Ave. Continue on Western Ave until just past Victor Steinbrueck Park; the parking structures are immediately ahead.

Orientation

Pike Place is made up of several buildings, covering about eight warrenlike blocks at the top of the bluff overlooking the Waterfront. It's easy to get lost here – in fact, experiencing a slight sense of mayhem and dislocation is part of the charm of your initial acquaintance with this leviathan. Don't let the sometimes seedy nature of the neighborhood bother you; the streets around the market are still centers for sex shops and off-putting vagrancy, but there's very little real danger in the area. To help you find your way around, pick up a copy of *Welcome to the Pike Place Market,* a brochure with a map and directory of market shops. It's available throughout the market and at the information booth (see below).

If you're coming from downtown, simply walk down Pike St toward the Waterfront; you can't miss the huge 'Public Market' sign etched against the horizon. Incidentally, the sign and clock, installed in 1927, constituted one of the first pieces of outdoor neon on the West Coast. From the top of Pike St and 1st Ave, stop and survey the bustle and vitality of the market: buskers strum and sing, baguettes stick out of shoppers' backpacks, towers of artichokes loom in market stalls and bouquets of flowers bloom in the arms of passersby. Walk down the cobblestone street, past perpetually gridlocked cars (don't even think of driving down to Pike Place) and, before walking into the market, stop and shake the bronze snout of Rachel the Market Pig, the de facto mascot and presiding spirit of the market. The life-size piggy bank, carved by Whidbey Island artist Georgia Gerber and named after a real pig, collects about $6000 dollars each year. The funds are pumped back into market social services. Nearby is the market information booth (☎ 206-682-7453; Pike St & 1st Ave), which has maps of the market and information about Seattle in general. It also serves as a Ticket/Ticket booth (p131), selling discount tickets to various shows throughout the city.

Pike Place Market is on the western edge of downtown, off 1st Ave. Bus Nos 15, 18, 21, 22 and 56 run up and down 1st Ave from Pioneer Square. You can also take any bus along 3rd Ave and get off at the University Street Station, then walk west, toward the water. Along the Waterfront Streetcar route, Pike St Station is the stop for Pike Place Market; from there you need to climb the hill to the market itself. On foot, the market is just minutes from most downtown hotels. Walk down Pike, Pine or Stewart Sts toward the Waterfront and you're there.

CORNER & SANITARY MARKET BUILDINGS Map pp238-9
Pike Pl & Pike St

Across Pike Place from the Main Arcade is the 1912 Corner Market Building and the Sanitary Market Building, so named because it was the first of the market buildings in which live animals were prohibited. It's now a maze of ethnic groceries and great little eateries, including the Three Girls Bakery, with a sit-down area (it's always packed) and a take-out window with some of the best breads and sandwiches around. This is also the home of **Left Bank Books** (p170), an excellent source for all your socialist reading needs.

DOWN UNDER Map pp238-9

As if the levels of the market that are aboveground weren't enough, below the Main Arcade are three labyrinthine lower levels called the Down Under. Here you'll find a fabulously eclectic mix of pocket-size shops, from Indian spice stalls to magicians' supply shops and military-button booths.

ECONOMY MARKET BUILDING Map pp238-9
1st Ave & Pike St

Once a stable for merchants' horses, the Economy Market Building on the south side of the market entrance has a wonderful Italian grocery store, DeLaurenti's – a great place for any aficionado of Italian foods to browse and sample. There's also Tenzing Momo, one of the oldest apothecaries on the West Coast, where you can pick up herbal remedies, incense, oils and books. Tarot readings are available here on occasion. Look down at the Economy Market floor, and you'll see some of the 46,000 tiles that line the floor. The tiles were sold to the public in the 1980s for $35 apiece. If you bought a tile, you'd get your name on it and be proud that you helped save the market floor. Famous tile owners include *Cat in the Hat* creator Dr Seuss and former US president Ronald Reagan.

MAIN & NORTH ARCADES Map pp238-9
Western Ave

Rachel the Market Pig marks the main entrance to the Main and North Arcades, thin

Transportation

Bus Take Nos 15, 18, 21, 22 and 56.
Streetcar Get off at Pike St Station, then climb the hill.
Parking There are two parking structures immediately below the market on Western Ave; see p56.

shedlike structures that run along the edge of the hill; these are the busiest of the market buildings. With banks of fresh produce carefully arranged in artful displays, and fresh fish, crab and other shellfish piled high on ice, this is the real heart of the market. Here you'll see fishmongers tossing salmon back and forth like basketballs (many of these vendors will pack fish for overnight delivery). You'll also find cheese shops, butchers, tiny grocery stalls and almost everything else you need to put together a meal. The end of the North Arcade is dedicated to local artisans and craftspeople – products must be handmade to be sold here. The Main Arcade was built in 1907, the first of Frank Goodwin's market buildings.

POST ALLEY Map pp238-9

Between the Corner Market and the Triangle Building, tiny Post Alley is lined with more shops and restaurants. Extending north across Stewart St, this street offers two of the area's best places for a drink: the Pink Door Ristorante (p138), an Italian hideaway, and an Irish pub called Kells (p133). In Lower Post Alley beside the market sign is the **LaSalle Hotel**, the first

Top Five Pike Place Market & the Waterfront

- **Left Bank Books** (p170) Socialist & anarchist lit.
- **Odyssey Maritime Discovery Center** (p59) Become a virtual scallywag.
- **Pike Place Market** (p55) Flying fish and stacks of apples in the Main and North Arcades.
- **Pike Place Pub & Brewery** (p135) Lift a pint of Kilt Lifter in the South Arcade.
- **Seattle Aquarium** (p59) See under the sea.

Neighborhoods – Pike Place Market & the Waterfront

Market Tours

bordello north of Yesler Way; it was originally the Outlook Hotel, but was taken over in 1942 by the notorious Nellie Curtis, a woman with 13 aliases and a knack for running suspiciously profitable hotels with thousands of lonely sailors lined up nightly outside the door. (She's the namesake for the Pike Place Pub & Brewery's equally tempting Naughty Nellie's Ale.) The building, rehabbed in 1977, now houses commercial and residential space.

SOUTH ARCADE Map pp238-9
1411 1st Ave
If you continue past DeLaurenti's, you'll come into the South Arcade, the market's newest wing, home to upscale shops and the lively **Pike Place Pub & Brewery** (p135).

TRIANGLE BUILDING Map pp238-9
Pike Place & Post Alley
All in a row in the Triangle Building are Mr D's Greek Deli, Mee Sum Pastries (try the great pork buns), a juice bar and Cinnamon Works – all great choices for a quick snack.

VICTOR STEINBRUECK PARK Map pp238-9
Western Ave & Virginia St
When you've had enough of the market and its crowds, wander out the end of the North Arcade and cross Western Ave to Victor Steinbrueck Park, a grassy area designed in 1982 by Steinbrueck and Richard Haag. You'll find benches, a couple of totem poles designed by Quinault tribe member Marvin Oliver, a few shuffling vagrants and great views over the Waterfront and Elliott Bay. Rallies and political demonstrations are often held here.

THE WATERFRONT

Seattle's beginnings are indelibly tied to its waterfront area, where thousands of Klondike fortune hunters left on ships for Alaska in 1897 to seek gold, many returning with the wealth that served to boom the town into one of the foremost cities along the Pacific Rim (p39). Seattle's Waterfront is still a busy place, although, today, tourist facilities far outnumber actual port activities. Most of Seattle's considerable traffic in containers and imports is handled at the port area south of the historic Waterfront.

Visitors can catch the flavor of a major seaport by walking along the Seattle Waterfront. This is also a fun, if tacky, place to eat seafood and shop for souvenirs. Most of the piers are now enclosed with endless tourist shops and clam-chowder venues. If you're looking for that 'I ♥ Seattle' T-shirt, a souvenir coffee mug or a mass-produced trinket, this is the place.

During summer months, outdoor concerts by nationally known music acts are presented by Summer Nights at the Pier. Open-air performances are held on Piers 63–64. Call **Ticketmaster** (☎ 628-0888) for tickets and a concert schedule.

For the past few years, the Port of Seattle has been redeveloping much of the Waterfront area to the north of Seattle Aquarium. **Pier 66**, also known as the Bell Street Pier, is home to the Bell Harbor International Conference Center and new Odyssey Maritime Discovery Center (p59). This is also where you'll find Anthony's Pier 66, one of Seattle's best seafood restaurants. This area is a lot less touristy than the main Waterfront, though further expansion is likely to change that.

Take a break from the carnival atmosphere of the Waterfront by walking north on Alaskan Way, past Pier 71, to **Myrtle Edwards Park**, a fringe of lawn and trees along Elliott Bay. The path is a favorite of joggers and power-walkers pursuing lunchtime fitness. In warm weather, the park, with stupendous views over the Sound to the Olympic Mountains, is a good place for a picnic.

Along the length of the Waterfront – amid the horse-drawn carriages, pedicabs and cotton-candy vendors – are a number of companies that offer harbor tours and boat excursions (p43).

Orientation

The Waterfront is relatively cut off from the rest of downtown Seattle, although the nicely landscaped Hillclimb Corridor (at the end of Pike St) serves as a handy people-funnel between the Waterfront and Pike Place Market. Still, the steep hillsides make access problematic for some; it can be as much as an eight-story descent down open stairways from 1st Ave to Alaskan Way. Also, when city planners elevated the Alaskan Way viaduct – essentially a freeway – between downtown and the Waterfront, they created a psychological barrier that's hard to ignore. While it in no way infringes upon getting from one place to the other, Alaskan Way is incredibly noisy, and the parking areas under the freeway can be a bit scary at night. Be sure not to leave anything valuable in your car if you park here.

The main tourist areas of the Waterfront are between Piers 52 and 59. Waterfront Park is the name given to Pier 57; it's just a boardwalk on the pier, but at least you can get out onto the Sound and get a feeling for the area. It's also the best place to tote your corn dogs and fish-and-chips from the adjacent piers and take a seat on a waterside bench. Keep your eyes on your fries, however, as Waterfront seagulls can resemble a pack of hungry bears. Piers 54, 55 and 56 are devoted to shops and restaurants, including novelty venues such as the 100-year-old Ye Olde Curiosity Shop, a bizarre cross between a museum and a souvenir shop.

The Waterfront Streetcar runs along Alaskan Way, the Waterfront's main thoroughfare. These trolleys are especially handy for visiting the Waterfront; they run from the area near Seattle Center (from the base of Broad St), along the Waterfront (including near Pike Place Market) and on to Pioneer Square and the International District. If you're anywhere downtown, it is an easy downhill walk westward to the Waterfront.

Washington State Ferries operates transport to Bainbridge Island and Bremerton from the piers, while privately owned ferries travel to the San Juan Islands and Victoria, BC. For more information on ferry operators and routes, see the Directory (p203) and Excursions (p187) chapters.

ODYSSEY MARITIME DISCOVERY CENTER Map pp238-9

☎ 206-374-4001; www.ody.org; 2205 Alaskan Way at Pier 66; adult/child/senior $7/2/5; ☺ 10am-5pm Tue-Sat, noon-5pm Sun

This unique museum in Waterfront Park is part of the Bell Street Pier, a huge complex that also houses convention space, restaurants and a marina. A haven for boat enthusiasts, the Discovery Center is also a wonderful place for families. The four galleries and more than 40 hands-on exhibits include a simulated kayak trip around Puget Sound, a chance to navigate a virtual ship through Elliott Bay and a visual re-creation of the cruise up the Inside Passage to southeast Alaska. You can find out about boat construction and high-tech contributions to boating, learn about oceanography and environmental issues and hear audio simulations of ocean animals. One section of the museum is devoted to fishing and another to ocean trade. Anyone with a nose for the nautical should check this place out.

Fisherman, Waterfront Park

SEATTLE AQUARIUM Map pp238-9

☎ 206-386-4320; 1483 Alaskan Way at Pier 59; adult/child 3-5/child 6-12 $11/5/7, with Imax $16.50/5/11.75, with Odyssey Maritime Discovery Center $15.50/7/10.50; ☺ 10am-5pm

Probably the most interesting site in the Waterfront area, this well-designed aquarium offers a view into the underwater world of Puget Sound and the Pacific Northwest coast. Exhibits include re-creations of ecosystems in Elliott Bay, Puget Sound and the Pacific Ocean, including tide pools, eelgrass beds, coral reefs and the sea floor. The centerpiece of the aquarium is a glass-domed room where sharks, octopi and other deepwater denizens lurk in the shadowy depths. The passages eventually lead outdoors to a salmon ladder and a pool where playful sea otters and northern fur and harbor seals await your attention. Combination tickets with the Imax theater and the Discovery Center are available at each site. If you're tired of lugging all your Waterfront purchases around, you can rent a locker at the aquarium for 50¢.

SEATTLE IMAX DOME THEATER Map pp238-9
☎ 206-622-1868; Pier 59; adult/child 6-12 $7/6, additional film on same day $2; ☽ 10am-5pm
Called the Omnidome until recently, this 180° surround-screen theater adjacent to the

aquarium usually has four shows playing daily though not all at once. The ongoing favorite is The Eruption of Mt St Helens, which features a helicopter ride over an exploding volcano (the film received an Academy Award nomination for best short documentary). Most features are 45 minutes long, and the first show begins at 10am; call for show times.

WATERFRONT STREETCAR Map pp238-9
☎ 206-553-3000; Pier 70 to the International District; adult peak/off-peak hr $1.25/1, child free; peak hrs ☽ 6-9am & 3-6pm Mon-Fri
Metro Transit runs Seattle's Waterfront system of vintage streetcars imported from Australia. The 15-minute trip goes from the International District through Pioneer Square to Pier 70 and is a fun, relaxing way to check out both the Waterfront scene and the cityscape across Alaskan Way.

BELLTOWN

Eating p115; Shopping p171; Sleeping p182
Belltown is a textbook illustration of the progress of the urban eco-system. A featureless area of warehouses and low-slung office build-ings, this neighborhood was dismissed by many in the 1970s. But one of city planning's greatest mysteries is the way seedy, low-rent neighborhoods tend to be spawning grounds for raw musical and artistic talent – and so become cool, then gradually more expensive, and then 'ruined' by the influx of cash-slinging yuppies. Eventually, the cachet wears off and the neighborhood settles into a comfort-able balance between the funky, artsy people who made it cool in the first place and the new crowd of condo-buying salary earners who keep the chic restaurants and boutiques in business, thereby drawing visitors. This is the phase Belltown seems to be in at the moment.

The area is also known as the Denny Regrade, for the massive sluicing project that re-duced what was Denny Hill to a more convenient flat grade, intended to open up Belltown for a business explosion and rapid economic growth. It didn't work; the area languished. Yet underground musicians and artists were part of an explosion of creative ferment that catapulted Seattle to international noteworthiness in the early 1990s: Belltown gave birth to grunge music.

Many of the old clubs are still here, but the area went seriously upscale for a few years, making Belltown one of the hottest neighborhoods. These days, while part of the area still clings to its grungy, punky roots, the other part marches onward toward yuppie heaven.

Signs of the old-and-new mix are everywhere. Some of the city's finest restaurants mingle with great cheap eateries (p116), the warehouses are converting to lofts; designer boutiques are now common. You're as likely to see businesspeople in suits as you are itinerant artists with nose rings. Many locals thought this neighborhood was 'ruined' a few years back. But the tenacity of places such as Shorty's (p147), the Frontier Room (p137), Singles Going Steady (p171) and the Crocodile Café (p61), and the air of excitement among the people crowding the streets, restaurants and clubs every night, indicate that reports of Belltown's death have been exaggerated.

Transportation
Bus Take Nos 1, 2, 3, 4,13,15, 16,18, 21, 22, 56, 39 and 42.
Parking There's metered street parking – good luck finding any at night, though.

Orientation

Belltown is immediately north of Pike Place Market and bordered by the downtown business district; it stretches from Virginia St to Denny Way and from the east side of Elliott Ave to 4th Ave. Bus Nos 15, 18, 21, 22 and 56 pass along 1st Ave. Traffic on 2nd Ave is one-way southbound; bus Nos 39 and 42 run along it. Routes on 3rd Ave include Nos 1, 2, 3, 4, 13 and 16, which link Belltown to downtown, Seattle Center and outlying neighborhoods. See the Downtown Metro Transit map (p250) to see where to catch your bus. Belltown is an easy walk from downtown hotels and lies just north of Pike Place Market.

Top Five Belltown

- **Buenos Aires Grill** (p115) Tango-dancing waitstaff.
- **Crocodile Café** (see below) Live music and grunge history.
- **Roq la Rue** (see below) Gutsy underground art.
- **Shorty's** (p147) Pinball heaven.
- **Singles Going Steady** (p171) Punk records the old-fashioned way.

CROCODILE CAFÉ Map pp238-9
☎ 206-441-5611; 2200 2nd Ave; admission $5-10
This club, a landmark of '90s rock whose stage has showcased virtually every important Seattle band during the grunge years and since (including, of course, Nirvana), has become one of the best rock clubs in the country. The ever-present lines of people waiting to get to the bar are a who's-who of Seattle's music scene; and if you get bored of looking at them, you can check out the indie-rock art tacked to the walls.

DENNY PARK Map pp238-9
This park was originally part of the official Seattle Cemetery – a hotly contested designation that ended up being rather morbidly temporary; see the boxed text, p62. The park is currently just a park – or so we're told.

ROQ LA RUE Map pp238-9
☎ 206-374-8977; 2224 2nd Ave; ⊙ 2-6pm Tue-Fri, noon-4pm Sat & by appointment
This Belltown gallery is notable for the risks it takes – the work on view here skates along the edge of urban pop-culture. It's more often provocative than attractive, which makes it perfect for Belltown, where gritty art and rough-hewn music have always been part of the scene.

SEATTLE CENTER

Eating p117; Shopping p171

In the early 1960s, Seattle was confident and ready for company. And the 1962 World's Fair gave the city the perfect opportunity to display its self-assured, high-tech vision of itself and of the future. The fair, also known as 'Century 21 Exposition,' was a summer-long exhibition that brought in nearly 10 million visitors from around the world. A 74-acre warehouse area north of downtown was leveled; a futuristic international enclave of exhibition halls, arenas and public spaces sprang up.

Today, that 74-acre site has been set aside as the Seattle Center, a mecca for museums, entertainment and cultural venues. Varnished by time, the place now evokes a distinctly 1960s notion of tomorrow's world; like relics from World's Fair expos everywhere, the buildings here still seem 'futuristic,' but in a nostalgic, science-fiction, *Jetsons*-esque way. There's no better example of this than the Space Needle, the 605ft-high observation tower and restaurant that has become emblematic of Seattle. If you think it looks otherwordly now, spiking out of the skyline, try picturing it in its original color of bright orange.

The Monorail, a 1½-mile experiment in mass transit, was another signature piece of the 1962 fair. Like it, a number of the exhibition halls have been adapted for civic use, such as the Opera House (renovated and reopened in 2003 as the Marion Oliver McCaw Hall, home of the Seattle Opera and Pacific Northwest Ballet) and the Bagley White, Intiman and Seattle Children's Theaters. Two sports complexes were also created, including the Key

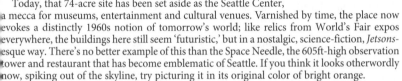

Graveyard Hopping

Most of Seattle's early pioneers were in their 20s when they arrived on Alki Point. These were visionaries and probably the last thing on their minds was where, when needed, they would bury their dead. It took a while for this problem to be laid to rest.

Seattle's first cemetery, on land near 2nd Ave and Stewart St in Belltown, was a casually-operated affair where nuisances like keeping records of burial plots were simply bypassed. However, when the body count reached 20, people began to worry a little. In 1860, the city asked Arthur Denny to donate the spot as an official cemetery, but Denny refused: he didn't want a bunch of corpses in the middle of Seattle's growing business district (it didn't quite fit with his vision). David Denny resolved the matter in 1884 by setting aside 5 acres for the official Seattle Cemetery (now Denny Park). The bodies were dug up and moved to the new cemetery (well, most of them – workers later found two unidentified skulls had been left behind).

The better-organized Seattle Cemetery was divvied up into individual plots that sold for $10 apiece. Deaths were recorded, and careful markers on each grave kept track of who was where. People with no family or money were buried in the 'Potter's Field.' In 1882, however, a small fire blew through and burned all the wooden markers. By then, the city had grown even more, and planners decided they didn't want a cemetery here either. Instead, they commissioned Denny Park as the first city park. But what about the dead people? A gravedigger was hired to dig up the bodies once again. However, because of the burnt markers and confusing records, a male corpse would turn up in a plot thought to be occupied by a woman, identities got mixed up, and no-one knew what to do with the Potter's Field bodies. In all, 223 corpses were moved up to Capitol Hill. When that spot also turned into a park called City Park (today Volunteer Park), the bodies were moved again, this time to Lakeview Cemetery at the northern end of Volunteer Park, where they finally got a chance to rest in peace.

Lakeview Cemetery (p78) now holds actors Bruce Lee and his son, Brandon Lee; Doc Maynard and one of his wives, Catherine, whose epitaph reads 'She did what she could'; and Princess Angeline, the daughter of Chief Seattle, in a canoe-shaped coffin.

Arena, home of the Seattle Supersonics NBA franchise. Other public buildings include the Pacific Science Center and the Seattle Children's Museum. Various other museums and art spaces are also remnants of the World's Fair; the Fun Forest Amusement Park, near the Monorail stop, is replete with carnival rides.

Additions to Seattle Center include the Experience Music Project (p63), a skateboard park and a public basketball court. The Seattle Center's Opera House was renovated in 2003 to the tune of $127 million and reopened as the Marion Oliver McCaw Hall (p133).

The Seattle Center also hosts many of the city's major annual events, including the popular Bumbershoot music festival, the Northwest Folklife Festival (p9) and the Seattle International Children's Festival (p9). On a nice day, Seattle Center is a pleasant place to wander around, and no matter what season you're here, there's always lots going on.

Orientation

Seattle Center is bounded by Denny Way, Mercer St, 1st Ave N and 5th Ave N. It's linked to downtown by a number of bus routes; see the Downtown Metro Transit map (p250). Be aware that Seattle Center is outside the downtown Ride Free Area.

You'll find that the most entertaining way to get back and forth to Seattle Center is by Monorail. This service provides frequent transportation between downtown's Westlake Center, at Pine St and 4th Ave, and Seattle Center; cars run about every 10 minutes.

It's about a 10-minute walk from Seattle Center to the Waterfront Streetcar terminus at Broad St and Alaskan Way.

Information booths, a number of fast-food venues, restrooms and other public facilities are in Center House near the Monorail Terminal. Some useful telephone numbers include ☎ 684-7200 for general information, ☎ 684-8582 for a recording of events and attractions, and ☎ 233-3989 for parking and transportation information.

Also helpful is the Seattle Center website at www.seattlecenter.com, which has has links to all Seattle Center attractions Parking can be limited around Seattle Center when more than one large event takes place. The biggest parking lots are on Mercer St, between 3rd and 4th Aves N, and on 5th Ave N between Mercer and Harrison Sts.

No admission is charged to enter the Seattle Center area.

CHILDREN'S MUSEUM & THEATER
Map pp240-1
Museum ☎ 206-441-1768, theater ☎ 206-441-3322; basement of Center House; adult & child/senior $6/5.50; ☺ museum 10am-5pm Tue-Sun & Mon in summer

In the basement of Center House near the Monorail stop, the Children's Museum is a learning center that offers a number of imaginative activities and displays, many focusing on cross-cultural awareness and hands-on art sessions. The play area includes a child-size neighborhood, a play center and an area dedicated to blowing soap bubbles. Also in Seattle Center is the Seattle Children's Theater, a separate entity with summer performances in the Charlotte Martin and Eve Alvord Theaters.

EXPERIENCE MUSIC PROJECT Map pp240-1
EMP; ☎ 206-367-5483; www.emplive.com; 325 5th Ave N; adult/child/student & senior $19.95/14.95/15.95; ☺ 9am-6pm Sun-Thu, 9am-9pm Fri & Sat summer; 10am-5pm Sun-Thu, 10am-9pm Fri & Sat winter

In a building that echoes Jimi Hendrix's smashed guitar – and also contains one – the EMP is a unique museum devoted to rock and roll, from its roots in jazz and the blues to its later incarnations as punk, riot grrl and grunge. The vast collection includes some of Nirvana frontman Kurt Cobain's handwritten notes, as well as an impressive sound and video archive. Kids will love the chance to record and mix their own song or make a video. See the boxed text on p64 for more information.

INTERNATIONAL FOUNTAIN Map pp240-1
☎ 206-684-7200; ☺ call for light-show times

This is the place to be on sunny days. With 287 jets of water pumping in time to a computer-driven music system, the International Fountain at the heart of the Seattle Center is a great place to rest your feet or eat lunch on sunny days. On summer nights, there's a free light-and-music show.

PACIFIC SCIENCE CENTER Map pp240-1
☎ 206-443-2001; 200 2nd Ave N; adult/child 2-5/child 6-13 $8/4/5.50, Imax Theater & Laserium with general admission extra $3, without general admission $6.75; ☺ 10am-5pm Mon-Fri, 10am-6pm Sat & Sun

This interactive museum of science and industry once housed the science pavilion of the World's Fair. Today, the center features virtual-reality exhibits, a tropical butterfly house, laser shows, holograms and other wonders of science, many with hands-on demonstrations. Also on the premises is the vaulted-screen **Imax Theater** (☎ 206-443-4629), a laserium and a planetarium.

SPACE NEEDLE Map pp240-1
☎ 206-905-2100; adult/child/youth/senior $12.50/5/10/11; ☺ 10am-10pm Sun-Thu, 10am-midnight Fri-Sat

Seattle's signature monument, the Space Needle was designed by Victor Steinbrueck and John Graham Jr, reportedly based on the napkin scribblings of World's Fair organizer Eddie Carlson. The part that's visible aboveground weighs an astounding 3700 tons. The tower takes advantage of its 520ft-high observation deck – offering 360° views of Seattle and surrounding areas – to bombard visitors with historical information and interpretive displays. On clear days, zip to the top on the elevators (43 seconds) for excellent views of downtown, Lake Union, Mt Rainier and the Olympic Range mountains way across Puget Sound; don't bother spending the cash on cloudy days. If you're coming up to take aerial photos, be

---

Transportation
Bus Take Nos 1, 2, 3, 4, 8, 13, 15, 16, 18, 19, 24, 33, 81 and 82. Note that Seattle Center is outside the downtown Ride Free Area.
Monorail From Westlake Center it's $1.50 one way.
Streetcar About 10 minutes' walk from the Waterfront Streetcar terminus, Broad St & Alaskan Way.

Glass Blowing, Belltown (p60)

forewarned that there's fencing around the observation deck's perimeter, making clear shots impossible. Back in 1962, the Space Needle surfed the wave of the future with its two revolving restaurants, and you had a choice between pricey and moderate dining. But today there's only one restaurant, **Sky City** (p117) which, in line with the views, is astronomically expensive. Reservations in the dining room do however, give you a free ride up the elevator.

QUEEN ANNE

Eating p118; Shopping p171; Sleeping p184

Rising above Seattle Center, Queen Anne is an old neighborhood of majestic redbrick houses and apartment buildings, sweeping lawns manicured to perfection and gorgeous views of the city and Elliott Bay. It has some of the most prestigious addresses in Seattle.

Queen Anne Hill was one of the original seven hills of Seattle. At 456ft, it's also the steepest and highest, rising precipitously above Elliott Bay and Lake Union. Named for the prominent Queen Anne–style houses first built on the neighborhood's lower slopes, the area attracted affluent folks looking for views of the city. But unlike the First Hill neighborhood, whose residents dripped with money when they got here, Queen Anne was open to new wealth, too. As such, when walking around, you'll see a mix of architectural styles reflecting the varying tastes and incomes of the neighborhood's first residents. Most of the original Queen Anne houses are gone or have

Are You Experienced?

The lovechild of a fat wallet and a rock-and-roll heart, the Experience Music Project (EMP) is worth a look for the architecture alone; whether it's worth the admission price is another story. The shimmering, abstract building – designed by Frank O Gehry and paid for by Microsoft cofounder Paul Allen and his sister Jody Patton – houses 80,000 music artifacts, including handwritten lyrics by Nirvana's Kurt Cobain and a Fender Stratocaster demolished by Jimi Hendrix.

The $450 million EMP, an ambitious tribute to rock-and-roll, opened in June 2000. No expense was spared in creating the collection, which features such items as Janis Joplin's pink feather boa, the world's first steel guitar and Hendrix's signed contract to play at Woodstock. Inspired by Allen's passion for Hendrix's music and initially intended as a tribute to only Hendrix, the project quickly blossomed into the gigantic display of excess you see today.

Gehry, most notable for designing the famed Guggenheim Museum in Bilbao, Spain, reportedly went out and bought a bunch of Stratocaster guitars, smashed them up and used the resulting pile of guitar bits to inspire the building's design. More than 3000 panels of stainless steel and painted aluminum shingles cover the exterior in crazy shades of purple, red, blue, silver and gold, and there isn't a right angle in sight. The building won praise among architectural circles but was fervently criticized by Seattleites, who called it everything from a 'pukish pile of sheet metal' to 'the ugliest building in Seattle.' Gehry has also been criticized for wasting space – of the building's 140,000 sq ft, only 35,000 constitute usable exhibit space. But standing, for example, in the soaring-ceilinged Sky Church and complaining about such practicalities is a bit like telling Mozart his pieces contained 'too many notes.'

Upon entering the museum, you'll get your own 'virtual companion' dubbed Meg (Museum Exhibit Guide), a rather clunky handheld computer that you strap over yourself and lug around, using it to access oral histories and exhibit descriptions. Staff train technophobes on how to use it. Though it's supposed to be easy and efficient, Meg is heavy and prone to technical difficulties, so you'll often see people walking around banging into each other because they're too busy fiddling with their Megs. Like many people before you, you'll learn less but might find it more enjoyable if you dump Meg altogether.

The best exhibits include the Hendrix Gallery, a major tribute to Jimi; the Northwest Passage, displaying everything from Ray Charles' debut album (recorded in Seattle) to Heart's stage apparel; and a long hallway that details the evolution of grunge. The Artist's Journey is a virtual roller coaster ride, complete with loud music and seats that roll as if you were on the real thing. Upstairs is the Sound Lab, a futuristic studio that lets you lay down vocal tracks and play guitars, drums and keyboards. The extensive exhibits will keep you busy for a few hours. There is also a bar and a couple of live-music venues, including Sky Church (p132).

To serious music fans, the exhibits may seem a little basic, although the video archive is excellent. The Sky Church theater, Liquid Lounge bar and Turntable restaurant are accessible free of charge, and if you're on the fence about paying the $20 admission, you could do worse than ponder that question from a barstool inside Gehry's remarkable building.

een divided into duplexes and apartments to absorb the neighborhood's quickly growing population, but there are still plenty of fabulous historic homes to gawk at.

The Queen Anne neighborhood has two distinct sides – roughly speaking, the bluebloods ve up top and the young urbanites down below. Funky Lower Queen Anne (or as it's more interestingly known, the Bottom of Queen Anne) flanks Seattle Center to the west and butts up against Belltown on the other side of Denny Way. This area has a pleasant, old-fashioned nd lived-in quality despite its busy urban locale. The old redbrick apartment buildings house generally youthful population that spends its time on Queen Anne Ave N between Mercer nd W Harrison Sts.

Favorite Queen Anne hangouts include the **Uptown Espresso Bar** (p149; ☎ 206-281-8669) nd the art deco Uptown Cinemas, an old theater converted into a movie triplex. Nearby, he **Behnke Center for Contemporary Performance** (p29) has excellent live theater. **Larry's Market** (p108) s a big draw. Because of their proximity to Seattle Center, bars and restaurants in Lower Queen Anne get quite a workout before and after home games at Key Arena or when there's performance at the Opera House.

Upper Queen Anne, on top of the hill, has lots of pretty gingerbread houses, excellent iews of the city and some great restaurants.

Up on the hilltop, the neighborhood of Upper Queen Anne reeks much more of the establishment and old money. Public ordinances decree that no-one should sit or lie down n public sidewalks, so if you're thinking about it, make sure there's a bench between you nd the curb. Laws like this, combined with Upper Queen Anne's position as something of destination (you don't just stumble upon it), make the absence of panhandlers obvious.

Though it may sound like a snooty place, the shops and restaurants are patrician without eeming too pretentious. Upper Queen Anne is quite a restaurant hub, especially for upscale Asian and Spanish food.

Other than to eat, the main reason to visit Upper Queen Anne is to check out the old mansions and spectacular views. Top to bottom, the whole neighborhood has a quaint feel, hanks to its well-preserved architecture and mostly small businesses.

Orientation

Between Upper and Lower Queen Anne runs Queen Anne Ave N, a very steep 18%-grade ill that'll give even avid hikers a workout. n the old days, trolley companies had to se counterbalances to pull the trolley cars p the hill. The main commercial strip is on Queen Anne Ave N between W Galer and V McGraw Sts.

Bus Nos 2, 13 and 45 go up Queen Anne Ave N, passing near the vista points on W Highland Dr. Though they take a more circuitous route, bus Nos 1, 3 and 4 also go up to Queen Anne; bus No 1 travels on the west side of the hill along 10th Ave W, while Nos 3 nd 4 go up Taylor Ave N on the east side. Check out the Downtown Metro Transit map p250) to see where to catch your bus. If you're driving from downtown, travel north on st Ave, which turns into Queen Anne Ave N.

For both views and architecture, take W Highland Dr, one of Seattle's most prestigious treets. You'll find it about halfway up Queen Anne Hill on the west side. Bigelow Ave N, n the east side of Queen Anne Hill, offers more views and period architecture; Bigelow Ave nd Highland Dr constitute part of 'the Boulevard,' a scenic ring of tree-lined streets that oops around the crest of Queen Anne Hill.

GABLE HOUSE Map pp240-1
W Highland Dr at Queen Anne Ave N

his 14-gabled house was built in 1905 by larry Whitney Treat, a friend of William F Buffalo Bill' Cody. Treat also built the Golden ardens Park (p88).

KERRY PARK Map pp240-1
211 W Highland Dr

Almost every tourist comes to get postcard-perfect photos of the Seattle skyline, Mt Rainier and the Space Needle from Kerry Park, along the stroll-friendly and prestigious Highland Dr.

This is one of the three best views in town (the others are from Gas Works Park near Wallingford and Duwamish Head in West Seattle). It's a magical vista, especially at night or sunset. Going a little further along W Highland Dr will take you to the lesser-known **Betty Bowen Park**, an excellent spot for views across Puget Sound to the Olympic Mountains. Across the way, check out **Parsons Garden**, a public garden that's especially popular for summer weddings.

QUEEN ANNE COUNTERBALANCE

Map pp240-1
Queen Anne Ave N north of W Roy St
The streetcar that chugged up and down the steep grade along Queen Anne Ave started operating on overhead-wire electricity in 1900, but it still needed some help to manage the hill. So engineers designed a system of counterweights – a 16-ton train that ran in tunnel beneath the street would go up whe the cablecar went down, and vice versa. The cablecars were retired in 1943, but the under ground tunnels are still there.

TURRET HOUSE Map pp240-1
W Halladay St & 6th Ave W
This adorable castle-like building, with gable and (appropriately enough) turrets galore was once the home of the Love Israel Famil a commune of ex-hippies turned religious cul Love Family members were famous for huffin noxious gasses, refusing to cut their hair an believing they were each part of the bod of Jesus Christ. At one point the Seattle cla numbered some 400 members in 15 house in this area. The Turret House has since bee converted to apartments.

LAKE UNION

Shopping p171; Sleeping p184

Lake Union is known for having the largest houseboat population in the US, and it isn't really a typical neighborhood. The Y-shaped lake's waters lap up against the shores of many traditional neighborhoods, including Fremont, southern Wallingford, Eastlake and the eastern slopes of Queen Anne. What ties this area together is the number of restaurants, lodgings and recreational facilities clustered around the lake. Lake Union is also a transportation hub for flights by seaplane to the San Juan Islands (p193) or Victoria, BC.

South Lake Union is perennially in the news, and never more than the past few years. It has mostly been left to its own devices, kind of a back-yard neighborhood, full of unglamorous storefronts and low-income housing. Then, 10 years ago, ther was an effort to raze many of this area's small businesses and transform 61 acres of land int Seattle Commons park. The neighborhood fought it and won, but the end result was tha Microsoft co-founder Paul Allen (he of the Experience Music Project) wound up ownin 11 acres here. Since then, rumor has it that Allen's company, Vulcan, has spent about $20 million buying up land bit by bit over the intervening years; Allen could now control 5 acres in the area – an astounding amount of real estate. Residents, needless to say, are o their guard.

Allen's vision, to be completed over the next 15 years, has already started taking shape. Th plan calls for 10 million sq ft of offices, apartments, condos, hotels, restaurants and shop plus – importantly – major new centers for biotechnology research. The idea is that th industry eventually could reshape the city – just as Boeing and Microsoft did before it.

For the visitor, all this means for the next few years is a possible construction-site tangl But eventually, this neighborhood could take an entirely different shape, one that include a much-needed make-over of the traffic patterns around Mercer St (the 'Mercer Mess,' a locals call it) and the addition of a park near the Center for Wooden Boats.

Orientation

The main arterials for access to Lake Union are Westlake and Eastlake Aves, which, unsu prisingly, follow the west and east shores of the lake. Westlake Ave N begins downtown nea

(Continued on page 75)

1 'Waiting for the Interurban', Fremont (p84) **2** Taking a closer look at the International Fountain, Seattle Center (p63) **3** Sleepless in Seattle: the view from the Seattle to Bremerton Foot ferry

1 Jonathon Borofsky's 'Ha
mering Man': 48 feet tall,
Seattle Art Museum (p47)
Chihuly's Benaroya Hall G
chandalier (15m long by
wide), finished in 1998 3 T
Sorrento Hotel, First Hill (p

THE WING LUKE ASIAN MUSEUM

1 *Wing Luke Asian Museum, The International District (p54)*
2 *Totem, carved by Duane Pascoe (1974), Occidental Park (p50)*
3 *Dragon mural, designed by John Woo, in Hing Hay Park in the International District (p54)* 4 *Entrance to the former sidewalks and first floors of the old Pioneer Square, in Pioneer Place Park (p48)*

1 Asian-themed columns, The International District (p52) 2 Resident of Capitol Hill (p75) 3 Window onto the world of Toys in Babeland, Pike/Pine Corridor (p173) 4 Detail of public art, 'The Broadway Dance Steps' by Jack Mackie, Capitol Hill (p76)

le Lounge nightspot,
(p147) **2** Lenin Statue,
(p83) **3** The Fremont
mont (p84)

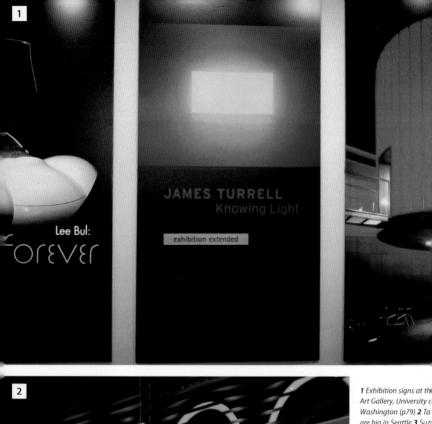

Lee Bul:
FOREVER

JAMES TURRELL
Knowing Light

exhibition extended

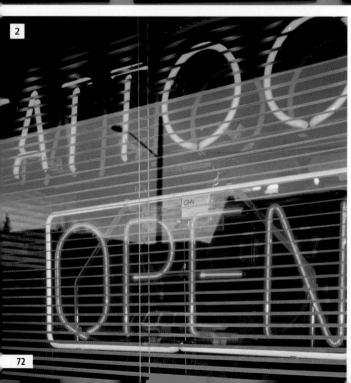

TATTOO

OPEN

1 Exhibition signs at the
Art Gallery, University of
Washington (p79) **2** Ta
are big in Seattle **3** Suz
Library, University of W
ton (p80)

1 *Pike Place Market, Pike Place (p55)* 2 *Local specialty, the Dungeness crab, Pike Place Market* 3 *Ivar's Acres of Clams (p113)* 4 *'To market to market': Rachel, the Pike Place Market Pig (p56)*

1 *Nightspot, Belltown (p134)* 2 *Coffeehouse, Fremont (p148)* 3 *Ivar's Acres of Clams' signage (p113)* 4 *5 spot cafe (p118)*

94

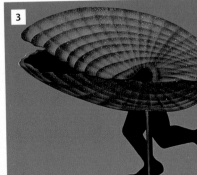

(Continued from page 66)

the intersection of Stewart St and 6th Ave. Eastlake Ave E is the continuation of Fairview Ave N, from Denny Way. Bus Nos 70, 72 and 73 serve Eastlake Ave.

CENTER FOR WOODEN BOATS Map pp240-1
☎ 206-382-2628; 1010 Valley St

If you have an interest in the history and craft of wooden boats, then the Center for Wooden Boats is somewhere you'll definitely want to visit. This museum and enthusiast's center features vintage and replica boats and it also offers sailing lessons and classes on subjects such as sail repair and boat building. As an added bonus you can rent sailboats and rowboats here. For more information on boat and kayak rentals, see p157.

Top Five Lake Union

- **Canlis** (p118) Old-school elegance.
- **Center for Wooden Boats** (see above) Soak up some history, then set sail.
- **Chandler's Crabhouse & Fresh Fish Market** (see above) Ship something to the folks back home.
- **Lobo Saloon** (p133) Sweaty rock shows; bring your earplugs.
- **REI** (see opposite) Even if you're not buying, the scale is impressive.

Transportation

Bus Take Nos 70, 72 and 73.
Parking There's metered and time-limited street parking.

CHANDLER'S CRABHOUSE & FRESH FISH MARKET Map pp240-1
☎ 206-223-2722; 901 Fairview Ave N

Here you can dine on crab or fresh fish prepared in a variety of ways, then buy the raw materials and have them shipped home.

REI Map pp240-1
☎ 206-323-8333; 222 Yale Ave N

As much an adventure as a shopping experience, this giant REI store has its own climbing wall – you can check out the rainproofing of various brands of gear by entering a special rainstorm shower; or road-test hiking boots on a simulated mountain trail. REI also rents various ski packages, climbing gear and camping equipment – call for daily and weekly rates.

CAPITOL HILL & VOLUNTEER PARK

Eating p119; Shopping p172; Sleeping p185

Northeast of downtown, Capitol Hill is probably Seattle's most diverse and lively neighborhood because of its distinct dual personality. Long a counterculture oasis, Capitol Hill's Broadway probably boasts more nose rings, tattoos and poetry readings than anywhere else in the Pacific Northwest. Trendy young students and urban homeless street kids share the sidewalks and café tables, although most people probably wouldn't immediately spot the difference. East of Broadway, on 15th Ave E, is a more subdued commercial area. It serves some of the city's wealthiest residents, who live in the grand old mansions along the tree-lined streets. Add to these demographics Capitol Hill's thriving gay and lesbian community, and you have a very lively and colorful mix of residents.

When Capitol Hill was still thick forest, Seattle pioneer Arthur Denny claimed land here in the hope that the area would become the Washington state capital. Though that hope was never realized (that honor went to Olympia, south of Seattle), Henry Yesler had already set to work logging the area, and soon people were building elaborate mansions on the slope that overlooks the east side of Lake Union. A streetcar route was installed up Broadway from Yesler Way to City Park, later renamed Volunteer Park (p77), and the area grew quickly. Some fantastic vestiges of the early architecture are well worth exploring.

Capitol Hill boasts three major commercial areas, each of which attracts a different kind of crowd. The main commercial street is **Broadway**. It is lined with coffeehouses, inexpensive restaurants, bars, trendy boutiques, book-stores and well-concealed supermarkets. Dilettante Chocolates, decked out in pink and umbrellas, is well known for confection truffles and 'adult' milkshakes. All along Broadway are good, inexpensive ethnic res-taurants, many of which cater to a student or long-haul traveler's budget. This is where the crowds are thickest and the vitality most en-gaging. Running perpendicular to Broadway is the so-called **Pike–Pine Corridor**. With most of the city's gay and lesbian bars, dance and live-music clubs, all-night coffeehouses, an increasing number of restaurants and more than a few tattoo and piercing salons, this is

Top Five Capitol Hill

- **Asian Art Museum** (p78) One of the top 10 Asian art collections outside Asia.
- **Cha-Cha Lounge** (p134) Except for the bath-rooms, you'll want to move in.
- **Lakeview Cemetery** (p78) Morbid tourism in a parklike setting.
- **Linda's** (p138) Casual Seattle hipster scene.
- **Wall of Sound** (p173) Rare records, vital under-ground reading material.

nightlife central for Seattle. East of Broadway, the quieter business district along **15th Ave E** has health-food stores, bookstores and ethnic restaurants.

You get a hint that this isn't Kansas anymore when the brass inlaid dance steps along Broadway propel you into a rumba or a waltz. Actually, the dance-step diagrams set in the pavement are *The Broadway Dance Steps,* a public artwork designed by Jack Mackie. If you decide to attempt a tango on a street corner, you assuredly won't be the most unusual sight on Broadway.

In fact, a sense of spectacle is what Broadway is all about; people don't visit here for the food or the shopping (though you can indulge in both quite happily) but for the scene. You'll see any and every color of hair, semi-clothed bodies with all manner of tattooing and piercing, men in both business suits and dresses, gray-haired widows carrying bags of groceries and homeless people walking their dogs. While the chances are good that you'll get panhandled by street kids or get an eyeful of pierced nipples, there's nothing particularly threatening about this in-your-face pageant. The slackers along Broadway manage to seem youthful and slightly menacing while never actually losing their decorum. It's all just part of the spectacle.

Equally thronging with people, especially very chic young nightlife seekers, is the Pike–Pine Corridor, a stretch of aging brick warehouses and former 1950s car dealerships. The 'Cor-ridor' doesn't look like much in the daylight, but after dark the area becomes Party Central. This was once a predominantly gay- and lesbian-oriented area, and it's still the location of most of the good queer clubs, but sexual orientation has taken a back seat lately to catwalk fashions and sleek 'concept' bars. At any rate, being straight here certainly won't make you feel unwelcome.

There seem to be a few bars on every block, but there's more to do here than just drink and dance. For every after-hours bar, there's a late-night coffeehouse, many of which fea-ture live music, poetry readings or pool tables. Here and there are antique stores and more unusual shops, including **Toys in Babeland** (p173) and **Beyond the Closet Bookstore** (p172), with a good collection of gay, lesbian and transgender books. This area is also the center of the city's tattoo culture – what better way to capture the Seattle experience than to buy a double espresso and head into a body piercing salon?

Anchoring each end of the Pike–Pine Corridor are two of Seattle's best brewpubs: the **Six Arms Pub & Brewery** (p135) and the **Elysian Brewing Company** (p135).

The sense of urban disenfranchisement along 15th Ave E isn't nearly as strong as on Broad-way, and the crowds aren't as thick. Instead, with an organic grocery store and a couple of mellow bars as its anchors, 15th Ave feels like an ex-hippie enclave and a real, settled-in com-munity. One of Seattle's favorite places for breakfast and brunch, **Coastal Kitchen** (p119), is here.

Orientation

To find the center of street life on Capitol Hill, you must head to the junction of E Broadway and E John St (the continuation of Olive Way from downtown). The Broadway commer-cial strip extends to the north to E Roy St; just to the south is Seattle Central Community College. The best way to enjoy Broadway is to buy a cup of coffee, lounge along the street, poke around in the shops and watch the crowds.

Public restrooms are upstairs in the Broadway Market shopping center (between E Harrison and E Republican Sts), along with a Ticket/Ticket booth, where you can buy discount tickets to live shows. Broadway's commercial activity ends at E Roy St.

The Pike–Pine Corridor extends roughly between Minor Ave and 16th Ave along E Pike and E Pine Sts.

The center of activity on 15th Ave E is the stretch between E Thomas and E Mercer Sts, with its center at E Republican St.

Transportation

Bus Take Nos 7, 10 and 43.
Parking There's metered off-street parking.

CENTER ON CONTEMPORARY ART

Map pp242-3
COCA; ☎ 206-728-1980; 1420 11th Ave btwn E Pike & E Union Sts; admission by suggested donation $5; ☺ 2-8pm Tue-Thu, noon-5pm Fri-Sun

This gallery space has been a strong force in Seattle's art scene for two decades. After floundering for a few years, it has recently moved to a new, harder-edged space on Capitol Hill, where it seems to be thriving on once again countercultural art shows.

CORNISH COLLEGE OF THE ARTS

Map pp242-3
☎ 800-726-ARTS; 1000 Lenora St

The south campus of the ornamental Cornish College of the Arts, built in 1921, has survived many bouts of debt and is now a top-notch school for music, art, dance and drama.

JIMI HENDRIX STATUE Map pp242-3

1600 Broadway

Guitar genius of last century and Seattle's favorite son, Jimi Hendrix rocks out eternally in this bronze sculpture by local artist Daryl Smith, made in 1997. Hendrix fans have been known to leave flowers, candles and notes at the base of the kneeling statue.

RICHARD HUGO HOUSE Map pp242-3

☎ 206-322-7030; 1634 11th Ave at E Olive St

Established in honor of famed Northwest poet Richard Hugo, this 1902 Victorian house, a former mortuary, is now the center of an active segment of Seattle's literary life. The house contains a library, conference room, theater and café with a small stage. It hosts readings and performances, writer-in-residence programs, reading groups and writing classes.

ST MARK'S CATHEDRAL Map pp242-3

☎ 206-323-0300; 1245 10th Ave E, cnr 10th Ave E & E Galer St; performances ☺ 9:30pm Sun

Go north on Broadway (as the chaos turns to well-maintained houses with manicured lawns) until it turns into 10th Ave E, and you're within a block of Volunteer Park. At the neo-Byzantine St Mark's Cathedral, a choir performs Gregorian chants on Sunday, accompanied by a 3700-pipe Flentrop organ. The performance is free and open to the public.

VOLUNTEER PARK

This stately 45-acre park above downtown on Capitol Hill began as pioneer Seattle's cemetery. But as Seattle grew and the need for water became more pressing (particularly after the Great Fire of 1889), the city created Volunteer Park, with its water tower and reservoir. Originally called City Park, it was renamed in 1901 to honor volunteers in the Spanish-American War (1898–1902).

Roads and paths wind around the park, with green meadowlike lawns descending to the mansion-rich neighborhoods that flank the area. Because the park has existed in one form or another since 1876, the trees and landscaping here reflect a kind of maximum growth of the Seattle urban ecosystem.

Orientation

Take bus No 7, 10 or 43 from Pike St downtown to get to Broadway E; the No 7 turns north and follows Broadway E, while the No 10 goes on to 15th Ave E and then turns north to follow that street. Bus No 43 continues on to the university via 24th Ave E.

If you're driving, the best streets up Capitol Hill from downtown are E Madison St, E Pike St or Olive Way. Be warned that parking is often difficult along Broadway, and many narrow side streets are zoned for residential parking only. The best bet is to park in the pay lot behind the Broadway Market (under the well-camouflaged Fred Meyer store), one block west of Broadway on Harvard Ave E. To reach Volunteer Park from 15th Ave E, travel north to E Galer St and turn west.

LAKEVIEW CEMETERY Map pp242-3

One of Seattle's oldest cemeteries and the final resting place of many early settlers, Lakeview Cemetery borders Volunteer Park to the north. Arthur Denny and his family, Doc and Catherine Maynard, Thomas Mercer and Henry Yesler are all interred here. This is also the gravesite of Princess Angeline, the daughter of Duwamish Chief Sealth after whom Seattle was named. Most people, however, stop by to see the grave site of martial arts film legends Bruce Lee and Brandon Lee. Flowers from fans are usually scattered around Brandon's red and Bruce's black tombstones, which stand side by side in a tiny part of the cemetery. The graves are not so easy to find: enter the cemetery at 15th Ave E and E Garfield St; follow the road in and turn left at the Terrace Hill Mausoleum. At the crest of the hill you'll see the large Denny family plot on your left. Look a little further along the road, and you'll find the Lees. If you're not usually into graveyards, you'll at least enjoy the beautiful views at this one.

LOUISA BOREN LOOKOUT Map pp242-3

15th Ave E at Garfield St

Outside the Volunteer Park boundaries, the Louisa Boren Lookout provides one of the best views over the university and Union Bay. The small park is named after the longest-surviving member of the party that founded Seattle in 1851.

SEATTLE ASIAN ART MUSEUM Map pp242-3

☎ 206-654-3100; Volunteer Park; adult/child $3/free; ☯ 10am-5pm Tue-Sun, 10am-9pm Thu

For almost 60 years the Seattle Art Museum occupied a prestigious Carl Gould–designed space in Volunteer Park. When it moved downtown in the early 1990s, the Seattle Asian Art Museum moved in. The museum now houses the extensive Asian art collection of Dr Richard Fuller, who donated this severe art moderne–style gallery to the city in 1932. The collection ranks among the top 10 Asian art collections outside Asia. Be sure to pick up a headset for the audio tour of the museum. Hang onto your ticket – it's good for $3 off the admission to the Seattle Art Museum if used within a week.

VOLUNTEER PARK CONSERVATORY

Map pp242-3

☎ 206-684-4743; 1400 E Galer St; ☯ 10am-7pm summer, 10am-4pm winter

The conservatory is a classic Victorian greenhouse built in 1912. Filled with palms, cacti and tropical plants, it features five galleries that represent different world environments.

WATER TOWER OBSERVATION DECK

Map pp242-3

1400 E Prospect St

Keen seekers of views can climb 107 steep steps to the top of Volunteer Park's 75ft water tower. Built in 1907, it provides wonderful vistas of the Space Needle and over Elliott Bay.

THE U DISTRICT

Eating p120; Shopping p173; Sleeping p186

The U District, named for the 'U Dub' (what locals call the University of Washington), feels like its own little college town. The streets are full of tiny, cheap eateries, thrift stores, record stores, second-hand bookshops, tattoo parlors and a couple of bars. Everyone who wanders around here seems to be between the ages of 18 and 24. The campus is beautiful and lends itself to leisurely, tranquil walks. There used to be a thriving drug trade along the Avenue, which made nighttime strolling unpleasant at times, but the city has cracked down and the number of down-and-outers has decreased dramatically.

The number of cheap places to eat, especially Indian and Asian, make the Avenue the best place to find an inexpensive meal. Coffeehouses grow like weeds in this area, and owners are used to students buying one coffee and sitting around for three hours. The absolutely cavernous University Bookstore (p174; ☎ 206-634-3400; 4326 University Way NE) takes up an entire city block. It has an excellent selection of general books and more scholarly tomes, along with a giant section of yellow and purple Huskies clothing.

At the Avenue and NE 50th St, the **Grand Illusion Cinema** (p152), an excellent though tiny theater, shows foreign and art films. The coffee shop next door is a popular place to have a latte and settle into a novel. At 25th Ave NE you'll find the **University Village**, an upscale, semi-outdoor mall geared more toward the parents of the UW students than the students themselves. People actually come here from all over town to shop at the highbrow chains such as Eddie Bauer and Pottery Barn.

Orientation

The University of Washington campus sits at the edge of a busy commercial area known as the U District. The main streets here are University Way, also known as 'the Avenue,' and NE 45th St. On these busy streets are innumerable cheap restaurants and cafés, student-oriented bars, second-hand clothing shops, cinemas and bookstores. Along NE 45th St, east of the Ave, are some of UW's sorority and frat houses.

Buses converge on the university from throughout the city. Nos 71, 72 and 73 offer the most direct routes to the university from the downtown bus tunnel. If you're driving, take I-5 north to the 45th St exit and travel east. A great way to explore the campus is on a bicycle. The Burke-Gilman Trail follows the south side of campus, providing an excellent arterial for getting to and from the university.

BURKE MUSEUM Map pp244-5

☎ 206-543-5590; 16th Ave NE & NE 45th St; adult/student/senior $6.50/3/5, 1st Thu each month free; ⏱ 10am-5pm Fri-Wed, 10am-8pm Thu

This museum of natural history and anthropology is on the UW campus. There's a good collection of dinosaur skeletons, but the real treasures here are the North Coast Indian artifacts, especially the collection of cedar canoes and totem poles. On the ground level of the museum is the pleasant **Museum Café** (☎ 206-543-9854), a high-ceilinged, atmospheric place with warm pine paneling and wooden tables. The Burke/Henry Dollar Deal means that if you buy a ticket for one museum, you can get into the other the same day for $1.

one museum, you can get into the other the same day for $1. College students with valid ID get in free.

RAVENNA PARK Map pp244-5

Just north of the U District is Ravenna, a residential neighborhood that's home to a lot of professors and university staff. At its heart is Ravenna Park, a lush and wild park with two playgrounds on either side of the mystery-drenched ravine carved by Ravenna Creek.

HENRY ART GALLERY Map pp244-5

☎ 206-543-2280; 15th Ave NE & NE 41st St on campus; adult/student/senior $8/free/6, 1st Thu each month free; ⏱ 11am-5pm Tue-Sun, 11am-8pm Thu

The university's sleek fine-art gallery, expanded and renovated in 1997, mounts some of the most intelligent exhibits and installations in Seattle. The focus is on 20th-century art and artists, with dedicated spaces for video and digital art. There's a small permanent collection, but the changing shows (35 a year) are usually noteworthy. Don't miss the newly completed Skyspace by James Turrell; an artist whose medium is light. Turrell's installation over the sculpture garden will alter the way you look at the ever-changing Seattle sky. The gallery also has an artsy café. The Burke/Henry Dollar Deal means that if you buy a ticket for

New Opera House, Queen Anne (p64)

Transportation

Bus Take Nos 71, 72 and 73.
Bicycle The Burke-Gilman Trail goes right along the edge of campus.
Parking There's both metered and time-limited street parking along the Avenue and its side streets.

UNIVERSITY OF WASHINGTON Map pp244-5

Visitors' center ☎ 206-543-9198; 4014 University Way; ⏱ 9am-5pm

Established in 1861, the University of Washington was first built downtown on the site of the present Fairmont Olympic Hotel. The university moved to its present location along Lake Washington's Union Bay in 1895. Much of the 639-acre site constituted the grounds of the 1909 Alaska-Yukon-Pacific Exposition. Dozens of new buildings were constructed for this World's Fair–like gathering.

Today, the university is the largest in the Northwest, with around 35,000 students, 211 buildings and 4000 faculty members. Noted programs include law and medicine; it's also highly regarded for computer science and liberal arts. More than half of its students are in graduate programs. The university publishes its own daily paper, aptly named the *Daily*. In it, you'll find out about whatever's currently causing the angst around campus, details about campus events and U District classifieds.

The collective name given to all the U Dub sports teams is the **Huskies**. They compete in 25 intercollegiate sports, most notably basketball and football. Most teams play at Husky Stadium and the Edmundson Pavilion, both on the east side of campus. To find out about athletic events and tickets, call ☎ 206-543-2200.

The university's main arts venue is the 1200-seat Meany Hall. Live dance, theater and musical performances also take place at U Dub's other three theaters – The Penthouse, The Playhouse and The Studio. For information and tickets, call or stop by the **UW Arts Ticket Office** (☎ 206-543-4880; cnr University Way NE & NE 40th St).

The university is a lovely, lively place; it is definitely worth touring the campus, especially in spring when bulbs and azaleas paint the verdant campus with brilliant colors. Maps are available from the **UW Visitors' Information Center** (☎ 206-543-9198; 4014 University Way NE). The center also offers free 90-minute campus tours that start at its offices at 10:30am weekdays.

UW CENTRAL PLAZA Map pp244-5

The center of campus is more commonly referred to as Red Square because of its base of red brick. It's not the coziest, but it fills up with cheerfully sunning students on nice days. *Broken Obelisk*, the 26ft-high stainless-steel sculpture in the square, was made by noted colorfield painter Barnett Newman. Just below Red Square is a wide promenade leading to lovely **Rainier Vista**, with spectacular views across Lake Washington to Mt Rainier.

UW DRUMHELLER FOUNTAIN Map pp244-5

Also known as 'Frosh Pond' because freshmen are traditionally initiated with an involuntary swim in it, Drumheller Fountain is one of the few remaining pieces leftover from the 1909 expo that beefed up the university. It consists of four columns standing in a tiny grove.

UW QUAD Map pp244-5

The Quad is home to many of the original campus buildings. When the ivy turns red in the autumn, the effect is much more reminiscent of New England than the Northwest.

UW SUZZALLO LIBRARY Map pp244-5

Those architecturally minded will be interested in the UW Suzzallo Library. Designed by Carl Gould around 1926, this bibliophile's dream was inspired by Henry Suzzallo, UW's president at the time. Suzzallo wanted it to look like a cathedral, because 'the library is the soul of the university.' Unfortunately for him, his bosses disagreed; on reviewing the building, they deemed it too expensive and fired Suzzallo for his extravagance. Gould was the founder of the university's architecture program; he created the plans for 18 campus buildings. Unfortunately you have to be a student of the university to access library materials.

Top Five U District

- **Agua Verde Café** (p121) Fish tacos and foosball on the deck.
- **Burke Museum** (p79) Totem pole collection.
- **Cedars Restaurant** (p120) Curry so lovely it'll make you cry.
- **Henry Art Gallery** (p79) Especially the Sky-space.
- **UW Suzzallo Library** (see above) A cathedral of books.

FREMONT

Eating p122; Shopping p174

Probably the most fun-loving of the northern neighborhoods, Fremont is known for its unorthodox public sculpture, junk stores, summer outdoor film festivals and general high spirits. In the evenings, the pubs, restaurants and coffeehouses fill with a lively mix of old hippies, young professionals and gregarious students. Except for the odd glitch, chain stores stay away from Fremont. If there's any rule of thumb to the growth of the retail center here, it's this: 'I have this weird idea for a store/restaurant/ coffeehouse/bar...' Unlike the flashy, urban disenfranchisement that gives Capitol Hill its spirit, life in Fremont is conducted with more humor and a sense of community well-being. Fremont's motto '*De Libertas Quirkas*' gives it the 'Freedom to be Peculiar,' and its residents happily live up to that proclamation. Though some of its quirks have been smoothed over recently by an influx of deep-pocketed real-estate investors, this district is still one of the more entertaining to visit.

Named by its first claim-holders after Fremont, Nebraska, the area was logged with the aid of oxen in the late 1890s. Once a working-class town, filled with employees of the Stimson shingle mill in Ballard, Fremont didn't really flourish until the building of the Fremont Bridge in 1916. The Hiram M Chittenden Locks opened a year later, allowing boat traffic to travel from the lakes to Puget Sound via the ship canal (p86).

Fremont wasn't always cool and, like a child who lacks natural talent, had to work hard to get to where it is. The completion of the high-flying Aurora Bridge (officially known as the George Washington Memorial Bridge, a fact unknown even to most Seattleites) in the 1930s meant people didn't need to come through Fremont anymore, which sent its commercial district into a sharp decline. Through the 1950s and '60s, Fremont experienced a tragic architectural blight, when many of the old mill-workers' houses were converted into cookie-cutter duplexes and cheaply built apartment buildings. Through the 1960s, Fremont had more vacant stores than occupied ones and it lacked neighborhood necessities, such as a grocery store or pharmacy. The low-rent buildings attracted a rather dowdy and rowdy bunch who didn't have much energy for making Fremont a better place.

In the 1970s things started to change. The first Fremont Fair danced its way along the neighborhood streets in 1972. The **Fremont Public Association** (☎ 206-694-6700), today the envy of every neighborhood association, was created in 1974 to provide shelter, food and help to disadvantaged residents. The association did (and still does) wonders for Fremont and its formation spawned a number of other thriving community associations, including the **Fremont Arts Council** (☎ 206-547-7440).

In 1994, Fremont citizens declared that they had seceded from Seattle, and the neighborhood was thenceforward the 'Republic of Fremont, Center of the Known Universe.' Public art, often wacky and unconventional, decorates neighborhood streets.

Fremont thrives today, but now it's got other problems. Like a teenager who suddenly becomes popular, everyone wants to hang out with it. Rents have skyrocketed here, stores and restaurants are pricier, and prime real estate is being sold to people who can afford it – generally not Fremont locals. The U-Park lot behind the former Redhook Brewery long held the infamous Fremont Almost-Free Outdoor Cinema, where movies played on a building wall and filmgoers brought couches from home, sat back in the parking lot and watched movies. That lot was bulldozed in 2001. The ever-expanding Lake Union Center, which houses software giant Adobe among others, brought more than 500,000 sq ft of office space to the once building-free Fremont waterfront.

For a fun-loving tour of Lake Union and its houseboats, join the **Sunday Ice Cream Cruise** (☎ 206-889-0306; adult/child 6-13/senior $7/4/6) aboard the *Fremont Avenue*. Tours leave every hour between 11am and 5pm. Catch the boat at the foot of Aurora Ave by the lower parking lot at Lake Union Center.

Another great Fremont must-attend is the **Fremont Fair** (☎ 206-633-4409; www.fremontfair .com), a colorful, musical and beer-filled event that takes place on the weekend nearest the summer solstice in June. The fair kicks off with the Solstice Parade, where human-powered floats traipse through the neighborhood in a lively tribute to quirkiness. A 'spookier' annual event, **Trolloween**, features a candlelight procession of costumed locals on Halloween night (October 31), followed by a dance. Throw a costume on and join the fun. But be warned: don't even think about parking in Fremont during either of these events.

Orientation

Fremont is located where Lake Union pours into the shipping canal. Anyone coming from downtown to the locks over the Fremont Bridge lands directly in the heart of Fremont. Consequently, the commercial hub of the neighborhood sits at the north end of the bridge at Fremont Ave N at N 35th St. To drive to Fremont from downtown, take Westlake Ave N north along Lake Union and follow signs for the Fremont Bridge. Bus Nos 26 and 28 go to Fremont from 4th Ave downtown.

Transportation

Bus Take Nos 26 and 28.
Parking There's parking on the street, both metered and time-limited.

APATOSAURS Map pp246-7

Along the banks of the ship canal, Fremont Canal Park extends west following the extension of the Burke-Gilman Trail. Right at the start of the park, at the bottom of Phinney Ave N, you'll see two giant, life-sized 'apatosaurs.' These are the world's largest known topiaries, given to Fremont by the Pacific Science Center.

DELUXE JUNK Map pp246-7

☎ 206-634-2733; 3518 Fremont Pl N

Stop in and look around one of Seattle's most kitschy secondhand shops. Located in a former funeral parlor, Deluxe Junk sells everything from retro sundresses and fluffy feather boas to homewares and furniture from the 1950s.

FREMONT BRIDGE Map pp246-7

Look across Fremont Ave N and you'll see the Fremont Bridge, not exactly a spectacular structure or piece of art, but interesting nonetheless. The bridge was built in 1916 when construction of the Washington Ship Canal sliced a gully between Fremont and the northern reaches of Queen Anne. The bridge went up, providing a vital link across the canal. It was painted industrial green – after all, this was long before Fremont became so colorful. When the revitalization of the neighborhood began in 1972, the bridge was to be repainted with the same shade of green. In the process, a coat of orange primer was painted on

the bridge and a few people thought, 'Hey, that orange isn't bad!' Of course just as many people thought the orange was awful, but it won out and the bridge stayed orange until the mid-1980s, when it needed yet another repainting. The orange-haters were still adamant and the decision about what color to repaint the bridge was put to a vote. Orange wasn't even on the ballot, and an acceptable shade of blue won. But the orange-lovers were still adamant, and a group of Fremont rebels went out in the middle of the night and painted orange accents on the blue bridge. This orange-and-blue combination stuck and is now the official color scheme every time the bridge gets repainted.

FREMONT OUTDOOR MOVIES Map pp246-7

☎ 206-781-4230; N 34th St & Phinney Ave N; admission by suggested donation $5

The original Fremont Almost-Free Outdoor Cinema is gone, but you can still watch films outside at Fremont Outdoor Movies. Films are shown in the parking lot across from the old location (the now-vacant Redhook Brewery, 3400 Phinney Ave N) and start at dusk on Saturday nights all summer.

FREMONT SUNDAY MARKET Map pp246-7

☎ 206-781-6776; Stone Way & N 34th St;
☯ 10am-5pm Sun

Despite recent changes, Fremont is still a great place to hang out, especially on Sunday at the Fremont Sunday Market. The market features fresh fruits and vegetables and an incredible variety of artists and people getting rid of junk. The outdoor summer market is held in the parking lot at the corner of Stone Way and N 34th St; in winter, it moves inside. Fremont's market has joined forces with its sister market in Ballard, which also runs every Sunday but is more of a traditional farmer's market.

FREMONT ROCKET Map pp246-7
Evanston Ave N off N 36th St
Fremont has adopted this phallic and slightly zany-looking rocket as its community totem. Constructed in the 1950s for use in the Cold War, the rocket was plagued with difficulties and never actually went anywhere, leaving the engineering team with the unfortunate problem of 'not being able to get it up.' Before coming to Fremont, the rocket was affixed to an army surplus store in Belltown. When the store went out of business, the Fremont Business Association snapped it up. Beneath the rocket and you'll find a coin box affixed to the building. Drop 50¢ in and the rocket will 'launch' by blowing a bunch of steam, but true to its under-performing nature, it won't go anywhere.

HISTORY HOUSE Map pp246-7
☎ 206-675-8875; 790 N 34th St; admission $1;
☺ noon-5pm Wed-Sun

The History House contains rotating exhibits focused on the history of Seattle neighborhoods. It's a good place to see photos of early Seattle. The building's colorful metal fence is another piece of public art, built by blacksmith and welder Christopher Pauley. The fence features brightly colored houses with open doors, a reflection of Fremont's welcoming attitude.

STATUE OF LENIN Map pp246-7
N 36th St & Fremont Pl N
This is the latest and most controversial addition to Fremont's collection of public art. This bronze, 16ft statue of former communist leader Vladimir Lenin weighs 7 tons. It was brought to the USA from Slovakia by an American, Lewis Carpenter, who found the statue in a scrap pile after the 1989 revolution. Carpenter spent a fortune to bring it over, sure

Top Five Fremont
- **Fremont Rocket** (see above) Sound and fury, signifying nothing.
- **Fremont Troll** (p84) Everyone loves the Troll.
- **Fremont Sunday Market** (p82) One man's trash might be your treasure.
- **Sunday Ice Cream Cruise** (p81) A fun tour of Lake Union (above).
- **Waiting for the Interurban** (p84) The human-faced dog.

'Public Art', Pike-Pine Corridor, Capitol Hill (p76)

The Fremont Troll

People get a little weird about the Fremont Troll. Understandably, of course. It's an unlikely city site, or rather, it *would* be unlikely anywhere but in Fremont. The troll is a mammoth, 18ft-high cement figure, constructed with 2 tons of ferro-concrete, and it's in the process of consuming a whole (real) Volkswagen Beetle. The troll's creators – artists Steve Badanes, Will Martin, Donna Walter and Ross Whitehead – won a competition sponsored by the Fremont Arts Council in 1990. The team took seven weeks to complete the troll, whose menacing chrome eye keeps watch over Fremont. This incredible piece of public art will instantly become a beloved icon for anyone interested in the peculiar things in life.

that some crazy American would want to buy it. No-one did, so here it stands biding its time in Fremont, still on sale for $150,000.

STILL LIFE IN FREMONT Map pp246-7
☎ 206-547-9850; 705 N 35th St

One of the city's best coffee shops, Still Life is a haven on rainy days and one of the greatest places in town to curl up with a good book, a coffee and a bowl of homemade soup. It now has a slightly more upscale dinner menu, but

the overall vibe is still comfy-granola-hangout. The mismatched chairs, couches and tables, the large windows and friendly staff all invite you to spend hours here if you want.

WAITING FOR THE INTERURBAN
Map pp246-7
N 34th St & Fremont Ave N

Seattle's most popular piece of public art, this lively sculpture in recycled aluminum, depicts people waiting for a train that never comes. The train that once passed through Fremont stopped running in the 1930s, and the people of Seattle have been waiting for a new train – the Interurban – ever since. Finally, in 2001, Sound Transit trains started to once again connect Seattle with Everett, much like the original train did. The sculpture is prone to regular 'art attacks,' where locals lovingly decorate the people in outfits corresponding to a special event, the weather, someone's birthday, a Mariner win – whatever. Rarely do you see the sculpture 'undressed.' Take a look at the human-faced dog peeking out between the legs of the people. That face belongs to Armen Stepanian, one of the founders of today's Fremont and its excellent recycling system. Sculptor Richard Beyer and Stepanian had a disagreement about the design of the piece, which resulted in Beyer's spiteful yet humorous design of the dog's face.

WALLINGFORD & GREEN LAKE

Eating p123; Shopping p175

Wallingford has blossomed from an old working-class neighborhood into a pleasant district of interesting shops, bookstores and inexpensive eateries, all just across the I-5 freeway from the University of Washington. The best thing about Wallingford is that it's not built upon a gimmick or tourist draw. This is as real as a neighborhood gets. The people who hang out here live here; you can still find an old-fashioned hardware store and a locals' pub among the espresso shops. Some excellent ethnic restaurants line N 45th St, along with some cool shops you don't want to miss.

Teahouse **Kuan Yin** (p125) is a great stop for a pot of exotic tea. Seattle's best travel bookstore is **Wide World Books** (p175). Another bookstore worth noting is **Open Books** (p175), which is devoted entirely to poetry; call to ask about readings and events. If you're not up for shopping, the **Guild 45th St Theater** (☎ 206-633-3353; 2215 N 45th St) shows mainstream and artsy flicks.

Orientation

Wallingford's west–east extent is from Stone Way N to roughly I-5, and you can walk its entire commercial district along N 45th St and back in less than an hour. It's also a very easy stroll across the I-5 overpass from the U District. Bus Nos 16 and 26 go to Wallingford from downtown 3rd and 4th Aves respectively; bus No 44 travels along N 45th St to and from the university.

Gas Works Park is at the southern end of Meridian Ave at N Northlake Way. To reach it, take bus No 26 from downtown.

To reach Wallingford by car from downtown, take I-5 north; exit at 45th St and turn west. Alternately, take Aurora Ave N (Hwy 99), get off at the Stone Way exit and follow it east to N 45th St.

EROTIC BAKERY Map pp246-7
☎ 206-545-6969; 2323 N 45th St; ☽ 10am-7pm Mon-Sat

Be prepared to blush when you stop in at the Erotic Bakery, where phallus-shaped desserts are made to order.

Top Five Wallingford & Green Lake

- **Erotic Bakery** (see above) Come on, you know you want to.
- **Gas Works Park** (see above) The weird industrial relic has a strange charm.
- **Green Lake** (see below) It's an algae-filled jewel, but a jewel nonetheless.
- **Murphy's Pub** (p138) Throw darts in the daytime, throw back pints by night.
- **Woodland Park Zoo** (p86) Pretend you're going for the kids' sakes.

GAS WORKS PARK Map pp246-7
Meridian Ave at N Northlake Way

Despite its history of contamination during the first 50 years of last century (p88), this park is still one of Seattle's best-loved parks. People come here to fly kites, picnic near the lake, or simply to take in the view. And it *is* like nothing else you've ever seen. Be sure to climb the small hill in order to see the clever sundial at the top. This is notorious as one of the best places from which to photograph Seattle's skyline, especially at sunset when you can see the sun glistening in the windows of downtown buildings.

WALLINGFORD CENTER Map pp246-7
Wallingford Ave N & N 45th St

This boutique and restaurant mall, inhabiting the nearly-condemned, refurbished old Wallingford grade school, is the hub of the area. Out front, the *Wallingford Animal Storm Sculpture,* created by artist Ronald Petty, depicts wildlife found in and around the neighborhood.

GREEN LAKE

Just north of Fremont and Wallingford is Green Lake, a small natural lake that's the hub of a large park complex and a pleasant low-key neighborhood. The lake is packed with crowds in summer, but it's even better in fall, when the leaves are changing, or on a rare rain-free day in winter. Any time of the year, it's a great spot for a walk or a run or to sit back on a bench and watch the rowers on the water. People circling the lake seem pretty serious about getting their exercise – if you just show up for a stroll in your street clothes, you might get some funny looks.

If you want to get away from the lakefront crowds, the small but serviceable business district, just to the east along NE Ravenna Blvd, offers the requisite coffee shops and cheap restaurants.

Below Green Lake, the Woodland Park Zoo is absolutely a must-see. Head on up to Phinney Ridge, the hilltop neighborhood north of the zoo along Phinney Ave N, as it also has some good restaurants (p123).

Orientation

To get to Green Lake, use bus No 16 or 358 going north on 3rd Ave. No 16 will drop you on the east side of the lake, by the restaurants and shops, while No 358 will take you to the west side, by the sports fields. Catch bus No 5 from downtown at 3rd Ave and Pine St (Westlake Station) to reach the zoo. If you're driving to Green Lake, use the N 45th St exit off I-5 north from downtown, head west through Wallingford and follow signs to the park; take the next exit at N 50th St for the zoo.

Transportation
Bus Take Nos 16, 26 and 44.
Parking There's metered street parking.

GREEN LAKE PARK Map pp232-3

One of the most popular spots in the city for recreationalists and sunbathers, scenic Green Lake Park surrounds Green Lake, a small natural lake created by a glacier during the last ice age. In the early 1900s, city planners lowered the lake's water level by 7ft, increasing the shoreline to preserve parkland around the lake. After the lowering, however, Ravenna Creek, which fed the lake, no longer flowed through. Green Lake became stagnant and filled with stinky green algae. Massive dredging efforts to keep Green Lake a lake (instead of a marshy wetland) continue. The lake is prone to algae blooms, which can cause an unpleasant condition called 'swimmer's itch' to anyone venturing into the water. Warning signs are usually posted on the beach if this is a risk.

Two paths wind around the lake, but these aren't enough to fill the needs of the hundreds of joggers, power-walkers, cyclists and in-line skaters who throng here daily. In fact, competition for space on the trails has led to altercations between speeding athletes; the city government now regulates traffic on the paths.

Green Lake also has a soccer field, bowling green, baseball diamond, basketball and tennis courts, and boat, bike and in-line skate rentals. Two sandy swimming beaches line the north end of the lake, but on sunny days the entire shoreline is massed with gleaming pale bodies.

BATHHOUSE THEATER Map pp232-3

The Bathhouse Theater, on the west side of the lake, is a 1928 bathing pavilion that turned into a live-performance venue in 1970.

WOODLAND PARK ZOO Map pp232-3

☎ 206-684-4800; 5500 Phinney Ave N; adult/child/student/senior $9/4.25/6.50/8.25, parking $3.50; ⊗ 9:30am-dusk

In Woodland Park, up the hill from Green Lake Park, the Woodland Park Zoo is one of Seattle's greatest tourist attractions, consistently rated as one of the top 10 zoos in the country. It was one of the first in the nation to free animals from their restrictive cages in favor of ecosystem enclosures, where animals from similar environments share large spaces designed to replicate their natural surroundings. Feature exhibits include a tropical rain forest, two gorilla exhibits, an African savanna and an Asian elephant forest. In November 2000, the zoo celebrated the birth of its first baby elephant; Hunsa, which means 'supreme happiness,' was named by a seven-year-old Redmond girl in a statewide naming contest.

SEATTLE ROSE GARDEN Map pp232-3

admission free

The 2½-acre Seattle Rose Garden, near the entrance road to the zoo off N 50th St, contains 5000 plants. Varieties include heirloom roses and All-American Rose selections.

BALLARD & DISCOVERY PARK

Eating p125; Shopping p175

Ballard, settled by Scandinavian fishermen in the early 20th century, at first feels like your average lutefisk-flavored blue-collar neighborhood. Once a seedy district where people spilled out of bars at 6am only to puke on the sidewalk and go back in, Ballard has, in recent years, learned how to hold its own. Unlike other former lowbrow-turned-fashionable neighborhoods, such as Belltown or Fremont, Ballard still attracts folks looking for no-nonsense venues, where they can eat a greasy breakfast, drink $3 beers and listen to good down-home folk or rock-and-roll. How long historic Ballard's well-guarded seediness lasts in the face of the current hipster invasion, however, is anyone's guess.

Though just a bridge away, Ballard seems distant from urban Seattle. Settled principally by Swedes, Norwegians and Danes (incorporated in 1890 and annexed to Seattle in 1907), this area has long been a Scandinavian enclave. Early Nordic settlers came to work sawmills – Ballard held the Seattle area's largest – and to fish. These seafaring immigrants were instrumental in establishing greater Seattle's fishing fleet. Today, boats no longer leave Ballard to fish the high seas; they depart from **Fishermen's Terminal** (p88), just across the shipping canal.

Ballard still maintains a decidedly Nordic air, though only about a third of today's population is of Nordic descent. Along NW Market St, you can pop into Olsen's Scandinavian Foods and buy some fresh *lefsa* (potato pancakes), or shop for trinkets at Norse Imports.

Most of the names on local businesses' signs are of Scandinavian origin, and many of the older folks on the streets and in the shops speak with distinct accents, if they're not actually speaking their mother tongue.

The heart of old Ballard is centered along Ballard Ave NW, which seems to have hardly changed aesthetically from the 1890s. Seven blocks here have been named a Historic Landmark District, but fortunately the buildings have not been thoughtlessly glamorized; the structures in this district are old, not 'olde.' Some are still hardware stores or meat markets, while others are brewpubs and bars. This is where you'll find Ballard's notable concentration of live music venues.

The 'Historic' designation helps protect Ballard from over commercialization or other undesirable growth. Any proposed development has to be approved by a board of locals, and the locals are pretty picky about who they let in. Ballard is fun and casual; here you can let your proverbial hair down, do shots with a fisherman, eat cheap food, get a tattoo or sit in a bar and get drunk all day – in Ballard, you won't be the only one.

Orientation

The Historic Landmark District along Ballard Ave NW extends seven blocks, starting from its intersection with Market St. Pick up a copy of the 'Historic Ballard Avenue Walking Tour' pamphlet for background on the buildings. The **Ballard Historical Society** (☎ 206-782-6844) also gives occasional tours.

Bus No 17 goes to Ballard from downtown at 4th Ave at Union. To drive to Ballard, you can take I-5 north to the 45th St exit and turn west, away from the university. Follow NW 45th St; it will become Shilshole Ave along the docks before it runs into NW Market St, which is the main commercial strip for Ballard. From downtown, you can also take Westlake Ave N toward Fremont, but continue west past Fremont Bridge on W Nickerson St to Ballard Bridge and over the ship canal.

BALLARD BUILDING Map p248
2208 NW Market St
Built in the 1920s by the Fraternal Order of Eagles, this imposing structure is the only major terra-cotta building in Ballard. It once held a community hospital and now houses the *Ballard News-Tribune* offices.

CORS & WEGENER BUILDING Map p248
5000-4 20th Ave NW
Once a wine bar and the offices of the early local broadsheet, the *Ballard News,* this grand building was one of the first in the area to be revitalized. It's now apartments and office space.

Transportation
Bus Take No 17 or 18.
Parking There's street parking.

FISH LADDER Map p248
3015 NW 54th; ⏰ 24hr, gardens 7am-9pm, visitors' center 10am-7pm Jun-Sep, 11am-5pm Thu-Mon Oct-May
On the southern side of the locks (p88), the ladder was built in 1976 to allow salmon to fight their way to spawning grounds in the Cascade headwaters of the Sammamish River, which feeds Lake Washington. Visitors can watch the fish from underwater glass-sided tanks or from above (nets are installed to keep salmon from over-leaping and stranding themselves on the pavement). Ironically, you can also watch sea lions munch on the salmon while the fish attempt to negotiate the ladder. Just what to do about the sea lions has stymied environmentalists, anglers and the local Fish & Wildlife Department. The best time to visit is during spawning season, from mid-June to September.

On the northern entrance to the lock area is the **Carl English Jr Botanical Gardens**, a charming arboretum and specimen garden. Trails wind

Top Five Ballard
- **Ballard Locks & the Fish Ladder** (see opposite & p88) Inexplicably fascinating.
- **Golden Gardens Park** (p88) Wonderful for a picnic.
- **Hattie's Hat** (p125) For breakfast with beer.
- **Nordic Heritage Museum** (p89) Walk through Old Ballard.
- **Sunset Tavern** (p132) Movie night! Or a cheap afternoon punk show.

Gas Works Park

Urban reclamation has no greater monument in Seattle than Gas Works Park. On a grassy point on the northern end of Lake Union, the former power station here produced gas for heating and lighting from 1906 to 1956. The gas works was thereafter understandably considered an eyesore and an environmental menace. However, the beautiful location of the park – with stellar views of downtown over Lake Union, while sailboats and yachts slide to and from the shipping canal – induced the city government to convert the former industrial site into a public park in 1975.

Rather than tear down the factory, however, landscape architects preserved much of the old plant. Painted black and now highlighted with rather joyful graffiti, it looks like some odd remnant from a former civilization. It also makes a great location for shooting rock album covers and music videos.

A major drawback of this ode to industrial art is that the soil and groundwater beneath the park contain chemical contamination. Though this apparently poses no health risks to humans, state government and environmental agencies occasionally close the park to complete various cleanup and research projects. During the latest closure, from November 2000 to June 2001, a new soil cover and irrigation system was installed to avoid further contamination of Lake Union.

Before the trail was extended to Fremont and Ballard, the Burke-Gilman Trail started in Gas Works Park. This is still a great spot to pick up the trail, which you can follow east to the University of Washington.

through gardens filled with labelled, mature trees and flower gardens. Commune with imploring squirrels and haughty geese.

Flanking the gardens is a small museum and **visitors' center** documenting the history of the locks. Free tours are offered at 1pm and 3pm daily mid-May to mid-September, with an added tour of the locks at 11am on weekends. The rest of the year, tours are offered at 2pm Thursday to Monday.

FISHERMEN'S TERMINAL Map p248
19th Ave & W Nickerson St; bus 15, 17 or 18

Seattle's fishing fleet resides at Fishermen's Terminal, in a wide recess in the ship canal called Salmon Bay on the south side of the Ballard Bridge at 19th Ave and W Nickerson St. About 700 fishing boats dock here, making this the largest halibut and salmon fleet in the world. Fishermen's Terminal is a popular moorage spot because the facility is in freshwater, above the Chittenden Locks. Freshwater is much less corrosive to boats than saltwater.

It's great fun to wander the piers, watching crews unload their catch, clean boats and repair nets. Many of these fishing boats journey to Alaska in summer and return to dry dock while they wait out winter. Outdoor interpretive displays explain the history of Seattle's fishing fleet, starting with the Natives who first fished these waters in canoes, to the Slavs and Greeks, who dominated salmon fishing in the early 1900s. A statue, the bronze **Seattle Fisherman's Memorial** at the base of the piers, commemorates Seattle fishers lost at sea. This memorial is also the site of the ceremonial blessing of the fleet, held annually on the first Sunday in May.

In the two shed-like terminal buildings are a couple of good restaurants specializing in the freshest seafood in Seattle, a tobacconist, a ship chandler and a charts and nautical gifts store. Stop at the **Wild Salmon Fish Market** (p176) to buy the freshest pick of the day's catch.

GOLDEN GARDENS PARK Map pp232-3
8498 Seaview Pl NW

Golden Gardens Park, established in 1904 by Harry W Treat, is a lovely 95-acre beach park with sandy beaches. There are picnic facilities, restrooms, basketball hoops, volleyball nets, gangs of Canadian geese, lots of parking and plenty of space to get away from all the activity. Rising above Golden Gardens is **Sunset Hill Park** (NW 77th St & 34th Ave), a prime perch for dramatic sunsets and long views.

HIRAM M CHITTENDEN LOCKS
Map p248
Visitors' center ☎ 206-783-7059; 3015 NW 54th St; ☻ 24hr; bus No 17 from downtown at 4th Ave & Union St

These locks, also known as the Ballard Locks, are about a half mile west of Ballard off NW Market St. Watching boats traverse the two locks on the Lake Washington Ship Canal exerts a strange Zen-like attraction for locals and tourists alike. The process takes between 10 and 30 minutes, depending on tides and lake levels and on whether the large or the small lock is used. Walkways along the locks allow an intimate look at the workings of these water elevators and a chance to view the vessels that are coming and going from Puget Sound to Lakes Union and Washington.

NORDIC HERITAGE MUSEUM Map p248

☎ 206-789-5707; 3014 NW 67th St; adult/child/
senior/child/child under 5 $6/4/5/free; ⏰ 10am-4pm
Tue-Sat, noon-4pm Sun

This museum preserves the history of the northern Europeans who settled in Ballard and the Pacific Northwest, as well as bringing in special exhibits of new work by contemporary Scandinavian artists. It's the only museum in the USA that commemorates the history of settlers from all five Scandinavian countries. A permanent exhibit, with one room for each country, features costumes, photographs and maritime equipment, while a second gallery is devoted to changing exhibitions. The museum also offers Scandinavian language instruction, lectures and films.

To get here, take bus No 17 from downtown at 4th Ave & Union St, get off at 32nd Ave NW & walk one block east on NW 67th St.

SHILSHOLE BAY MARINA Map p248
Seaview Ave NW

The Shilshole Bay Marina, about 2 miles west of the locks along Seaview Ave, offers nice views across Puget Sound and, as Seattle's primary sailboat moorage, a glittery collection of boats. Inside the marina, you can rent sailboats or

Coffeeshop, Wallingford (p148)

Neighborhoods – Ballard & Discovery Park

take classes at **Wind Works** (☎ 206-784-9386; 7001 Seaview Ave NW).

DISCOVERY PARK

Eating p125

Discovery Park is 534 acres of urban wilderness northwest of downtown Seattle and just southwest of the mouth of Chittenden Locks. Locals love to come here escape the ever-present manicure of city gardens and get windswept along the park's many trails. Though it's easy to reach, it feels utterly remote; there are good walking trails, long beaches, picnic areas and a helpful visitors' center.

The park was originally Fort Lawton, an army base established in 1897 to protect Seattle from unnamed enemies. Fort Lawton didn't see much activity until WWII, when it was used as barracks for troops bound for the Pacific. Over the course of the war it held up to 1400 German and Italian prisoners. When the fort was declared surplus property in the 1960s, the City of Seattle decided to turn it into a park (although significant areas of the park are still used for military housing). The fort was finally proclaimed public parkland in 1972.

Orientation

You can simply take bus No 33 from downtown or Seattle Center. Though they take a more circuitous route, bus Nos 19 and 24 also come here from downtown (4th Ave and Union St). To reach Discovery Park by car from downtown, take Elliott Ave north, which will turn into 15th Ave W. Take the W Dravus St exit and turn left. Turn right onto 20th Ave W and proceed until it turns into Gilman Ave W, and eventually into W Government Way. For a map of the park's trail and road system, stop by the visitors' center (☎ 503-386-4236; ⏰ 8:30am-5:30pm) near the Government Way entrance. The park runs educational programs including Saturday nature walks, day camps for children and bird-watching tours.

DAYBREAK STAR INDIAN CULTURAL CENTER Map p248
W Cramer St

In 1977, native groups laid claim to the land in this area, and 17 acres of parkland were decreed Native land on which now stands the Daybreak Star Indian Cultural Center, a community center for Seattle-area Native Americans. Discovery Park has over 7 miles of hiking trails, several of which lead to the Daybreak Star Center. Except for a small art gallery, there are few facilities for outside visitors.

The vista point in front of the center affords beautiful views of the Sound, and several steep trails lead down through the forest to narrow, sandy beaches.

WEST POINT LIGHTHOUSE Map p248

About a mile off from the 3-mile paved loop that circles the park, a trail skirts the water's edge all the way to the still-functioning West Point Lighthouse. It's a great spot for panoramic views of the Sound and mountains to the west.

CENTRAL DISTRICT, MADRONA & MADISON PARK

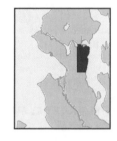

Eating p126

Running down the east slope of First Hill to the upscale neighborhoods that flank Lake Washington, the Central District – or 'the CD' – represents the heart of Seattle's African American community. Few blacks lived in Seattle until WWII, when they moved to the area in large numbers to work in the shipyards and contribute to the war effort. Today the CD is overrun with empty storefronts, which is ironic considering the high price of real estate in nearby Capitol and First Hills. During the day the CD is a friendly place, where you can find some great soul food and barbecue joints (p126), but you'll probably want to avoid walking alone in the CD at night.

Madrona is one of Seattle's more ethnically diverse neighborhoods, blending elements of the CD's African American community to the west with the predominantly white neighborhoods that ring Lake Washington proper. Once a relatively unheard-of neighborhood, Madrona has been gentrified recently and now draws crowds from around the city, notably at one of the most popular brunch places in Seattle, the **Hi Spot Café** (p126).

If you follow Madison St from downtown (or take bus No 11), you're following the old trolley line that once served the eastern side of Capitol Hill and the amusement park and beach at Madison Park. Today these tranquil neighborhoods are quietly upscale, home to little commercial hubs lined with understated shops and good restaurants. When it gets hot in the summer – yes, Seattle can get hot – locals make the pilgrimage to Lake Washington to sprawl out on the small sandy-grassy beaches. Just driving or cycling around is a good respite – the houses along Lake Washington Blvd boast old money or new corporate wealth.

The first neighborhood you come to is Madison Valley, where the biggest attractions are two notable restaurants: **Rover's** (p126), considered one of the best restaurants in Seattle, and **Café Flora** (p126), a vegetarian's dream restaurant. Continue toward Lake Washington to reach Madison Park, another neighborhood with the usual hub of trendy restaurants and cafés.

In the 1890s Madison Park proper comprised an amusement park, bathhouse, ballpark and racetrack. Ferries left from here to cross Lake Washington to Bellevue. Nowadays, Madison Park is a much quieter place and very genteel. The park proper is the most northerly of the public parks and beaches along Lake Washington's western shore. In summer, the popular beach sees a sizable gay male contingent mixed in with local families. The beach here is one of the more pleasant places to swim and sunbathe.

Orientation

The Central District's principal commercial areas are along E Madison St from 12th to 18th Aves and along E Union St around 26th Ave. To get here, take bus No 11 outbound on Madison St from downtown. From downtown or Pioneer Square, the best streets to walk along (about 20 blocks) are E Union or E Cherry.

Madrona's small business district is on 34th Ave, between E Pike and E Spring Sts. Take bus No 2 outbound on Spring St from downtown to get here. No bus routes serve the whole length of Lake Washington Blvd, though you can get to Madrona Park by bus No 2. By car, follow Union or Cherry Sts from downtown to get to Madrona.

Access to parks and beaches along the western shores of Lake Washington is primarily along Lake Washington Blvd, which isn't exactly easy to get to. From the north or downtown, it's easiest to follow Madison St out to the Washington Park Arboretum (p92). Lake Washington Blvd E intersects E Madison St before descending onto the lakeshore.

COLMAN PARK Map p249

Continue south along the Lake Washington Blvd E through the very upscale Madrona Park neighborhood, and you'll end up at Colman Park. The entire lakefront stretch between here and Seward Park is parkland. This is an especially good area for bike riding; on the weekends the boulevard is closed to cars.

DENNY BLAINE PARK Map p249

South of Madison Park toward the tail of Lake Washington Blvd is Denny Blaine Park, found at the end of a looping tree-lined lane. This predominantly lesbian beach is surrounded by an old stone wall, which marked the shoreline before the lake level was dropped 9ft during construction of the ship canal. Just a little further south on your right-hand side, you'll find the two-tiered **Viretta Park**, from which you can see the mansion once owned by Nirvana's Kurt Cobain and Courtney Love (it's the house on the north, or left, side of the benches if you're facing the water). Seattle sweetheart Cobain took his life with a shotgun in the mansion's

greenhouse in April 1994. The greenhouse is long gone and Love no longer owns the house, but Nirvana fans still make the pilgrimage to this small park to give their tribute to the angst-ridden king of grunge and scribble messages on the benches in the lower part of the park.

HOWELL PARK Map p249

Just south of Viretta Park is a small beachfront called Howell Park. It is usually less crowded due to the park's lack of parking. If you're on foot, look for a small sign and trailhead that leads to the beach.

MADRONA PARK BEACH Map p249

Madrona Park Beach, down from the business district in Madrona Park, is one of the nicest along the lake. In clear weather, the views of Mt Rainier are fantastic. Swimming is only for hardy souls, however; the water's icy cold even in summer. Further south, past the yacht moorage, is **Leschi Park**, a grassy green space with a children's play area.

Neighborhoods – Central District, Madrona & Madison Park

City skyline from Alki Beach (p93)

MOUNT ZION BAPTIST CHURCH

Map p249

☎ 206-322-6500; 1634 19th Ave at E Madison St

One of the cornerstones of this neighborhood is Mount Zion Baptist Church, a 2000-member congregation with a choir that has reached national acclaim through its gospel recordings. The church is over a century old.

WASHINGTON PARK ARBORETUM

This wild and lovely park offers a wide variety of gardens, a wetlands nature trail and 200 acres of mature forest threaded by paths. More than 5500 plant species grow within the arboretum's boundaries. In the spring Azalea Way, a jogger-free trail that winds through the arboretum, is lined with a giddy array of pink- and orange-flowered azaleas and rhododendrons. Trail guides to the plant collections are available at the **Graham Visitors' Center & Gift Shop** (2300 Arboretum Dr E; ☺ 10am-4pm). Free guided tours of the grounds are available at 1pm on Saturday and Sunday from January to November.

Orientation

The Washington Park Arboretum is just south of the University of Washington across Union Bay. Public transportation to the arboretum isn't great. The No 11 Madison St bus delivers you to the base of the park at Lake Washington Blvd, but there's still quite a walk (albeit through the park) to the visitors' center. To MOHAI, it's probably better to catch one of the buses to the university and walk from there (p80).

To reach the visitors' center and hiking trails at the north end of the park by car, take Hwy 520 east from I-5, then take the first exit (for Montlake/UW). This intersection can be confusing: stay in the right lane and go straight through the first intersection. This lane becomes Lake Washington Blvd. Follow this street for about a quarter mile, and then turn onto Foster Island Rd (not 26th Ave E). Follow signs for the visitors' center. If you're trying to get to MOHAI, follow the signs for Montlake and the university, but turn immediately left (east) on E Hamlin St or E Shelby St before crossing the Montlake Bridge.

Access from the south is somewhat less confusing. Follow Madison St from downtown until it intersects with Lake Washington Blvd E. Turn left at the junction. Take Arboretum Dr E to the visitors' center.

JAPANESE GARDEN Map p249

☎ 206-684-4725; adult/senior & student $3/2;
☺ 10am-6pm Mar-Nov

At the southern edge of the arboretum, this 3½-acre formal garden has koi pools, waterfalls, a teahouse and manicured plantings. Granite for the garden's sculptures was laboriously dragged in from the Cascades. Tea ceremony demonstrations are frequently available; call for a schedule.

FOSTER ISLAND WETLANDS TRAIL

Map p249

The northern edge of the arboretum includes this wonderful trail around Foster Island in Lake Washington's Union Bay, a picnic spot that once was a burial ground for Union Bay Indians. The waterfront trail winds through marshlands and over floating bridges to smaller islands and reedy shoals. Bird-watching is popular here, as is swimming, fishing and kayaking (for kayak rentals, see p157). It's just too bad that busy, elevated Hwy 520 roars above the island. The nature trail is best accessed from the MOHAI parking lot (see above).

Top Five Central District, Madrona & Madison

- **Café Flora** (p126) Veggie heaven.
- **Catfish Corner** (p126) For a whole different breed of seafood.
- **Hi Spot Café** (p126) For brunch.
- **Rover's** (p126) Splurge on dinner.
- **Washington Park Arboretum** (see above) Gardens galore.

MUSEUM OF HISTORY & INDUSTRY

Map p249
MOHAI; ☎ 206-324-1126; 2700 24th Ave E; adult/
senior & student $7/5; ⏰ 10am-5pm Fri-Wed, 10am-
8pm Thu
This museum at the northwest corner of the
arboretum documents the history of Seattle
and the Puget Sound in terms of its lumber,
fishing and shipping industries. There's also,
no surprise, a big Boeing presence, including
a 1920s mail plane. Usually called by its acro-
nym, MOHAI has an entertaining collection of
historic photos, old planes, memorabilia from
the Great Fire and artifacts and lore from Seattle's great seafaring era.

WEST SEATTLE

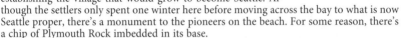

Eating p127; Shopping p176
West Seattle is the nose of land across Elliott Bay to the west of
downtown Seattle, beyond the Port of Seattle and Harbor Island.
West Seattle hasn't succumbed to gentrification and still feels
working class. Although access to downtown is good, it seems removed from the rest of the city. From here the views can be stellar,
both of the city center and of the islands to the west.

Alki Point, the westernmost point of the peninsula, attracted
the Denny party, who landed in the schooner *Exact* in 1851,
establishing the village that would grow to become Seattle. Al-
though the settlers only spent one winter here before moving across the bay to what is now
Seattle proper, there's a monument to the pioneers on the beach. For some reason, there's
a chip of Plymouth Rock imbedded in its base.

The main reason to visit West Seattle, especially in good weather, is to go to **Alki Beach Park**.
The sober and purposeful settlers who landed here wouldn't recognize the place today. This 2-
mile stretch of sandy beach is a madhouse in summer. Like southern California, the volleyball
nets go up, sunbathing occupies the strand and teens in souped-up cars prowl the streets. Still,
it's Seattle's only real beach scene, and the views of Seattle from **Duwamish Head**, at the northern
end of the beach, are spectacular. Perhaps avoid Alki on summer weekends, but good beach-
side cafés, quaint fish-and-chips joints, the miniature replica of the Statue of Liberty on the
beach and the Alki Point Lighthouse make this area a nice getaway most other times.

The main commercial strip on West Seattle is along California Ave SW, centering at the
junction of SW Alaska St. There's nothing particularly compelling about the shops here, except
that they seem at least a generation and 200 miles removed from the rest of Seattle. Old five-
and-dime stores slumber next to old diners, neither having changed much since the 1950s.

If you're interested in a ferry ride, follow Fauntleroy Way SW down through West Seattle
to Fauntleroy Ferry Terminal at Henderson St SW, south of Lincoln Park. Here you can take
a half-hour ferry ride to Vashon Island, a semi-rural island that also serves as a bedroom
community to Seattle.

Orientation

To get to Alki Beach by public transportation, catch bus No 37 or 56 heading southbound
from anywhere along 1st Ave downtown. Route Nos 54, 116, 118 and 119 go to the Vashon
Ferry departure point at Fauntleroy Ferry Terminal. Catch No 116, 118 or 119 from any
of the designated stops along 2nd Ave downtown. Catch No 54 westbound on Union St,
or southbound on 1st Ave.

By car, take Hwy 99 or I-5 south from Seattle to the West Seattle Freeway; for Alki Beach,
take the exit for Harbor Ave SW and travel north (it later changes its name to Alki Ave SW
and then Beach Dr SW on its way around the promontory). For the Vashon Ferry, follow
the signs for Fauntleroy Way SW.

ALKI BEACH PARK Map pp232-3

Alki Beach has an entirely different feel from
the rest of Seattle; this 2-mile stretch of sandy
beach could almost fool you into thinking it's

California, at least on a sunny day. There's a
bike path, volleyball courts on the sand, and
rings for beach fires. Look for the miniature
Statue of Liberty, donated by the Boy Scouts.

A pylon marking the Arthur Denny landing party's first stop, in 1851, now contains a shard of Massachusetts' Plymoth Rock in its base.

ALKI POINT LIGHT STATION Map pp232-3
☎ 206-217-6123; btwn Beach Dr & Point Pl, Alki Beach
The US Coast Guard maintains this lighthouse. It has limited public hours, but tours are available by appointment; call for a current schedule and more information.

DUWAMISH HEAD Map pp232-3
Popular for its views of Elliott Bay and downtown, this is the former site of Luna Park.

In its days as an over-the-top amusement center, the park covered more than 10 acres and boasted the 'longest bar on the bay'. This grand assertion unfortunately led to claims of debauchery and carousing, and the park was eventually closed in 1913 by the conservative powers-that-were.

FAUNTLEROY FERRY DOCK Map pp232-3
☎ 206-464-6400; Fauntleroy Way SW & Henderson St
Washington State Ferries to Vashon Island leave daily from this dock.

HIGH POINT Map pp232-3
SW Myrtle St & 35th Ave
This intersection marks the highest point in Seattle, at 518ft above sea level.

SOUTH SEATTLE
South Seattle isn't exactly a neighborhood in the traditional sense; basically, the term describes everything south of downtown and the Pioneer Square area. But both of the sites we've listed here make nice mini-excursions from the city. Both of them are reached by going south outside of town on I-5.

SEWARD PARK Map pp232-3
No 39 bus from 2nd Ave downtown
For wilderness, go to Seward Park, dominating the 277-acre Bailey Peninsula, which juts into Lake Washington like a hitchhiking thumb. The park preserves what is just about the only old-growth forest anywhere in the vicinity of Seattle and is known for its wildlife, including a nesting pair of bald eagles. Hikers and bikers will be interested in the 2.5-mile paved lakeside trail. Other trails lead to a fish hatchery, beach access and several picnic areas. On the weekends the lakefront boulevard between here and Colman Park (p91) is closed to cars and makes an especially good area for bike riding. Seward Park can be dangerous after dark, so be attentive.

By car, take I-5 south to I-90 (exit 164), then exit 1 for Rainier Ave S; stay on Rainier Ave S until it intersects with S Orca St after about 2 miles; turn left (east) and follow signs to the park.

MUSEUM OF FLIGHT Map pp232-3
☎ 206-764-5720; 9494 E Marginal Way S, Boeing Field, about 10 miles south of downtown; adult/child/senior $11/6.50/10, 5-9pm 1st Thu each month free; ☽ 10am-5pm Fri-Wed, 10am-9pm Thu; bus No 174 from downtown
In many ways, aviation and aircraft manufacturing have been integral to the growth of modern Seattle. Unfortunately that fact alone doesn't

justify this rather gratuitous paean to Boeing. While this vast museum has no formal ties to the aircraft giant, the local boosterism is implicit. It'll be interesting to see how much of that remains in the wake of 2001's massive layoffs and the company headquarters' move to Chicago.

Aviation buffs wholeheartedly enjoy the Museum of Flight, while others traipse through suppressing yawns, so be choosy about who you come with. The museum presents the entire history of flight, from da Vinci to the Wright Brothers to the NASA space program. More than 50 historic aircraft are displayed, including a recently aquired British Airways Concorde. The restored 1909 Red Barn, where Boeing had its beginnings, contains exhibits and displays. The six-story glass Great Gallery has 20 airplanes suspended from its ceiling. Vintage fliers reside on the grounds outside the buildings. There's also a hands-on area where visitors get to work the controls and sit in the driver's seat. Films about flight and aircraft history are shown in the small theater, and there's a gift shop and café.

To get here by car, take I-5 south from downtown to exit 158, turn west & follow East Marginal Way north.

Walking &
Cycling Tours

Walking & Cycling Tours

These six themed tours – four walking, one cycling and one very likely stumbling – are designed to give you a feel for these areas of the city as a whole, rather than just seeing one or two sights out of context. For companies that offer guided tours, see p43.

EXPLORING BELLTOWN WALKING TOUR

Belltown is at its best in the wee hours of the night. This tour should start between 8pm and 9pm, and it can take as much or as little time as you and your liver are willing to invest. Don't forget to drink plenty of water along the way.

Most of Belltown's shops and fancy restaurants are along 1st Ave, while 2nd Ave is the home of the bars and nightclubs. It's easy enough to explore on your own, so don't feel tied to this itinerary.

Start the tour by fueling up with an enormous mushroom-swiss burger at the **Two Bells Tavern 1** (p117; 2313 4th Ave), on 4th Ave between Bell and Battery Sts. If the

weather's nice, have your burger and a beer in the garden out back; otherwise, enjoy the conviviality of the main room, full of people who all seem to know and like each other.

When you're sated, wander down 4th Ave toward Blanchard St. On the right, between Bell and Blanchard, is the site of Seattle's legendary laundromat-slash-bar-slash-café-slash rock venue, Sit & Spin, now reinvented as rock club the Hideaway.

Take a right on Blanchard and walk down to 2nd Ave. On the corner of 2nd Ave and Blanchard St, you'll see the snakeskin-green sign of the famed **Crocodile Café 2** (p132; 2200 2nd Ave), one of the best rock clubs in the country and a key venue in the rise of the grunge movement. Many an up-and-coming band has wooed or rocked the crowd from its stage. Nirvana played here in 1992, less than two years before Kurt Cobain's suicide. During the day the Croc is a decent greasy-spoon café. Check the posters on its window for upcoming shows.

Next to the Crocodile is Tula's, a great local jazz venue. If that sounds good, stop in and hear some of Seattle's best-kept secrets. If you're after more active pursuits, and you're thirsty, keep walking. Right in the middle of the block, you'll find **Shorty's 3** (p147; 2222 2nd Ave), otherwise known as pinball heaven. Grab a cheap beer or a slushy blue cocktail and head straight to the back room to test your reflexes.

When the pinball wears you out or simply beats you into submission, hop next door to the **Lava Lounge 4** (p138; 2226 2nd Ave), another groovy nightspot. Its comfy wooden booths and tiki décor will soothe your battered ego. On your way out, peek across the street at **Singles Going Steady 5** (p171; 2219 2nd Ave), an excellent punk-rock record store.

Continue on past legendary nosh spots the Noodle Ranch and Mama's Mexican Kitchen, both usually packed to the gills. In the next block you'll come to the **Rendezvous 6** (p138; 2320 2nd Ave), a classy place with a curvilinear bar and an adorable, recently gussied-up theater in the back. Head back a block, then up Bell St toward 3rd Ave to Regrade Park, where you'll usually find an unfortunate lot enjoying brown-bag beverages. Walk back down Bell St to 1st Ave: you'll see the gloriously flashing neon sign of the **Frontier Room 7** (p137; 2203 1st Ave), an institution in Belltown, a no-frills kind of tavern where you swig whiskey, ponder Kenny Rogers' *The Gambler* and don't ask too many questions. From here you can head toward Blanchard St and hit the **Axis 8** (p136; 2212 1st Ave) if you feel you're dressed well enough; or push northward, past the **Belltown Pub 9** (p136; 2322 1st Ave) to the corner of 1st Ave and Wall St. Here you'll find **Cyclops 10** (p137; 2421 1st Ave), half restaurant, half bar. If you're lucky enough to be staying at the Ace Hotel, you can chill at the Cyclops until your eyes match the bleary, bloodshot one hanging over the door, then stumble upstairs and fall into bed. End of tour.

CENTER OF THE UNIVERSE: FREMONT WALKING TOUR

Exploring Fremont can take as much or as little time and energy as you want. Start the walk on Evanston Ave N between N 35th and N 36th Sts at the rather conspicuous **Fremont Rocket 1** (p83). The rocket is Fremont's community totem. Beneath it is a coin box affixed to the building – drop 50¢ in and the rocket will 'launch' by blowing steam.

Walk north (away from the water) up Evanston Ave N to N 36th St. Take a right onto Fremont Place N. On N 36th St at Fremont Place N, you'll see the latest and most controversial addition to Fremont's collection of public art. This bronze, 16ft statue of former communist leader **Vladimir Lenin 2** (p83) weighs 7 tons. Brought to the USA from Slovakia, it's still waiting for a buyer.

Transportation

Bus No 26, 28.
Parking Street, both metered and time-limited.

Pioneer Building (1889), in Pioneer Square; Smith Tower on the right (p51)

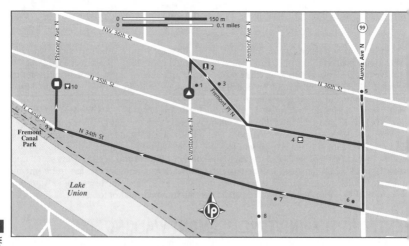

Walk half a block east along Fremont Place N. Stop in and look around one of Seattle' most kitschy secondhand shops, **Deluxe Junk 3** (p174; 3518 Fremont Place N), located in former funeral parlor.

Continue east along Fremont Place N, cross Fremont Ave N and go east on N 35th St, wher it's coffee time. In Seattle, no day is complete without a little caffeine. One of the city's bes coffee shops, **Still Life in Fremont 4** (p84; 705 N 35th St) is a haven on rainy days and one of th greatest places in town to curl up with a good book, a coffee and a bowl of homemade soup. Bu you're not lounging just now, so after sippin your coffee for a bit, get back on your feet This is, after all, a *walking* tour.

<table>
<tr><td colspan="2">

Walk Facts

Start Fremont Rocket
End Former Redhook Brewery
Distance About 0.5 miles
Duration 30 to 60 minutes

</td></tr>
</table>

Leave Still Life and take a right, follow ing N 35th St to Aurora Ave N. Here you' be underneath the Aurora Bridge. Turi left and head for the dark, shadowy spac where the bridge meets the ground.

Watch out! It's the **Fremont Troll 5** (p84) This incredible piece of public art is must-see for anyone interested in the peculiar things in life. He's an 18ft cement figur busily munching on a VW bug.

Back away slowly, then head back down Aurora Ave N to N 34th St. Turn right.

On your right, you'll see the colorful metal fence of the **History House 6** (p83; 790 N 34t St). The fence features colored houses with open doors. Inside are exhibits about the his tory of Seattle neighborhoods.

Follow N 34th St west, toward the Fremont Bridge. Here you'll find Seattle's most popula piece of public art, **Waiting for the Interurban 7** (p84), showing people waiting for a train tha never comes. Their clothes change regularly, as locals like to decorate them.

Continue west and look left down Fremont Ave N, and you'll see the **Fremont Bridge &** (p82), with an orange-and-blue color scheme that seems to fit perfectly in this slightl wacky neighborhood.

From the bridge, go west along N 34th St for two blocks until you get to Phinney Ave N Along the banks of the ship canal, Fremont Canal Park extends west following the exten sion of the Burke-Gilman Trail. Right at the start of the park, at the bottom of Phinne Ave N, you'll see two giant, life-size **apatosaurs 9** (p82), giant topiaries given to Fremont by the Pacific Science Center.

Near the corner of Phinney Ave N and N 35th St is the building that used to house the **Red hook Brewery 10** and the Trolleyman Pub; the brewery has moved, so the building sits empty Which means it's time for you to hunt down a beer – officially the end of our tour.

DOWNTOWN ARCHITECTURE WALKING TOUR

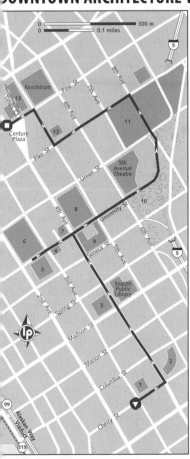

Start this walk on the south end of downtown at the **Arctic Building 1** (p46; Cherry St at 3rd Ave). Crane your neck to get a look at the walrus heads on the building's exterior. Then walk up Cherry St and take a left onto 4th Ave.

The **Bank of America Tower 2**, formerly the Columbia Seafirst Center, takes up the block between 4th and 5th Aves and Columbia and Cherry Sts. This is the tallest building on the West Coast. If you have time, check out the observation deck on the 73rd floor.

Follow 4th Ave to Madison St, to the **1001 Fourth Ave Plaza 3** (p46), one of the city's first real skyscrapers, built in 1969. Locals call it 'the box that the Space Needle came in.' In the plaza outside is Henry Moore's *Three Piece Sculpture: Vertebrae.*

Continue north on 4th Ave to University St and take a left, walk half a block and look up. Formerly the Northern Life Tower, the **Seattle Tower 4** (p47), an Art Deco skyscraper built in 1928, was designed to reflect the mountains of the Pacific Northwest. There's an 18-karat-gold relief map in the lobby.

Continue down University St across 3rd Ave. The beauty of the Seattle skyline is the blue-and-cream **Washington Mutual Building 5** at 3rd Ave at Seneca St, which changes colors with the clouds and sunsets. Don't be shy; enter off 3rd Ave to explore the building's stunning interior.

Cross University St to **Benaroya Concert Hall 6** (p46). Walk into the glass-enclosed lobby of the performance hall, where you can take in excellent views of Elliott Bay. Check out the 20ft-long chandeliers.

Walk back up University St, across 3rd Ave to the corner of 4th Ave. Look up at the 1910 **Cobb Building 7** and see remnants of an older Seattle. Peering out from the building is the dour terracotta head of a Native American chief.

Continue on University St across 4th Ave to **Rainier Tower 8**. Taking up an entire block between 4th and 5th Aves and University and Union Sts is Rainier Square, a shopping center connected to the top-heavy tower.

Cross University St and gaze in wonder at the **Fairmont Olympic Hotel 9** (p179; 411 University St). Formerly the Four Seasons, this is undoubtedly one of the classiest remnants of Seattle's early-20th-century heyday. The block-square building is sober and unrevealing on the outside, but journey through the revolving doors to discover a sumptuous lobby dominated by chandeliers, marble walls and exotic carpets – testimony to a distant, more glorious era. Peek into the Georgian Room to see a dining room right out of a stylish 1930s film. University St got its name because the original building of the University of Washington once stood

Walk Facts

Start Arctic Building
End Westlake Center
Distance About 1.5 miles
Duration 1 to 2 hours

Walking & Cycling Tours – Downtown Architecture Walking Tour

on the location of the hotel. The university still owns 10 acres of land in the city center, par of a land donation made by Seattle founder Arthur Denny in 1860.

Continue northeast on University St past 6th Ave; look ahead to **Freeway Park 10**. Th: lone downtown island of greenery is in fact built right over I-5's ugly trench along th eastern edge of downtown. Built in a series of steps, the park escapes the growl of engine. The sound of traffic is masked by the roar of tumbling water from the waterfall, fountair and gurgling streams. Meander through Freeway Park, then follow signs to the **Washingto State Convention & Trade Center 11** (p47), whic is attached to the park. Pick up whateve brochures and maps you need at the visito center inside.

Transportation

Bus Almost every bus in Seattle goes through down-town. Downtown is in the Ride Free Area.

Monorail The terminus is inside Westlake Center, at 4th Ave & Pine St; a Metro Transit information booth is also here.

Parking Metered street parking, some paid lots (but they're very expensive).

Leave the convention center through it front doors on Pike St. Follow Pike sout. (you'll see Pike Place Market at the end c the street) to 5th Ave.

You won't be able to miss the imposin Banana Republic store at the corner of 5t Ave and Pike St. It is located in the wonder ful old terracotta-faced **Coliseum Theater 1** a film palace dating back to 1916. In it heyday, the theater filled its 1700 seat with eager moviegoers. The theater unfortunately suffered from neglect over the year until it was saved by Banana Republic's multimillion-dollar rehabilitation project, whic was completed in 1985.

Take a right on 5th Ave to Pine St; turn left. You can't miss the steel-and-glass visio of **Westlake Center 13** (p47), beckoning for your attention and pulsating with the frenzy c happy shoppers. What better way to finish up this tour than to stop by Seattle's Best Cof fee kiosk in front of Westlake Center and settle in for some people-watching while yo sip your brew.

From here you have a couple of options: you can shop at the upscale boutiques, go t the top of the mall and catch the Monorail to Seattle Center, or head back south along 4t Ave to Cherry St where you started the tour.

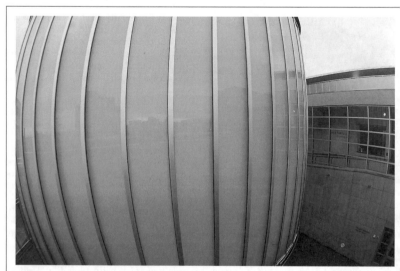

Henry Art Gallery, University of Washington (p79)

UNIVERSITY OF WASHINGTON WALKING TOUR

The 'U Dub,' as locals call it, is one of the nicest places in the city for a stroll. It has a parklike feel, with imposing buildings, quiet open areas and the understated buzz of a few thousand students studying fervently.

Walk Facts

Start Burke Museum
End Intersection of NE 45th St & University Way
Distance About 2 miles
Duration 2 to 3 hours, depending on museum stops

Start this tour at the **Burke Museum 1** (p79; NE 45th St at 15th Ave NE), which you may choose to visit now (this will add at least an hour to the tour time) or simply note to check out later. Its collection of Northwest native art is definitely not to be missed. From here, walk along NE 45th St to Memorial Way – take a right and amble into campus through the university's north gate.

Stroll along Stevens Way to Pierce Lane which leads to the center of campus. Here overlooking **Red Square 2**, you'll see the gorgeous, cathedral-like **Suzzallo Library 3** (p80). Admire it from the inside and out, then take a sharp left when you exit the library. Descend the stairs and walk straight ahead toward **Drumheller Fountain 4** (p80), which is also known as 'Frosh Pond.' On the way, along the pathway leading to the fountain, you'll be stunned (if it's a clear day) by the

Transportation

Bus 71, 72, 73.
Bicycle The Burke-Gilman Trail goes right along the edge of campus.
Parking There's both metered and time-limited street parking along the Ave and its side streets.

views from what is appropriately named Rainier Vista.

Head back toward Red Square, and bear left at the library. This will lead you to the **Henry Art Gallery 5** (p79), perhaps the best gallery in Seattle. The café downstairs is a good place for coffee and a panini. Or press on to 'The Ave,' bustling University Way NE, where there's a string of affordable coffeeshops and ethnic restaurants to kick back in (see the Eating chapter, p120).

Wander up the Ave, peeking in shops and cafés along the way. The tour concludes when you reach the busy intersection with NE 45th St; this is the core of the U District.

DISCOVERY PARK WALKING TOUR

Get out of the city and into what feels like utterly remote wilderness. Discovery Park is within easy reach of downtown Seattle, but it makes you feel like you've had a nice, long getaway. Bring a picnic lunch, plenty of water and good walking shoes for this tour. You might also want to dress in layers and be prepared for rapid weather changes. Extra socks are a good idea if you feel like soaking your feet in the surf midway through the walk.

Start the tour at the East Parking Lot of the **Discovery Park visitors' center 1** (for driving directions, see p89), at the intersection of W Government Wy and 36th Ave W. Ask for a map at the visitors center's front desk.

As this is basically a loop tour (in fact the main trail is called the Loop Trail, good to remember if you start to feel lost), you have several options, depending on how much you

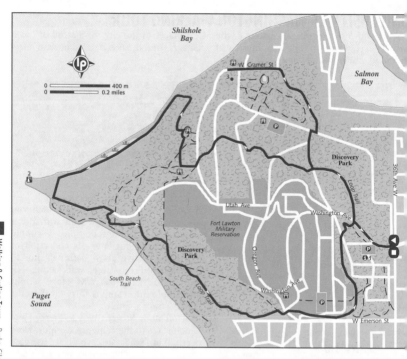

Walk Facts

Start Discovery Park visitors center East Parking Lot
End Back to visitors center East Parking Lot
Distance About 5 miles, depending on branches taken
Duration 1 to 3 hours

Transportation

Bus 33, 19, 24.
Parking There's a free lot near the visitors center (East Parking Lot) and another near the Daybreak Star Indian Cultural Center (North Lot).

feel like walking and what kind of weather you expect. If it's a warm, sunny day, don't miss the chance to see the **West Point lighthouse 2** (p90) over Shilshole Bay. To get to it, head south when you leave the visitors center's parking lot. This southern loop will take you past the South Parking Lot and onto the South Beach Trail. Follow signs to the lighthouse.

If you'd rather see the **Daybreak Star Indian Cultural Center 3** (p90), start with the northern route on the Loop Trail. Aim for the North Parking Lot, then follow the paved road to the cultural center. After your visit, you can either return to the East Parking Lot or pick up the Loop Trail where you left it and head west.

From here you may either simply complete the loop and head back to the visitors' center or branch off and see the lighthouse first.

BURKE-GILMAN TRAIL CYCLING TOUR

This tour can be hiked, but it's better if done on a bike. Seattle is a dream for cycling fanatics (for bike rental, see p159). This particularly popular and well-maintained route, a former railroad track, stretches 14 miles from Tracy Owen Station (a park at the top of Lake Washington) to Gas Works Park and beyond.

Start the hike or ride at **Gas Works Park 1** (p85), a cool industrial relic that has been (mostly) cleaned of its environmental contaminants and repainted – both officially, in bright primary

Ride Facts

Start Gas Works Park
End Tracy Owen Station
Distance 12.5 miles (one way)
Duration 1 hour and up, depending on stops

colors, and in highly entertaining graffiti. The park provides fantastic views of downtown Seattle.

Head northeast along the paved Burke-Gilman Trail. You'll follow the shore of Lake Union to the University District; if you feel like refueling already, there's an ideal spot for it right here. Where the trail loops down toward Boat St, look for the **Agua Verde Café 2** (p121), right at the edge of the water. You can fill up on tacos and beer, then watch the kayakers until you're ready to hit the trail again.

From here, the trail takes you through some residential areas and right past several parks. The first is **Ravenna Park 3** (p79), just north of the U District; reach it by taking a hard

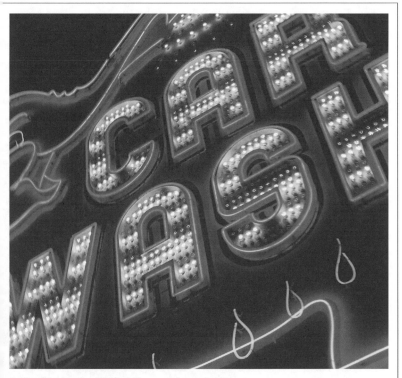

Design-winning sign (1956), Belltown nightspot (p60)

left (north) when the trail crosses 25th Ave NE about 1.25 miles north of the Agua Verde Café.

There's no shame in spending the rest of the day at Ravenna Park, but if you press on, you'll come to **Warren G Magnusen Park 4**, which sticks out into Lake Washington, followed shortly thereafter by **Mathews Beach Park 5**, a nice place to have a picnic lunch and dip your toes in the water.

This is essentially the halfway point. The rest of the trail clings to the shore of Lake Washington all the way up to the park at Tracy Owen Station, the official end of our tour (unless of course, you count the trip back). Note for the fit: the Burke-Gilman Trail here connects to the Sammamish Trail, allowing you to ride at least another 10 miles to the east.

Transportation

Bus 16, 26, 44.
Parking Limited parking near Gas Works Park.

Eating

Eating

With a long coastline, fertile valleys of fields and orchards, and miles of grassland devote
to livestock, the Pacific Northwest grows an abundance of high-quality food products. Loc
chefs appreciate this natural bounty and prepare indigenous foods with simple eleganc
along with an attitude that eating great food ought to be great fun. And Seattle residen
have begun to pick up on this attitude – going out to eat has become much more commo
as an activity, an evening-long event. When you see the terraces of sleek new Belltow
eateries jam-packed every night, rest assured, those aren't all out-of-towners.

Though the latest economic slump has put a slight damper on it, there was an explosio
of disposable income that came along with the Microsoft fortunes and the dot-com boo
in recent years. People here got accustomed to eating out, and they learned to apprecia
fine cuisine. The number of restaurants that have sprung up in the past five years or so
downright impressive.

For chic new places, Belltown can't be beaten; just stroll up and down 2nd Ave to have
look at the offerings. Make reservations for many of the newer, fancier places. Capitol H
also has several forward-looking new establishments. For the old-school treatment, a dar
wood-and-brass joint where starch-shirted waiters serve you steak and seafood in the class
style, Pioneer Square is still your best bet. For cheap ethnic food of all kinds, go straight
the U District and nosh with the budget-conscious students. If you want gourmet Chines
Vietnamese or dim sum, head for the International District. And for casual seafood joints, th
kind of places that compete for best-fish-and-chips honors, stroll along the Waterfront.

A lot of Seattle's gourmet restaurants describe their style of cuisine as 'Northwest'. But wh
does that actually mean? Besides the high quality of the raw materials found naturally in th
region, the thing that distinguishes Northwest cuisine from standard US food is the influence
Asian cooking traditions. Pan-Asian cooking, often referred to as Pacific Rim cuisine or fusio
food, is the blending of American or European standards with ingredients from Asia. It resul
in some unusual combinations – don't be surprised if you get wasabi on your French fries.

Not surprisingly, seafood is a cornerstone of Northwest cuisine. Crab, often Dungenes
fresh from the boat, is available almost
everywhere – you'll see stacks and stacks of
crabs at Pike Place Market. In restaurants,
crab is usually served in salad or with garlic butter, but you can also get crab cakes,
crab bisque or even crab burgers. The better seafood restaurants print a new list of
what's freshly caught each day; you might
love seared ahi, but if it's the (very limited)
season for native coho salmon, for example,
you'd be silly not to choose that instead,
and a good restaurant will tell you so.

Locally caught fish include red snapper,
flounder, sole, tuna, halibut and cod. Shrimp is another major catch. For most of the yea
salmon, still a menu staple, is as likely to be from Alaska as from the Northwest. Local trou
is also found in fish markets and on menus: watch for vibrantly yellow golden trout.

The chilly waters of the Pacific produce sweet-tasting, delicately tangy oysters, causin
oyster farms to spring up all along the coast. In the best places, discerning diners can choos
which Northwestern bay their oysters on the half-shell hail from. Clams, usually steamed
broth or seawater, and mussels, which cover practically every rock along the Pacific Coas
are common as appetizers, frequently in combination. The elongated, delicately flavore
razor clam, in particular, gets nobility status on the West Coast.

The Northwest offers an incredibly rich diversity of fruit, which the best chefs sprinkl
like jewels all over their creations, or whip into decadent sauces to drizzle over meat an

Top Five Eat Streets

- Belltown's 2nd Ave (p115)
- Broadway in Capitol Hill (p119)
- Anywhere in Pike Place Market (p112)
- Pioneer Square (p110)
- International District (p111)

fish. Blueberries thrive in the acidic soil, and they appear in pies, breads, muffins and scones. The mild climate is also good for strawberries and raspberries. Washington is the nation's largest producer of apples, and other notable orchard crops include pears, cherries and peaches. Blackberry brambles, which snag clothing and grab at the legs of hikers, are a great annoyance until late summer and early fall, when they produce a heady abundance of purple-black fruit. A favorite of black bears, wild huckleberries are found high up in mountain meadows. Washington state is also a major producer of tart, bright-red cranberries, which appear in a bewildering array of local dishes.

Rainy Washington is also a mushroom-lover's paradise. The best chefs use wild mushrooms gathered in the forest that morning. Don't miss a chance at the saffron-colored chanterelles, whose brief season, intense hue and unique flavor make them a sought-after commodity. Other mushrooms that grow in Northwest forests include the oyster, morel, porcini and shiitake, which are shipped worldwide.

No discussion of food from the Northwest would be complete without mentioning nuts. Filberts, or hazelnuts, grow profusely here, as do walnuts. For that special Northwest touch, look for hazelnut gift packs (some jazzed up in smokehouse- or jalapeno-style) or hazelnuts served in baked goods or with meat.

Opening Hours

The listings below list the meals served at each restaurant, breakfast, brunch, lunch and dinner. Unless otherwise noted in the review, breakfast is served 7am to 11am; brunch usually 7am to 2pm; lunch 11:30am to 2:30pm; and dinner 5pm to 10pm.

Restaurant hours in general, unless otherwise noted, are 7am to 10pm daily. In many cases, particularly with places that have an attached bar or stay open after midnight, the line between restaurant and bar starts to blur around 9pm. At that point several of the city's top eateries transform into buzzing hotspots, places where you'll want to grab a cocktail and a snack and watch the mating rituals of Seattle's beautiful people. Few restaurants serve their whole menu after 10pm; exceptions are noted in the reviews below.

How Much?

Expect to pay an average of $6 to $8 for breakfast, $8 to $12 for lunch, and $12 to $25 for a single dinner main course, plus $6 to $8 each for starters, salad or dessert. A steak à la carte at one of Seattle's old-school chophouses will cost about $25. Budget options ($4 to $7 for lunch, less than $10 for dinner) abound in the U District, Capitol Hill, Pike Place Market, the International District and the fish-and-chips joints along the Waterfront or at Alki Beach in West Seattle.

Booking Tables

Most Seattle restaurants don't require advance bookings, but many of the hottest spots fill up quickly, and calling ahead will save you waiting in line. Where reservations are recommended or mandatory, it's noted in the review.

Tipping

Tips are not figured into the check at a restaurant. In general, 15% is the standard minimum tip; 20% is common if you enjoyed the service. If you're just ordering coffee at a counter, you don't need to tip, but if someone makes you a specialty drink, it's polite to leave 10% to 15%. There's no need to tip when ordering takeout from a counter.

Groceries

Between restaurant hopping, it's always handy to know where a good supermarket is, and Seattle has plenty. The following local groceries pay special attention to high-quality produce and products often hard to find at regular grocery stores.

LARRY'S MARKET Map pp240-1

☎ 206-213-0778; 100 Mercer St; ☽ 6am-midnight

This Lower Queen Anne market carries high-end and hard-to-find gourmet ingredients and has a good fresh seafood department.

MADISON MARKET Map pp242-3

☎ 206-329-1545; 1600 E Madison St; ☽ 7am-midnight

This natural-foods co-op on Capitol Hill has a great deli and a good selection of wines at reasonable prices.

METROPOLITAN MARKET Map pp240-1

☎ 206-284-2530; 1908 Queen Anne Ave N; ☽ 24hr

Formerly a Thriftway, the Metropolitan Market has a small but high-quality selection of produce, wine, deli items and gourmet groceries. There's also a branch at **West Seattle** (Map pp232–3; ☎ 206-937-0551; 2320 42nd Ave SW).

RAINBOW NATURAL GROCERY

Map pp242-3

☎ 206-329-8440; 417 15th Ave E; ☽ 9am-9pm

Get a shot of wheatgrass juice along with a good selection of vitamins and natural foods at Rainbow.

Fab seafood

DOWNTOWN & FIRST HILL

You might have to empty your pockets to fill your belly in the central downtown area, where a majority of the restaurants are designed with business meetings and expense accounts in mind. But you get what you pay for – this is the place to find classic Northwest food in old-fashioned oyster bars and cavernous chophouses, as well as trendsetting haute cuisine in sleek new spaces with interiors as architecturally immaculate as the food on the plates. If you're on a budget and just want some grub, you're better off finding cheap eats in Pike Place Market, Belltown or the Pioneer Square area, which are all within walking distance from the downtown core.

DAHLIA LOUNGE Map pp234-5   *Northwest*

☎ 206-682-4142; 2001 4th Ave; starters $10, mains $25; ☽ lunch & dinner Mon-Fri, dinner until 11pm Sat & Sun

The Dahlia usually gets the credit for having invented Northwest cuisine. Owner Tom Douglas started fusing flavors at this Seattle institution in the late 1980s and single-handedly made Seattleites more sophisticated; this was probably the first place in town to serve foie gras with figs and lavender caramel. There's a bakery next door where you can pick up one of the Dahlia's fabulous desserts to go. Douglas also owns **Etta's Seafood** (p113) and **Palace Kitchen** (p109). It's best to reserve a table.

GEORGIAN ROOM Map pp234-5   *Continental*

☎ 206-621-7889; 411 University St; starters $13-20, mains $20-35; ☽ breakfast, lunch & dinner

A treat above treats, the Georgian Room at the Fairmont Olympic Hotel (formerly Four Seasons) is one of the most imposing restaurants in the city – the ornate high ceilings and dripping chandeliers, shiny silver and gilt details will have you swooning. The food is equally eye-catching and inspired by regional ingredients, such as scallops with truffles or roasted sea bass. Service is tops here, and it's one of the few places where Seattleites tend to be sharply dressed. Reservations are recommended.

HUNT CLUB Map pp234-5   *Northwest*

☎ 206-343-6156; Sorrento Hotel, 900 Madison St;
starters $8-13, mains $22-32; 🕑 breakfast & dinner
daily, lunch Mon-Fri

The Hunt Club ought to be on the short list if
you're looking for a special occasion, top-end
restaurant. The setting is absolutely beautiful:
an intimate mahogany-paneled dining room
shimmering with candles and decked with
flowers. The food is equally stellar, featuring
local lamb, fish and steaks from sustainable
farms, accentuated with inventive sauces and
regional produce.

Top Five Downtown & First Hill

- **Palace Kitchen** (opposite)
- **Georgian Room** (p108)
- **Mae Phim Thai Restaurant** (p110)
- **Top Pot Donuts** (p110)
- **Wild Ginger** (p109)

ICON GRILL Map pp234-5   *Northwest*

☎ 206-441-6330; 1933 5th Ave; starters $5-8, mains
$15-20; 🕑 lunch Mon-Fri, dinner daily

The Icon's pink-and-orange astoundingly busy,
sculpted glass décor here contrasts with the
simple comfort food on the menu. Try a grilled
pizza margherita made with fresh mozzarella, a
hearty rock shrimp penne, or the ever-popular
molasses-glazed meatloaf wrapped in bacon.
Swing music on the stereo keeps the place
hopping.

MCCORMICK'S FISH HOUSE & BAR

Map pp234-5   *Steak & Seafood*

☎ 206-682-3900; 722 4th Ave; starters $6-12, mains
$15-35; 🕑 lunch & dinner

A mainstay of traditional Seattle dining and the
flagship in a small Northwest chain, this classy,
wood-lined, brass-detailed place is a network of
cubbyholes that looks like an old-boys club. The
food is consistently good, with daily fresh fish
specials, mostly grilled with zesty sauces, and a
fine selection of local oysters, chops and steak.
Try the plump crab cakes or the seared ahi.

METROPOLITAN GRILL

Map pp234-5   *Steak & Seafood*

☎ 206-624-3287; 820 2nd Ave; starters $15, steaks
$35-45; 🕑 lunch & dinner

This handsome and atmospheric business favorite fills up with stock analysts and bankers

who pour out of nearby office towers. Though
you can get fish, 'portabella mignon' or even
Beluga caviar, beef's the big thing here; steaks
are custom-aged and grilled over mesquite
charcoal. Many consider this the top chop-
house in the city.

NIKKO Map pp234-5   *Sushi*

☎ 206-322-4641; 1900 5th Ave; sushi from $4, mains
from $12; 🕑 lunch & dinner

Nikko, in the basement of the Westin Hotel, has
a gigantic menu, with two pages for sushi alone.
It's neither cheap nor entirely transcendent, but
it's a fun place and the chefs habitually go out
on a limb. (Bits of apple in a California roll? Well,
why not?) Hot dishes are recommended, too.

PALACE KITCHEN Map pp234-5   *Northwest*

☎ 206-448-2001; 2030 5th Ave; starters $6-8, mains
$20; 🕑 dinner until 1am

Owned by the Dahlia's Tom Douglas, the Palace
is a see-and-be-seen hotspot that really picks
up for the late-night cocktail scene. Daily dinner specials present such wonders as spaetzle-
stuffed pumpkin or traditional pork loin. Snack
on appetizers – including a smoked salmon
and blue cheese terrine or a sampler plate of
regional cheeses – or go for the whole shebang
with grilled trout, leg of lamb or roasted chicken
with blackberries and nectarines.

WILD GINGER Map pp234-5   *Asian*

☎ 206-623-4450; 1403 3rd Ave; satay $3-5, lunch $8-12,
dinner $15-20; 🕑 lunch Mon-Sat, dinner daily, satay
bar until 1am

Seattle was more or less introduced to the
satay bar by this popular Indonesian restaurant, where throngs of diners sit and sample
bite-size, skewered bits of fiery grilled chicken,
vegetables or scallops, luscious soups and
daily specials. More substantial dishes include
Burmese curry crab and cinnamon- and-anise-
spiced duck. It used to be in an impossibly
small space – the wait was hours long – but
now it's moved to a building large enough
that you don't have to feel rushed through
your meal.

CHEAP EATS

CYBER-DOGS Map pp234-5 *Veggie Hot Dogs*

☎ 206-405-3647; 909 Pike St; dogs $2-5; Internet
free for first 20min, then $6/hr; 🕑 breakfast, lunch
& dinner

One of those all-things-to-some-people places,
like Easy Street in West Seattle, Cyber-Dogs is

an all-veggie hot-dog stand, espresso bar, Internet café and youngster hangout/pickup joint. Its advertising campaign is based on miniature hand-scribbled-and-stapled chapbooks with cute indie-rock-style cartoons. But the best thing about the place is trying out the weird, insanely imaginative non-meat 'not-dogs' with tastes-better-than-it-sounds toppings (eggplant, potatoes, hummus).

MAE PHIM THAI RESTAURANT

Map pp234-5   *Thai*
☎ 206-624-2979; 94 Columbia St; meals from $7;
☺ breakfast, lunch & dinner

And you thought *you* were in a hurry for lunch! Your order here arrives so quickly you wonder if the cooks are psychic, which is good, because the place is mobbed at lunchtime with people hooked on its huge, inexpensive Thai noodle dishes.

TOP POT DONUTS

Map pp238-9   *Coffee & Donuts*
☎ 206-728-1966; 2124 5th Ave; donuts $1-3;
☺ breakfast, lunch & dinner

OK, so maybe this should be filed under 'coffeehouses,' but frankly at Top Pot it's all about the donuts, and no, it is not wrong to eat them three meals a day. Top Pot donuts are hand-forged as quickly as the little Seattleites can gobble them up, and this huge new store (there's also one on Capitol Hill) means you can down them twice as often. Krispy what?

PIONEER SQUARE

Eating – Pioneer Square

Pioneer Square is the ideal place to be if you're looking for a meal in an old-school steak and seafood restaurant with loads of atmosphere and traditional service. It also has a good range of budget-friendly options that are inexpensive without lacking character (see below).

FX MCRORY'S STEAK, CHOP & OYSTER HOUSE Map pp236-7 *Steak & Seafood*
☎ 206-623-4800; 419 Occidental St S; mains $10-27
☺ lunch & dinner

This vast Pioneer Square landmark across from the sports stadiums is full of jocks and can get completely out of hand on days when the Seahawks or Mariners play. McRory's claims to have the largest selection of bourbon in the world; add 18 Northwest beers on tap and a stand-up oyster bar and you've got quite a party. Tuck into classic fare like prime rib or Dungeness crab, or share a seafood platter of raw oysters on the half shell, smoked salmon, prawns, crab, Penn Cove mussels and scallops.

IL TERRAZZO CARMINE Map pp236-7 *Italian*
☎ 206-467-7797; 411 1st Ave S; meals from $60;
☺ lunch Mon-Fri, dinner Mon-Sat

Often mentioned in discussions of Seattle's best restaurants, the very upscale Il Terrazzo Carmine is a showcase of European luxury that serves succulent Italian meals in multiple courses. A small fountain and the rustling of green ferns serenade the almost-hidden terrace out back: a really wonderful spot in summer. If you want to check the place out but you don't feel like staying for dinner, you can just have an appetizer and drink in the lounge while catching a glimpse of Seattle's elite.

TRATTORIA MITCHELLI Map pp236-7 *Italian*
☎ 206-623-3883; 84 Yesler Way; pasta $8-10;
☺ breakfast, lunch & dinner until 4am Tue-Sat, until 11pm Sun & Mon

Craving carbs after a night of Pioneer Square club-hopping? Mitchelli feeds the bleary-eyed masses with perfectly cooked pasta, pizza, calzones, salads and breakfast frittatas until the wee hours – a rarity in Seattle. The later you come here, the better the people-watching will be.

CHEAP EATS

BAKEMAN'S Map pp236-7 *Diner*
☎ 206-622-3375; 122 Cherry St; sandwiches $3-6;
☺ lunch

This is a rare find. It's an old-fashioned, zero-frills, formica-countered diner which serves up great American standards like meatloaf sandwiches, a drool-inducing roasted turkey sandwich, mashed potatoes, chili and hot apple pie.

ELLIOTT BAY CAFÉ

Map pp236-7   *Soup & Sandwich*
☎ 206-682-6664; 101 S Main St; salads $3-4,
sandwiches $5-7; ☺ breakfast, lunch & dinner

This cozy crypt underneath Elliott Bay Book Co is a great place to settle in with a book and a bowl of soup, an incredibly fresh salad, a hearty pastrami sandwich, or just cookies and a cup of coffee. Browse the book-lined walls while you eat.

GRAND CENTRAL BAKING CO
Map pp236-7   *Soup & Sandwich*
☎ 206-622-3644; 214 1st Ave S; sandwiches $5-7;
☽ breakfast, lunch & dinner until 6pm
This artisan bakery in the Grand Central Arcade builds sandwiches on its own peasant-style loaves and baguettes, with soups, salads, pastries and other treats.

SALUMI Map pp236-7   *Soup & Sandwich*
☎ 206-621-8772; 309 3rd Ave S; meals from $5
☽ lunch until 4pm Tue-Fri
This is an incredibly authentic, European-style deli/lunch café that's utterly lacking in pretension but turns out food you could cry over. Sit down at the communal table in back over pasta and wine and pretend you're in *The Godfather,* or take-out a gloppy sandwich made with hand-cured meat – it might stop your

Top Five Pioneer Square

- Il Terrazzo Carmine (p110)
- Elliott Bay Café (p110)
- Zaina (see below)
- Bakeman's (p110)
- Salumi (see below)

heart, but as long as you get to eat it first you won't even mind. Plan on a later lunch, as the wait is agonizing around noon.

ZAINA Map pp236-7   *Middle Eastern*
☎ 206-624-5687; 108 Cherry St; sandwiches $4-7, plates $9; ☽ lunch & dinner Mon-Sat, closed Sun
This friendly café, decorated with a mishmash of Middle Eastern themes, has juicy falafel sandwiches stuffed to overflowing, as well as shwarma plates with various healthy salads, creamy hummus, great baklava and killer lemonade.

INTERNATIONAL DISTRICT

The International District (ID) is a great neighborhood for cheap eats, or you can go all-out on a sumptuous eight-course dinner banquet. The many Vietnamese, Thai and Chinese restaurants that line Jackson St between 6th and 12th Aves give you plenty of options. East of 8th Ave S and I-5, Little Saigon takes over and the flavor becomes decidedly Vietnamese. In many of these restaurants, you'll have trouble spending more than $7 on lunch or $10 at dinner. In the ID, there are places where the tourists go and places where everyone else goes. The following suggestions emphasize local favorites over those with lines and, consequently, higher prices.

Dim Sum Delights

Dim sum is a fun way to get a taste (or several tastes) of Chinese-American culture. The phrase means 'a bit of heart,' and that's exactly what these little morsels are like. Even a beginner can't help but drop his or her inhibitions as trays of mysterious but cute little squares and triangles of food roll past the table. Novices might want to avoid the fried chicken feet, but good introductory options include a variety of steamed cakes, dumplings, potstickers, rice balls and shrimp toast.

Enjoying a leisurely dim sum is one of the best ways to spend a Sunday morning in Seattle – or, if you'd rather, a late Saturday night. In the International District (Map pp236-7), you can get excellent dim sum any day of the week. The following have regular menus too, but they are especially noted for their dim sum.

China Gate (☎ 206-624-1730; 516 7th Ave S; ☽ 10:30am-3pm & 9:30pm-2am) This is arguably the best place in town for dim sum. The Hong Kong–style menu offers a couple hundred choices. The real treat here is that you can get dim sum late into the night.

Four Seas (☎ 206-682-4900; 714 S King St) and Sun-Ya Seafood (☎ 206-623-1670; 605 7th Ave S) are two other excellent spots to pick at the floating trays of curiosities.

House of Hong (☎ 206-622-7997; 409 8th Ave S; ☽ 10am-5pm) If your hankering for dim sum hits in the middle of the day, head to House of Hong.

Top Gun (☎ 206-623-6606; 668 S King St) A close contender if you want to deal with huge crowds of locals, Top Gun serves turns out dim sum with such an authentic menu, you need to trust what you're ordering.

PHO BAC Map pp236-7 *Vietnamese*
☎ 206-323-4387; 1314 S Jackson St; meals from $5;
☺ lunch & dinner

Famously *the* place to go for pho, this little restaurant on the edge of 14th Ave and Jackson St has huge windows gazing onto Little Saigon, and nearly as massive bowls of steaming pho.

SAIGON BISTRO Map pp236-7 *Vietnamese*
☎ 206-329-4939; 1032 S Jackson St; mains from $7;
☺ lunch & dinner

This Vietnamese bistro is a favorite for its filling soups and special 'dry' noodles. It also serves up a killer Kung Pao chicken.

SEA GARDEN SEAFOOD
Map pp236-7 *Chinese*
☎ 206-623-2100; 509 7th Ave S; mains $7-12;
☺ lunch & dinner daily, until 3am Fri & Sat

A classic, the Sea Garden has a deft hand with fresh seafood – and it's open late, perfect for post-club noshing.

SHANGHAI GARDEN Map pp236-7 *Chinese*
☎ 206-625-1688; 524 6th Ave S; mains $10-12
☺ lunch & dinner

Hand-shaved noodles are the specialty of Shanghai Garden – try the 'barleygreen' noodle dish. If you're used to heavy, greasy Chinese

food, you're in for a revelation; Shanghai's food seems almost pristine.

THANH VI Map pp236-7 *Vietnamese*
☎ 206-329-0208; 1046 S Jackson St; starters from $1.50, mains $5-8; ☺ lunch & dinner

In Asian Plaza on the corner of S Jackson St and 12th Ave, Thanh Vi offers authentic Vietnamese cuisine at very reasonable prices. Check out the charbroiled pork chop or salted fried squid with a bottle of Vietnamese beer.

YOSHINOBO JAPANESE RESTAURANT
Map pp236-7 *Japanese*
☎ 206-405-4646; 520 S Jackson St; mains from $8;
☺ lunch & dinner

This place might make you feel dirty by comparison; everything is smooth and white and gleaming, including the tidy sushi rolls. Udon noodles are great here too, as is the interesting combination of the bento box. Check out the cool U-shaped bar.

Top Five International District

- **Shanghai Garden** (see opposite)
- **House of Hong** (p111)
- **Top Gun** (p111)
- **Saigon Bistro** (see above)
- **Pho Bac** (see above)

PIKE PLACE MARKET & THE WATERFRONT

For a wide selection of fresh produce, bakery products, deli items and takeout ethnic foods, head to Pike Place Market. Explore the market on an empty stomach and commit to a few hours of snacking; you'll be full by the time you leave, and it doesn't have to cost you much. However, if you're looking for serious dining, you can find it here, too; some of Seattle's favorite restaurants are tucked in mysterious corners in the market district. For a full directory and map of everything in the market, be sure to pick up a copy of *Welcome to the Pike Place Market*. Get it from the market information booth on 1st Ave at Pike St, in front of the main entrance.

ATHENIAN INN Map pp238-9 *Diner*
☎ 206-624-7166; 1517 Pike Place Market; mains $8-12; ☺ lunch & dinner

There's nothing fancy about the Athenian, but it's a landmark and a bastion of unpretentious, frontier-era Seattle, a holdover from the days before Starbucks and Grand Central Bakery (it opened in 1909). It's been a bakery and a lunch counter and now seems to have settled in as a diner/bar combination, where, especially in the off hours, you can snuggle into a window

booth and gaze over Elliott Bay with a plate of fried fish.

CAFÉ CAMPAGNE Map pp238-9 *French*
☎ 206-728-2233; 1600 Post Alley; mains from $12;
☺ lunch & dinner

At the casual younger sibling of the upscale Campagne (p113), the quality of the French-style cooking is what you'd expect from such a talented kitchen; the prices are more manageable, and you don't have to dress up for dinner.

Ivar's Acres of Clams (below)

CAMPAGNE Map pp238-9 *French*
☎ 206-728-2800; 86 Pine St; mains $25-35; ☽ dinner
You have to love a place that cut off part of its building to save the one tree in the Market, as the bar at Campagne did. Nestled in the courtyard of the Inn at the Market, it is Seattle's best traditional French restaurant, with an emphasis on the foods of Gascony – done, of course, with that good old Northwest twist. Try the pan-roasted sea scallops or the free-range beef tenderloin.

CHEZ SHEA Map pp238-9 *Mediterranean*
☎ 206-467-9990; upstairs, Corner Market Bldg; prix fixe menu $40; ☽ dinner
Another treasure hidden in one of the market's many corners, Chez Shea has great views over Puget Sound that combine with spectacular four-course meals to make this one of the city's most romantic restaurants. You can also skip dinner and have a snack at the seductive bar.

ETTA'S SEAFOOD Map pp238-9 *Seafood*
☎ 206-443-6000; 2020 Western Ave; mains $12-25; ☽ brunch 9am-3pm, lunch & dinner
Famous for its daily brunch, with such mouth-waterers as poached eggs with Dungeness crab and chipotle hollandaise, Etta's has a meat- and fish-focused dinner menu, but the king salmon is almost enough to convert even ardent vegetarians.

IL BISTRO Map pp238-9 *Italian*
☎ 206-682-3049; lower Post Alley; mains $20-27; ☽ dinner
At this atmospheric Italian café, the best and freshest of the market is incorporated into daily specials. Il Bistro's red lighting gives it a gangster-movie feel; even the Godfather would enjoy the roasted chicken or the herb-crusted pork loin, with pasta and red wine, of course.

IVAR'S ACRES OF CLAMS
Map pp238-9 *Seafood*
☎ 206-624-6852; Pier 54, 1001 Alaskan Way; mains $12-20; ☽ lunch & dinner
Ivar Haglund was a beloved local character famous for silly promotional slogans ('Keep clam!'), but he sure knew how to fry up fish-and-chips. A meal here won't blow your mind with wild innovations, but it's a Seattle tradition that started in 1938, and the outdoor seating on the wharf is lovely in nice weather.

113

LE PICHET Map pp238-9 *French*
☎ 206-256-1499; 1933 1st Ave; lunch $6-10, dinner $16-17; ☽ breakfast, lunch & dinner, until 2am Sat & Sun

This tiny French bistro and wine bar is elegant and tasteful, and yet it's casual enough to quickly become a favorite haunt. The reasonably priced menu features traditional French cuisine without the aorta-clogging heaviness that this often implies. Breakfast is simple and delicious, and the pommes frites are killer. For a treat, order the roasted chicken with apples and potatoes ($30); it's made only on request and takes an hour, but is worth the wait.

MATT'S IN THE MARKET
Map pp238-9 *Northwest*
☎ 206-487-7908; upstairs, Main Arcade; mains $8-18; ☽ lunch & dinner

Upstairs, in an intentionally small and hard-to-find spot, Matt's in the Market is a gem, which locals protect fiercely. If you're lucky enough to get a seat in this tiny place, sip some wine, have a snack (food, while delicious, is cooked on camping stoves) and admire the view over the bay.

MAXIMILIEN-IN-THE-MARKET
Map pp238-9 *French*
☎ 206-682-7270; behind the Main Arcade; starters $4-10, mains $10-30; ☽ lunch & dinner

This little place hanging off the back of the Main Arcade offers French bistro-style food in a warm and welcoming atmosphere, with, of course, fantastic views.

OLD SPAGHETTI FACTORY
Map pp238-9 *Italian*
☎ 206-441-7724; 2801 Elliott Ave; mains $8-12; ☽ lunch & dinner

This kid-friendly outfit is part of a small chain that revamps historic buildings, furnishes them with antiques and serves well-prepared, well-priced pasta; it's especially popular with families or large groups.

PINK DOOR RISTORANTE
Map pp238-9 *Italian*
☎ 206-443-3241; 1919 Post Alley; lunch $8-12, dinner from $14; ☽ lunch & dinner until 1am

There's no sign pointing to this perennial favorite, but it's easy to find; just follow your nose to the, um, pink door with the amazing

Italian aromas wafting out, and *eccolo!* Lunch is mostly pasta dishes and a soul-stirring *cioppino* (hearty seafood stew); at dinner, the food is accompanied by live jazz.

TYPHOON! Map pp238-9 *Thai*
☎ 206-262-9797; 1400 Western Ave; satay bar $2-5, lunch $7-9, dinner $12-14; ☽ lunch & dinner

Creative, colorful Thai food fills the menu at this successful food emporium. Lunch is your best bet – there are an array of curries and noodle dishes in two sizes. Dinner is offered in larger portions from the same menu. If you're not up for the full meal, slink up to the satay bar for a beer and a sampler of lemongrass pork or Portobello mushroom.

Top Five Pike Place Market & the Waterfront

- Campagne (p112)
- Ivar's Acres of Clams (p113)
- Il Bistro (p113)
- Le Pichet (see above)
- Pink Door Ristorante (see below)

CHEAP EATS
LOWELL'S RESTAURANT
Map pp238-9 *Diner*
☎ 206-622-2036; 1519 Pike Pl; mains $5-8; ☽ lunch & dinner

If you want a sit-down meal but nothing fancy, head to Lowell's, well loved by shoppers, businesspeople and fellow market operators for its classic, eye-opening breakfasts and cheap-and-cheerful lunches.

MEE SUM PASTRIES Map pp238-9 *Asian*
☎ 206-682-6780; 1526 Pike Pl; rolls $2-3; ☽ breakfast, lunch & dinner

This little market storefront is famed for its *hum baos* – meat- or vegetable-filled buns that make a great snack (like a pot sticker).

THREE GIRLS BAKERY Map pp238-9 *Bakery*
☎ 206-622-1045; 1514 Pike Pl; snacks $1-5; ☽ breakfast & lunch

A great place for cookies, bread and other baked goods. You can also buy sandwiches from the takeout window.

Pike Place Fish (p170)

BELLTOWN

This hip neighborhood, which flanks downtown, is the uncontested center of fine dining in Seattle. The beauty of Belltown is that you can spend a little or spend a lot and still get a fabulous meal. An abundance of delis, inexpensive pubs and low-budget hangouts frequented by arty musicians and starving students are still found throughout the neighborhood. The other advantage of Belltown is that you're more likely to be able to find late-night dining, thanks to an active cocktail scene that encourages many restaurants to serve at least a bar menu until 2am.

BUENOS AIRES GRILL

Map pp238-9 *Argentinean*
☎ 206-441-7076; 2000 2nd Ave; salads $8-12, mains $15-25; ☽ dinner daily, until 12:30am Fri-Sat

Tucked into a Belltown side street, this South American place serves elaborate cocktails, unusual salads (like hearts of palm) and huge portions of well-prepared steak. The cooking aromas will lure you in; the fun vibe and the staff's tendency to tango on request will make you linger.

Top Five Belltown

- Lampreia (p116)
- Buenos Aires Grill (see above)
- Queen City Grill (p116)
- Shiro's Sushi Restaurant (p116)
- Two Bells Tavern (p117)

CYCLOPS Map pp238-9 *Northwest*
☎ 206-441-1677; 2421 1st Ave; dinner from $20; ☽ breakfast Sat & Sun, dinner daily

This restaurant/bar at the heart of Belltown sits beneath the legendary Ace Hotel. Its décor is dominated by red vinyl, trippy art and good-looking hipsters eyeing each other. Leisurely weekend breakfasts here are a must.

EL GAUCHO Map pp238-9 *Steakhouse*
☎ 206-728-1337; 2505 1st Ave; sides $5, mains $28-40; ☽ dinner until 2am

What economic slump? No evidence of it at El Gaucho, a modern re-creation of a 1950s supper club where old-school flair meets cool retro swank, complete with massive steaks, a cigar room, dozens of single-malt scotches and a stylish clientele. Service is impeccable and an integral part of the show. Dining here is not a meal; it's a thrilling, educational event.

FANDANGO Map pp238-9 *Latin American*
☎ 206-441-1188; 2313 1st Ave; meals from $20;
☽ dinner

Owned by the chef Christine Keff, who is also the owner of Flying Fish (below), Fandango's (other) claims to fame are lively atmosphere and great Latin American food.

FLYING FISH Map pp238-9 *Seafood*
☎ 206-728-8595; 2234 1st Ave; small plates $7-10, mains $16-20; ☽ dinner until midnight, bar menu until 1am

This exciting restaurant specializes in using delicate spices and a little joie de vivre to transform an ordinary piece of salmon or tuna into something truly magical. Combine several small plates, share a platter of oysters, or go with a main dish, such as yellowtail with eggplant and soy ginger sauce, or monkfish in coconut peanut sauce. The dining room is bustling and energetic, the service friendly and top-notch. The menu changes daily depending on what's fresh.

LAMPREIA Map pp238-9 *Northwest*
☎ 206-443-3301; 2400 1st Ave; starters $8-14, mains $25-37, themed tasting menu $65; ☽ dinner Tue-Sat

A contender for the title of Seattle's best formal restaurant, Lampreia specializes in grilled meat and poultry and is known among serious food connoisseurs for its artfully constructed dishes, like foie gras with plums or kiwifruit, duck breast 'lacquered' in spices and mustard, or rack of lamb with sweet-pepper crust. Dinner here may be expensive, but it's an experience. Reservations are required.

MARCO'S SUPPERCLUB Map pp238-9 *Global*
☎ 206-441-7801; 2510 1st Ave; starters $8, mains $15; ☽ lunch & dinner daily, brunch Sun

Marco's travels the globe with its multi-ethnic menu, including Jamaican jerk chicken and eggplant masala; the deep-fried sage leaves are mandatory.

QUEEN CITY GRILL Map pp238-9 *Seafood*
☎ 206-443-0975; 2201 1st Ave; starters $9-15, salads $6, mains $18-20; ☽ lunch & dinner until 2am

This longtime Belltown favorite offers great seafood from its daily menu and a solid selection of meats and chicken from its seasonal menu. The goat cheese appetizer and the grilled ahi with red-pepper sauce are divine, and warm lighting makes the room feel cozy yet sophisticated. Reservations are recommended.

RESTAURANT ZOE Map pp238-9 *Northwest*
☎ 206-256-2060; 2137 2nd Ave; starters $8-10, mains $18-20; ☽ dinner Mon-Sat

This sleek, trendy new restaurant has minimalist décor and a well-edited menu that pairs fish, seafood and local meats with the freshest produce in wild new ways. Peppercrusted ahi tuna is paired with beets, lentils and watercress, for example, and a pan-seared sweetbreads appetizer comes with pickled pears. A prix-fixe menu is also available. Lines snake out the door at dinner; reservations are recommended.

SHIRO'S SUSHI RESTAURANT
Map pp238-9 *Japanese*
☎ 206-443-9844; 2401 2nd Ave; dinner $18-20, sushi rolls from $4; ☽ dinner

Sushi master Shiro Kashiba, who made his name at Nikko, uses only the freshest ingredients and takes his sushi very seriously. Get a seat at the bar if you can, and watch him work (he's the older guy with the cute smile). Reservations recommended.

WASABI BISTRO Map pp238-9 *Japanese*
☎ 206-441-6044; 2311 2nd Ave; dinners from $20; ☽ lunch Mon-Fri, dinner until 1am daily

The walls of this place are painted the color of its namesake – and, not coincidentally, of avocado, which the sushi chefs here use liberally in nearly all of their creations. Rolls are innovative, and the place has a chic, futuristic style that draws a crowd clearly hoping to be cool. But who cares, when the sushi's this good?

CHEAP EATS
BELLTOWN PIZZA Map pp238-9 *Italian*
☎ 206-441-2653; 2422 1st Ave; pizza $15; ☽ lunch & dinner

Walk past the door and try to resist the aromas tugging you inside. You just can't. These guys know how to make a pizza, and the price is right. A large is enough to feed four hungry people. You can also get salads, pasta and sandwiches.

BELLTOWN PUB Map pp238-9 *Northwest*
☎ 728-4311; 2322 1st Ave; mains $8-10; ☽ lunch & dinner

The easygoing, nonsmoking Belltown Pub is a longtime neighborhood favorite. The crowd tends to be on the bland side, but it's a nice, quiet place to meet for a beer, and the menu transcends usual pub fare, with inventive salads and sandwiches.

BUFFALO DELI Map pp238-9 *Deli*
☎ 206-728-8759; 2123 1st Ave; sandwiches $6-8;
☺ lunch

If you've got a craving for matzoh balls or a sub sandwich with Italian meat, this New York-style deli will take care of it.

CAFFE MINNIE'S Map pp238-9 *Diner*
☎ 448-6263; 101 Denny Way; breakfast $5-8;
☺ 24hr

At the northern end of Belltown, almost in Lower Queen Anne, is Caffe Minnie's – an appealingly seedy 1950s-style diner. It's an absolute blessing for insomniacs, bar-crawlers, truckers, fugitives or those with the munchies after 2am.

There's also the newer, Broadway branch, **Caffe Minnie's Too** (☎ 206-860-1360; 611 Broadway Ave), with the same deal and appeal.

CHERRY STREET COFFEE HOUSE
Map pp238-9 *Coffeehouse*
☎ 206-441-7176; 2121 1st Ave; bagels $1-3, sandwiches $4-6; ☺ breakfast, lunch & dinner

Relaxing and friendly, this high-ceilinged coffee shop will make you feel like you live in the neighborhood. Curl up in the bay window seat with a yummy salad, sandwich or smoothie, or start your day here with coffee and a bagel. They also serve beer.

LUX COFFEE HOUSE
Map pp238-9 *Coffeehouse*
☎ 206-443-0962; 2226 1st Ave; bagels $1-3, sandwiches $3-5; ☺ breakfast, lunch & dinner

A cool, blue, techno-pumping hangout where you can pick up your morning cuppa joe and a breakfast bagel, check out the local artwork and read the free weekly papers.

MACRINA
Map pp238-9 *Bakery*
☎ 206-448-4032; 2408 1st Ave; snacks $1-5;
☺ breakfast, lunch & dinner

You might have to wait in line, especially if you want to sit at a table, but as soon as you bite into your breakfast roll or panini sandwich, you won't care. Macrina makes some of the city's best artisan bread and decadent snacks.

MAMA'S MEXICAN KITCHEN
Map pp238-9 *Mexican*
☎ 206-728-6262; 2234 2nd Ave; burritos $6;
☺ lunch & dinner

Wildly popular, California-style Mama's Mexican Kitchen is always packed. But that's no surprise for a place that serves scrumptious burritos, huge combination plates and killer margaritas (during happy hour from 4pm to 6pm Monday to Saturday, margaritas go for $2.75). It's in a great location for people-watching, but the kitsch Mexican artifacts plastering the walls are equally absorbing.

NOODLE RANCH Map pp238-9 *Asian*
☎ 206-728-0463; 2228 2nd Ave; curries $8-10;
☺ lunch & dinner Mon-Sat

Every stop in Seattle should consider a visit to the Noodle Ranch. In the same block as Mama's, it's a hip diner with delicious pan-Asian noodle dishes, such as red curry with yams. Vegetarians will be in noodle heaven here.

TWO BELLS TAVERN
Map pp238-9 *Burgers*
☎ 206-441-3050; 2313 4th Ave; burgers $7.50;
☺ lunch & dinner until 10pm

This cozy, friendly, nonsmoking neighborhood hangout serves thick, hand-formed burgers on French rolls, loaded with cheese and creamy horseradish sauce. There's a cute beer garden/patio out back where you can sip at any of a dozen regional draft beers.

SEATTLE CENTER
SKY CITY Map pp240-1 *Northwest*
☎ 206-905-2100; 219 4th Ave N; starters $8-15, mains $30-40; ☺ lunch & dinner, breakfast Sat & Sun

No compilation of Seattle restaurants would be complete without a mention of Sky City, the revolving restaurant atop the Space Needle – but you don't really go there for the food, which locals deem uninspiring at best. Seafood dishes are your best bet; options include a mixed grill of salmon, tuna, scallops and prawns, seared ahi with wasabi mashed potatoes, Alderwood-smoked salmon and Dungeness crab. The views are tremendous from 500ft up in the air, although you pay dearly for them. Appetizers cost almost the price of a meal at a top-end restaurant, dinner is gouging, and lunch is only slightly less expensive, with a $15-per-guest minimum. The ride up the elevator is free if you have meal reservations.

QUEEN ANNE

Many of the dining options in Lower Queen Anne, just west of Seattle Center, are geared toward the pre- or post-game crowd attending games at Key Arena. Up on top of the hill, in Upper Queen Anne, restaurants are a bit fancier, with some very good ethnic restaurants vying for well-heeled customers.

Eating – Queen Anne

CANLIS Map pp240-1 *Northwest/American*
☎ 206-283-3313; 2576 Aurora Ave N; mains $20-30;
☻ dinner Mon-Sat
This place is old-school enough for either prom night or your grandma's birthday dinner. The traditional, classic food and service are both top-notch, and you can rest assured that none of the style is affected. Canlis has been around since 1950 and its authenticity shows. The view is lovely, too.

CHINOISE CAFÉ Map pp240-1 *Asian*
☎ 206-284-6671; 12 Boston St; mains $8-12;
☻ lunch & dinner
This is one outpost in a small chain of pan-Asian restaurants with dishes ranging from Korean barbecue to Japanese sushi to Vietnamese soups. Try the delicious lemongrass stir-fry.

KASPAR'S Map pp240-1 *French-Northwest*
☎ 206-298-0123; 19 W Harrison St; mains from $20;
☻ dinner
Chef Kaspar Donier has been nominated five times for Best Chef Pacific Northwest honors. He's known for blending French and Northwest flavors in new, ever-more-delicious ways; witness the popular quesadilla of smoked salmon and goat cheese. Reservations are required.

ORRAPIN THAI CUISINE Map pp240-1 *Thai*
☎ 206-283-7118; 10 Boston St; mains $8-12;
☻ lunch & dinner
Queen Anne's favorite place for excellent Thai curries and noodles, Orrapin also has great outdoor seating.

PARAGON BAR & GRILL
Map pp240-1 *American*
☎ 206-283-4548; 2125 Queen Anne Ave N; brunch $5-9, starters $6-10, lunch $8-10, mains $15-20;
☻ breakfast, lunch & dinner, bar until 2am
The Paragon is a bastion of American regional cooking, with a specialty in grilled fish and updated American classics. Try the avocado shrimp cakes, either as a starter or in a sandwich, or go with a classic cheese-burger. There's an open fireplace and a lively bar scene.

QUEEN ANNE CAFÉ Map pp240-1 *Northwest*
☎ 206-285-2060; 2121 Queen Anne Ave N; sandwiches $8, mains $10-12; ☻ breakfast, lunch & dinner
Locals flock to this trendy neighborhood spot for traditional comfort food, including broiled pork chops and various sandwiches.

SAPPHIRE KITCHEN & BAR
Map pp240-1 *Mediterranean*
☎ 206-281-1931; 1625 Queen Anne Ave N; mains from $18; ☻ brunch Sun, dinner until midnight Sun-Wed, until 2am Thu-Sat
A groovy spot for nightlife in Upper Queen Anne, the Sapphire has a well-stocked bar and serves Spanish-influenced Mediterranean fare in a chic dining room with sapphire, red and purple walls. The black-painted façade and the neon sign outside might not fit with Queen Anne's style, but don't let it turn you off.

Top Five Queen Anne

- **Canlis** (see above)
- **5 Spot** (see below)
- **Paragon Bar & Grill** (see below)
- **Sapphire Kitchen & Bar** (see above)
- **Kaspar's** (see opposite)

CHEAP EATS

5 SPOT Map pp240-1 *Northwest*
☎ 206-285-7768; 1502 Queen Anne Ave N; breakfast scrambles $6-8; ☻ breakfast, lunch & dinner
In Upper Queen Anne, everyone's favorite breakfast and hangover diner is the 5 Spot. Good strong coffee keeps the staff ultra-perky. Try a local legend, like the red flannel hash, or get crazy with the devastating smoked salmon and cream cheese scramble. On weekends, go early to avoid the lines snaking out the door – or go for lunch or dinner; this is an excellent place for a quiet meal featuring good American cooking.

CAPITOL HILL & VOLUNTEER PARK

The scene on Capitol Hill is almost as much about style as food; it's no use enjoying a fabulous dinner if no one can see how chic you look while you're eating it. Then again, ambience hardly detracts from a fine dining experience, so who's complaining? The restaurants along Broadway and 15th Ave, and to a slightly lesser extent the Pike-Pine Corridor, offer the full range of Seattle dining options.

CAFÉ SEPTIEME Map pp242-3   Northwest
☎ 206-860-8858; 214 Broadway E; burgers $8, salads $10, mains $15; ⏰ breakfast, lunch & dinner

Strong drinks, good food and cold service reign at this trendy, arty, intensely minimalist café. Their homemade grub is sophisticated yet unfussy; the bacon-laden provolone cheeseburger or free-range chicken are worth trying. In nice weather, the outdoor tables provide first-rate people watching. It's a nice coffee shop in the morning, and turns into a classy bar with artfully mixed cocktails at night.

CAPITOL CLUB Map pp242-3   North African
☎ 206-325-2149; 414 E Pine St; mains $15; ⏰ dinner until 2am

This gorgeously decorated restaurant, with its elegant, mosquito-netted windows and brocade pillows everywhere, takes classic North African dishes and updates the sauces and flavors into nouvelle cuisine.

CASSIS Map pp242-3   French
☎ 206-329-0580; 2359 10th Ave E; mains $15-20; ⏰ dinner

The fish soup is a highlight of the seasonally rotating menu at this French bistro, which is traditional but never boring. A four-course prix-fixe dinner is offered before 7pm Sunday to Thursday.

COASTAL KITCHEN Map pp242-3   Eclectic
☎ 206-322-1145; 429 15th Ave E; starters & tapas $4-8, mains $10-18; ⏰ breakfast, lunch & dinner until midnight

This longtime favorite turns out some of the best food in the neighborhood – it has an eclectic mix of Cajun, Mayan and Mexican inspirations. It also rotates its themed menus, such as a recent Catalan ensemble that included fish stew and pan-seared chicken in Amontillado sherry-mushroom sauce. The Barbados grill of prawns and fish with sweet-potato pancakes is a regular favorite, and so are the Rasta rollups. There's also a great 'blunch' ($8.75) between 8:30am and 3pm on weekdays.

KINGFISH CAFÉ Map pp242-3   Southern
☎ 206-320-8757; 602 19th Ave E; mains $10-15; ⏰ lunch & dinner

The Coaston sisters' café, opened in 1997, turns out fried chicken that has locals lined up for miles, every night. Don't forget to save room for the sweet potato pie.

Top Five Capitol Hill & Volunteer Park

- Bimbo's Bitchin' Burrito Kitchen (p120)
- Kingfish Café (see above)
- Café Septieme (see opposite)
- Cassis (see opposite)
- Ristorante Machiavelli (see below)

RISTORANTE MACHIAVELLI
Map pp242-3   Italian
☎ 206-621-7941; 1215 Pine St; mains $12-18; ⏰ dinner Mon-Sat, closed Sun

One of the city's cutest restaurants, the no-fuss Ristorante Machiavelli specializes in full-flavored Italian cooking without any of the trappings of a high-attitude restaurant. Old-world touches, such as putting chicken livers in the lasagne, help keep it real. Half of the small space is reserved for an incredibly romantic bar, where you can sip wine and wait for a table or just stop in for a cocktail or coffee and dessert.

SIX ARMS PUB & BREWERY
Map pp242-3   American
☎ 206-223-1698; 300 E Pike St; sandwiches $6-8, specials $6-12 ⏰ lunch & dinner

Part of the Portland-based McMenamins chain, this charming old tavern is resplendent with high ceilings, cool antique lighting fixtures, friendly staff and funky art. There's a good selection of sandwiches and burgers and a few specials, such as pasta or halibut-and-chips. And, of course, there's a selection of the McMenamins' microbrewed beer.

CHEAP EATS
BIMBO'S BITCHIN' BURRITO KITCHEN

Map pp242-3   *Mexican*
☎ 206-329-9978; 506 E Pine St; meals $3-6; ☺ lunch
& dinner until 2am

A godsend for anyone prowling Capitol Hill late at night, Bimbo's slings fat tacos ($3-$4), giant burritos ($5-$6) and juicy quesadillas at hipster-friendly prices. Every inch of the tiny space is decked out in kitschy knickknacks, including velvet matador portraits, oil paintings with neon elements, and a hut-style thatched awning. Have a margarita with your meal (happy hour, with drinks at $2, is from 4pm to 7pm) or check out the adjoining **Cha-Cha Lounge** (p134).

ELYSIAN BREWING CO

Map pp242-3   *Northwest*
☎ 206-860-1920; 1221 E Pike St; sandwiches $6-8;
☺ lunch & dinner

This spacious brewpub is as much a restaurant as a beer hall, with a full menu of light meals that strays from the ordinary. The *pahjola* sandwich – grilled ahi with wasabi sauce – is an excellent alternative to a burger. There are also yellowfin fritters, an eggplant sandwich, and specials of pasta or rice bowls. The pub serves eight to 10 of its own beers and has a well-crafted list of guest taps.

GRAVITY BAR Map pp242-3   *Vegetarian*
☎ 206-325-7186; 415 Broadway E; juices $3-5, salads
$5-8; ☺ breakfast, lunch & dinner

For vegetarian meals and fresh juices in a Jetsons-like futuristic interior, go to the Gravity Bar in the Broadway Market. Don't be in a hurry or expect a warm welcome, but do expect healthy food, tofu in every form, salads, organic brown rice and mysterious potions

that clean all your organs and magically give you energy.

GREEN CAT CAFÉ Map pp242-3   *Vegetarian*
☎ 206-726-8756; 1514 E Olive Way; mains $5-9;
☺ breakfast, lunch until 4pm

One of the best places in town for vegetarian food, the Green Cat serves up such scrumptious dishes as the Buddha Bowl – rice, veggies and curry noodles – or the Green Eggs Sans Ham, scrambled eggs with pesto.

HONEYHOLE Map pp242-3   *Sandwiches*
☎ 206-709-1399; 703 E Pike St; sandwiches $6-10;
☺ breakfast, lunch & dinner

Cozy by day, irresistible at night, the Honeyhole has a lot to recommend it: great sandwiches with cute names (the turkey-cranberry is called The Pilgrim), a full bar, DJs and cool cubbyhole atmosphere at night; the rule is, if you beat the high score on its pinball machine, you get a free sandwich.

LA COCINA & CANTINA MEXICAN
RESTAURANT Map pp242-3   *Mexican*
☎ 206-323-1675; 432 Broadway E; buffet lunch/
dinner $6/9; ☺ lunch & dinner

If you want to get full and drunk, La Cocina & Cantina has delicious margaritas and an all-you-can-eat Mexican buffet. It's also a great place to sit and watch the entertaining street scenes.

SATELLITE LOUNGE Map pp242-3 *American*
☎ 206-324-4019; 1118 E Pike St; burgers $7-10;
☺ lunch & dinner

This clean and friendly place, the gussied-up sibling of the **Comet** (p137), is a good spot for dinner or a cocktail at the bar. It serves generous portions of standard American food.

THE U DISTRICT

This is one of the best districts in Seattle for cheap, delicious, authentic ethnic food, and it's easy to find vegetarian options at most places. When you're browsing for lunch or dinner, don't be put off by unappetizing-looking storefronts; some of the most interesting food comes from places that have the outward appearance of rundown five-and-dime stores. The adventurous will be rewarded.

CEDARS RESTAURANT

Map pp244-5   *Indian & Middle Eastern*
☎ 206-527-5247; 4759 Brooklyn Ave NE; starters $4,
mains $9-12; ☺ lunch & dinner Mon-Sat, 3-9pm Sun
Possibly the best Indian restaurant in Seattle, Cedars serves enormous curries and vindaloos

so smooth and creamy you want to dive into them. Eat here just once and you will dream about it later. Cedars also offers shish kebabs, falafel and gyros, and there are plenty of vegetarian options. The namesake wooden patio is wonderful in nice weather.

FLOWERS Map pp244-5 *Eclectic*

☎ 206-633-1903; 4247 University Way NE; lunch buffet $7, mains $9-12; ⏲ lunch, dinner until 2am

One of the most stylish places in the U District, Flowers has a lunchtime vegetarian buffet, and dinners include meat choices. After hours, it becomes an inviting place to sip a cocktail, munch on an appetizer and 'do homework' with a promising study partner.

Top Five U District

- Cedars Restaurant (p120)
- Ruby (p121)
- Agua Verde Café (p121)
- Flowers (p121)
- Café Allegro (p121)

RUBY Map pp244-5 *Global*

☎ 206-675-1770; 4241 University Way NE; starters $5-7; ⏲ breakfast & lunch, dinner until 2am

The menu at this gorgeous space next to Flowers reflects the room's Casablanca feel. With fragrant jasmine rice bowls ($8 to $9), a ginger-onion-chili breakfast omelet ($6) and soups like yellow dhal with tofu, spinach, lemon, garlic and ginger or lemongrass miso with shiitake mushrooms. The bar is hopping at night, and drinks are large and well crafted.

CHEAP EATS

AGUA VERDE CAFÉ Map pp244-5 *Mexican*

☎ 206-545-8570; 1303 NE Boat St; taco plates $6.50; ⏲ lunch & dinner Mon-Sat, takeout only Sun

On the shores of Portage Bay at the southern base of University Avenue, Agua Verde Café is a wonderful little gem that overlooks the bay and serves mouth-watering, garlic-buttery tacos of fish, shellfish and portabella mushrooms, plus other Mexican favorites. There's usually a line, but you can have a drink and sit on the deck while you wait for a table; in summer there are outdoor foosball tables to play while you wait. You can also rent kayaks in the same building, in case you want to work off your dinner later.

ARAYA PLACES Map pp244-5 *Vegetarian Thai*

☎ 206-524-4332; 4732 University Way NE; mains from $7; ⏲ lunch & dinner

This whimsically decorated place, with slogans painted all over its exterior, serves good, cheap vegan and vegetarian Thai food.

CAFÉ ALLEGRO Map pp244-5 *Sandwiches*

☎ 206-634-2310; 4002 University Way NE; sandwiches $6-8; ⏲ breakfast, lunch & dinner

A nice spot for a sandwich, Allegro offers better food than most quick-serve places on the Ave, and it has a funky little smoking loft upstairs with a big window usually full of students literally hanging out.

Agua Verde Café, above

Café Allegro (p121)

2am, with fries and a shake, and you want it all for less than $5. At Dick's, you can – plus a bonus sideshow of parking-lot hijinks that peak right after the bars close. It's not just fast food; it's an institution. There are other locations around town; their bright orange signs are hard to miss. The most theatrically rewarding, of course, is in **Capitol Hill** (Map pp242–3; ☎ 206-323-1300; 115 Broadway Ave E).

NEELAM'S Map pp244-5 _Indian_
☎ 206-523-5275; 4735 University Way NE; buffet $6; ⏱ lunch & dinner
This favorite for East Indian curries has an all-you-can-eat lunch buffet.

ORANGE KING Map pp244-5 _Burgers_
☎ 206-632-1331; 1411 NE 42nd St; burgers $2-5; ⏱ lunch & dinner
At this old-fashioned greasy spoon, miraculously, you can still get a burger and fries for less than $4. It's not gourmet, but it's good, fast and cheap.

SCHULTZY'S SAUSAGES
Map pp244-5 _Sausage_
☎ 206-548-9461; 4142 University Way NE; sausages $3-6; ⏱ lunch & dinner
A meat emporium in the midst of the U District's many vegan and vegetarian options, Shultzy's is the place to go for all sorts of grilled–sausage sandwiches.

DICK'S DRIVE-IN Map pp244-5 _Burgers & Fries_
☎ 206-632-5125; 111 NE 45th St; meals $1-5; ⏱ breakfast, lunch & dinner
Sometimes you don't want gourmet. Sometimes you just want a big, greasy burger at

FREMONT
Fun-loving Fremont is changing fast, but is still known for its lively mix of old hippies, young professionals and gregarious students who fill the neighborhood's pubs, restaurants and coffeehouses every evening.

CAFFÉ LADRO Map pp246-7 _Coffeeshop_
☎ 206-675-0854; 452 N 36th St; pastries $2-5; ⏱ breakfast, lunch & dinner
The Fremont branch of this coffee shop chain has a nice patio that fills up with interesting-looking people sipping coffee, nibbling pastries and thinking deep thoughts.

STILL LIFE IN FREMONT
Map pp246-7 _Northwest_
☎ 206-547-9850; 709 N 35th St; breakfast $2-5, lunch $3.50-7, starters $4-9, mains $8-12; ⏱ breakfast, lunch & dinner
Embodying the quickly changing Fremont neighborhood, this once funky café has gone

sophisticated; it's still quirky, but now it serves dinner to sleek salad-nibblers more often than Birkenstock-clad hippies. But it's not a total change; dishes like tofu with brown rice co-exist on the rotating menu with more upscale items like the steak salad, roasted half-chicken and squash-stuffed ravioli.

SWINGSIDE CAFÉ Map pp246-7 _Italian_
☎ 206-633-4057; 4212 Fremont Ave N; starters $5-12, mains $12-16; ⏱ dinner Tue-Sat, open some Sun (call ahead)
This place _is_ Fremont – it has an affinity for hippies, kids, randomly altered schedules, folk music and dogs. The food is Italian, but it has

a Fremont twist, too; you might find a hazelnut pasta. Nothing is strictly traditional, and it's great that way. The well-chosen wine list won a Wine Spectator Award of Excellence in 2002.

TRIANGLE LOUNGE Map pp246-7 *American*
☎ 206-632-0880; 3507 Fremont Place N;

starters $4-8, pasta $10; ☺ lunch & dinner until 2am
Interesting American dishes and outdoor seating make this arrowhead-shaped café a bustling crossroads. You should try the White Lightning pizza, with garlic sauce, grilled chicken, red peppers and fresh mozzarella ($9 to $10), or the portabella mushroom burger ($7.50).

WALLINGFORD & GREEN LAKE

In Wallingford, North 45th St stretches past a long strip of inexpensive, mostly ethnic restaurants, giving this charming neighborhood a low-key international feel. Both quality and prices are a step up from what you'll find in the U District, and you'll see more soccer moms than students. Further north, Green Lake is a pleasant neighborhood, centered on a large park complex, and has some good coffee shops and cheap restaurants.

74TH STREET ALE HOUSE
Map pp232-3 *American*
☎ 206-784-2955; 7401 Greenwood Ave N; mains $6-10;
☺ lunch & dinner
This favorite neighborhood pub also serves good food, including a spicy gumbo and good quesadillas. The pub is nonsmoking.

ASTEROID CAFÉ Map pp246-7 *Italian*
☎ 206-547-2514; 1605 N 45th St; pasta $12-15, specials $16-22; ☺ lunch & dinner
It looks like a quirky coffee shop with an asteroid inexplicably perched on its rooftop, but this café actually serves sophisticated, rather upscale Italian food. The wine list is as large as the place is small. Political screeds, many from before the US-Iraq war, cover the windows, making it clear that this café, cute as it may be, is not just another pretty face.

BESO DEL SOL Map pp246-7 *Mexican*
☎ 206-547-8087; 4468 Stone Way N; mains $8-12;
☺ lunch & dinner
For Southwest Mexican cuisine, Beso del Sol attracts a lively crowd, especially for the salsa dancing on Friday and Saturday nights.

BETH'S CAFÉ *Breakfast*
☎ 206-782-5588; 7311 Aurora Ave N; omelets $6-9;
☺ 24hr
The best hangover breakfast in the world is at Beth's, and you can get it almost all day long. Key words: all-you-can-eat hash browns. There are also giant burgers perfect for soaking up booze. You can smoke in here, too (the staff certainly does), further easing the transition from closing time to daytime. Unless you

are a professional, do not attempt to eat the 12-egg omelet on your own. Do, however, contribute a piece of scribbled artwork to the wall – look for the miniature art-feud between pirate cartoons in the front room.

BIZZARRO Map pp246-7 *Italian*
☎ 206-545-7327; 1307 N 46th St; mains $12-16;
☺ dinner
With a name like Bizzarro you'd never guess that this Wallingford hotbed is an excellent neighborhood Italian café. When you learn that it's actually someone's garage crammed with kitschy art and weird antiques, the name makes sense.

KABUL Map pp246-7 *Afghani*
☎ 206-545-9000; 2301 N 45th St; mains $12-15;
☺ dinner Mon-Sat
You don't find Afghani food on every street corner, and if you'd like to give it a try (it's like a blend of Pakistani and Middle Eastern cooking, with lots of yoghurt and stewed eggplant, grilled lamb kebabs, and korma, a mild and creamy curry) then head to Kabul. Vegetarians have plenty of great options here.

Top Five Wallingford & Green Lake
- **Asteroid Café** (see below)
- **Bizzarro** (see below)
- **Kabul** (see below)
- **Beth's Café** (see below)
- **Patty's Eggnest** (p124)

Eating – Wallingford & Green Lake

MAE'S PHINNEY RIDGE CAFÉ

Map pp232-3 *American*

☎ 206-782-1222; 6412 Phinney Ave N; mains $6-9;
☺ breakfast & lunch

Breakfast is heavenly, and the tasty milkshakes make it a worthwhile trip any time. Have the best of both worlds and go for the 'shake and eggs' breakfast, served until 3pm daily.

MANDALAY CAFÉ Map pp246-7 *Asian*

☎ 206-633-0801; 1411 N 45th St; mains $11-17;
☺ dinner

Explore such delights as lemongrass curry in the yellow house, where the unfussy décor makes room for the excellent menu. Again, this is a great choice for vegetarians.

MUSASHI'S Map pp246-7 *Japanese*

☎ 206-633-0212; 1400 N 45th St; ☺ lunch & dinner Mon-Fri, dinner only Sat

This tiny, unpretentious storefront is constantly jammed with locals in the know; you can scarcely find cheaper eats in Seattle. Skewers of teriyaki beef, chicken or veggies are the best bet ($1 to $3), or you can go with a bento box for a nice meal. Miso soup ($1 to $2) is also excellent and dirt-cheap. The sushi rolls are fine but not stunning; serious connoisseurs might find it worthwhile to pay a little more elsewhere.

NELL'S Map pp232-3 *Continental*

☎ 206-524-4044; 6804 E Green Lake Way N; mains $18-22, 5-course menu $52; ☺ dinner

For fine dining near Green Lake, Nell's serves up classic European dishes with Northwestern flair. It inhabits the space formerly occupied by Saleh al Lago, and it actually maintains one of that beloved eatery's dishes – the calamari with aioli – to widespread critical acclaim. Opt for seafood dishes, and don't skip dessert.

PATTY'S EGGNEST Map pp246-7 *Breakfast*

☎ 206-675-0645; 2202 N 45th St; omelets $8-10;
☺ breakfast 8am-3pm

Nestle in for a breakfast scramble or gourmet omelet in this homey little café, reportedly beloved by actor Tim Robbins.

TANGLETOWN PUB Map pp232-3 *Northwest*

☎ 206-547-5929; 2106 55th St N; mains $7-12;
☺ breakfast Sat & Sun, lunch & dinner daily

Elysian Brewing Company's new outpost takes over the space that was once the worshiped Honey Bear Bakery, and it has proved to be good enough to win neighborhood approval.

It's a more child-friendly space than Elysian's Capitol Hill brewery, and the building itself is gorgeous: when afternoon sunlight comes streaming into the leaded-glass windows and hits those burgundy walls, look out! Glorified pub food (chicken wings, an eggplant panini, and Elysian beer carries the day. This pub promises to remain a cornerstone of the tiny cluster of activity known as Tangletown.

CHEAP EATS

BOULANGERIE Map pp246-7 *Bakery*

☎ 206-634-2211; 2200 N 45th St; pastries $2-5;
☺ breakfast & lunch

None of the restaurants in Wallingford is expensive, but if you're interested in keeping within your budget, you could do worse than heading to one of Seattle's best neighborhood bakeries. Boulangerie is as close as Seattle gets to a real French bakery; the pastries are fantastic.

CHILE PEPPER Map pp246-7 *Mexican*

☎ 206-545-1790; 1427 N 45th St; mains $6-10;
☺ dinner

For the neighborhood's best Mexican food, go to Chile Pepper, where the food always tastes homemade and appropriately fiery. Try the mole, a unique version that's the most popular dish on the menu.

JITTERBUG CAFÉ

Map pp246-7 *Italian & American*

☎ 206-547-6313; 2114 N 45th St; frittatas $7-9;
☺ brunch 11am-3pm, lunch & dinner

If your kind of breakfast is a Bloody Mary and a goat cheese and sun-dried tomato frittata, then stop by the zippy Jitterbug Café. This is also a comfortable, smoke-free spot for lunch or dinner, when the menu is divided between New American and Roman (as from Rome) cooking. Vegetarians can find lots to eat here.

JULIA'S OF WALLINGFORD

Map pp246-7 *American*

☎ 206-633-1175; 4401 Wallingford Ave N; mains $8-10; ☺ breakfast, lunch & dinner

The most popular stop for breakfast in the outlying neighborhoods, Julia's is ideal if your idea of an eye-opener is a stack of pancakes and gallons of coffee. It's also good for lunch or an uncomplicated dinner. You'll find a decent menu of salads, fried chicken and other standbys here.

RED MILL BURGERS Map pp232-3 *Burgers*
☎ 206-783-6362; 312 N 67th St; burgers $4-6;
⊗ lunch & dinner
This place is constantly collecting accolades for grilling up the best burger in town. Red Mill Burgers also fries up the fattest, yummiest onion rings. There's always a line out the door.

TEAHOUSE KUAN YIN Map pp246-7 *Tea*
☎ 206-632-2055; 1911 N 45th St; tea $2-6, snacks $2-6; ⊗ 10am-11pm Sun-Thu, 10am-midnight Fri & Sat
For a switch from the coffee shop routine, the Teahouse Kuan Yin has an impressive selection of black, oolong, green and herbal teas, as well as all the paraphernalia you need to enjoy a pot of same.

BALLARD & DISCOVERY PARK

Ballard is known for its waterfront restaurants, but there are also several good places to eat in the charmingly hip historic area. Nothing is terribly extravagant, this being an old Scandinavian settlement, after all. But the offerings are solid, the places neighborly and often surprisingly affordable.

Top Five Ballard & Discovery Park

- Old Town Ale House (see below)
- Madame K's (see below)
- Anthony's Homeport (see below)
- Chinook's at Salmon Bay (see below)
- Ray's Boathouse (see below)

ANTHONY'S HOMEPORT
Map p248 *Seafood*
☎ 206-783-0780; 6135 Seaview Ave NW; mains $10-20;
⊗ lunch & dinner
Right next door to Ray's Boathouse, Anthony's Homeport boasts much the same menu and views as Ray's. If you can't get into one, try the other.

BURK'S CAFÉ Map p248 *Cajun*
☎ 206-782-0091; 5411 Ballard Ave NW; mains $12-16;
⊗ dinner
Though you won't mistake red-brick Old Ballard for New Orleans, the Cajun and Creole food at Burk's is good enough to set this cool Scandinavian 'hood on fire.

CHINOOK'S AT SALMON BAY
Map p248 *Seafood*
☎ 206-283-4665; 1900 W Nickerson St; mains $12-20; ⊗ lunch & dinner Mon-Fri; breakfast, lunch & dinner Sat & Sun
Across the Ballard Bridge in the Fisherman's Terminal, Chinook's is where fish practically leap out of the water and into the kitchen. You can't get it much fresher than this, and the selection of fish and range of preparations is vast. Another plus is watching the fishing fleet coming in or fishers mending their nets from the massive restaurant windows or the sundeck in summer.

MADAME K'S Map p248 *Italian*
☎ 206-783-9710; 5327 Ballard Ave NW; starters $6.50, pasta $10, pizza $12-20; ⊗ dinner
An elegant, red-and-black pizza parlor with an old bordello feel (the building was once a brothel), this small, chic place is packed at dinner. It's also popular for drinks and desserts. There's a nice patio out back, or you can let history repeat itself in the upstairs dessert room with a decadent 'Chocolate Chip Orgasm.'

RAY'S BOATHOUSE Map p248 *Seafood*
☎ 206-789-3770; 6049 Seaview Ave NW; mains from $16; ⊗ lunch & dinner, bar until midnight
OK, so it's a cliché, but Ray's offers views over the Olympics, nautical décor and an exhaustive fresh fish menu. It offers tourists everything they think of when they ponder Seattle. Reservations are required; if you can't get in for dinner, at least come for a drink on the sundeck. Ray's is about a mile west of the Ballard Locks.

CHEAP EATS

HATTIE'S HAT Map p248 *American*
☎ 206-784-0175; 5231 Ballard Ave NW; burgers $6-8; ⊗ breakfast all day, lunch, dinner until 2am
When you say the words 'greasy spoon' do they linger on your tongue and make your mouth water? Well then, Hattie's Hat is the place for you. It's a former dive that's been infiltrated by the first wave of hipsters. Hattie's serves beer and breakfast all day, and it's drip coffee, baby; don't even think about asking for a cappuccino.

OLD TOWN ALE HOUSE Map p248 *American*
☎ 206-782-8323; 5233 Ballard Ave NW; sandwiches $8, starters $3-6; ☺ lunch & dinner

This cavernous, warmly lit, red-brick pub serves giant sandwich 'wedges,' stacks of delicious fries and microbrewed beer.

CENTRAL DISTRICT, MADRONA & MADISON PARK

You'll look a while before you find decent barbecue in Seattle, but the Central District has a couple of places worth checking out. They may not look like much from the outside, but open your mind and your stomach will be happy. On the other end of the scale, locals come for sophisticated vegetarian and tasty brunch spots.

CACTUS Map p249 *Tapas/Mexican*
☎ 206-324-4140; 4220 E Madison St; lunch $8-10, dinner $10-15; ☺ lunch & dinner Mon-Sat, 4-10pm Sun

Cactus is a popular, not-too-pricey eatery that's half tapas bar and half Southwestern Mexican fine dining. Hollywood stars have reportedly been spotted cuddling over giant mojitos here.

CAFÉ FLORA Map p249 *Vegetarian*
☎ 206-325-9100; 2901 E Madison St; mains from $12; ☺ lunch & dinner daily, breakfast Sat & Sun

If you're looking to convert a meat-eater in your life, take him or her to Café Flora; it's vegetarian, but the food is so good your friend might not even notice, much less miss the meat. Sure, Flora does some of the usual vegan tricks, like the portabella mushroom burger, but most of its food is not trying to compensate: roasted squash with saffron couscous or breaded coconut tofu dipped in chili sauce do fine on their own. Brunch is legendary (vegan doughnuts!).

MADISON PARK CAFÉ Map p249 *American*
☎ 206-324-2626; 1807 42nd Ave E; brunch $6-10, starters $8, mains $18; ☺ dinner Tue-Sat, brunch Sat & Sun

Down in Madison Park, at the end of Madison St just before you hit Lake Washington, the Madison Park Café is a favorite breakfast and lunch spot in an old converted house. Homemade pastries are very good, as are the frittatas.

ROVER'S Map p249 *French*
☎ 206-325-7442; 2808 E Madison St; meals from $20; ☺ dinner Tue-Sat

Many locals consider this Seattle's best restaurant. Chef Thierry Rautureau offers three prix-fixe menus a day (usually one vegetarian); the food is upscale French with a Northwest twist.

The cozy space is one of the few in Seattle where you'll want to dress up, and reservations are definitely advised. Don't hold back when surveying the luscious wine list.

CHEAP EATS
ATTIC ALEHOUSE & EATERY
Map p249 *American*
☎ 206-323-3131; 4226 E Madison St; burgers $6-8; ☺ lunch & dinner until 2am Thu-Fri, breakfast Sat & Sun

The Attic Alehouse & Eatery is a friendly neighborhood pub and a good spot for a beer 'n' burger.

CAFÉ SOLEIL Map p249 *Global*
☎ 206-325-1126; 1400 34th Ave; frittatas & sandwiches $6-8; ☺ lunch & dinner daily, breakfast Sat & Sun

Café Soleil is a good, cheap eatery with outdoor tables and friendly service; the hearty brunch, soups and sandwiches are filling, and dinner's subtle spice is influenced by the cuisine of café owner Kuri Teshome's native Ethiopia.

CATFISH CORNER Map p249 *Southern*
☎ 206-323-4330; 2726 E Cherry St; meals $4-10; ☺ lunch & dinner Mon-Sat

For traditional, inexpensive Southern-style fare, head for Catfish Corner. Catfish strips are the specialty here, and you can accessorize them with all the trimmings, including collards, red beans and rice.

EZELL'S FRIED CHICKEN
Map p249 *Southern*
☎ 206-324-4141; 501 23rd Ave; meals $6-8; ☺ lunch & dinner

You'll forget industrial fried chicken after tasting the great crusty, spicy takeout chicken at

Top Five Central District, Madrona & Madison Park

- Catfish Corner (p126)
- Ezell's Fried Chicken (p126)
- Hi Spot Café (p126)
- Rover's (p126)
- Café Flora (p126)

Ezell's. Side dishes, like the coleslaw and sweet potato pie, are also good. This place boomed after Oprah Winfrey hyped the fried chicken here as some of the best in the country.

HI SPOT CAFÉ Map p249 *Breakfast*
☎ 206-325-7905; 1410 34th Ave; breakfast & lunch $5-8, dinner under $12; 🕑 breakfast, lunch & dinner

The Hi Spot basks in fame for its incredible

cinnamon rolls, Torrefazione coffee and filling breakfasts, including creative omelets served with potatoes. The sandwich-and-salad lunch is just as good, and dinner is affordable as well.

MS HELEN'S SOUL FOOD
Map p249 *Southern*
☎ 206-322-6310; 1133 23rd Ave E; mains $6-10; 🕑 lunch & dinner

Ms Helen's Soul Food is another favorite for Southern USA specialties such as gumbo, fried catfish and smothered oxtails, followed by peach cobbler.

R & L HOME OF GOOD BAR-B-QUE
Map p249 *Southern*
☎ 206-322-0271; 1816 E Yesler Way; barbecue $6-8; 🕑 lunch & dinner Tue-Sat

This neighborhood joint makes good on its name, delivering exactly what it promises.

WEST SEATTLE

Most of the action in West Seattle is found along a short strip across from Alki Beach or along California Ave SW.

ALKI CAFÉ Map pp232-3 *Northwest*
☎ 206-935-0616; 2726 Alki Ave SW; breakfast & lunch $8-12, dinner $10-15; 🕑 breakfast until 2pm, lunch, dinner until 9pm

One of Seattle's favorite spots for breakfast and brunch, the Alki serves fresh baked goods, vegetable-filled omelets and hot-cakes. Once the beach crowd goes home, come here for a relaxed dinner of grilled fish, meats or pasta.

BOCA Map pp232-3 *Caribbean*
☎ 206-933-8000; 2516 Alki Ave SW; lunch $6-8, dinner $10-12; 🕑 lunch & dinner daily, brunch Sat & Sun

This Alki Beach mainstay offers Caribbean- and Latin-style food; the jerked ribs are excellent, and the grilled sea bass in banana leaf is a house specialty.

PHOENICIA AT ALKI
Map pp232-3 *Mediterranean*
☎ 206-935-6550; 2716 Alki Ave SW; mains $12-18; 🕑 lunch & dinner

Mediterranean and North African food is the focus at Phoenicia. The best dishes here are the house specialties, which mix and blend Italian and Moroccan flavors with a bounty of fresh local seafood.

SALTY'S ON ALKI
Map pp232-3 *Steak & Seafood*
☎ 206-937-1600; 1936 Harbor Ave SW; starters $12, mains from $20; 🕑 lunch & dinner, brunch Sun 9am-2pm

While many restaurants afford views onto Alki Beach and its strutting revelers, most people drive to West Seattle for the view at Salty's on Alki. This steak and seafood house looks across Elliott Bay onto downtown Seattle; at sunset, the spectacle of lights, shining towers and the rising moon is amazing. The food is secondary, but still quite good.

CHEAP EATS

ALKI BAKERY Map pp232-3 *Bakery*
☎ 206-935-1352; 2738 Alki Ave SW; snacks $1-3; 🕑 breakfast & lunch

The blossoming offspring of the busy Alki Café (above) is worth the line for a cinnamon roll, fresh cookie and coffee. Order takeout sandwiches and salads to eat on the beach.

ALKI'S PEGASUS PIZZA & PASTA
Map pp232-3 *Italian*
☎ 206-932-4849; 2758 Alki Ave SW; mains $5-8, pizzas $10-12; 🕑 lunch & dinner

In competition for Alki's best pizza award, this place draws a crowd from all over the beach.

SPUD FISH & CHIPS Map pp232-3 *Seafood*
☎ 206-938-0606; 2666 Alki Ave SW; fish & chips $4-7; ☻ lunch & dinner

The competition is fierce over which Alki institution has the best fish-and-chips. Spud gets the tourist vote, with its crisp, beachy interior, friendly staff and large portions of fried fish, clam strips and oysters.

SUNFISH Map pp232-3 *Seafood*
☎ 206-938-4112; 2800 Alki Ave SW; fish & chips $4-7; ☻ lunch & dinner

Locals swear by this fish and chips institution. Options include cod, halibut or salmon and chips, fried oysters, clam strips, or any combination thereof. Sit at one of the outdoor tables and enjoy the boardwalk feel.

Top Five West Seattle

- **Alki Café** (see below)
- **Salty's on Alki** (see opposite)
- **Phoenicia at Alki** (see below)
- **Sunfish** (p128)
- **Spud Fish & Chips** (p128)

Entertainment

Entertainment

Seattle's options for after-hours fun run the gamut from silly to sophisticated. A dedicated thrill-seeker can find everything here from opera to pinball. Shake your groove thing at a dance club downtown, stagger along on a Pioneer Square pub crawl or slink through the chic cocktail scene in Capitol Hill. Get beer-splattered and sweaty at a punk-rock dive, sip a pint of microbrew in one of Seattle's excellent brewpubs, or check out an art film in a jewelbox theater. It's all here.

Live music is a good bet on any given night in Seattle. The city gave birth to Jimi Hendrix, and Quincy Jones and Ray Charles spent their formative years carousing in the clubs along Jackson St. During the late '80s, underground garage rock transformed into grunge, bringing local bands like Nirvana, Mudhoney and Pearl Jam to worldwide prominence. These days, you can find electronica, indie-rock, folk, punk, blues, jazz, the occasional hip-hop or reggae performance, and even one genuine honky-tonk bar.

Maybe it's because of all the rain, but Seattleites read a lot. The **Elliott Bay Book Company** (p149) is a mandatory stop in any major author's book tour, and people turn out in droves to go to readings there. Underground readings and poetry slams are also common and enthusiastically attended.

Live theater runs the gamut from big productions, like Ibsen at the **Intiman** (p149), to staged readings of obscure texts in cobbled-together venues or coffeeshops, depending on your taste.

The Seattle Symphony has become nationally known and widely respected, primarily through its excellent recordings. And with its new home in McCaw Hall, the **Seattle Opera** (p152) continues to strengthen and grow.

Film is big news in Seattle these days; the Seattle International Film Festival is among the most influential festivals in the country, and a thriving independent film scene has sprung up in a few underground venues, including the **Alibi Room** (p151).

Some of the city's more interesting cultural events, whether film, music, theater or a combination, occur in makeshift venues, galleries, warehouses and the like. To find a current listing, check the *Stranger, Seattle Weekly* or *Tablet,* all available free at various points around town. For listings and reviews of more mainstream performances, consult the arts sections of the city's daily newspapers.

Top Five Drinking Establishments

Seattle offers a vast range of places to imbibe, from sweaty and smoky beer joints to tres chic cocktail factories. Here's a sampling of the best.

- **Alibi Room** (p135) A dark, smoky hideaway tucked in a corner of Pike Place Market.
- **Cha-Cha Lounge** (p134) Cute hipster staff, cozy corners, great happy hour, bitchin' burritos next door.
- **Baltic Room** (p136) Sophistication on Capitol Hill.
- **Linda's** (p138) Hipsters cram in like sardines for strong drinks and $1 cans of beer on the tiki-themed patio.
- **Shorty's** (p147) Cheap beer, hotdogs, people-watching out front, pinball heaven in back.

Tickets & Reservations

Tickets for big events are available through **TicketMaster** (☎ 206-628-0888, 206-292-2787), by phone or at ticket centers located in retail shops around Seattle; call for locations. Ticket centers are open 8am to 9pm Monday to Saturday and 10am to 6pm Sunday. But if you can buy tickets at the door and there's no risk of the show being sold out, do so; it'll save you the service fee TicketMaster tacks on (usually $6 to $10). **TicketsWest** (☎ 800-325-7328) is a regional ticketing service, with outlets at Rudy's Barbershops and QFC grocery stores. For

Downtown, TicketMaster discount ticket booth at **Westlake Center** (☎ 206-233-1111; ☺ 10am) has last-minute seats. Day-of-performance tickets are usually cheaper; pay by cash.

Ticket/Ticket (☎ 206-324-2744) is a half-price, day-of-performance ticket outlet; you can't get information on ticket availability over the phone, but there are locations at the Market Information Booth at Pike Place Market (Map pp238–9) and on the upper level of the Broadway Market (Map pp242–3) on Capitol Hill.

LIVE MUSIC

Don't even say the G-word. These days, grunge is little more than a mummified corpse taking up a hefty chunk of the Experience Music Project, and most Seattleites would prefer to forget about the national music media's brief love affair with their city. Nevertheless, grunge rock's influence was tremendously important to Seattle's live music scene, and many of the clubs it spawned are still around in some form or another, helping local bands get established and providing medium-size venues for touring indie-rock bands, see also p22.

As anywhere, the club scene here is pretty capricious – name changes and small-venue closures happen frequently, so check live-music listings and ads in the *Stranger, Tablet* or *Seattle Weekly* before heading out. The free papers also have club directories that list phone numbers and addresses for local venues, and they're good places to find out about up-and-coming new bands, all-ages shows, house parties and one-off performances in galleries or warehouses, often the best way to get an insider's view of the local music scene.

Typically, live music starts between 9pm and 10pm and goes until 1am or 2am. For most of the venues below, you can pay admission at the door; larger venues sell advance tickets through **TicketMaster** (p130) or **TicketWeb** (www.ticketweb.com).

Summer music festivals include the **Seattle Chamber Music Festival** (☎ 206-283-8808; at Lakeside School, 14050 1st Ave NE), held outdoors in July with a smaller festival at Benaroya Concert Hall in winter. At the University of Washington, the **International Chamber Music Series** (☎ 206-543-4880, 800-859-5342) brings six concerts to Meany Hall in autumn and winter. During summer months, open-air performances by nationally known pop and rock acts are presented by **Summer Nights at the Pier** (TicketMaster ☎ 206-628-0888). Concerts are performed at the Waterfront on Piers 62-64.

Children, hipsters and hippies alike enjoy the **Northwest Folklife Festival** (☎ 206-684-7300; www.nwfolklife.org). Held at Seattle Center in May on the Memorial Day long weekend, this is a fun event with music, dance, food and crafts.

The absolutely best way to kiss the sweetness of Northwest summer goodbye is at **Bumbershoot** (☎ 206-281-8111; www.bumbershoot.com). Held in September on the Labor Day long weekend, Bumbershoot brings hundreds of musicians to 25 stages throughout Seattle Center, as well as readings, artwork and other performances.

Generally, music venues are open from 5pm to 1am or 2am; most performances start around 9pm. At mega-venues like the Gorge, facilities are open only at events.

ROCK

BALLARD FIREHOUSE Map p248
☎ 206-784-3516; 5429 Russell Ave NW;
cover charge $8-30
This versatile old brick fire station books everything from rock to reggae, though recently it's been leaning more toward the latter.

CATWALK CLUB Map pp236-7
☎ 206-622-1863; 172 S Washington St;
cover charge $5-15
Famous for its weekly goth night (check listings), the Catwalk also books bands, usually touring acts of the goth-metal ilk.

Top Five Clubs

- **Chop Suey** (p132) The silly faux-Asian décor somehow works perfectly.
- **Crocodile Café** (p132) A landmark of the grunge era, still going strong.
- **Re-Bar** (p149) Just try to come here and not have a good time – you can't!
- **Sunset Tavern** (p132) Hipster haunt with indie-rock bands and cult movies.
- **Tractor Tavern** (p133) Classy, amber-lit acoustic theater.

CHOP SUEY Map pp242-3
☎ 206-860-5155; 1325 E Madison St;
cover charge $5-15
With its slightly facetious Asian theme achieved via a giant pagoda-like stage prop and a few Chinese lanterns over the bar, this wide-open, uncluttered space hosts national and local rock bands, DJs and karaoke nights. The crowd and the atmosphere depend on who's playing.

CROCODILE CAFÉ Map pp238-9
☎ 206-441-5611; 2200 2nd Ave; cover charge $5-10
One of the best rock clubs in the country and a Seattle institution, this Belltown space helped launch the grunge and alt-rock scenes and is now home to most of the city's best indie-rock shows, whether local or touring bands. It also serves a decent greasy-spoon breakfast, lunch and dinner.

EXPERIENCE MUSIC PROJECT Map pp240-1
EMP; ☎ 206-367-5483; 325 5th Ave N;
cover charge free-$25
The EMP at Seattle Center boasts two stellar venues: the soaring-ceilinged, acoustically brilliant Sky Church just inside the entrance, and the Liquid Lounge upstairs. The Sky Church is the main venue for big-name concerts; it has loads of atmosphere, thanks to laser-light and video mosaics. The Liquid Lounge usually has minimal or no cover charge, so it's a great way to check out the building's style and architecture without blowing your budget.

GRACELAND Map pp240-1
☎ 206-381-3094; 109 Eastlake Ave E; cover charge $5-10
Formerly the Off-Ramp, Graceland has lots of history echoing around its walls – and lots

of sweaty, beer-drenched bodies bouncing off them. Save your clean shirt for another night, and don't expect perfect sound quality at every show, but this is probably your best bet for the kind of live music scene that put Seattle on the map.

MOORE THEATER Map pp238-9
☎ 206-443-1744; 1932 2nd Ave; cover charge $10-25
Bands love playing this 1500-seat Belltown venue for its classy style and great acoustics.

RAINBOW Map pp244-5
☎ 206-634-1761; 722 NE 45th Ave; cover charge $2-8
Next-door to the Blue Moon in the U District, this is a semi-decrepit old club that played an important role in the early days of garage and grunge bands. It now leans more toward 'rawk' and metal, interspersed with hip-hop and DJs.

SHOWBOX Map pp238-9
☎ 206-628-3151; 1426 1st Ave; cover charge $18-35
This cavernous showroom, hosting everything from indie rock to hip-hop, but mostly national touring acts, reincarnates itself every few years. Smaller shows happen in the attached **Green Room** (cover charge $5-6), which also has a decent café.

SUNSET TAVERN Map p248
☎ 206-784-4880; 5433 Ballard Ave NW;
cover charge free-$7
The Sunset is a Ballard dive that's been revived by hipsters, but not in a bad way. The current booking agent has great taste in slightly dirty punk and gutsier indie rock bands. Wednesdays are Rock-a-raoke, in which a live band plays while you sing; there are

Entertainment – Live Music

Macro Amounts of Microbrews

The microbrew explosion rocked the Northwest around the same time as the gourmet coffee craze – not coincidentally, Seattle's Redhook brewery was co-founded in 1981 by Gordon Bowker, one of the guys who founded Starbucks. Redhook is no longer brewed in Seattle itself; the former Trolleyman brewpub, on 34th Ave in Fremont, now sits empty. The beer is brewed in two other breweries, one in Woodinville, WA, 20 miles east of Seattle, and one in New Hampshire.

Most local microbreweries started out as tiny craft breweries that produced European-style ales. Many of these small producers initially lacked the capital to offer their brews for sale anywhere but in the brewery building itself, hence the term brewpub – an informal pub with its own on-site brewery.

Though you can find microbrews at practically every bar in town, brewpubs often feature signature beers and ales not available anywhere else. It's worth asking about specialty brews or seasonal beers on tap. Most of the brewpubs listed in this chapter offer a taster's selection of the house brews. The brewpubs listed are generally open 11am to midnight daily; exceptions will be noted. Pints range in price from $3 to $5.

These days, many of Seattle's' breweries are no longer very 'micro,' but their operations and quality of beer are still a far cry from Anheuser-Busch or Coors.

Tickets for these major concert and event venues can generally be purchased from TicketMaster, or by calling the box office of the venue at the number listed.

- **Benaroya Hall** (Map pp240-1; ☎ 206-215-4747; 3rd Ave & Union St) The Seattle Symphony's home venue.
- **Gorge Amphitheater** (754 Silica Road NW, George, WA) A 20,000-person venue for shows and festivals like Lolla-palooza and HORDE.
- **McCaw Hall** (Map pp240-1; ☎ 206-684-7200; 321 Mercer St) A brand-new hall for the Seattle Opera.
- **Meany Hall** ☎ 206-543-4880; University of Washington)
- **Paramount Theater** (Map pp234-5; ☎ 206-682-1414; 901 Pine St) B. Marcus Priteca designed this performance hall after the Paramount in New York; hydraulic seats enable the space to morph into a concert hall, theater or banquet facility.
- **Washington State Exhibition Center** (Map pp236-7; ☎ 206-461-5840; 800 Occidental Ave S)
- **White River Amphitheater** (☎ 360-825-6200; 40601 Auburn Enumclaw Road, Auburn, WA) This giant outdoor arena opened in June 2003 and serves the entire Seattle/Tacoma region.

lso movie nights and ultra-cheap afternoon punk shows. Check the papers for a current chedule, or just take your chances – it'll be un, regardless.

CELTIC, FOLK & COUNTRY

KELLS Map pp238-9
☎ 206-728-1916; 1916 Post Alley
Kells is part of a small regional chain of Irish pubs, but it feels completely authentic, with its old wood, nooks and crannies and rosy-cheeked crowd. The perfectly poured Imperial pints of Guinness are divine, and there's live Irish (or Irish-inspired) music nightly (no cover charge).

LITTLE RED HEN
☎ 206-522-1168; 7115 Woodlawn Ave NE; cover charge from $3
This is Seattle's only venue devoted to authentic, live country music. Nightly entertainment includes country karaoke and good timehonky-tonk bands – or you can make like Billy Ray Cyrus with weekly line-dancing lessons.

OWL & THISTLE Map pp236-7
☎ 206-621-7777; 808 Post Alley; cover charge free-$5
The schedule here varies, but most nights it books Celtic folk bands or acoustic singer-songwriters.

TRACTOR TAVERN Map p248
☎ 206-789-3599; 5213 Ballard Ave NW; cover charge $8-15
The premier venue for folk and acoustic music, the elegant Tractor Tavern also books local songwriters, touring acts of a folk persuasion such as Joe Henry or the Meat Purveyors, and

(really) old standbys like Dead Moon. A gorgeous room, usually with top sound quality.

JAZZ & BLUES

CENTRAL SALOON Map pp236-7
☎ 206-622-0209; 207 1st Ave S; cover charge free-$5
One of the city's best blues clubs, the Central has a long history of all kinds of live music. It tends to get uncomfortably crowded on weekends.

DIMITRIOU'S JAZZ ALLEY Map pp234-5
☎ 206-441-9729; 2033 6th Ave; cover charge free-$15
Hidden in an unlikely spot behind a boring-looking office building is Seattle's most sophisticated and prestigious jazz club. Dimitriou's hosts the best of the locals and many national acts passing through.

NEW ORLEANS CREOLE RESTAURANT
Map pp236-7
☎ 206-622-2563; 114 1st Ave S; cover charge free-$7
This old-school hang-out in Pioneer Square has Basin Street-style jazz, blues and zydeco.

TULA'S Map pp238-9
☎ 206-443-4221; 2214 2nd Ave; cover charge free-$8
Kick back to Heart-and-soul jazz musicians who never made the fame-seeking trip to New York or New Orleans, but easily could have.

PUNK

LOBO SALOON Map pp240-1
☎ 206-223-9204; 433 Eastlake Ave; cover charge free-$5
The Lobo is a prime venue for down-and-dirty punk shows shows full of skater boys,

The Seattle Music Scene   by Jennifer Maerz

Seattle is host to a thriving music community, and almost every genre has a place to call home here. You can see anything from old school hip-hop to avant jazz to black metal at a venue that fits your style almost any night of the week, continuing the city's reputation as a destination for bands and fans from all over the world.

Places like **Graceland** (p132), the **Crocodile Café** (p132), the **Showbox** (p132), **Chop Suey** (p132) and **Vera Project** (☎ 206-956-8372; 1916 4th Ave), a no-alcohol all-ages venue, are the city's musical mainstays, hosting everything from *Rolling Stone*-anointed buzz bands of all genres to unsigned local acts, while the **Tractor Tavern** (p133) is ground zero for alt-country and the **Sunset Tavern** (p132) is home to wild garage rock. For the adventurous types, don't miss the **Fun House** (☎ 206-374-8400; 206 5th Ave N) or the **Hideaway** (no phone; 2219 4th Ave), both in Belltown, and the **Comet** (p137), on Capitol Hill, colorful dive bars that book the cool up-and-comers (mostly punk/noise/garage) way before their time. Various art galleries and collective living spaces also have sporadic shows. Read the club weeklies and check out fliers plastered around Capitol Hill for those events. If you're more into the DJ thing, the intimate **Baltic Room** (p136) offers a mix of electronic and hip-hop nights, along with an amazing view of the Space Needle from its dance floor.

For a more highbrow night out, the cozy non-profit **Polestar Gallery** (☎ 206-329-4224; 1412 18th Ave), in the Central District, hosts international avant-garde/experimental talent, the **Benaroya Hall** (p46) is home to the Seattle Symphony, and both Cornish College and the University of Washington have classical and jazz performances. (Skip the Triple Door's yuppie supper club vibe.)

Pioneer Square is Seattle's version of the 'bridge and tunnel' area and their clubs attract the meat market types. For those looking to hook up on the cheap, many of the bars offer a joint entry cover, but you often get what you pay for there – a mix of cover bands and dated rock.

On the nights when you skip the show but still hang out with the bands, the **Cha-Cha Lounge**, located on Seattle's scenester-stocked Pike–Pine corridor, employs a good portion of the local rock population and gets them drunk. Touring bands will often stop in as well, as the compact watering hole has quite the hipster reputation.

Jennifer Maerz is the music editor at Seattle's the Stranger *and a freelance music writer for various national publications.*

frayed black T-shirts, intentional feedback and beer cheap enough to throw at the bands. The little balcony is a major bonus on hot nights.

MONKEY PUB Map pp244-5
☎ 206-523-6457; 5305 Roosevelt Way NE; cover charge free

This U-District dive is one of the few places in town where you can slug beer, shoot pool and see live punk bands on weekends. The strip-

mall exterior is uninspiring, but the staff and clientele are super friendly, and the frat boys seem to get along with the punks just fine.

STUDIO SEVEN
☎ 206-286-1312; 110 S Horton St, just off 1st Ave S one block N of Spokane St; cover charge free-$7

This all-ages club books local and touring punk shows; bring your ID to get into the bar, where there's $2 Pabst Blue Ribbon at all times.

DRINKING

Drinking in Seattle falls into two basic categories: brewpubs, and everything else. The focus at the former is distinctly on the beer; décor, dress and atmosphere are all very casual. Other bars are more about the scene – the vibe can vary from grubby hipster to gold lamé. Most brewpubs are open for lunch and dinner, closing around midnight.

BREWPUBS

Maybe it's due to all the rainy days, maybe it's because of the great microbrew selection or maybe it's because Seattleites simply enjoy a pint. Whatever the reason, this city has some great brewpubs. Most of

the places listed here also offer something to eat, ranging from simple snacks to full menus – a few places incorporate their house-made beer into the food, or, in the tradition of wine pairings, suggest the ideal brew to accompany each dish on the menu. It's that serious.

BIG TIME MICROBREW & MUSIC
Map pp244-5

☎ 206-545-4509; 4133 University Way NE

A fun hang-out in the U District, this expansive brewpub is quiet and casual in the daytime, but gets hopping at night. During the school year, it can be crowded with students still testing their alcohol limits.

DAD WATSON'S RESTAURANT & BREWERY Map pp246-7

☎ 206-632-6505; 3601 Fremont Ave N

This place is Fremont's representative of the McMenamins brewpub chain based in Portland. It doesn't have as much old-world charm as its Six Arms pub, but it's roomy and comfortable, and there's a patio where you can watch the street life on this quirky corner of town.

ELLIOTT BAY BREWERY & PUB Map pp232-3

☎ 206-932-8695; 4720 California Ave SW

Long and narrow, with a loft at the back of the room and a beer garden outdoors, this comfortable brewpub makes a nice retreat after a day at Alki Beach. The food is well-priced and substantial, perfect for soaking up a stellar IPA.

ELYSIAN BREWING COMPANY Map pp242-3

☎ 206-860-1920; 1221 E Pike St

At the far end of Capitol Hill, this spacious pub has comfortable booths across from a massive central bar, or more communal tables on a lower level. Huge windows make for great people-watching. There are always seasonal beers to try, plus at least one nitro tap; the Loki Lager and the Dragon's Tooth Oatmeal Stout are recommended standbys. Food here is more upscale than you'd think; see p120.

HALE'S BREWERY & PUB Map pp246-7

☎ 206-782-0737; 4301 Leary Way NW

Hale's makes some fantastic beer, notably its Ambrosial Cream Ale, but this brewpub has the feel of a corporate hotel lobby. It's definitely worth a quick stop, though; ask the friendly staff about the personalized mugs hanging above the bar. There's a miniature self-guided tour in the entryway.

JOLLY ROGER TAPROOM Map p248

☎ 206-782-6181; 1514 NW Leary Way; ☯ closed Sun

A secret treasure tucked away off busy Leary, Maritime Pacific Brewing's Jolly Roger Taproom is a tiny, pirate-themed bar with a nautical chart painted onto the floor. Its delicious handcrafted beer comes in real, 20-ounce pints, or you can try a sampler of five types. There are about 15 taps, all serving Maritime Pacific brews. The strong winter ale, called Jolly Roger, is highly recommended.

PIKE PLACE PUB & BREWERY Map pp238-9

☎ 206-622-6044; 1415 1st Ave

At this Pike Place Market–area brewpub, tourists and locals alike dig into amazing burgers (try the mushroom-swiss), brats or pizza (from $7.95 each) and peruse a list of stellar beers. Highlights include the XXXXX Stout, the popular Kilt Lifter and the perfectly sweet Naughty Nellie's. There's also a finely curated selection of bottled beers from the UK, Belgium and Bavaria.

PYRAMID ALE HOUSE Map pp236-7

☎ 206-682-3377; 1201 1st Ave S; ☯ tours 2pm & 4pm Mon-Fri, 1pm, 2pm & 4pm Sat & Sun

This brewpub has the cleaned-up-industrial feel most often associated with Northwest brewpubs in the public imagination. It's across from Safeco Field; stop in for a Hefeweizen after the game.

ROCK BOTTOM BREWERY Map pp234-5

☎ 206-623-3070; 1333 5th Ave

Rock Bottom doesn't get tons of respect in the Northwest, partly because its beers are all rather on the light side, but mostly because it's part of a chain based in Colorado. Nevertheless, it's the only brewpub in this part of downtown, and the food is excellent.

SIX ARMS PUB & BREWERY Map pp242-3

☎ 206-223-1698; 300 E Pike St; ☯ until 1am Mon-Sat, midnight Sun

One of the classiest of the McMenamins outposts, the Six Arms has comfy booths and couches upstairs with a lived-in feel. Antique lighting helps set the mood. Beer is the standard McMenamins fare; the Terminator is a good stout, and Hammerhead's a perennial favorite.

BARS

Bars are usually open 5pm to 2am, unless there's a restaurant attached, in which case they're often also open for lunch.

ALIBI ROOM Map pp238-9

☎ 206-623-3180; 85 Pike Pl

The perfect place to hide from the perfect crime, the Alibi attracts a crowd of mysterious strangers huddling over cigarettes, savoring

135

stiff drinks and killer views. The pasta dishes are great, too. The basement has been known to host Super 8 film viewings; ask at the bar for upcoming events.

AXIS Map pp238-9
☎ 206-441-9600; 2212 1st Ave

This self-reflecting pool in Belltown attracts gorgeous salivating singles looking to hook up with salivating singles of the opposite sex. Wear something shimmery.

BAD JUJU LOUNGE Map pp242-3
☎ 206-709-9951; 1518 11th Ave

Black-lipsticked poets are often seen spouting grim verse at this dark, smoky goth bar. The booths are comfy, and the black walls are graced with cool art.

BALTIC ROOM Map pp242-3
☎ 206-625-4444; 1207 Pine St; admission free-$12

Classy and high-ceilinged, this expansive Capitol Hill space oozes sophistication, with ultra dim lighting, plush if minimal décor and an excellent mix of DJs spinning jungle, Brit-pop or dance tunes.

BARÇA Map pp242-3
☎ 206-325-8263; 1510 11th Ave

Velvet couches, filmy curtains, plush booths – this is one sexy, decadent bar. Settle in among the other pretty people for seduction or quiet conversation.

BELLTOWN PUB Map pp238-9
☎ 206-728-4311; 2322 1st Ave

Also a great place for a meal, this friendly, unpretentious pub offers many local beers and a low-key atmosphere. Even shy people will inevitably share a conversation while sitting at the bar.

BLUE MOON TAVERN Map pp244-5
☎ 206-633-626; 712 NE 45th St

This U-District dive, marked by its own miniature Hammering Man-type sculpture (more like Hammered Man?), is an institution made famous by the people who sat here, like Kerouac and Ginsberg. Novelist Tom Robbins did his time here as well.

BOOKSTORE BAR & CAFÉ Map pp234-5
☎ 206-382-1506; 1007 1st Ave

Next to the Alexis Hotel, this book nook is a relaxing spot to kick back with a snifter of cognac and a stogie. The bookshelves are filled with newspapers, magazines, and books about beer, wine and cigars.

BUNGALOW WINE BAR & CAFÉ Map pp246-7
☎ 206-632-0254; 2412 N 45th St

Above the Open Books store in Wallingford, this balcony nook offers a light menu and 2oz tasters of wine (about $4 each). The cozy atmosphere makes it a great spot to do some sipping.

Moore Theater and Hotel (p132)

CANTERBURY ALE & EATS Map pp242-3

☎ 206-322-3130; 534 15th Ave E

British-style pub divided into four small rooms, this well-loved bar is always filled with friendly locals sipping one of the many beers on tap. A knight in shining armor guards the entrance.

COMET Map pp242-3

☎ 206-323-9853; 922 E Pike St

This joint doesn't care if the rest of the Capitol Hill bars are putting on their Sunday best; it pays sincere homage to the beautiful simplicity of draft beer. An institution on the Hill, the Comet takes no-frills seriously, with cheap pool, cheap beer, bright lights and loyal locals. Unless you're already deaf from rock'n'roll, you might want to avoid it on karaoke nights.

CONOR BYRNE'S Map p248

☎ 206-784-3640; 5140 Ballard Ave NW

Conor Byrne's is a traditional Irish pub where the Guinness flows to the tune of live Celtic music on Wednesday and weekends.

CYCLOPS Map pp238-9

☎ 206-441-1677; 2421 1st Ave

A happening hang-out that is a bar on one side and a restaurant (p115) on the other. Maintains its cool with lava lamps and friendly staff. Look for the single bloodshot eye above the door.

DRAGONFISH ASIAN CAFÉ Map pp234-5

☎ 206-467-7777; 722 Pine St

Dragonfish, in the Paramount Hotel, is a great place to meet for drinks. It stirs up wonderful cocktails, such as a Lemongrass Lime Rickey (vodka infused with lemongrass) or Dragon's Breath Martini (vodka infused with hot pepper).

ELITE Map pp234-5

☎ 206-324-4470; 622 Broadway E

This small gay bar gets crowded, mostly with slightly older men.

FENIX UNDERGROUND Map pp236-7

☎ 206-405-4323; 109 S Washington; cover charge $5-12

The original Fenix, partly owned by actor John Corbett (*My Big Fat Greek Wedding*), was destroyed in Seattle's 2001 earthquake. It has risen again across the street, this time without the movie-star connection. The new Fenix is an 18,500-sq-ft, three-level DJ and dance club with five bars, three dance floors and a café, plus a stage for live bands. It's a cornerstone of the Pioneer Square circuit (p148).

Top Five Pubs

- **Jolly Roger Taproom** (p135) A nautical map on the floor helps you find your way to the bar.
- **Pike Place Pub & Brewery** (p135) Great views, delicious food and pints of Naughty Nellie's.
- **Elliott Bay Brewery & Pub** (p135) An ideal post-beach retreat in West Seattle.
- **Elysian Brewing Company** (p135) Almost mythical beer, Capitol Hill crowd-watching.
- **Six Arms Pub & Brewery** (p135) Loads of creaky old-world atmosphere.

FIVE POINT CAFÉ Map pp234-5

☎ 206-448-9993; 415 Cedar St; ⏰ 24hr

Not 'retro,' just old, the Five Point Café in Tillicum Square has been around since 1929, and so have many of its patrons. It's too small, smoky and worn-in to be obnoxiously hip; this is more of a hang-out for old-timers, bikers and youngsters allergic to chic places like Axis. Check out the men's bathroom (if you can) – while standing at the urinal you can get a periscope view of the Space Needle.

FRONTIER ROOM Map pp238-9

☎ 206-441-3377; 2203 1st Ave

The real deal, this uncorrupted Belltown mainstay is the kind of place you slam your fist on the counter and demand a scotch, just because you can. There aren't a lot of frills in this long, skinny room, but after one or two of the Frontier's knock-you-down drinks you wouldn't be able to focus on decorations anyway.

HATTIE'S HAT Map p248

☎ 206-784-0175; 5231 Ballard Ave NW; ⏰ breakfast Sat & Sun

This is the kind of comfortable, down-home place where you're a regular on your second visit. Check the scenic nature mural and keep an eye out for bartenders you recognize from the stages of local rock clubs. Food is of the equally unpretentious burgers-and-fries variety (p125).

HILLTOP ALE HOUSE Map pp240-1

☎ 206-285-3877; 2129 Queen Anne Ave N

Hilltop is a comfy neighborhood hang-out on Queen Anne Hill.

HOPSCOTCH Map pp242-3

☎ 206-322-4191; 332 15th Ave E

A whisky drinker's heaven, Hopscotch has more than 130 types of scotch to choose from.

Entertainment – Drinking

LAVA LOUNGE Map pp238-9
☎ 206-441-5660; 2226 2nd Ave

The only downside of this cute, fun tiki-themed bar is that it's beer-and-wine-only. Everything about the décor makes you want a tropical drink – but games of all kinds and over-the-top art on the walls make up for the lack of booze. The booths invite all-night lingering, and the staff is super friendly.

LIQUID LOUNGE Map pp240-1
☎ 206-367-5483; EMP, 325 5th Ave N

You'd expect any bar at the Experience Music Project (EMP) to be wildly overpriced, but the Liquid Lounge is a cool spot and the drinks and snacks are reasonably priced, especially during happy hour (4pm to 6pm weekdays). The high ceilings, blue lights and energy of the EMP – as well as the occasional live acts (no cover) – make this a good spot to kick back with a cocktail. If you're on a tight budget, this is the best way to get a good look at the incredible architecture of Frank Gehry's building.

LINDA'S Map pp242-3
☎ 206-325-1220; 707 E Pine St

This bar is constantly thronged with hipsters and rockers; in summer months it's nearly impossible to squeeze onto the patio out back, but worth trying. It's also reportedly one of the last places anyone saw Kurt Cobain alive.

MECCA CAFÉ Map pp240-1
☎ 206-285-9728; 526 Queen Anne Ave N

The Mecca's a tiny, dark bar with a diner atmosphere that attracts a loyal, late-night crowd.

MURPHY'S PUB Map pp246-7
☎ 206-634-2110; 1928 N 45th St

This charming, many-windowed Irish pub could almost have been airlifted directly from Ireland to Wallingford. There's live Irish music on weekends; the rest of the time the place is filled with dart players and devotees of the perfect pint.

NOC NOC Map pp234-5
☎ 206-223-1333; 151 2nd Ave

The Noc Noc is stylish but unpretentious, and it crams everything needed for a good bar into its small, velvet-curtained space: good grooves, a dance floor, a pool table, funky artwork, friendly staff and amazingly cheap happy-hour drinks and nightly specials. The goth-leaning crowd all seem to know each other, but they're friendly nonetheless.

O'SHEA'S Map pp246-7
☎ 206-547-832; 309 NE 45th St

A grittier version of the typical stateside r creation of traditional Irish pubs, O'Shea's small and welcoming, with weekly deals o Irish-themed drinks (shots of Bushmills, pin of Guinness etc).

PALACE KITCHEN Map pp234-5
☎ 206-448-2001; 2030 5th Ave

As much a **restaurant** (p109) as a bar, Palace ge packed with hungry club goers looking for late-night snack and cocktail. Tall window make it appealing for those who want to b seen on the scene.

PARAGON BAR & GRILL Map pp240-1
☎ 206-283-4548; 2125 Queen Anne Ave N

The Paragon is a fun place where the in-you face pickup scene is mellowed by the war wood, cozy fireplace and strong drinks. Jaz blues and acoustic live-music acts play he Tuesday, Wednesday, Thursday and Saturd nights (also see the Eating chapter, p118).

PINK DOOR RISTORANTE Map pp238-9
☎ 206-443-3241; 1919 Post Alley

The Pink Door is a popular Italian restaurant day, but in the evening it's also a pleasant plac for a glass of wine; try to catch the live cab ret or jazz offered nightly (also see the Eatir chapter, p114).

R PLACE Map pp242-3
☎ 206-322-8828; 619 E Pine St

This is an easygoing place to sip a microbre and check out the Capitol Hill scene. Th friendly crowd is primarily gay guys in th mid-20s, but sexual orientation here is se ondary to good beer and pool.

RENDEZVOUS Map pp238-9
☎ 206-441-5823; 2320 2nd Ave

The Rendezvous is a classy place with a curve bar up front and a small theater in the ba room. Emblematic of the chic makeover of Be

Top Five Smoke-Free Bars

- 74th Street Ale House (p147)
- Hilltop Ale House (p137)
- Liquid Lounge (see above)
- Tost (p147)
- Virginia Inn (p147)

(Continued on page 14

SEATTLE

~~places unique~~ I'd go

Fishermen's Terminal
The Waterfront + Aquarium
Pike Place Market
Monorail
Lake Union
Downtown (Nordstrom)?
Pioneer Square
REI
Volunteer Park (Conservatory)
Museum of Flight
Burke Museum
Washington Park (Japanese garden)
The Boeing Tour

Seattle 1sts

gas station 1907
Public golf course
 1915
General Strike in US 1919
Circumnavigational Flight
 from sandpoint 1924
Woman Mayor 1924
Water Skis 1928
Concrete "Floating"
 bridge 1939
Full Scale Monorail
 1962
Covered Mall 1950

1 *State Ferry arriving at the Colman dock (p205)* 2 *Sailboats, Lake Union (p156)* 3 *On board a state ferry* 4 *Olympic mountain range, across the water*

1 Action in the kItchen at one of Seattle's many great eateries 2 Get some pork on your fork! 3 Agua Verde Café (p121) 4 Madame K's (pizza bistro) (p125)

FOO

OPEN

1 The bar at the Bar Icon Grill (p109) **2** Interior, Bar Icon Grill (p109) **3** Chinese Bakery, The International District (p111) **4** Cosy and out of the rain at one of Seattle's many coffeehouses

1 *FX McRory's nightspot (p*
2 *McMenamin's pub, Quee*
Anne (p135) *3* *The Moore*
Theater and Hotel (p132 &
p183)

1 Union Square Grill **2** Pinball at Shorty's, Belltown (p147) **3** The Cha-Cha Lounge, Pike–Pine Corridor (p134) **4** Seattle: tolerance, community and dance music ... gay heaven.

IF YOU ARE:
· RACIST
· SEXIST
· HOMOPHOBIC
· OR AN ASSHOLE
DO NOT COME IN

1 Mural on Burke-Gilman [...]
painted by AEII School, ro[...]
17– 5th grade (2000-2001[...]
Seattle Rose Garden, Woo[...]
land Park Zoo (p86)
3 Watching the rowers, G[...]
Lake (p86)

Kayaking, Lake Union (p156)
Union and Seattle
from Gas Works Park
Along the waterfront
ashington Park Arbore-
02)

1 Dead Horse Trail, Paradise
area of Mount Rainier National
Park (p196) 2 Puget Sound
(p192) 3 Bridal Veil Falls,
Mount Rainier National Park
(p196)

Continued from page 138)

ing chapter, p113) has views over Pike Place Market and Puget Sound; there are only a few tables, so come early.

SHORTY'S Map pp238-9
☎ 206-441-5449; 2222¾ 2nd Ave

A bastion of lowbrow fun in the same stretch of Belltown as Lava Lounge and the Crocodile, Shorty's has cheap beer and hotdogs, cool blue slushy drinks, and a super-friendly crowd (half of whom also work there). The booths have tabletops made of old pinball tables, and the back room has about a dozen pinball games old and new.

TINI BIGS LOUNGE Map pp240-1
☎ 206-284-0931; 100 Denny Way

The gigantic martini list at this vast corner bar gives the crowd here a happy glow.

TOST Map pp246-7
☎ 206-547-0240; 513 N 36th St

This swanky new lounge in Fremont (pronounced toast) has sleek décor just this side of pretentious, a suave clientele and local DJ-spun tunes most nights.

TRIANGLE LOUNGE Map pp246-7
☎ 206-632-0880; 3507 Fremont Pl N

The neon red 'Prescriptions' sign above the bar doesn't hide the fact that locals come here to get loaded. The Triangle is a good stop for snacks, too, with a down-to-earth menu (p123).

TS MCHUGH'S Map pp240-1
☎ 206-282-1910; 21 Mercer St

This great-looking faux-English tavern in lower Queen Anne gets packed during events at Seattle Center.

TWO BELLS TAVERN Map pp238-9
☎ 206-441-3050; 2313 4th Ave

In Belltown, but removed from the hipster scene, the Two Bells is a casual, TV-free neighborhood pub in which to sip a beer and ponder your next move. The burgers are excellent (p117).

VIRGINIA INN TAVERN Map pp238-9
☎ 206-728-1937; 1937 1st Ave

Near Pike Place Market is one of Seattle's most likable bars. The Virginia Inn serves every walk of life in a lively, nonsmoking atmosphere. Lots of draft beers, a nice interior and friendly staff make this a good rendezvous point and a great staging area for forays elsewhere.

Gay & Lesbian Seattle

Seattle is a progressive, gay-and-lesbian-friendly place with a club scene that's much less segregated than in many American cities. We've included listings of gay and lesbian bars and clubs throughout this chapter. For eating, sleeping and shopping, the following are noteworthy.

Eating
- Café Septieme (p119)
- Still Life in Fremont (p122)
- Elysian Brewing Company (p120)

Sleeping
- Ace Hotel (p182)
- Bacon Mansion B&B (p185)
- Gaslight Inn B&B (p185)

Shopping
- Beyond the Closet Books (p172)
- Left Bank Books (p170)
- Toys in Babeland (p173)

own, the Jewel Box Theater was once a slightly grubby venue for punk bands but now sparkles enough to live up to its name. It hosts a variety of music, film and performances (p152).

4TH STREET ALE HOUSE Map pp232-3
☎ 206-784-2955; 7401 Greenwood Ave N

This nonsmoking ale house up on Phinney Ridge is one of the best pubs in the city. It offers a friendly vibe and a good menu.

SAPPHIRE KITCHEN & BAR Map pp240-1
☎ 206-281-1931; 1625 Queen Anne Ave N

The sleek facade sticks out like a sore thumb in stately Queen Anne, but the Sapphire is a top-end Spanish restaurant (p118) with a hopping bar scene.

SATELLITE LOUNGE Map pp242-3
☎ 206-324-4019; 1118 E Pike St

Purple curtains, big windows and candlelit booths make the Satellite a great place to meet for a drink before a rock show at Chop Suey. Alternatively, you can just relax with a beer and a burger and watch Capitol Hill go by. See the Eating chapter for more information, p120.

SHEA'S LOUNGE Map pp238-9
☎ 206-467-9990; 94 Pike St

A favorite for a romantic drink, this intimate lounge beside Chez Shea restaurant (see Eat-

Entertainment – Drinking

WILDROSE Map p242-3
☎ 206-324-9210; 1201 E Pike St

The Wildrose is a comfortable lesbian bar that has theme nights (no-panty Tuesdays!). Pool tables, a light menu, Wednesday night karaoke and occasional live music keep this place jumping.

COFFEEHOUSES

With the opening of the first Starbucks in Seattle in 1971, the city became something of a hub for the coffee craze that overtook the nation. It's a cold and rainy corner of the world; not only did the first few espresso bars give Seattleites a taste for cappuccino and latte, it gave them something warm to hang on to. Soon the entire city was buzzing for more. Standards for coffee quality and strength grew, and soon no one was willing to put up with anything but the best.

In addition to creating a new class of high-brow caffeine addicts, the city's coffee fanaticism has also served to revitalize the coffeehouse as a social meeting place that offers entertainment in the form of poetry readings, theatrical performances and acoustic music sessions. The following java joints are known for more than just food and brew. Also see the Eating chapter (p105) for coffee and tea shops with serious eats, listed by neighborhood.

Coffeehouses are generally open from 7am until 7pm; a few of the hipper places stay open as late as 10pm or midnight.

B&O ESPRESSO Map pp238-9
☎ 206-322-5028; 204 Belmont Ave E

A one-stop shop for leisure activities, this Belltown hang-out is an Internet café with benefits (espresso, microbrews, a cigar shop). If you tire of staring at the monitor, take in one of the performances or readings occasionally held here.

BAUHAUS Map pp242-3
☎ 206-625-1600; 301 E Pine St

Bauhaus looks like the most beatnik library in the world (and the books are for sale); wear black clothes and a ponderous expression, and prepare for heavy conversation.

Pioneer Square Party Pass

Designed with the barhopper in mind, this deal gets you into eight Pioneer Square nightspots for one flat fee. A joint cover fee of $5 (Sunday to Thursday) or $10 (Friday or Saturday) buys you in-and-out privileges at the following clubs: Doc Maynard's Public House; Old Timer's Café; Larry's Greenfront; Bohemians Backstage Café & Lounge; The Fenix & Fenix Underground; New Orleans Creole Restaurant; and the Central Saloon. If you go between 8pm and 9pm on weekends, the price drops to $8, but remember, pace yourself – you've got a long night ahead of you! Pay the cover at the first club you visit.

CAFÉ ALLEGRO Map pp244-5
☎ 206-633-3030; 4214 University Way NE

This exposed-brick café, tucked in the alle between NE 42nd and NE 43rd Sts, east c University Way, helped launch the Seattle co fee scene. It's full of students scribbling ove papers or mooning over professors. Upstai has a large-windowed smoking area.

CAFFÉ VITA Map pp242-3
☎ 206-325-2647; 1005 E Pike St; ☾ 6am-midnight Mon-Fri, 7am-midnight Sat & Sun

The patrons here have fluorescent hair, pierce tongues and plenty of attitude, and the coffe is a worshiped all over town.

CAPITOLHILL.NET Map pp242-3
☎ 206-860-6858; 216 Broadway E

This quiet spot has moved across the street fron its former location. It offers brews of all sorts, var ous events, and Internet access for $6 per hou

COFFEE MESSIAH Map pp242-3
☎ 206-861-8233; 1554 E Olive Way

If caffeine is your personal deity, you'll di this funky coffee hang-out loaded with pop culture crucifixes and over-the-top religiou kitsch. Started by an ex-Mormon ex-Catholi 'getting over some issues,' the Messiah host open-mike nights, rock shows and cabarets.

GRAND ILLUSION CAFÉ & ESPRESSO
Map pp244-5
☎ 206-525-2755; 1405 NE 50th Ave

In the courtyard outside an art movie theate this is a nice, quiet spot for coffee and con versation. There's a bookstore downstairs, i case you forget to bring something to rea with your latte.

ONLINE COFFEE COMPANY Map pp242-3

☎ 206-328-3713; 1720 Olive Way

This mellow place offers good respite from the chaos of Broadway. Have a beer or glass of wine while you check your email.

UPTOWN ESPRESSO BAR Map pp240-1

☎ 206-285-3757; 525 Queen Anne Ave N

This is the place to meet in Lower Queen Anne; it's always crowded with filmgoers and refugees from Seattle Center, but still has an intimate neighborhood feel.

VIVACE Map pp242-3

☎ 206-860-5869; 321 Broadway E

Vivace is a tiny espresso stand where you can pay your respects to the Sacred Shrine of Caffeina, Goddess of the Working Day, or sit outside and watch the world go by.

ZEITGEIST Map pp236-7

☎ 206-583-0497; 161 S Jackson St

This arty café gave birth to the local literary-performance troupe Typing Explosion, a trio of drone-like secretaries who madly churn out poetry on demand. The clientele is divided between black-turtleneck notebook-scribblers and swank-suited architects with laptops.

Neon sign for Palace Kitchen and Cocktails (p148)

DANCE CLUBS

Flexibility reigns in Seattle's clubs; many of Seattle's live-music venues also have DJ nights, which transform them into dance clubs. The gay discos have the hottest dance scene in town, including Re-Bar, though distinctions of sexual orientation tend to disappear on the best dance nights, when everybody goes everywhere in search of that sweet groove. Most of these clubs charge a cover ($5 to $10) on Thursday through Saturday nights.

CC ATTLE'S Map pp242-3

☎ 206-726-0565; 1501 E Madison St

A self-proclaimed 'drinkin' bar,' CC Attle's is a little cheesy, but it's a longstanding favorite gay hang-out for men.

NEIGHBOURS Map pp242-3

☎ 206-324-5358; 1509 Broadway E

Referred to on one occasion as a 'Big, soulless, cha cha palace,' Neighbours has a mostly gay male disco scene.

RE-BAR Map pp234-5

☎ 206-233-9873; 1114 Howell St

Arguably Seattle's best dance club, Re-Bar attracts a lively crowd that comes to boogie on various theme nights. It's currently the site of madly popular dance/DJ/band night 'Pho Bang' (check listings in the weekly papers for updates), as well as a monthly showcase run by *Tablet*. Whether you're gay, lesbian, bi or straight (or still unsure), you'll have fun at the classic weekly Queer Disco, where everyone shakes a little ABBA booty.

VOGUE Map pp242-3

☎ 206-443-0673; 1516 11th Ave

At its former location in Belltown, it was one of the first clubs where grunge bands like Nirvana and Soundgarden played to slam-dancin' crowds. Today the Vogue has mostly DJ music, and the atmosphere varies greatly depending on who's spinning.

READINGS

Seattle is a tremendously literary city; a lot of authors live here, and people read constantly, whether it's the latest literary novel, an underground comic book or a home-stapled zine. Certain author appearances at bookstores are standing-room-only, and the annual **Northwest Bookfest** (late October; www.nwbookfest.org) is an annual event which draws authors and readers from the Northwest and beyond for panel discussions, readings and a trade show. Several bookstores and coffeeshops host readings on a regular basis. For schedules, and to find offbeat events at non-major venues, check listings in the *Stranger* or the *Seattle Weekly*, or look for events calendars posted in bookstores around town. Most readings and open-mike events are free.

BORDERS BOOKS & MUSIC Map pp234-5
☎ 206-622-4599; 1501 4th Ave

Borders stages readings by touring authors, plus occasional live music and children's events, mostly during the day.

CAFFÉ VITA Map pp242-3
☎ 206-709-4440; 1005 E Pike St

Vita hosts weekly poetry readings (currently every Tuesday, but check listings) by Northwest authors. For more information see p148.

ELLIOTT BAY BOOK COMPANY Map pp236-7
☎ 206-624-6600; 101 S Main St

The greatest bookstore in town also holds the best readings, with nationally touring authors as well as some local literary stars (Tom Robbins, Sherman Alexie, David James Duncan

and so forth). Readings are usually free; most start at 7pm.

GLOBE CAFÉ Map pp242-3
☎ 206-547-4585; 1531 14th Ave

The Globe has long held poetry readings and open-mike performances. Stop by and mingle with the pierced Capitol Hill crowd for an all vegetarian breakfast on the weekends.

RICHARD HUGO HOUSE Map pp242-3
☎ 206-322-7030; 1634 11th Ave

This nexus of Seattle's literary community, with its own library, writer's room and gallery space, hosts an experimental reading series called Subtext as well as various events both in-house and around town. The great zine collection invites all-day lingering.

THEATER & COMEDY

Seattle has one of the most vibrant theater scenes on the West Coast, from weird experimental troupes to full-scale, elaborate productions of Shakespearean classics. Check the local newspapers for openings.

A CONTEMPORARY THEATER (ACT)
Map pp234-5
☎ 206-292-7676; 700 Union St; box office ☯ noon-7pm Tue-Sun; admission $25-40

One of the three big companies in the city, ACT fills its $30 million home at Kreielsheimer Place with excellent performances featuring Seattle's best thespians and occasional big-name actors.

THE ANNEX THEATER
☎ 206-728-0933; 1122 E Pike St

Seattle's main experimental/fringe theater group is the Annex; it produces shows and a monthly cabaret at various locations, including the adorable, swanked-up **Jewel Box Theater** (Map pp238–9; 2320 2nd Ave) at the Rendezvous in Belltown.

5TH AVENUE THEATER Map pp234-5
☎ 206-625-1900; 1308 5th Ave

Built in 1926 with an opulent Asian motif, the 5th Avenue opened as a vaudeville house; it was later turned into a movie theater and closed in 1979. An influx of funding and a heritage award saved it in 1980, and now it's Seattle's premier theater for Broadway musical revivals. It's worth going just for a look at the architecture.

INTIMAN THEATER COMPANY Map pp240-1
☎ 206-269-1900; 201 Mercer St, Seattle Center; admission $27-42

Intiman Theater is Seattle's mainstay for classic dramas and heavy-hitting, serious theater (Henrik Ibsen, Langston Hughes, for example), although artistic director Bartlett Sher, who joined Intiman in 2000, has amped up the edginess of the theater company's schedule to include striking new work.

MARKET THEATER Map pp238-9
☎ 206-781-9273; 1428 Post Alley
The Market Theater hosts improvisational comedy, called Theater Sports, on Friday and Saturday night; call for the schedule.

SEATTLE REPERTORY THEATER
Map pp240-1
☎ 206-443-2222; 155 Mercer St, Seattle Center; adult $15-46, child $10
The Seattle Repertory Theater (the Rep) won a Tony Award in 1990 for Outstanding Regional Theater. It's known for large, elaborate productions of big-name dramas and second-run Broadway hits.

FILM

Although colossal multiscreen cinema complexes are plentiful in Seattle, there are still a number of small independent theaters that go out of their way to feature the unusual and obscure. Some of the first-run houses, including those listed below, also show foreign and smaller independent films alongside mainstream smash hits. To really delve into Seattle's film culture, though, you have to seek out the tiny independent festivals and screenings. Check listings in the weekly papers, or ask around at **Consolidated Works** (Map pp240-1; ☎ 206-860-5245; 410 Terry Ave N), **911 Media Arts Center** (Map pp240-1; ☎ 206-682-6552; 117 Yale Ave N), the **Alibi Room** (Map pp238-9; ☎ 206-623-3180; 85 Pike St) or the Grand Illusion Cinema (p146).

The biggest event of the year for cinephiles is the **Seattle International Film Festival** (☎ 206-464-5830; www.seattlefilm.com/siff; admission $8.50, matinees $6). Film geeks wait all year for this annual three-week extravaganza of international art films, including many new directors

Coffee Craze

Anyone who's spent any time in the Northwest can sympathize with comedian Denis Leary's manic diatribe about trendy coffee drinks. You've got lattes, cappuccinos, soy frappuccinos, caramel flavor, hazelnut flavor – the one thing you can't seem to get these days is plain old coffee-flavored coffee. Standing in line at Starbucks or SBC gives you front-row seats in the theater of the absurd. Nobody orders a regular cuppa joe. It takes the average customer longer to place an order than it takes the frantic baristas to whip up the concoction. It makes you wonder – someone who's capable of walking up to a counter first thing in the morning and ordering a double-tall extra-hot skinny soy caramel latte on the dry side – well, does that person really *need* coffee?

In Seattle, if you want a large cup of regular coffee (heaven forbid), ask for 'a large drip,' otherwise they'll look at you funny. Some other tips to help you navigate the surprisingly complicated world of the Northwest coffeeshop menu:

- There's no such thing as small, medium and large. This is America; the tiniest available size is enormous. Many places offer either 'short' (small) or 'tall' (huge). At Starbucks, a 'small' is a Tall (12oz), a 'medium' is a Grande (16oz) and a 'large' is a Venti (20oz). If you want an 8oz drink, ask for a 'short.'
- Ordering a cappuccino 'dry' means you want more foam than liquid; 'wet' means the opposite.
- It's considered acceptable to specify whether you want your drink extra-hot or on the cooler side.
- 'Skinny' means you want your latte made with nonfat milk. Soy, naturally, means you want soy milk instead of dairy.
- A 'single' contains just one shot of espresso; a double has two shots, and yes, if you're not planning on sleeping that day, you can even get a triple or a quad.
- When the server looks at you and says 'Room?' it's not a come-on; he's asking if you want him to leave room for cream in the cup.
- A nice alternative to coffee is a Chai latte, a hot drink made of sweetened Chai syrup (tea and spices) in steamed milk.

Ordering coffee may be difficult, but finding it is simplicity itself. Seattle has a ridiculous number of coffee shops; every downtown block has at least one, and almost every major building has an espresso cart out front. Even out-of-the-way gas stations and fast-food restaurants offer espresso. Starbucks, which started the whole thing, is both loved and loathed in Seattle. The rapidly metastasizing company has also recently purchased two of its former competitors, Seattle's Best Coffee (SBC) and Torrefazione Italia.

and exciting premieres. The festival starts in mid-May. The **Seattle Lesbian & Gay Film Festival** (☎ 206-323-4274; admission $6-8), a popular festival in October, shows new gay-themed films from directors worldwide, primarily at the Harvard Exit and the Egyptian.

For a full listing of theaters, times and locations, check the *Stranger* or *Seattle Weekly* or the arts sections of the daily papers.

OPERA, CLASSICAL MUSIC & DANCE

Seattle is a sophisticated city with a well-regarded symphony, an ever-strengthening opera and a vibrant dance scene. It's hard to go wrong with any of the following options. Keep an eye out for the **World Dance Series** (☎ 206-543-4880, 800-859-5342; University of Washington), where six major works annually blow audiences away.

NORTHWEST CHAMBER ORCHESTRA

☎ 206-343-0045; www.nwco.org; admission $12-32
The top professional chamber orchestra in the Northwest focuses on chamber music of the 17th to 20th centuries. The orchestra performs at various venues throughout the city, including Benaroya Concert Hall. Call or check listings in local newspapers for schedule and venue information.

PACIFIC NORTHWEST BALLET Map pp240-1

☎ 206-441-9411; McCaw Hall, Seattle Center
The ballet is the foremost dance company in the Northwest. Its annual performance of the Nutcracker is practically mandatory.

SEATTLE MEN'S CHORUS

☎ 206-323-2992; www.seattlemenschorus.org
One of the nation's most active gay choral groups, with nearly three dozen engagements throughout the year, the Seattle Men's Chorus does a popular annual Christmas concert.

SEATTLE OPERA Map pp240-1

☎ 206-389-7676; McCaw Hall, Seattle Center; admission $37-92
Celebrating the construction of its new home, McCaw Hall, the opera continues to grow stronger under the directorship of Speight Jenkins. The company features a program of four or five full-scale operas every season, including a summer Wagner's *Ring* cycle that draws sellout crowds.

Top Five Movie Theaters

- **Egyptian** (Map pp242-3; ☎ 206-323-4978; 801 E Pine St)
- **Grand Illusion Cinema** (Map pp244-5; ☎ 206-523-3935; 1403 NE 50th St)
- **Metro Cinemas** (Map pp244-5; ☎ 206-633-0055; NE 45th St at Roosevelt Way)
- **Rendezvous Jewel Box Theater** (Map pp238-9; ☎ 206-441-5823; 2320 2nd Ave)
- **Varsity Theater** (Map pp244-5; ☎ 206-632-3131; 4329 University Way NE)

SEATTLE SYMPHONY Map pp240-1

☎ 206-215-4747; Benaroya Concert Hall, 200 University St; admission from $30
Under maestro Gerard Schwartz, the symphony has earned its reputation as the heart of the Seattle classical music scene. It has presented several successful series since Schwartz came aboard in 1984 and released a number of recordings to critical acclaim. Worth noting is the symphony's Discover Music Series – concerts designed to introduce children to various aspects of classical music.

Sports, Health & Fitness

Sports, Health & Fitness

For a city that is, at least in the popular mind, perennially drenched in rain, Seattle is a very outdoorsy community. Of course, with the Olympic and North Cascade mountains and Mt Rainier National Park just out the back door – and the fingers of Puget Sound protruding everywhere – you won't have to drive far to find pristine wilderness or calm waters. But Seattle is rare for a large city in that many forms of outdoor recreation (hiking, kayaking, biking and windsurfing) are available within the city itself. If you'd rather watch other people sweat, there's plenty to do in the way of spectator sports, too.

When it comes to finding out where to go, what to do or where to rent equipment, a couple of places deserve special notice. Recreational Equipment Inc, better known as REI (Map pp240–1; ☎ 206-223-1944; 222 Yale Ave N), is a Seattle native and is one of the largest sporting and recreational gear and equipment outfitters in the nation. Gearheads go giddy at this flagship store, a wild paean to the outdoor spirit, with a mock mountain-bike trail, a rock gym, simulated hiking trail (to test boots) and more tents, canoes and rucksacks than you've probably ever seen in one place. The eager staff are very knowledgeable about area recreation, and there are several bulletin boards with information on talks, gatherings, outings, clubs and courses. REI's good selection of books and maps on regional recreation is helpful, especially the topographic maps of regional mountains. The rental department can rent you most kinds of equipment or tell you where to go to do so. REI Adventures (☎ 800-622-2236) organizes trips.

<aside>

Top Five Seattle Activities

- Watch a **Mariners game** (see below).
- Head to **Husky Stadium** (p156).
- Bicycle the **Burke-Gilman Trail** (p158).
- Kayak **Puget Sound** at sunrise or sunset (p157).
- Hit the slopes at **Snoqualmie** (p161).

</aside>

Upstairs at REI, the **Forest Service/National Park Service** (Map pp240–1; ☎ 206-470-4060) runs an Outdoor Recreation Center, and its staff can tell you anything you need to know about nearby national parks.

Another excellent Seattle-based travel resource, the **Mountaineers** (Map pp240–1; ☎ 206-284-6310; 300 3rd Ave W) in Lower Queen Anne, specializes in Northwest recreation. The organization offers courses in hiking, mountaineering, kayaking, every type of snow sport and other outdoor skills, such as first aid and backcountry travel. Events such as film and slide shows are enough to tickle anyone's adventurous spirit, and the Mountaineers bookstore boasts an unbeatable collection of outdoor books, maps and videos, many of which are available to borrow through the Mountaineers library.

You can buy tickets for the teams listed under Sports through **TicketMaster** (☎ 206-628-0888) or **Pacific Northwest Ticket Service** (☎ 206-232-0150).

WATCHING SPORT

With the new stadiums and teams that flirt with glory, Seattle is a great town to watch the pros play. College games, too, are hugely popular with locals and a fun way to spend an afternoon.

BASEBALL

SEATTLE MARINERS Map pp236-7
☎ 206-628-3555; www.mariners.org; admission $17-50

There was a time when Seattle's professional baseball team was nothing but an annoying itch on the upper right shoulder of the USA but not anymore. The Mariners won a division title in 1995 and promptly moved into the shiny new $417 million open-air Safeco Field. In 2000, the Ms (as they are fondly referred to) missed a World Series berth by a hair, but snagged even more love from their devoted

Taking in a Game *by Virginie Boon*

Seattle's grungy sensibilities and predilection for caffeine mask what has quietly become a bona fide sports town. We're not talking Philly or Chicago here, but with the addition of a couple of state-of-the-art downtown ball parks and a sophisticated fan base, Seattle is a fantastic place to catch a game.

The town's sports renaissance was capped by the 2002 opening of Seahawks Stadium, in the city's oldest neighborhood, Pioneer Square. It is home to both the NFL Seahawks and the Sounders semi-pro soccer team. Construction took two years, financed via a public/private partnership, which included money from Paul Allen, the Microsoft billionaire and Seahawks owner, who specifically wanted the facility to be closer in feel to an open-air European soccer stadium than a stodgy cement football dome. The builders' exceeded and then some – creating an arching, open-steel frame roof with cantilevered views of downtown, snow-capped Mount Rainier and the blue-green gorgeousness of Puget Sound. With a 72,000-person capacity, over 70% of the seats are protected from the rain. The playing surface (a funny amalgam called FieldTurf, the same turf now being used by the New Zealand All Blacks, Arsenal Football Club, Oakland Raiders and more) is made from recycled tennis shoes and tires, yet retains the look and feel of natural grass.

Not 20 steps away is Safeco Field, home to the Seattle Mariners baseball team, which was among the first to sign a Japanese pro, Ichiro Suzuki, who has quickly become a favorite adopted son. The intimate ball yard is the ideal sublimation of old and new, with antique steel work set in contrast against a retractable dome even Stanley Kubrick couldn't have imagined. Opened in 1999, the traditional grass field is surrounded by a wide concourse with views of the action below, as well as the city and its natural elements all around. Every seat's a good one, and the tempting food options range from hot dogs to fresh salmon, with microbrew beers on tap.

The atmosphere in and around the new stadiums has the air of a grand street party. With plenty of parking and public transportation streaming into the area, folks often come by just for the fun of it all. Better than a farmers' market, but with a similar sense of community, street vendors sell everything from T-shirts and hacky sacks to popcorn and gourmet sausages, and the neighborhood bars and coffee shops offer shelter from the rain.

A former LP author, Virginie Boone now covers the San Francisco 49ers for ESPN's SportsTicker. She travels regularly to Seattle to see Ichiro in action.

fans. The season runs April to August (October if they make the playoffs), and games are played at 7:05pm or 7:35pm weeknights; 1:05pm or 6:05pm Saturday; and 1:35pm Sunday. There are also occasional midday games during the week.

BASKETBALL

SEATTLE SUPERSONICS Map pp240-1
☎ 206-283-3865; www.nba.com/sonics; admission $9-120

Seattle's National Basketball Association (NBA) franchise, the Seattle SuperSonics, provides plenty of excitement at Key Arena in Seattle Center. The Sonics' season runs November to late April. Games start at 7pm.

FOOTBALL

SEATTLE SEAHAWKS Map pp236-7
☎ 425-827-9777; www.seahawks.com; admission $15-68

The Northwest's only National Football League (NFL) franchise, the Seattle Seahawks have enjoyed both roaring success and dismal slumps, one of which prompted former

Seahawks stadium, Sodo District (see above)

owners to put the team on the selling block, which left Seattlelites fearing its relocation. In 1997 Microsoft co-founder Paul Allen saved the day by purchasing the Seahawks franchise, with the stipulation that the Hawks get a new stadium. Beyond that, the Hawks' former home, the Kingdome, quickly became a pile of rubble, replaced in 2002 by the new 72,000-seat Seahawks Stadium.

UNIVERSITY OF WASHINGTON HUSKIES Map pp244-5
☎ 206-543-2200; www.gohuskies.com; admission $7-25

The University of Washington Huskies football and basketball teams are another Seattle obsession. The Huskies football team plays at Husky Stadium; you'll find the men and women's basketball teams at the Edmundson Pavilion, both of which are on campus. The women's basketball team draws massive crowds.

HOCKEY

SEATTLE THUNDERBIRDS Map pp240-1
☎ 206-448-7825; admission $10-22

Also playing at Key Area, the Seattle Thunderbirds rip around the ice in the Western Hockey League (WHL) from September to March. The games are lively and well attended, and tickets are very reasonable.

SOCCER

SEATTLE SOUNDERS Map pp236-7
☎ 206-622-3415; www.seattlesounders.net; admission $10-15

Soccer's no stranger in Seattle either. The A-League Seattle Sounders play at Seahawks Stadium, admittedly looking a little lost in the gigantic facility; soccer has yet to become huge in the US, but those who love it, *really* love it. The soccer season runs May to mid-September.

OUTDOOR ACTIVITIES
WATERSPORTS

Rumor has it that one in three people who live in Seattle owns a boat of some sort. It could be a rubber dinghy, a crusty kayak or a salty sailboat, but, regardless, the locals here love to play in the water. Whether you learn to windsurf on Green Lake, kayak past the houseboats on Lake Union or hoist the sails on Lake Washington, there are plenty of organizations here that are geared toward having fun on the water. For organized boat trips, see p43.

Sea kayaking can soothe your soul or wake up your adventurous spirit and, if you don't know how, it's one of the easiest sports to pick up. Seattle's many waterways are ideal for kayak exploration, and it doesn't take long before controlling your paddle is as natural as waving your arm. White-water kayaking on area rivers is also popular, though a little more challenging to pick up. But have no fear, many organizations offer excellent lessons.

Despite the flood of water in Seattle, the sailing isn't that great; in fact, you're lucky if the calm summer days cough up enough of a breeze to keep you moving bow ward. However, in the spring, fall and winter a soft wind exhales over the sound, and sailing becomes a spectacular way to be outside. But even when the calm days keep the motor running, sailing offers views and perspectives you can only get on the water. More adventurous sailors head out on Puget Sound and along its inland waterways, or all the way up the coast to British Columbia.

Windsurfing is a big sport in Seattle; it's part of that quintessential Seattle mix of being in a band, having a job at an espresso stand and putting your sail up on the lake. As such, windsurfing draws more locals than tourists. Lake Washington is the most popular place to sail; it's big enough to accommodate traffic and out-of-control windsurfers. The warm waters of Green Lake are good for beginners, but it can get pretty congested in summer. Between the sailboats, floatplanes and motorboat traffic, Lake Union is not good for anyone but expert windsurfers with full control. Usual launch spots are Magnuson and Mount Baker Parks. In summer, the calm waters of Puget Sound are good for experienced windsurfers; try setting out from Alki Beach in West Seattle, or from Golden Gardens northwest of Ballard.

Some people shy away from the chilly waters surrounding Seattle, but local divers will tell you that the marine biodiversity in the Northwest beats any tropical clime. Sure, you're not likely to see colorful tropical fish, but dive sites in Puget Sound and along the Northwest coast offer year-round diving and regular sightings of octopus, huge ling cod, cabezon, cathedral-like white anemones and giant sea stars.

Most of Seattle's best dive sites are actually out of Seattle, in sheltered coves and bays up and down the coast. Popular spots include Alki Cove, on the eastside of Alki Point, Saltwater State Park, south of Seattle in Des Moins, and Edmonds Underwater Park near the Edmonds Ferry Dock north of Seattle. Other popular spots include Port Angeles, Keystone and the San Juan Islands. For more information on area dive sites, look for *Northwest Shore Dives*, by Stephen Fischnaller, a helpful guide – considered the dive site bible by locals – to nearby sites.

MOSS BAY ROWING & KAYAK CENTER Map pp240-1
☎ 206-682-2031; www.mossbay.net; 1001 Fairview N
Moss Bay offers rentals, extensive lessons and tours on Lake Union.

NORTHWEST OUTDOOR CENTER
Map pp240-1
☎ 206-281-9694; www.nwoc.com; 2100 Westlake Ave N, Lake Union
The center offers a vast selection of rentals, guided tours and instruction in sea and white-water kayaking.

PUGET SOUND KAYAK COMPANY
☎ 206-933-3008; www.pugetsoundkayak.com
This active organization, which is located on both Bainbridge and Vashon Islands, offers classes, clinics and guided trips. These include the popular Harbor Moonlight Paddle in Vashon's Quartermaster or Bainbridge's Eagle Harbors.

STARFISH ENTERPRISE Map pp246-7
☎ 206-286-6596; 600 W Nickerson St
This is one of several Seattle dive shops offering instruction and rentals for all levels on the south side of the Washington Ship Canal in northern Queen Anne.

UNDERWATER SPORTS Map pp232-3
☎ 206-362-3310; 10545 Aurora Ave
This is the best place to go for gear repair; it also offers courses in its on-site pool.

WASHINGTON KAYAK CLUB
☎ 206-433-1983l; www.washingtonkayakclub.org
The Kayak Club provides both white-water and sea kayaking courses. It's also in the business of educating in matters of conservation and safety awareness.

Gear Rental
In addition to the above, water sport equipment rentals are available at the following establishments.

AGUA VERDE PADDLE CLUB Map pp232-3
☎ 206-545-8570; 1303 NE Boat St; ☺ 10am-dusk Mar-Oct, 10am-6pm Sun; single kayak per hr/day $10/45, double kayak $15/60
On Portage Bay, near the university, you can rent kayaks from this friendly place right at the edge of the water. When you get back from your paddle, be sure to visit the café upstairs (p121) for the best fish tacos in town.

CENTER FOR WOODEN BOATS Map pp240-1
☎ 206-382-2628; www.cwb.org; 1010 Valley St; small/large sailboat Mon-Fri $16/23.50, Sat & Sun $25/37.50; small/large rowboat Mon-Fri $12.50/18.75, Sat & Sun $20/30; beginner sailing course $250
This museum offers sailboat lessons and rentals on Lake Union. One person in your party has to know how to sail and must do a checkout before you'll be permitted to rent. It's pretty straightforward; you need to demonstrate tacking, jibing and docking. The center also offers sailing lessons, including an excellent beginner course that gives you as many lessons as it takes in a four-month period (usually eight to 12 lessons). Seasoned sailors who are a little rusty can take a one-on-one lesson for $30 per hour.

GREEN LAKE SMALL CRAFT CENTER
Map pp232-3
☎ 206-527-0171; 7351 E Green Lake Dr
Green Lake's still waters help keep beginner kayakers calm, though the crowds might also keep you waiting. Run by Seattle Parks & Recreation Department, it rents kayaks, canoes, rowboats and paddleboats from March to October, and also provides lessons.

Kayakers, Portage Bay (p157)

SAILING IN SEATTLE Map pp240-1

☎ 206-289-0094; www.sailing-in-seattle.com; 2040 Westlake Ave; lessons per hr $100

On Friday evenings Sailing in Seattle holds races on Lakes Washington and Union. Anyone can come join a racing crew and, though you should be somewhat fit, no experience is necessary; they'll show you what to do. For information on hiring Sailing in Seattle's 33ft *Whoodat* see Organized Tours p44.

UW WATERFRONT ACTIVITIES CENTER Map pp244-5

☎ 206-543-9433; ☽ approx 10am-7pm; canoe & rowboat per hr $6.50

Another good way to explore the waters surrounding the Arboretum is to rent a canoe or rowboat from the University of Washington's facility. You need a current driver's license or passport. The center is in the southeast corner of the Husky Stadium parking lot.

CYCLING

Despite frequent rain and hilly terrain, bicycling is still a major form of both transportation and recreation in the Seattle area. Both bicycle touring and mountain biking are widespread, so whether you're a clipless mudhound or a casual cruiser, you'll find plenty of places to ride.

In the city, commuter bike lanes continue to get painted on city streets, city trails are well maintained, and the friendly and enthusiastic biking community is happy to share the road. The wildly popular 16.5 mile **Burke-Gilman Trail** winds from Ballard to Log Boom Park in Kenmore on Seattle's Eastside. There, it connects with the 11-mile **Sammamish River Trail**, which winds past the Chateau Ste Michelle winery in Woodinville before terminating at Redmond's Marymoor Park. This route is described in more detail in the Walking Tours chapter (p102). Marymoor Park boasts the only **velodrome** (☎ 206-675-1424) in the Pacific Northwest. You'll need to be a trained velodrome rider before you can get on the track, but the untrained can watch the exciting races, which are held at 7pm Wednesday and Friday mid-May to September. Admission to the amateur races is free Monday and Wednesday; when the pros hit the track on Friday, admission costs $3.

More cyclists than you can imagine peddle the loop around **Green Lake**, making it downright congested on sunny days. Closer to downtown, the scenic 2.5 mile **Elliott Bay Trail** runs along the waterfront through Myrtle Edwards and Elliott Bay Parks. The eight-mile **Alki Trail** in West Seattle makes a pretty ride as it follows Alki Beach before connecting up with the 11-mile **Duwamish Trail** that heads south along W Marginal Way SW.

Though they are not specified trails, the tree-lined roads winding through the **Washington Park Arboretum** and along **Lake Washington Blvd** make for lovely road rides. The bike trail around **Seward Park** gives cyclists the sensation of looping a forested island. The 14-mile **Mercer Island Loop** is another residential ride along E and W Mercer Way around the perimeter of the island.

Bainbridge and Vashon Islands are popular with cyclists and are just a ferry ride away, offering near-rural isolation on rolling country back roads. Bike shops and the usually friendly folks who work there are always gushing fountains of good information. Most shops stock cycling publications and can point you in the right direction for public rides, trails and places to avoid. Anyone planning on cycling in Seattle should pick up a copy of the *Seattle Bicycling Guide Map*, published by the City of Seattle's **Transportation Bicycle and Pedestrian Program** (☎ 206-684-7583) and available at bike shops. Alternatively you can order the map free of charge over the phone or online at www.cityofseattle.net/transportation/bikemaps.htm.

Bike Rentals

The following places are recommended for bicycle rentals and repairs. The average rental cost is about $20 for a half day, and up to $35 for a full day.

AL YOUNG BIKE AND SKI Map pp244-5
☎ 206-524-2642; 3615 NE 45th St
Al's is convenient to the University of Washington and the Burke-Gilman Trail.

BLAZING SADDLES Map pp238-9
☎ 206-341-9994; 1230 Western Ave
This shop on the Waterfront rents higher-end mountain bikes.

GREGG'S GREENLAKE CYCLES
Map pp232-3
☎ 206-523-1822; 7007 Woodlawn Ave NE
Gregg's is among the friendliest and most helpful bike shops in town.

Cycling Clubs

Seattle's active biking community thrives because of organized clubs.

BACKCOUNTRY BICYCLE TRAILS CLUB
☎ 206-293-2995; www.bbtc.org
Fat-tire riders will want to contact this club, which organizes mountain-biking trail rides and offers bike repair and technical-riding courses.

CASCADE BICYCLE CLUB
☎ 206-522-2453; www.cascade.org
With more than 5500 members, this is the largest cycling club in the USA. It holds organized rides daily as well as various special events, such as races and long-distance rides. It publishes the *Cascade Corner*, a newsletter that describes what's happening in the bike world.

HIKING

In Seattle, it's possible to hike wilderness trails without ever leaving the city. **Seward Park** (Map pp232–3) offers several miles of trails in a remnant of the area's old-growth forest, and an even more extensive network of trails is available in 534-acre **Discovery Park** (Map p248), northwest of downtown. At the northern edge of Washington Park Arboretum, **Foster Island** (Map p249) offers a 20-minute wetlands trail winding through marshlands born upon the opening of the Lake Washington Ship Canal. This is a great place for bird watching, fishing and swimming. The trail begins at the bottom of the Museum of History and Industry (MOHAI) parking lot.

Outside the city, hiking opportunities are practically endless in the Olympic Range; the north, central and south Cascades; and in the Issaquah Alps. For specific trail information, contact **REI** (p154) or the **Mountaineers** (p154) or the following groups.

SIERRA CLUB Map pp232-3
☎ 206-523-2019; 8511 15th Ave NE
The Cascade chapter of the Sierra Club is a busy and active group. Its extremely diverse offerings range from beachcombing and botany walks at Alki to weekend day-hiking and car-camping trips along the Pacific Crest Trail. Call for a recording of future events. Most day trips are free; longer trips may have minimal fees.

WASHINGTON TRAILS ASSOCIATION

☎ 206-625-1367; www.wta.org
This nonprofit group organizes hiking trips, conservation efforts and trail-building jaunts into local mountains.

RUNNING

With its many parks, Seattle offers a number of good trails for runners. If you're in the downtown area, the trails along **Myrtle Edwards Park** – just north of the Waterfront along Elliott Bay – make for a nice run, with views over the sound and of the downtown skyline. **Green Lake** has two paths, the 2.75 mile paved path immediately surrounding the lake and a less-crowded, unpaved path on the perimeter of the park. The **Washington Park Arboretum** is another good choice, as the trails lead through beautiful trees and flower gardens. Trails in the arboretum connect to the Lake Washington Blvd trail system, which extends all the way south to Seward Park, just in case you are training for a marathon. Most of the bicycling routes listed earlier are also good running routes.

Running Clubs

Runners looking to hook up with running mates can contact a number of Seattle's running clubs, most of which offer organized runs that usually turn into social events. Active clubs include the **Puget Sound Hash Harriers** (☎ 206-528-2050), **Seattle Frontrunners** (☎ 206-322-7769) and the **West Seattle Runners** (☎ 206-938-2416). **Super Jock n' Jills** trains runners of all levels and maintains a running **hotline** (☎ 206-524-7867). Also, check sports stores for *Northwest Runners,* a monthly publication and a good resource for running-related information.

IN-LINE SKATING

Call 'em in-line skaters, rollerbladers or just kickbacks from the disco era, but skaters swoosh everywhere, wearing everything from Nike's latest trends to groovy pink legwarmers. Seattle's paved paths are perfect except when it rains, which is why you should beware the skating storm on sunny days. Popular skating spots include the Burke-Gilman Trail, around Green Lake, Alki Point, Lake Washington Blvd and the Sammamish River Trail on the Eastside. **Gregg's Greenlake Cycle** (p159) rents in-line skates for $5 per hour.

SKIING & SNOWBOARDING

When the winter rains make you squint in Seattle, you can bet that fluffy, blessed snow is kissing (make that 'making love to') the alpine peaks on the nearby Cascade mountains. If you're planning on a ski trip out of Seattle it will require driving from 90 minutes to a few hours out, depending on which resort you want to go to. A couple of the ski resorts offer a shuttle from downtown, which is a convenient way to avoid driving the snowy roads on high-elevation mountain passes.

If you are taking a car, be sure to call ☎ 425-368-1944 for a report on current road conditions. If you're heading into the backcountry, contact the **Northwest Avalanche Information Hotline** (☎ 206-526-6677) and be absolutely certain you have a good understanding of trails and backcountry first-aid. Contact the **Mountaineers** (p154) for training and advice before heading deep into the mountains. Also call the **Cascade Ski Report** (☎ 206-634-0200) for the latest conditions on all the local mountains.

CRYSTAL MOUNTAIN RESORT

☎ 360-663-2265, snow report ☎ 888-754-6199; 75 miles southeast; 3-lesson package $150, lift ticket per adult/child/senior/youth $45/5/15/40, ski/snowboard rental $35/30
One of the largest and most popular ski areas in Washington, Crystal Mountain Resort offers year-round recreational activities. Downhill skiers give Crystal Mountain high marks for its variety of terrain, including some very steep chutes and remote, unpatrolled backcountry trails for advanced skiers. Its summit (Silver King) tops out at 7012ft; the vertical drop is 3120ft. Crystal has 2300 acres of skiable terrain and 50 named runs, more than 50% of which are rated intermediate. The slopes are served by 10 lifts, including four high-speed chairs. Snowboarding in the deep bowls is also popular here. There's night skiing until 8pm Friday to Sunday.

STEVENS PASS

☎ 360-973-2441, snow report ☎ 360-663-7711; 75 miles east of Seattle, Hwy 2; lift ticket per adult/child/youth/senior $44/5/28/31, night skiing only $28/5/23/26, adult/child rental packages $32/23
Stevens Pass, which has 37 runs, 11 lifts and a vertical drop of 1774ft, is the state's second-largest downhill venue.

Seasoned skiers will love the dry snow, run variety and stellar views over the Cascades.

Northern Slopes

The skiing and snowboarding at nearby British Columbia's mountain resorts draws snow enthusiasts from around the world, many of whom fly into Sea-Tac and drive to the wintry bliss. The following BC ski resorts are easily accessible in a few hours by car from Seattle.

Cypress Bowl Ski Area

Just 20 minutes from downtown Vancouver, the wide, snow-filled **Cypress Bowl** (☎ 604-926-5612, conditions ☎ 604-419-7669; www.cypressbowl.com) sits between Strachan and Black Mountains in the heart of Cypress Provincial Park. Great night skiing.
Driving time from Seattle 3½ hours
Nearest town/city West Vancouver, BC

Grouse Mountain Resort

A 20-minute drive from downtown Vancouver, **Grouse Mountain** (☎ 604-984-0661; www.grousemountain.com) is a favorite for its night skiing. An aerial tram whisks you to the mountaintop, offering incredible views along the way. There's a half pipe for boarders.
Driving time from Seattle 3½ hours
Nearest town/city North Vancouver, BC

Mount Seymour

Another local Vancouver area mountain (just 15 minutes from downtown Vancouver), **Mount Seymour** (☎ 604-986-2261; www.mountseymour.com) is a haven for boarders, who come to rip it up in Seymour's three snowboard parks. A good place for beginner skiers and snowboarders, as well as families.
Driving time from Seattle 3½ hours
Nearest town/city North Vancouver, BC

Whistler/Blackcomb

A world-famous, dual-mountain paradise, **Whistler/Blackcomb** (☎ 604-932-3434, 800-766-0449; www.whistler-blackcomb.com) has enough lifts to accommodate up to 59,000 skiers and snowboarders an hour. With 5278 vertical feet, 18 sq miles of bowls, glades and steeps, the exploration seems endless. You could stay here for an entire season – and plenty of people do – and still not explore it all. Legendary nightlife, university-caliber ski school.
Driving time from Seattle 4½ hours
Nearest town/city Whistler, BC

Sports, Health & Fitness – Outdoor Activities

Snowboarders cut trails through the powder and swoop around on the half-pipe. In addition, there is night skiing from 4pm to 10pm daily.

Just 5 miles east of the downhill resort is the **Stevens Pass Nordic Center**, which maintains 25 miles of groomed cross-country ski trails, a rental center and a restaurant.

SUMMIT AT SNOQUALMIE

☎ 425-434-7669, snow report ☎ 236-1600; 40 miles east of Seattle, I-90; lift ticket per adult/child/ concession $42/8/28, midweek $37/8/28, 4-10pm only $27/8/21, adult/concession rental package $30/25
This ski and snowboard resort encompasses four different ski areas: Alpental, Summit West, Summit Central and Summit East. The four areas vary greatly in difficulty and

somewhat in conditions. Alpental is generally considered the most difficult, with steep slopes and a vertical drop of 2200ft. Alpental also offers access to the backcountry. Summit West boasts one of the best snowboarding half-pipes in the Northwest, along with good terrain for beginner and intermediate skiers. Summit Central's lower slopes cater to families and beginner skiers, while its upper reaches offer treed runs and moguls. Summit East has a Nordic Center, with miles of trails for snowshoers and cross-country skiers. Full rental and ski instruction options are available, and night skiing until 10pm is offered daily except Sunday. One lift ticket is good at all four ski areas; free buses link the runs, as do trails on the slopes.

ROCK CLIMBING

There's plenty of climbing and mountaineering to be had in the Olympics and the Cascades, but even if your travel plans don't allow time for an excursion to the mountains, you can keep in shape by clambering up the faces at Seattle-area rock walls.

REI Map pp240-1
☎ 206-223-1944; 222 Yale Ave N

The REI Pinnacle climbing wall is a 65ft rock pinnacle to the side of the store's entryway. The wall is open for scrambling at various times daily except Tuesday, when it's reserved for private groups. You can climb free of charge, but be prepared to wait your turn.

STONE GARDENS: THE CLIMBERS GYM Map p248
☎ 206-781-9828; 2839 NW Market St

This is a full climbing gym with 14,000 sq ft of climbing surface on more than 100 routes. The gym also has weights, lockers and showers. Courses, from beginner climber to anchoring, are also offered. The drop-in rate is $12. If the weather is good, head to Marymoor Park in Redmond (on the Eastside), where there's a 45-ft outdoor climbing structure for all levels of climbers.

ULTIMATE FRISBEE

Ultimate is hugely popular in the Northwest, and the many co-ed leagues offer games for players of every level. The Potlatch tournament, held annually in Redmond in July, attracts the West Coast's top players.

DISC NORTHWEST
☎ 206-781-5840; www.discnw.org

Disc Northwest runs a summer and winter league and is the primary resource for ultimate in the Seattle Area. Both give updates on league and pick-up games. Long-running pick-up games include 1pm Saturday and 6pm Wednesday at Dahl Field at 25th Ave NE and NE 77th St, above Ravenna Park and the U District. Pick-up games are also played at noon Sunday at Sand Point in Magnuson Park, and 1pm Saturday at Discovery Park. For directions to ultimate games, check the map section of the Web site.

TENNIS

Many of Seattle's public parks have tennis courts and you don't have to wait long to play. Seattle Parks & Recreation (☎ 206-684-4075) maintains a number of courts in parks throughout the city: most are on a first-come, first-served basis. Play tennis on four courts in Volunteer Park on Capitol Hill, on 10 courts in lower Woodland Park, adjacent to Green Lake, or on the four courts in Magnolia Playfield on 34th Ave W and W Smith St. For a full listing of public tennis courts contact Seattle Parks & Recreation.

SEATTLE TENNIS CENTER Map p249
☎ 206-684-4764; 2000 Martin Luther King Jr Way; singles/doubles games $15/20

The giant Seattle Tennis Center in the Central District has 10 courts, the only indoor ones in the city.

GOLF

Seattle Parks & Recreation (☎ 206-684-4075) runs three public golf courses in Seattle, along with a short (nine-hole) course at Green Lake (☎ 206-632-2280; 5701 W Green Lake Way N), a fun spot if you're just learning or lack the patience for a full round.

JACKSON PARK GOLF COURSE
Map p232-3
☎ 206-363-4747; 1000 NE 135th St

The most popular municipal course, Jackson Park is on the far northern edge of Seattle. This 18-hole course is best on weekdays, when there are fewer lines at the first tee.

JEFFERSON PARK GOLF COURSE
Map pp232-3
☎ 206-762-4513; 4101 Beacon Ave S

Another convenient tee spot, Jefferson Park is an 18-hole course with short fairways and lots of lovely and mature (but sometimes troublesome) trees and bushes.

WEST SEATTLE MUNICIPAL GOLF COURSE Map pp232-3
☎ 206-935-5187; 4470 35th Ave SW

With 18 holes and superior views across Elliott Bay, this is one of the area's best public courses. Green fees for city courses are $25 per person on weekdays and $28 on weekends.

When they are not booked, the courses offer reduced rates in the evenings.

SWIMMING

When summer temperatures rise, there's no more popular place to be than on one of Seattle's beaches. One of the most popular is **Alki Beach** (p93) in West Seattle, a real scene with beach volleyball, acres of flesh and teenagers cruising in their cars. **Green Lake Park** (p86) has two lakefront swimming and sunbathing beaches, as do several parks along the western shores of Lake Washington, including **Madison Park** (p90), **Madrona Park** (p91), **Seward Park** (p94), **Magnuson Park** and **Mt Baker Park**. Lifeguards are on duty at public beaches between 11am and 8pm mid-June to Labor Day (beginning of September).

Swimming is a great way to keep in shape. Many pools host swim clubs or masters programs. The following are public pools that offer a variety of open swim sessions, lessons and lap swimming. Drop-in fees are about $3. For information on other pools, contact **Seattle Parks & Recreation** (☎ 206-684-4075), or try:

Evans Pool at Green Lake (Map p232-3; ☎ 206-684-4961; 7201 E Green Lake Drive N)

Medgar Evers Aquatic Center (Map p249; ☎ 206-684-4766; 500 23rd Ave)

Queen Anne Pool (Map p240-1; ☎ 206-386-4282; 1920 1st Ave W)

HEALTH & FITNESS

Most of Seattle's large hotels have workout facilities available to guests. But if you're looking for more expansive facilities, including group classes and personal trainers, try one of the following gyms.

24-HOUR FITNESS Map pp234-5
☎ 206-624-0651; 1827 Yale Ave; day/month pass $15/99; 🕑 24hr

Downtown, with an indoor pool, spa, sauna and steam room, child care, classes and tanning, plus the usual weights and cardio equipment. Ask about specials or check online before you go; free 10-day passes are often available.

DOWNTOWN SEATTLE YMCA Map pp234-5
☎ 206-382-5010; 909 4th Ave; day pass $10-15; 🕑 5am-9pm Mon-Fri, 7am-6:30pm Sat, 11am-6:30pm Sun

The Y is notably traveler-friendly, and this location has clean, classy, updated equipment including a pool, free weights, cardiovascular equipment and day care.

Seattle: city of cyclists

GOLD'S GYM Map pp234-5

☎ 206-583-0640; 825 Pike St; day pass $10;
🕑 5:30am-10pm Mon-Fri, 8am-8pm Sat & Sun

The downtown Seattle branch of this chain has first-rate facilities for cardio and strength training, plus classes in aerobics, yoga, pilates, dance, kickboxing, and karate. Massage, personal training, a sauna and a women-only section are also available.

SOUND MIND AND BODY Map pp246-7

☎ 206-547-3470; 437 N 34th St; day pass $12, 10-visit card $90; 🕑 5:30am-10pm Mon-Thu, 5:30am-9pm Fri, 8am-7pm Sat, 9am-7pm Sun

You'll find the branch of Sound Mind & Body located in Fremont vast but quiet. It has an unbelieveable 40,000 sq ft of weight training and cardio equipment, and basketball and volleyball courts. It has a sauna and steam room. In addition it has group classes in yoga, pilates and kickboxing. Most unusual is that there's hardly a blaring television or stereo to be found (viewers must wear headphones while working out).

Shopping

Shopping

Seattle has the best of both worlds, shopping-wise. You can power-shop at all the big-name highbrow chain stores in City Centre Mall – Barney's, Tiffany, FAO Schwarz, Louis Vuitton, Ann Taylor – or you can seek out the quirky, ultra-independent, one-of-a-kind shops hidden away in someone's garage with a spray-painted sign tacked to the door. Besides the upscale malls and locally based chains, such as Nordstrom and Bon Marche, there are a few Seattle shopping experiences that are worth seeking out. The city has some of the greatest bookstores in the country, and a considerable number of them. Also, with Seattle's rich music culture, record stores are a good bet, although you won't find amazing deals – the owners know people will come here looking for that rare, limited-edition Green River single, and they'll charge a pretty penny for it. If you're mourning one of the best record stores that ever existed, Fallout Records, check out Wall of Sound instead in its new home on Capitol Hill; the owner stocks cool obscurities and a well-chosen selection of imported mags, underground comics and zines.

Left Bank Books, Pike Place Market (p170)

Naturally, any shopping excursion in Seattle must include Pike Place Market. From stacks of crabs to used books to spiced teas to goth toys, the selection here pretty much runs the gamut. And browsing this landmark labyrinth is just as much fun as buying.

Shopping Areas

Downtown dominates Seattle's retail scene with glamorous malls that in themselves are works of art. But take a look in the corners of Pioneer Square for splendid art and antique shops, or in the many nooks and crannies of Pike Place Market for everything from embroidered tea towels to lollypop condoms. Make the Waterfront your stop for obligatory souvenirs, become a gear junkie at one of many outdoor outfitters. Several of the outlying neighborhoods display quirky local wares, and Seattle lives up to its literary reputation with an excellent selection of general and specialty bookstores.

Top Five Shopping Strips

- Pike Place Market (p169)
- Downtown (p167)
- Broadway (p172)
- Pioneer Square (p168)
- University Way (p173)

Opening Hours

Most city stores, especially the ones geared toward tourists, are open every day (though some close on Sunday), typically 9am or 10am to 6pm. Malls and department stores keep later hours, often staying open until 8pm or 9pm. Where there are no hours listed in a review, you can assume these general hours apply. Exceptions will be noted in the reviews.

Consumer Taxes

An 8.8% sales tax is added to all purchases except food to be prepared for consumption (ie groceries). Unlike the European VAT or Canadian GST, the sales tax is not refundable to tourists.

DOWNTOWN

The main shopping area in Seattle is downtown between 3rd and 6th Aves and between University and Stewart Sts. If you're anywhere nearby, you can't miss it.

BON-MACY'S Map pp234-5   *Clothing*
☎ 206-344-2121; 3rd Ave & Pine St
Seattle's oldest and largest department store, the 'Bon' – formerly Bon-Marché, but renamed in August 2003 when it was bought by Macy's – is still a classic.

CAMERAS WEST Map pp234-5   *Cameras*
☎ 206-622-0066; 1908 4th Ave
The foremost selection of film and photographic supplies in Seattle is Cameras West, right downtown.

CITY CENTRE MALL Map pp234-5   *Mall*
☎ 206-223-8999; 5th Ave btwn Pike & Union Sts
This fancy mall has a higher class of tenant, including **Barney's New York** (☎ 206-622-6300) for luxurious and trendy men's and women's clothing, **Ann Taylor** (☎ 206-623-4818) for elegant women's wear and **FAO Schwarz** (☎ 206-442-9500) for over-the-top toys. The treasure in here is the local company **Design Concern** (☎ 206-623-4444), which has a creative selection of upscale office tools and toys, watches, soaps and local jewelry.

HEAVENS ON 2ND Map pp234-5   *Records*
☎ 206-443-9373; 1914 2nd Ave; ☻ closed Sun & Mon
A great selection of Olympia-style indie-rock records and CDs.

KITS CAMERAS Map pp234-5   *Cameras*
☎ 206-682-3221; 806 3rd Ave
For one-hour photo developing, this is a good bet; it also has a branch at Westlake Center.

NIKETOWN Map pp234-5   *Clothing*
☎ 206-447-6453; 1500 6th Ave
The ridiculously huge Niketown has its roots in the Northwest.

Top Five Record Stores

- **Wall of Sound** (p173) Obscurities and great publications.
- **Singles Going Steady** (p171) Totally punk rock.
- **Easy Street Records & Café** (p176) A fun place to hang out and browse.
- **Sonic Boom** (p173) Alt-rock and indie rock essentials.
- **Platinum Records** (p172) Technoheads and DJs treasure this shop.

NORDSTROM Map pp234-5   *Clothing*
☎ 206-628-2111; Pine St btwn 5th & 6th Aves
Born and raised in Seattle, this chain department store occupies a giant space in the former Frederick and Nelson Building. Closer to Pike Place Market, **Nordstrom Rack** (☎ 206-448-8522; 1601 2nd Ave) offers closeouts and returns from the parent store.

NORTH FACE Map pp234-5   *Outdoors*
☎ 206-622-4111; 1023 1st Ave
For hardcore camping, climbing and hiking equipment, go to the North Face, downtown toward the Waterfront.

PACIFIC PLACE Map pp234-5   *Mall*
☎ 206-405-2655; 600 Pine St
Seattle's newest boutique mall ranks at the top. Clothiers include **J Crew** (☎ 206-652-9788), **Club Monaco** (☎ 206-264-8001) and **BCBG** (☎ 206-447-3400). The large stores of **Pottery Barn** (☎ 206-621-0276) and **Williams-Sonoma** (☎ 206-621-7405) are fun to look around in. Take a moment to gape in the window at **Tiffany & Co** (☎ 206-264-1400), or saunter inside for a special gift. The mall's top level features a movie theater, a pub and a couple of restaurants.

RAINIER SQUARE Map pp234-5   *Mall*
☎ 206-373-7119; btwn 4th & 5th Aves & Union & University Sts
A mall where you'll find it all. Upscale clothing stores include Oregon's famed **Northwest Pendleton** (☎ 206-682-4430), which sells its trademark plaid wool shirts and blankets. The cool **Channel 9 Store** (☎ 206-682-8198) is filled with educational videos and games, while **Fox's Gem Shop** (☎ 206-623-2528) displays its Tiffany collection and **Louis Vuitton** (☎ 206-749-0711) oozes with luxury leather goods.

WESTLAKE CENTER Map pp234-5 *Mall*
☎ 206-467-3044; 4th Ave & Pine St

This decorative boutique mall is one of the megamall Rowse developments that are cropping up in big US cities. Here you'll find specialist shops like **Crabtree & Evelyn** (☎ 206-682-6776) and the **Galleries of Neiman Marcus** (☎ 206-447-0901). There are some local stores as well, including an outlet of **Fireworks** (☎ 206-682-6462), which offers inexpensive funky and arty products by regional craftspeople – they make great gifts.

PIONEER SQUARE

Not surprisingly, given its historic importance to the city, Pioneer Square is where to shop for antiques. It's also a good place to find reasonably priced artwork and crafts by local artists, particularly blown glass and traditional art by coastal Native artists. And, of course, you can't miss a chance to browse through Elliott Bay Books.

BUD'S JAZZ RECORDS
Map pp236-7 *Records*
☎ 206-628-0445; 102 S Jackson St

Whether you're looking for recordings of Coltrane or the Duke, you'll have a good shot of finding them here. Bud specializes in vintage vinyl recordings of early and hard-to-find jazz.

ELLIOTT BAY BOOK COMPANY
Map pp236-7 *Books*
☎ 206-624-6600; 101 S Main St

One of the best general bookstores in the Northwest is the Elliott Bay Book Company. This rambling bookstore takes up an entire block of historic storefronts in Pioneer Square. The interior, all exposed red brick and high ceilings, is absolutely stuffed full of new books and browsing customers. Downstairs is a popular **café** (p110). Elliott Bay is the local leader in author appearances, with some writer appearing at a reading or signing almost nightly (p150).

FLORA & FAUNA BOOKS
Map pp236-7 *Books*
☎ 206-623-4727; 121 1st Ave S

Seattle has some great theme bookstores. Flora & Fauna is good for books on natural history and local field guides.

FOSTER/WHITE GALLERY Map pp236-7 *Art*
☎ 206-622-2833; 123 S Jackson St

The famed Foster/White Gallery features glassworks, paintings and sculpture by mainstream Northwest artists.

GLASSHOUSE STUDIO Map pp236-7 *Art*
☎ 206-682-9939; 311 Occidental Ave S

The Seattle area is known for its Pilchuck School of glassblowing art. Glasshouse Studio is the city's oldest glassblowing studio – stop by to watch the artists in action.

JACKSON STREET GALLERY
Map pp236-7 *Antiques*
☎ 206-447-1012; 108 S Jackson St

Find all manner of antiques and collectibles at Jackson Street Gallery. Also nearby are **Jean Williams Antiques** (☎ 622-1110; 115 S Jackson St), which sells English and French period antiques, and **Elliott Bay Antiques** (☎ 340-0770; 165 S Jackson St), which features Asian furniture and art.

LEGACY LTD GALLERY
Map pp236-7 *Arts & Crafts*
☎ 206-624-6350; 1003 1st Ave

Northwest Coast Indian and Inuit art and artifacts, including baskets and jewelry, are sold at Legacy Ltd.

METSKER MAPS Map pp236-7 *Maps & Books*
☎ 206-623-8747; 702 1st Ave

The definitive source for maps is this shop near Pioneer Square. It has a good selection of regional recreation, adventure, camping and hiking books.

PIONEER SQUARE ANTIQUE MALL
Map pp236-7 *Antiques*
☎ 206-624-1164; 601 1st Ave

Little antique shops pop up all around the city, though the highest concentration is found around Pioneer Square. This Antique Mall is a warren of little shops right across from the pergola; it's actually part of the Seattle 'underground' (p38) and can be somewhat claustrophobic.

SEATTLE MYSTERY BOOKSHOP
Map pp236-7 *Books*
☎ 206-587-5737; 117 Cherry St

The name gives it away – Seattle Mystery Bookshop is a specialty store for page-turners and whodunits.

STONINGTON GALLERY Map pp236-7   *Art*
☎ 206-405-4040; 119 S Jackson St
The Stonington Gallery focuses on intricate arts by coastal Native artists from Washington to Alaska.

TRADITIONS & BEYOND
Map pp236-7   *Arts & Crafts*
☎ 206-621-0655; 113 Cherry St
Affordable and authentic Native American crafts are available at Traditions & Beyond, where part of the proceeds goes to Native programs and education.

INTERNATIONAL DISTRICT

KINOKUNIYA Map pp236-7   *Books*
☎ 206-587-2477; 600 5th Ave S
For books in Japanese, on Japanese culture (in both English and Japanese) and Japanese works translated into English, go to Kinokuniya, above Uwajimaya.

UWAJIMAYA Map pp236-7   *Food*
☎ 206-624-6248; 600 5th Ave S
This cornerstone of the International District is a wonderful supermarket filled with everything needed to prepare Japanese and other

Stonington Gallery, Pioneer Square (left)

Asian foods, including many different kinds of fish, meats, fruits and vegetables. Cooking vessels, hard-to-find spices and other flavorings, and even the necessary cookbooks can be found at the market as well.

PIKE PLACE MARKET & THE WATERFRONT

No visit to Seattle is complete without several hours of wandering in the atmospheric market. For the compulsive browser, amateur chef, hungry traveler on a budget or student of the human condition, Seattle has no greater attraction than Pike Place Market. This is shopping central in Seattle: dozens of market food stalls hawk everything from geoduck clams to fennel root to harissa. (For suggestions on where to eat in the market, see p112.) Everything pertaining to food – cooking utensils, spices – is also available in the market.

The North Arcade of the market is mostly given over to craftspeople, who sell their own goods from tables and benches; this is a good place to pick up something that is uniquely 'Seattle'. Beneath the market is a maze of little shops which sell everything from comic books to crystals. If you enjoy browsing, you can spend hours here: the shops just don't end.

But sometimes you really want something utterly typical of the city, a classic souvenir. In Seattle, that could mean anything from a good selection of locally made crafts to local food products and regional wines. For the full gamut of souvenirs, you need simply stroll up and down the boardwalk along the Waterfront.

ANTIQUES AT PIKE PLACE
Map pp238-9   *Antiques*
☎ 206-441-9643; 92 Stewart St
This is a charming store for small antiques, including jewelry, toys and dishes.

DELAURENTI'S Map pp238-9   *Food*
☎ 206-454-7155; Pike Place Market
Even if you don't have a kitchen handy, shopping for food is great fun in Pike Place Market; you can channel your shopping urges

into buying local jams or syrups, hunting for obscure spices and condiments or picking out a bottle of local wine for drinking later. DeLaurenti's is a mandatory market stop for the Italian chef or Continental food enthusiast. Not only is there a stunning selection of cheeses, sausages, hams and pastas, but there's also the largest selection of capers, olive oils and anchovies that you're likely to find this side of Genoa. The wine selection is also quite broad.

EL MERCADO LATINO Map pp238-9 *Food*
☎ 206-623-3240; Pike Place Market
El Mercado Latino has a wide array of chilies and other products needed to make authentic Caribbean and Central American foods.

GOLDEN AGE COLLECTIBLES
Map pp238-9 *Toys*
☎ 206-622-9799; downstairs, Pike Place Market
A haven for geeks, kids, and especially geeky kids, this shop has comic book-inspired toys, novelty items (hopping nuns etc), costumes and loads of goth-style knickknacks.

GREAT WIND UP Map pp238-9 *Toys*
☎ 206-621-9370; North Arcade, Pike Place Market
This kids' heaven in the market has every wind-up toy and gizmo known to humankind, and then some.

JACK'S FISH SPOT Map pp238-9 *Food*
☎ 206-467-0514; Pike Place Market
Perhaps the gift that says I 'heart' Seattle the most is a whole salmon or other fresh seafood from the fish markets. All the markets will prepare fish for transport on the plane ride home, or you can just call and have them take care of the overnight shipping. In Pike Place Market, you also can try **Pike Place Fish** (☎ 682-7181, 800-542-7732).

Top Five Seattle Bookstores

- **Elliott Bay Book Company** (p168) Faultless selection, drenched in atmosphere.
- **Bailey/Coy Books** (p172) Smaller but extremely well-edited selection.
- **Magus Books** (p174) Used treasures in the U District.
- **Twice Sold Tales** (p173) Don't ask about the cats.
- **Left Bank Books** (see above) A light in the darkness.

LEFT BANK BOOKS Map pp238-9 *Books*
☎ 206-622-0195; Pike Place Market
This legendary bookstore/distributor is small but fierce, with an essential collection of political theory, off-center fiction and surrealist literature. A sign in the anarchist section humbly requests that, if you're going to steal books, you do it from a corporate chain store, not a workers-run collective.

MADE IN WASHINGTON
Map pp238-9 *Souvenirs*
☎ 206-467-0788; 1530 Post Alley
If you're looking for something more authentically Northwest than what most souvenir shops offer, head to Made in Washington.

MARKET CELLAR WINERY
Map pp238-9 *Wine*
☎ 206-622-1880; 1419 1st Ave
Market Cellar Winery, located at the southern end of the market, makes its own wine and sells do-it-yourself home brew kits.

MARKET MAGIC SHOP
Map pp238-9 *Novelty*
☎ 206-624-4271; North Arcade, Pike Place Market
Feeling enchanted? Stop by for magic and conjuring supplies.

MJ FEET'S BIRKENSTOCK STORE
Map pp238-9 *Shoes*
☎ 206-624-2929; 1514 Pike Pl
Feet's has all the latest in hippie footwear. Don't forget your try-on socks!

PETER MILLER ARCHITECTURE & DESIGN BOOKS Map pp238-9 *Books*
☎ 206-441-4114; 1930 1st Ave
This store, whose window arrangements can make a bibliophile or a design fiend drool, specializes in luxurious architecture books.

PHOENIX RISING GALLERY
Map pp238-9 *Art*
☎ 206-728-2332; 2030 Western Ave
Relatively inexpensive if looking for local arts and crafts. This place is right near the market.

PIKE & WESTERN WINE SHOP
Map pp238-9 *Wine*
☎ 206-441-1307; 1937 Pike Pl
If a present of regional wine seems an appropriate gift, check out Pike & Western Wine

Shop at the northern end of Pike Place Market. Its selection and friendly service make this a great place to get introduced to the wines of the Northwest.

SOUK Map pp238-9 *Spices*
☎ 206-441-1666; Pike Place Market
Supplies here include Middle Eastern and North African spices and foods.

SUR LA TABLE Map pp238-9 *Cookware*
☎ 206-448-2244; 84 Pine St
It's hard to miss this gigantic, excellent cookware store. It's a chain, but a darn good one, with books, gear and gadgets to entice any foodie, gourmand or gourmet.

TENZING MOMO Map pp238-9 *Apothecary*
☎ 206-623-9837; Economy Market Bldg, Pike Place Market
One of the coolest shops in Pike Place Market, Tenzing Momo, in the Economy Market Building, is a unique natural apothecary, with shelves of glass bottles filled with herbs and tinctures to cure any ailment.

YE OLDE CURIOSITY SHOP
Map pp238-9 *Souvenirs*
☎ 206-682-5844; Pier 54
Ideally, begin your souvenir-shopping foray at the landmark Ye Olde Curiosity Shop, on Pier 54. This is where you'll find all the best in goofy Seattle mementos.

BELLTOWN
Belltown's shopping runs the gamut from a punk-rock record store to the polar-fleece-happy Patagonia. Be prepared for anything, and you'll probably find something.

ELLIOTT BAY BICYCLES Map pp238-9 *Bicycles*
☎ 206-441-8144; 2116 Western Ave
Elliott Bay Bicycles aims more at pro or hardcore cyclists who are prepared to slap down big bucks for bikes. Custom-made bikes are a renowned specialty.

PATAGONIA Map pp238-9 *Clothing & Outdoors*
☎ 206-622-9700; 2100 1st Ave
The fashionable outdoor clothing at Patagonia may seem to be only for the very adventurous, but experience a sodden winter in Seattle and you'll understand why this is where the locals shop for rain gear and outdoor apparel.

SEATTLE CELLARS Map pp238-9 *Wine*
☎ 206-256-0850; 2505 2nd Ave
A good source for regional wines, Seattle Cellars can help you find gifts to take back home.

SINGLES GOING STEADY
Map pp238-9 *Records*
☎ 206-441-7396; 2219 2nd Ave
Singles Going Steady specializes in hardcore punk, hip-hop and ska, mostly in the form of 7-inch vinyl singles, as well as posters, patches and other accessories.

SEATTLE CENTER
NORTHWEST CRAFT CENTER
Map pp240-1 *Arts & Crafts*
☎ 206-728-1555; 305 Harrison St
The Northwest Craft Center is mostly dedicated to ceramics by regional craftspeople.

TOWER RECORDS Map pp240-1 *Records*
☎ 206-283-4456; 500 Mercer St
Seattle has some good specialty stores for recordings but, oddly, no locally owned comprehensive source for mainstream or classical music. For that, you need to go to Tower Records.

QUEEN ANNE
MOUNTAINEERS Map pp240-1 *Outdoors*
☎ 206-284-6310; 300 3rd Ave
For outdoor activities guides, the Mountaineers in lower Queen Anne has one of the best selections anywhere. In addition to books, it also has CDs, videos, maps and technical manuals. It also offers a range of outdoor courses; see p154.

QUEEN ANNE AVENUE BOOKS
Map pp240-1 *Books*
☎ 206-283-5624; 1811 Queen Anne Ave N
This cozy little nook is a good neighborhood bookstore, with special events and a nice selection of children's materials.

LAKE UNION
FEATHERED FRIENDS
Map pp240-1 *Outdoors*
☎ 206-292-2210; 119 Yale Ave N
Near REI, Feathered Friends stocks high-end climbing equipment, made-to-order sleeping bags and backcountry ski gear.

PATRICK'S FLY SHOP Map pp240-1 *Outdoors*
☎ 206-323-3302; 2237 Eastlake Ave E

Patrick's Fly Shop, located near Lake Union, has been around as long as anyone can remember. It offers workshops on fly-fishing, sells equipment and gladly gives advice.

REI Map pp240-1 *Outdoors*
☎ 206-223-1944; 222 Yale Ave N

The state-of-the-art REI store is right by I-5 south of Lake Union. This outdoor recreation megastore has become a tourist destination: the store has its own climbing wall; you can check out the rain-proofing of various brands of gear by entering a special rainstorm shower; or road-test hiking boots on a simulated mountain trail. You can get almost every kind of outdoor equipment and gear here, from hiking boots to kayaks, and pitons to bicycle tires. REI rents all forms of ski packages, climbing gear and camping equipment – call for daily/weekly rates. For more on REI, see p154.

CAPITOL HILL

Shopping on Capitol Hill makes you instantly hipper. Anything you pick up is bound to increase your cool quotient; just looking at the funky shops is an education in cutting-edge popular culture. This is the place to find great record stores, unusual bookstores, vintage clothing shops and fun, risqué toy stores.

BAILEY/COY BOOKS Map pp242-3 *Books*
☎ 206-323-8842; 414 Broadway E

This is a general bookstore with a good gay and lesbian section and a really classy, well-chosen supply of literary fiction.

BEYOND THE CLOSET BOOKS
Map pp242-3 *Books*
☎ 206-322-4609; 518 E Pike St

Beyond the Closet is the city's primary gay-focused bookstore.

DILETTANTE CHOCOLATES
Map pp242-3 *Chocolate*
☎ 206-329-6463; 416 Broadway E

If you have a sweet tooth to satisfy, try the confection truffles at Dilettante Chocolates. Great selection of desserts, too.

MARCO POLO Map pp242-3 *Books*
☎ 206-860-3736; 713 Broadway E

Marco Polo is a small, intimate travel bookstore; lots of maps and globes, too.

MULTILINGUAL BOOKS & SOFTWARE
Map pp242-3 *Books*
☎ 206-328-7922; 1205 E Pike St

Multilingual Books & Tapes sells materials in 100 different languages.

ORPHEUM Map pp242-3 *Records*
☎ 206-322-6370; 618 Broadway

The Orpheum is another source for cutting-edge local and alternative music. The second floor is stocked with vinyl.

Clothing Sizes

Measurements approximate only, try before you buy

Women's Clothing						
Aust/UK	8	10	12	14	16	18
Europe	36	38	40	42	44	46
Japan	5	7	9	11	13	15
USA	6	8	10	12	14	16
Women's Shoes						
Aust/USA	5	6	7	8	9	10
Europe	35	36	37	38	39	40
France only	35	36	38	39	40	42
Japan	22	23	24	25	26	27
UK	3½	4½	5½	6½	7½	8½
Men's Clothing						
Aust	92	96	100	104	108	112
Europe	46	48	50	52	54	56
Japan	S		M	M		L
UK/USA	35	36	37	38	39	40
Men's Shirts (Collar Sizes)						
Aust/Japan	38	39	40	41	42	43
Europe	38	39	40	41	42	43
UK/USA	15	15½	16	16½	17	17½
Men's Shoes						
Aust/ UK	7	8	9	10	11	12
Europe	41	42	43	44½	46	47
Japan	26	27	27½	28	29	30
USA	7½	8½	9½	10½	11½	12½

PLATINUM RECORDS Map pp242-3 *Records*
☎ 206-324-8032; 915 E Pike St

Platinum's the source for high-quality vinyl techno and various electronica – DJs comb its shelves constantly.

RED LIGHT Map pp242-3 *Clothing*
☎ 206-329-2200; 312 Broadway E

Looking for groovy stuff but don't want to pay a lot? Red Light sells a good collection of stylish, painstakingly selected second-hand clothes; you can also sell to them, but your stuff had better be good. Nearby is the less expensive but also generally less cool **Crossroads Trading Co** (☎ 206-328-5867; 325 Broadway E). Red Light also has a store in the **U District** (Map pp244-5; ☎ 206-545-4044; 4560 University Way NE).

SONIC BOOM Map pp242-3 *Records*
☎ 206-568-2666; 514 15th Ave E

This location of the local chain store has cool atmosphere and a wide selection of rock CDs.

TOYS IN BABELAND Map pp242-3 *Adult*
☎ 206-328-2814; 707 E Pike St

The delightful Toys in Babeland is a sex-positive toy store for women (looking for a glass dildo? You've found the spot).

TWICE SOLD TALES Map pp242-3 *Books*
☎ 206-324-2421; 905 E John St; 🕒 24hr Fri

Twice Sold Tales' Capitol Hill location is a rambling space full of used books; it stays open late most nights and never closes on Friday. Dinosaur heads and rockets stick out of the walls, and you'll likely see one of the store's eight cats roaming the rafters. Look for the bubble machine outside.

URBAN OUTFITTERS Map pp242-3 *Clothing*
☎ 206-322-1800; 401 Broadway E

If you're looking to fit in with the crowd on Capitol Hill, Urban Outfitters in the Broadway Market sells clothing geared toward young folks looking to score points on the hip scale.

VELO STORES Map pp242-3 *Bicycles*
☎ 206-325-3292; 1533 11th Ave

Velo Stores has a good selection of road and mountain bikes, along with a helpful staff.

WALL OF SOUND Map pp242-3 *Records*
☎ 206-441-9880; 315 E Pine St

This place, moved from its former location in Belltown, is one of the best things about Capitol Hill; it stocks music you've never heard of, from obscure noise artists to gypsy folksongs, but nothing the owners and staff wouldn't listen to at home. And the wall of magazines, zines, comics and small-press books is purely cream of the crop.

THE U DISTRICT

Shops located in the U District, not surprisingly, cater to youth culture and the student budget. Bookstores and record stores are the main thing here, although everyone should make time to explore the bins at Hardwick's Hardware Store.

Magus Books, the U District (p174)

Shopping – The U District

ALL FOR KIDS Map pp244-5 *Books*
☎ 206-526-2768; 2900 NE Blakely

Near the University District, All For Kids has one of the largest selections of children's books in town, and it also stocks a lot of children's music.

BULLDOG NEWS & ESPRESSO
Map pp244-5 *Newsstand*
☎ 206-632-6397; 4208 University Way NE

The newsstand of choice at the university is Bulldog News & Espresso. Terminals here offer Internet access at 50¢ for 10 minutes. The small monitors are no good for Web surfing, but if you want to check your email, they work just fine.

CELLOPHANE SQUARE Map pp244-5 *Records*
☎ 206-634-2280; 4538 University Way NE
Locally based chain Cellophane Square can special order anything.

CONTINENTAL STORE Map pp244-5 *Food*
☎ 206-523-0606; 5014 Roosevelt Way NE
By 'the continent,' they mean Germany; here's where to pick up imported foods, books and knickknacks. There's also a great deli.

DREAMING Map pp244-5 *Comic Books*
☎ 206-525-9394; 5226 University Way NE
If you recognize where the name of this store comes from (hint: Neil Gaiman), you will delight in the comics and graphic novels it offers.

HARDWICK'S HARDWARE STORE
Map pp244-5 *Cool Junk*
☎ 206-632-1203; 4214 Roosevelt Way NE
Locals in the know come to Hardwick's to explore the rows and rows of buckets filled with bizarre little gadgets and gizmos. Some people probably know what purposes these objects are meant for, but most shoppers are looking for things to use in their art projects. It's a hive of a place that's fun just to explore.

MAGUS BOOKS Map pp244-5 *Books*
☎ 206-633-1800; 1408 NE 42nd St

One of two great used-book stores in the area, Magus Books specializes in scholarly books. The other great one is **University Used & Rare Books** (☎ 206-632-3738; 4213 University Way NE), the place to look for tomes long out of print – you'll have good luck finding them here.

RECYCLED CYCLES Map pp244-5 *Bicycles*
☎ 206-547-4491; 1007 NE Boat St
Recycled Cycles, at the bottom of the U District along Lake Union, sells used and consignment bikes. It also has a wide selection of parts including cranks, forks, pedals, tires and tubes.

SATISFACTION RECORDS & CDS
Map pp244-5 *Records*
☎ 206-783-0222; 5214 University Way NE
This place sells goth-punk CDs in the Misfits vein and has a huge number of music videos and cult films crammed into its tiny storefront.

UNIVERSITY BOOKSTORE
Map pp244-5 *Books*
☎ 206-634-3400; 4326 University Way NE
University Bookstore is vast and all-purpose, though lacking in the time-worn atmosphere of many of Seattle's other bookstores. It does have absolutely everything, though. There's a smaller outlet **downtown** (Map pp234–5; ☎ 206-545-9230; 1225 4th Ave).

FREMONT
Fremont's quirky personality is reflected in the shops that line its streets. The antiques here are a little more off-beat, the arts and crafts a little more out-there, the bookstores a little more unorthodox. Again, it's a fun place to browse regardless of whether you're in the mood to spend money.

DELUXE JUNK Map pp246-7 *Cool Junk*
☎ 206-634-2733; 3518 Fremont Pl N
A local landmark, Deluxe Junk carries an interesting collection of, well, junk. But nice junk, retro and glitzy and sometimes fabulous.

FRANK AND DUNYA
Map pp246-7 *Arts & Crafts*
☎ 206-547-6760; 3418 Fremont Ave N
For funky jewelry and 'functional art' by local artists, check out Frank and Dunya.

FREMONT ANTIQUE MALL
Map pp246-7 *Antiques*
☎ 206-548-9140; 3419 Fremont Ave N
Weed and rifle through the junk at the Fremont Antique Mall – you just might find

a unique gift or something you can't live without.

FREMONT PLACE BOOK CO
Map pp246-7 *Books*
☎ 206-547-5970; 621 N 35th St
The Fremont Place Book Co is a friendly little place with a relatively small but interesting collection.

LOUD MUSIC
Map pp246-7 *Music Gear*
☎ 206-547-1981; 223 N 36th St; ☯ noon-7pm Wed-Sat
Another mainstay of the Fremont neighborhood, this friendly store sells used music equipment.

WALLINGFORD & GREEN LAKE

Some of the city's most interesting bookstores are in this area – don't miss Wide World Books & Maps, for travelers, and Open Books for anyone interested in poetry. And, of course, there's always the Erotic Bakery.

ASTROLOGY ET AL Map pp246-7   *Books*
☎ 206-548-1095; 1711 N 45th St
Astrology et al sells everything from horoscope guides to tarot cards.

CITY CELLARS Map pp246-7   *Wine*
☎ 206-632-7238; 1710 N 45th St
In Wallingford, there's no snobbery at City Cellars, which has great wines at reasonable prices. In the adjoining storefront, check out **Bottleworks Inc** (☎ 206-633-2437; Suite 3, 1710 N 45th St), which sells mostly imported bottled beer.

COMICS DUNGEON
Map pp246-7   *Comic Books*
☎ 206-545-8373; 250 NE 45th St
Nestled right between the U District and Wallingford, Comics Dungeon stocks a good selection of comics and graphic novels.

EROTIC BAKERY Map pp246-7   *Novelty*
☎ 206-545-6969; 2323 N 45th St
Lovers of sweet things should check out Wallingford's Erotic Bakery, where erection confections and other exotic desserts are made to order. Ask for a business card so you can mail

it home and shock a loved one. It also sells a few sex-toy novelty items.

GREGG'S GREENLAKE CYCLES
Map pp232-3   *Bicycles*
☎ 206-523-1822; 7007 Woodlawn Ave NE
Seattle's largest bicycle dealer is Gregg's, near Green Lake. It has a huge stock of all kinds of bikes and accessories and a very helpful staff. Gregg's also hires out bicycles; see Bike Rental p159.

OPEN BOOKS Map pp246-7   *Books*
☎ 206-633-0811; 2414 N 45th St 🕙 noon-6pm Tue-Sun
Open Books in Wallingford is devoted totally to poetry; call to ask about readings and events.

WIDE WORLD BOOKS & MAPS
Map pp246-7   *Maps & Books*
☎ 206-634-3453; 4411 Wallingford Ave N
Travelers will want to make a pilgrimage to Wide World Books & Maps. In addition to a great selection of travel guides, this pleasant store offers a full array of travel accessories and a staff of seasoned globetrotters. Watch for occasional slideshows and author events.

BALLARD

Ballard is a fun place to browse. Make sure to allow plenty of time for Archie McPhee's, especially if you have kids or enjoy pretending to be one. Another good children's store is Secret Garden Bookshop, where the selection of books for young readers is hard to beat. You can also pick up Scandinavian foods and knickknacks at several shops in the area.

ARCHIE MCPHEE'S Map p248   *Cool Junk*
☎ 206-297-0240; 2428 NW Market St
Famous for its mail-order catalog, Archie McPhee's is the source for all your weird gift items. It's a browser's heaven, and you'll almost certainly wind up buying something you never realized you needed.

OLSEN'S SCANDINAVIAN FOODS
Map p248   *Food*
☎ 206-783-8288; 2248 NW Market St
If you've had a hankering for authentic Swedish hardbread or Kalle's Kaviar in a squeeze

tube – and who hasn't? – this is the place to cure it. Olsen's also stocks Nordic-flavored knickknacks and gift items.

SECOND BOUNCE Map p248   *Outdoors*
☎ 206-545-8810; 5209 Ballard Ave NW
A unique store that has moved from its former location in Fremont, Second Bounce sells used outdoor gear, such as clothing, boots, backpacks and camping gear. This is a good way to save some money if you've decided on an impromptu hiking trip, but you don't have the gear with you.

SECRET GARDEN BOOKSHOP

Map p248   *Books*

☎ 206-789-5006; 2214 NW Market St

The children's collection, especially the fiction selection, is excellent here, and the staff will order you anything they don't have.

WILD SALMON FISH MARKET

Map p248   *Food*

☎ 206-283-3366, 888-222-3474

At the Fishermen's Terminal, on the south side of the Ballard Bridge, Wild Salmon Fish Market sells the freshest salmon and shellfish in town. The market also will ship fresh fish at very reasonable prices.

WEST SEATTLE
EASY STREET RECORDS & CAFÉ

Map p232-3   *Records*

☎ 206-938-3279; 4559 California Ave SW

This place has everything: rock-and-roll, coffee, beer, food...and even better it has an open, airy place to hang out while enjoying all of the above. Any place where you can shop for new import records, have a beer and then kick back on the couch for a while is bound to attract attention, and you might have to elbow some hipsters out of your way to grab that coveted album – just try not to spill.

Sleeping

Sleeping

Hotels in Seattle run the gamut from functional motor inn to incredibly plush places that make you feel decadent just by peeking into the lobby. Some of the finest accommodations are in older, restored hotels such as the Sorrento and the Fairmont Olympic. But there are also several options for slightly less expensive, equally charismatic hotels, particularly in Belltown and among the B&Bs in Capitol Hill. Seattle also has two great hostels, the gigantic Hostelling International (HI) facility – which is right in the middle of the Pike Place Market action – and the slightly grungier, but friendly and casual, Green Tortoise downtown. Keep in mind that the hostels fill up well in advance during summer, and sometimes throughout the year, so be sure to book ahead.

Parking is a major hassle in Seattle – it's been said that much of the population of Portland, Oregon, consists of people who couldn't find a place to park in Seattle, so they kept driving in ever-widening circles until they wound up in Portland. Downtown Seattle real estate is at a premium, and finding a hotel here with free parking is like discovering an extra $20 in your pocket while doing laundry. We've noted in each review whether the place offers parking; if there's a fee, it's noted after the Ⓟ icon. If there's no Ⓟ icon in the review, you're on your own for parking (you'll find street meters and paid parking garages downtown).

Lodging can get tight in the popular summer months, specifically July, August and September. During other times of the year, large conventions or special events can make finding a room difficult, especially if you want to stay in central Seattle. It pays to plan ahead when you're booking a room.

Hotel prices also soar in summer: midrange hotels cost $90 to $170 a night; classier hotels easily double that. But a few older hotels yet to be infused with renovation dollars offer cheap accommodations right in town. These offer good value and loads of atmosphere, but be prepared to book in advance in summer. The 'cheap sleeps' designation in this chapter ranges from $18 for a dorm bed up to $80 for a hotel room. The rates listed are what you

Top Five Places to Sleep

- Ace Hotel (p182)
- Fairmont Olympic Hotel (p179)
- Hotel Monaco Seattle (p179)
- Sorrento Hotel (p180)
- Moore Hotel (p183)

can expect to pay in peak season. Be aware, though, that prices can vary wildly depending on demand and whether there are festivals or events going on in town. Seattle hotel rooms are also subject to a variable room tax of at least 14%.

Options for out-of-season travelers are excellent. From mid-November through March 31, most downtown hotels offer Seattle Super Saver Packages. These rates are generally 50% off the rack rates, and they come with a coupon book that offers savings on dining, shopping and attractions. To obtain a Super Saver Package, or to get help finding a hotel when Seattle is all booked up, call the **Seattle Hotel Hotline** (☎ 206-461-5882, 800-535-7071). You can also get information or make reservations on its website at www.seattlesupersaver.com.

The **Seattle B&B Association** (☎ 206-547-1020; PO Box 31772, Seattle, WA 98103-1772) has a brochure listing B&Bs affiliated with the association.

DOWNTOWN & FIRST HILL

Most of the following downtown accommodations offer some kind of parking program with in-and-out privileges, but you'll pay handsomely for it, usually between $12 and $20 a day. If you have a car, you'll need to factor the parking fees into the cost of staying downtown. Instead consider staying near Seattle Center, where most lodgings offer free parking.

Hotel Monaco Seattle, Downtown & First Hill (below)

ALEXIS HOTEL Map pp234-5 *Hotel*
☎ 206-624-4844, 800-426-7033; 1007 1st Ave; r $250, ste with fireplace $460, d ste $725; **P** $20

A modern hotel tucked inside an old architectural exoskeleton, this place emphasizes quiet, high-quality service and amenities. The focus is on elegance rather than dramatic views or ostentatious glamour. The cool thing about the Alexis is that you can bring your dog for an extra $25; the staff will even walk Rover for you.

CLAREMONT HOTEL Map pp234-5 *Hotel*
☎ 206-448-8600, 800-448-8601; 2000 4th Ave; r/ste $145/190; **P** $18

An older hotel that hasn't lost its comforting vibe or become snobby through its restoration, the Claremont is well located, close to both Pike Place Market and the downtown boutique malls. Its suites are spacious and worth the money if you're traveling with friends or family.

DAYS INN TOWN CENTER
Map pp234-5 *Hotel*
☎ 206-448-3434, 800-225-7169; 2205 7th Ave; $80-135; **P** free

Rooms at this no-fuss, no-frills hotel, north of downtown toward Seattle Center, are spacious and comfortable.

FAIRMONT OLYMPIC HOTEL
Map pp234-5 *Hotel*
☎ 206-621-1700, Washington ☎ 800-821-8106, elsewhere ☎ 800-332-3442; 411 University St; s/d from $395/405; **P** $22

This hotel is unquestionably Seattle's doyen of old money and elegance. Imposing and luxurious, the Olympic was built in 1924, and subsequent remodels have worked to maintain the period glamour of its architecture. Until recently known as the Four Seasons Olympic, this 450-room hotel drips with opulence as bellhops, maids and concierges jump to your service. You'll feel like you've walked onto the set of an extra-suave Cary Grant picture. It's worth walking around the hotel even if you can't cough up the cash to stay here.

HOTEL MONACO SEATTLE
Map pp234-5 *Hotel*
☎ 206-621-1770, 800-945-2240; 1101 4th Ave; r $240-395; **P** $20

The exceedingly artistic and hip Hotel Monaco is housed in the old Seattle Phone Building, which sat vacant before the Kimpton group from San Francisco converted it. The spacious suite-style rooms are individually decorated and colorfully furnished.

HOTEL VINTAGE PARK Map pp234-5 *Hotel*
☎ 206-624-8000, 800-624-4433; 1100 5th Ave;
r $255-300, ste from $525; P $20

The rooms here are a little smaller than at some other downtown hotels and they get a bit more noise but it's a pleasant place to stay, especially if you get a west-facing room. The theme is wine; rooms are named after local varietals, and there's wine-tasting in the lobby every afternoon.

INN AT VIRGINIA MASON
Map pp234-5 *Hotel*
☎ 206-583-6453, 800-283-6453; 1006 Spring St, First Hill; r/ste $115/245; P $11

On First Hill, just above downtown near a complex of hospitals, this nicely maintained older hotel caters to families needing to stay near the medical facilities. It also offers quiet rooms to other visitors and has a nice rooftop garden with a view from First Hill overlooking the rest of the city. There are discounts if you are staying at the hotel for family medical reasons.

LOYAL INN BEST WESTERN
Map pp234-5 *Hotel*
☎ 206-682-0200; 2301 8th Ave; s/d $106/149;
P free

Slightly more plush than other options in the area, this chain hotel has a whirlpool and sauna, a small exercise room and complimentary continental breakfast.

MAYFLOWER PARK HOTEL
Map pp234-5 *Hotel*
☎ 206-623-8700, 800-426-5100; 405 Olive Way;
standard r from $190, ste $220-400; P $20

If you're coming to Seattle to shop, this is the hotel for you. Next door to the Westlake Center, it's also a good choice if you're going to take the Monorail out to Seattle Center for an event. The Mayflower was one of the first of the older downtown hotels to renovate and these days it doesn't quite match the class of more recent luxury renovations at other vintage Seattle hotels. Still, it's a very comfortable place to stay and is relatively good value for its location.

PACIFIC PLAZA HOTEL Map pp234-5 *Hotel*
☎ 206-623-3900, 800-426-1165; 400 Spring St;
r $110-135; P $16

The Pacific Plaza is centrally located, just a block from the Fairmont Olympic Hotel. Though small, the nicely remodeled rooms come with a big breakfast. There's no air-conditioning, so it's not a good choice in summer.

Top Five Views

- **Best Western University Tower** (p186)
- **Westin Hotel Seattle** (p181)
- **Hotel Edgewater** (p181)
- **Inn at Virginia Mason** (left)
- **Tugboat Challenger Bunk & Breakfast** (p185)

PARAMOUNT HOTEL Map pp234-5 *Hotel*
☎ 206-292-9500, 800-426-0670; 724 Pine St; r from $230; P $20

Although it doesn't look the part, the Paramount is a new hotel. Built with the elegant lines of a vintage historic structure, the hotel's 146 rooms are large and exquisitely furnished. The downstairs bar, Dragonfish, has a 'sushi happy hour' and is a great place to meet for a drink before hitting the town.

RAMADA INN DOWNTOWN
Map pp234-5 *Hotel*
☎ 206-441-9785, 800-272-6232; 2200 5th Ave; s/d $170/180; P $12

This well-located hotel is within the Ride Free Area, on the Monorail route and about equidistant from downtown and Seattle Center. The rooms here cater to the business crowd; it's a decent price for what you get, except that parking costs extra.

RENAISSANCE MADISON HOTEL
Map pp234-5 *Hotel*
☎ 206-583-0300, 800-468-3571; 515 Madison St;
r from $240; P $15; ⌘

Located in the former Stouffer Madison, this is one of the city's nicest hotels, with large rooms and a rooftop pool.

SHERATON SEATTLE HOTEL
& TOWERS Map pp234-5 *Hotel*
☎ 206-621-9000, 800-325-3535; 1400 6th Ave; ste $200-389; P $20

This is the best of the several large hotel chains with facilities in Seattle. It offers business travelers and convention-goers modern rooms with a wide range of amenities.

SORRENTO HOTEL Map pp234-5 *Hotel*
☎ 206-622-6400, 800-426-1265; 900 Madison St, First Hill; d/ste $250/280; P $19

Seattle's finest hotel when it was built in 1909 for the Alaska-Yukon-Pacific Exposition (after substantial and continual refurbishing, this beautiful Italian Renaissance-style hotel bejeweled with chandeliers and lined with mahogany, is again one of Seattle's best.

TRAVELODGE SEATTLE CITY CENTER
Map pp234-5 *Hotel*
☎ 206-624-6300, 800-578-7878; 2213 8th Ave; s/d $105/120; Ⓟ free
The rooms here are basic but clean, with free breakfast and friendly staff.

WESTCOAST VANCE HOTEL
Map pp234-5 *Hotel*
☎ 206-441-4200, 800-426-0670; 620 Stewart St; r $120-150; Ⓟ $15
The WestCoast Vance Hotel is another nicely restored older hotel in a classic European style. The hotel's 165 rooms aren't the largest in Seattle, but they're well appointed and comfortable. In winter, there's a special reduced B&B rate that includes a free breakfast.

WESTIN HOTEL SEATTLE Map pp234-5 *Hotel*
☎ 206-728-1000, 800-228-3000; 1900 5th Ave; r from $190; Ⓟ $20; 🖳 🕿
This impossible-to-miss, two-cylinder luxury business hotel has almost 900 rooms, some of which contain whirlpools and CD players. There's a heated pool, exercise room, gift shop, Internet access and a business center, and the restaurant, **Nikko** (p109), has great sushi.

CHEAP SLEEPS
GREEN TORTOISE BACKPACKERS' GUESTHOUSE Map pp234-5 *Hostel*
☎ 206-340-1222, 888-424-6783; 1525 2nd Ave; dm $17, s/d $20/45
The hostel will arrange free pickup at the ferry terminal or bus and train stations, and breakfast is included. Reservations are recommended.

KING'S INN Map pp234-5 *Hotel*
☎ 206-441-8833, 800-546-4760; 2106 5th Ave; $65/75; Ⓟ free
Just beyond the downtown core along the Monorail track, the King's Inn is a classic older motel that has somehow managed to resist the gentrification all around it. The walls are a bit thin and the rooms are incredibly basic, but the place is clean and a great deal, especially if you factor in the free parking.

SIXTH AVENUE INN Map pp234-5 *Hotel*
☎ 206-441-8300, 800-648-6440; 2000 6th Ave; s/d $80/110; Ⓟ free
There's on old-fashioned glamour at this motor inn just five minutes north of the downtown shopping frenzy. Though the décor won't win any awards, it's clean and ideally located, the price is right and there's free parking.

YWCA OF SEATTLE Map pp234-5 *Hostel*
☎ 206-461-4888; 1118 5th Ave; s/d $33/44, r with/ without bathroom $60/50
Seattle's central YMCA no longer lets rooms, but the YWCA of Seattle rents rooms to women.

PIONEER SQUARE
Options are limited for accommodations in Pioneer Square.

BEST WESTERN PIONEER SQUARE HOTEL Map pp236-7 *Hotel*
☎ 206-340-1234; 77 Yesler Way; s/d from $160/180; Ⓟ $15
This older hotel is one exception in the historic heart of Seattle. Recently refurbished it has some nicely appointed rooms, and nightlife, restaurants and shopping are just steps from the door.

PIKE PLACE MARKET & THE WATERFRONT
Unsurprisingly, the Waterfront and the Market areas are considered prime real-estate, and hotels here tend to be on the expensive side, but you can't beat the location – or the fantastic views.

HOTEL EDGEWATER Map pp238-9 *Hotel*
☎ 206-728-7000, 800-624-0670; 2411 Alaskan Way; waterfront r from $325; Ⓟ $16
Only one Seattle hotel actually faces Elliott Bay directly, and that's on the Waterfront at Pier 67. Hotel Edgewater boasts excellent views over Puget Sound. When this hotel was first built, people paid a premium to stay in the rooms so they could literally hang over the bay and fish from the windows. Times have changed, and fishing is no longer allowed, but if you came to Seattle to experience the tang of sea air, this might be the hotel for you. Prices are steep and range quite a bit, depending on your proximity to the saltwater. During rainy winters, room rates drop significantly.

Getting Up/Down to the Waterfront

A hint to those who plan to walk: Seattle is as hilly as a Hollywood starlet, and the area between Pike Place Market and the Waterfront is one of the most precipitous parts of town. There's an eight-story drop from the market down to the boardwalk. This makes for great views, but it's an exhausting climb or descent for those on foot.

To give your feet a break when walking up from the Waterfront, take the elevator in the parking complex to the top, cross Western Ave and look for the sign with a pointing hand; the elevator to the market level is just below it, and you can take this up to the market. On the return journey, take the well-hidden elevator behind the fish markets in Pike Place to the bottom, then head into the parking structure across Western Ave and take the elevator down four stories to the Waterfront.

If you'd rather walk, you can take the Hillclimb Corridor up many steps from the aquarium at the Waterfront; it exits out the back of the market's Main Arcade. The good news is that the entire trajectory is flanked by shops, eateries and potted greenery. You can also take the Harbor Steps, a landscaped cascade of stairs that sweeps up to below the Seattle Art Museum. In the middle of it all is the rotating Schubert's Sonata, a sculpture by Mark di Suvero.

INN AT THE MARKET Map pp238-9   *Hotel*
☎ 206-443-3600, 800-446-4484; 86 Pine St; r $190-380; Ⓟ $17
Right in the thick of things at Pike Place, the Inn at the Market is an elegant and architecturally interesting hotel and the only lodging in the venerable Pike Place Market. This 70-room boutique hotel has large rooms, many of which enjoy grand views onto market activity and Puget Sound.

PENSIONE NICHOLS Map pp238-9   *B&B*
☎ 206-441-7125; 1923 1st Ave; s/d $75/95; Ⓟ $10
In a town with few cheap hotels and hardly any B&Bs right downtown, Pensione Nichols, at Stewart St, is a treat. Right in the urban thick of things between Pike Place Market and Belltown, this charmingly remodeled older hotel has 10 rooms that share four bathrooms and a large

common area that overlooks the market. Rooms come with a complete and tasty breakfast.

CHEAP SLEEPS
HOSTELLING INTERNATIONAL – SEATTLE Map pp238-9   *Hostel*
☎ 206-622-5443; reserve@hiseattle.org; 84 Union St; dm members/nonmembers $24/26, r $54
Housed in a former US immigration station, Seattle's International Hostel is in a prime location at the south end of Post Alley, near the Pike Place Market and just above the Waterfront. This bustling behemoth offers 199 beds in 23 rooms, including family and private rooms. A large common area with a TV, kitchen and laundry facilities are provided, along with information on Seattle events, attractions and excursions. Reservations are essential in summer.

BELLTOWN

It may be surprising considering that Belltown is one of Seattle's hippest areas, but this is where you'll find some of the best hotel deals. The extra advantage is that some of the city's best nightlife and hottest restaurants are right outside your door – or, in the case of the Ace and the Moore hotels, right downstairs.

ACE HOTEL Map pp238-9   *Hotel*
☎ 206-448-4721; 2423 1st Ave; r $67-90, with bathroom $130-175; Ⓟ $12
If you're looking for the absolutely coolest place in town and the best value, you've found it here, above Cyclops at 1st Ave and Wall St in the heart of Belltown. Each of the Ace's 34 immaculate, artsy rooms is unique and so fashionable you quickly get the feeling you're the star of an art film. Rooms, which range from European style with shared bathrooms to deluxe ones with private bathrooms, CD play-

ers and enough mirrors to make you almost paranoid, are also stocked with free condoms and a copy of the *Kama Sutra*. Obviously this isn't the place for the uptight – it's also no good for light sleepers, as the always-hopping **Cyclops** (p115) bar and restaurant is just downstairs.

COMMODORE HOTEL Map pp238-9   *Hotel*
☎ 206-448-8868, 800-714-8868; 2013 2nd Ave; s/d $49/59, d with bathroom $87; Ⓟ $3
This large but modest hotel, a bit older these days, offers inexpensive lodgings central to

downtown, Pike Place Market and Belltown. The rooms are best described as no-frills, but there's nothing scary about them, and you can't argue with the rates. The hotel has a deal with two nearby city parking garages, so you only pay $3 a day, a big plus in this part of Seattle.

MOORE HOTEL Map pp238-9 *Hotel*
☎ 206-448-4851, 800-421-5508; 1926 2nd Ave; s/d $39/49, with bathroom $65/75

The once grand Moore Hotel offers 135 bedrooms, small and not fancy but refurbished with an understated elegance. The turn-of-the-20th-century lobby, with its molded ceiling and marble accoutrements, speaks of the building's long history, which is echoed in the better rooms (ask for one with a view of the Sound). Don't miss the great little lounge next door, the Nitelite, whose clientele are a mix of young hipsters and regulars at least as old as the hotel.

WALL STREET INN Map pp238-9 *B&B*
☎ 206-448-0125, 800-624-1117; 2507 1st Ave; s/d $120/135, s/d luxury room $140/155; P $8

Right in the heart of all the dining and nightlife is the Wall Street Inn, which follows the neighborhood tradition of converting space. The building used to be a residence for sailors in the merchant marine. Now the space has been updated into 20 large guestrooms, some with period details (including some original Murphy beds), others with kitchens or killer views out the back onto Elliott Bay. You'll find robes and slippers in the rooms, and breakfast is included. This family-run inn offers a cozy and cheery respite from the bustle of Belltown. Furnishings are sleek and modern – there's no rickety antiques here.

SEATTLE CENTER

Staying around Seattle Center makes sense for a number of reasons: It's only five minutes from downtown on the Monorail or bus (and just slightly more to walk), and room prices are usually lower than those downtown (except when big concerts or festivals are on at Seattle Center). You can also park your vehicle free of charge at most hotels, and that's no small matter in Seattle – it'll save you the cost of a nice dinner out.

The following accommodations are no more than five minutes from the action at the Space Needle. Most of the hotels around here are fairly anonymous, motor-court type lodgings from the 1960s, but they are in good repair and offer no negative surprises. Many also cater to business travelers, so they are efficient, but devoid of much character.

BEST WESTERN EXECUTIVE INN
Map pp240-1 *Hotel*
☎ 206-448-9444, 800-351-9444; 200 Taylor Ave N; s/d from $111/126; P free

In the shadow of the Space Needle, the Executive Inn has an exercise spa and a complimentary shuttle to downtown.

HOLIDAY INN EXPRESS Map pp240-1 *Hotel*
☎ 206-441-7222; 226 Aurora Ave N; standard r from $129, ste $159-200; P free;

The gigantic Holiday Inn Express has 195 rooms, an indoor pool, weight room and free continental breakfast.

SEATTLE INN Map pp240-1 *Hotel*
☎ 206-728-7666, 800-255-7932; 225 Aurora Ave N; r from $79; P free;

The slightly rundown Seattle Inn has an indoor pool, exercise room and spa and a children's play area. Be warned that the roar of traffic rarely ceases on Aurora Ave. Ask for rooms on the west side of the hotel.

TRAVELODGE BY THE SPACE NEEDLE
Map pp240-1 *Hotel*
☎ 206-441-7878, 800-578-7878; 200 6th Ave N; r $109-119; P free;

Quieter than anything on Aurora Ave N, this hotel offers amenities including a year-round Jacuzzi, seasonal pool, coffeemakers and complimentary continental breakfast (though it's fairly skimpy).

VAGABOND INN Map pp240-1 *Hotel*
☎ 206-441-0400, 800-522-1555; 325 Aurora Ave N; r $94-105; P free

Youth 18 years and under can stay free here when accompanied by their parents, which is especially great when you're trying to scrounge enough dough to send your herd up the Space Needle.

QUEEN ANNE

Immediately to the west of Seattle Center is Lower Queen Anne, essentially an extension of Seattle Center. It's only a five-minute walk from here to the opera house or Key Arena and a 10-minute walk to the Space Needle.

HAMPTON INN Map pp240-1 *Hotel*
☎ 206-282-7700; 700 5th Ave N; standard s/d $179/189, ste s/d $209/289; **P** free

A couple of blocks north of Seattle Center, the Hampton Inn has 198 rooms, most of which have balconies. There's a wide variety of rooms, from standards to two-bedroom suites with fireplaces.

INN AT QUEEN ANNE Map pp240-1 *Hotel*
☎ 206-282-7357, 800-952-5043; 505 1st Ave N; standard/deluxe r $99/109; **P** $10

This place is a 1929 apartment building-turned-hotel. Rooms come with kitchenettes and continental breakfast; or grab a complimentary apple from the bowl in the lobby. The only difference between standard and deluxe is that deluxe rooms have air-conditioning.

MARQUEEN HOTEL Map pp240-1 *Hotel*
☎ 206-282-7407, 888-445-3076; 600 Queen Anne Ave N; standard s/d $150/160, deluxe s/d $175/185, ste from $195; **P** $16

Another old (1918) apartment building, the recently converted MarQueen Hotel has hardwood floors throughout and a variety of rooms, most of which have kitchenettes leftover from their days as apartments.

QUEEN ANNE HILL B&B Map pp240-1 *B&B*
☎ 206-284-9779; 1835 7th Ave W; r $99-109

On Queen Anne Hill, just north of Lower Queen Anne and Seattle Center, a clutch of nice older homes now serve as B&Bs. One of the best in the city is Queen Anne Hill B&B, on the west side of Queen Anne. It boasts majestic views of the Olympic Mountains over Puget Sound. Common areas include a sundeck, sun porch and a nice garden. There are four guestrooms that are decorated with Pacific Northwest art and antiques; three of the rooms have private bathrooms. Parking is on the street.

LAKE UNION

COURTYARD MARRIOTT Map pp240-1 *Hotel*
☎ 206-213-0100, 800-321-2211; 925 Westlake Ave N; r with/without view from $200/190; **P** free; ♨

Over on the southwest side of Lake Union, the Courtyard Marriott has all the big hotel amenities, including an indoor pool and restaurant.

MARRIOTT RESIDENCE INN
Map pp240-1 *Hotel*
☎ 206-624-6000, 800-331-3131; 800 Fairview Ave N; studio ste from $200, 2-bedroom ste from $230; **P** free; ♨

If you're in Seattle for any length of time and price isn't an object, consider the appealing all-suite Marriott Residence Inn. A lap pool, exercise room and spa let you work off all those excellent Seattle meals. All rooms have kitchens, and there's complimentary breakfast and evening desserts in the lobby. Rooms on the west side of the hotel have good views of Lake Union. Again, rates here vary depending on whether you get a view or not.

SILVER CLOUD INN LAKE UNION
Map pp240-1 *Hotel*
☎ 206-447-9500, 800-330-5812; 1150 Fairview Ave N; rooms $150-185, with view from $170; **P** free

This hotel has 184 rooms, some of which have stunning views of Lake Union. There's also a gym, indoor and outdoor pool, laundry facilities and complimentary breakfast, plus a free shuttle service to downtown, a handy amenity in this area.

Interior of Ace Hotel, Belltown (p182)

TUGBOAT CHALLENGER BUNK &
BREAKFAST Map pp240-1 *B&B*
☎ 206-340-1201; 1001 Fairview Ave N; s/d $55/85,
Admiral ste $185; **P** free

If you think you know what life on a tugboat is like, then get ready to be surprised by the Tugboat Challenger Bunk & Breakfast. The tugboat's eight rooms are small but perfectly charming. It has a common area with a fireplace, and the excellent breakfast included in the rates makes this a good place to meet people and start your day. Several of the rooms have views of the marina and the city skyline across the water. Get to the tugboat by taking Fairview Ave N to the Yale St Landing; it's directly behind the TGI Friday's restaurant.

Airport Accommodations

If you're flying in to Sea-Tac late at night or out early in the morning, you might want to stay near the airport for the sake of convenience. The following hotels all offer complimentary airport shuttles and do a good job of getting you to and from the airport on time.

The no-frills **Airport Plaza Hotel** (☎ 206-433-0400; 18601 Pacific Hwy S; s/d $50/55) offers basic rooms. The **Days Inn at Sea-Tac Airport** (☎ 206-244-3600, 800-325-2525; 19015 International Blvd S; s/d from $87/91) has 86 rooms, a small gym and free continental breakfast.

If you're looking for something fancier, the **Radisson Hotel Seattle Airport** (☎ 206-244-6000, 800-333-3333; 17001 Pacific Hwy S; r/ste from $109/199) has 308 rooms, a restaurant, lounge, outdoor pool, gym and sauna. The free shuttle will also take you to nearby restaurants or car-rental agencies.

The **Wyndham Seattle-Tacoma Airport** (☎ 206-244-6666; 18118 Pacific Hwy S) has 204 rooms, featuring dataports (some with high-speed Internet connections), CD players and in-room coffee. There's a pool, whirlpool, exercise room and a restaurant/bar.

CAPITOL HILL & VOLUNTEER PARK

Some of Capitol Hill's lovely old homes have converted into beautiful B&Bs and, once you consider the free breakfast, location and cozy rooms, you'll see that you get a lot for your money. Seattle's unique B&Bs are dwindling fast, though; as housing prices skyrocket, many homeowners find it more viable to sell. Soon, B&Bs could end up going the way of the hostels.

Capitol Hill used to have a couple of hostels that gave budget travelers a choice for cheap digs on the Hill. They've both since shut down, and now inexpensive accommodations are hard to come by. You'll have to park on the street when staying at these places.

BACON MANSION B&B Map pp242-3 *B&B*
☎ 206-329-1864, 800-240-1864; 959 Broadway E;
r $94-154

Bacon Mansion, a few blocks north of all the action on Broadway E, offers 11 unique guestrooms, nine of which have private bathrooms. The rooms at this 1909 Tudor-style mansion include TV and voicemail.

CAPITOL HILL INN B&B Map pp242-3 *B&B*
☎ 206-323-1955; 1713 Belmont Ave; r $120-170

This cozy B&B, on the west side of Capitol Hill, is a 1903 Victorian home with seven rooms.

GASLIGHT INN B&B Map pp242-3 *B&B*
☎ 206-325-3654; 1727 15th Ave E; r $78-178; 🔊

The Gaslight Inn has 15 rooms available in two neighboring homes, 12 of which have private bathrooms. In summer, it's refreshing to dive into the outdoor pool.

HILL HOUSE B&B Map pp242-3 *B&B*
☎ 206-720-7161, 800-720-7161; 1113 E John St;
r with/without bath from $95/80

Close to the hub of Capitol Hill, there are seven guestrooms in this restored 1903 home. Five of the rooms have private bathrooms, and all the rooms come with queen beds and down comforters. Fresh flowers add a nice touch.

MILDRED'S B&B Map pp242-3 *B&B*
☎ 206-325-6072; 1202 15th Ave E; r $135-150; 🔊

Mildred's is a Victorian home across the street from Volunteer Park. There are four guestrooms, each with a private bathroom.

SALISBURY HOUSE B&B Map pp242-3 *B&B*
☎ 206-328-8682; 750 16th Ave E; r $95-149

Salisbury House is near Volunteer Park. This 1904 home's five guestrooms all have bathrooms and include a delicious vegetarian breakfast.

SHAFER BAILLIE MANSION
Map pp242-3   *B&B*
☎ 206-322-4654, 800-922-4654; 907 14th Ave E;
r with with/without bathroom from $145/79

One of Capitol Hill's most fantastic homes, the Shafer Baillie Mansion has 11 rooms, three of which have a shared bathroom. Most rooms have great views.

THE U DISTRICT
This area is another good place to find good-value rates at hotels and B&Bs. Accommodations here are also more likely to include free parking, as real estate is less limited than it is downtown.

BEST WESTERN UNIVERSITY TOWER
Map pp244-5   *Hotel*
☎ 206-634-2000, 800-899-0251; 4507 Brooklyn Ave NE; r $89-179; Ⓟ free

One of the best bets in town, the art deco University Tower, in the former Meany Tower Hotel, is also one of the classiest places to stay in the U District. The same architect who designed the Old Faithful Lodge in Yellowstone National Park built this hotel in 1931. Recent renovations have given it a face-lift, modernizing the hotel's 155 comfortable rooms while keeping them decidedly unfussy. The lobby and the downstairs bar and breakfast area are as plush, luxuriously appointed and comfortable to relax in as the rooms themselves. Rooms come with dataport phones, mini fridges and microwaves. There's an exercise room, a semi-happening bar and free continental breakfast. Most rooms have good views of Mt Rainier.

CHAMBERED NAUTILUS B&B INN
Map pp244-5   *B&B*
☎ 206-522-2536, 800-545-8459; 5005 22nd Ave NE; r with/without bath from $104/99

The 1915 Georgian-style Chambered Nautilus B&B Inn has six guestrooms decorated with authentic British antiques. The communal living room has a welcoming fireplace, and the full gourmet breakfast is reason enough to stay here. One of Seattle's first B&Bs, it's still one of the best. Its location – in a quiet residential area between the university and Ravenna Park – can't be beat. Rooms come with down comforters, bathrobes and voicemail.

SILVER CLOUD INN
Map pp244-5   *Hotel*
☎ 206-526-5200, 800-205-6940; 5036 25th Ave NE; r $110-125; Ⓟ free

This hotel has spacious, tastefully decorated, clean rooms and comfortable family-size suites. In-room coffeemakers, dataports, and an exceptionally friendly, capable staff make it an appealing choice.

UNIVERSITY INN
Map pp244-5   *Hotel*
☎ 206-632-5055, 800-733-3855; 4140 Roosevelt Way NE; standard s/d $105/115, deluxe $117/127, ste from $139; Ⓟ free; ⓡ

One of the best-value hotels in town, the University Inn is three blocks from campus on the north side of the University Bridge. It has 102 rooms that are ironically reminiscent of university dorms, which gives this friendly place a campus-like bustle. You'll more than likely join an interesting conversation in the lobby. Other features include a whirlpool, outdoor pool, laundry facilities and dataports on the phones. There's also a free continental breakfast.

UNIVERSITY PLAZA HOTEL
Map pp244-5   *Hotel*
☎ 206-634-0100, 800-343-7040; 400 NE 45th St; standard s/d $99/109; Ⓟ free; ⓡ

Off I-5 exit 169, a number of moderately priced motels near the university and only a few miles from downtown cater to the U crowd and people visiting the Wallingford or Green Lake areas. The 135-room University Plaza Hotel is on the west side of the freeway, not far from campus. There's a heated swimming pool, gym, restaurant and an antique Steinway player piano in the lobby.

CHEAP SLEEPS
COLLEGE INN Map pp244-5   *Hostel/B&B*
☎ 206-633-4441; 4000 University Way NE; r $45-85

The closest thing this district has to a hostel, the College Inn is a great budget option. The building, built for the 1909 Alaska-Yukon-Pacific Exposition, has 25 European-style guestrooms: these have a sink, but the bathrooms are shared. This is a friendly, no-frills place that's a perfect spot to hang your hat while visiting UW. South-facing rooms get the most light. Rates include a continental breakfast served in the communal lounge. Stair-phobes should be aware that the old building lacks elevators, and you have to climb four flights up a narrow stairway.

Excursions

Excursions

Seattle's location makes it ideal for getting out of the city with ease and exploring the natural beauty of its surroundings. With very little effort, you can trade that caffeinated urban buzz for a tranquil island retreat, an orchard-strewn valley or a rugged mountain peak – even all three.

Puget Sound, the sparkling jewel that surrounds Seattle, is dotted with tiny islands once dismissed as agricultural backwaters but now among the most popular tourist destinations in the area. Visiting the islands does take some planning in the summer months, when everybody else wants to be there too, but you'll understand why as soon as you start paddling your rented kayak or sailboat out on the water. The sparse population of many of the islands makes them ideal places for bicycle fiends. Or, if you prefer, you can always sit at a dockside pub and sip a microbrew while you watch active people do their thing. Most of the hotels, B&Bs and restaurants in island towns are open all year, so if you'd like to avoid the crowds, plan on an off-season visit.

Those looking to take their minds off city life with a serious physical challenge also have a couple of options. The most tempting is Mt Rainier, mostly because its pointy peak beckons from the horizon almost everywhere you go in Seattle. Reaching the summit is no picnic (p198), but the whole Mt Rainier area has an abundance of hikes at all skill levels and distances.

Climbing the summit of Mt St Helens is another option for serious hikers. Or, for peace and quiet, enjoy your lunch along the shores of Coldwater Lake at the base of the dramatically scarred mountain.

Drive a bit further and feel infinitely more distant from urban chaos by visiting the Olympic Peninsula. This remote area feels steeped in mystery – partly because of its thick, misty, moss-laden forests and partly because there is only one major road going through it. Combine the wild nature of the Hoh River Rain forest with the charm of Victorian-era Port Townsend and you might just accidentally forget to catch that flight home.

For those with less time and energy, the Snoqualmie Valley makes a quick and easy escape from the city. Its pastoral landscape, dotted with orchards and imbued with an eerie feel, is a lovely place for a leisurely drive. In winter it offers some of the area's best skiing.

ITINERARIES

ISLANDS

It's almost criminal to be in Seattle and not get out on the water. Puget Sound has some of the most gorgeous islands in the country and it's a great area to explore by ferry. An outing on the sound makes a relaxing day trip, whether you're going by car or bike or just on foot.

Bainbridge Island (p192) makes an easy day or half-day trip from downtown Seattle. Explore the island's main town, Winslow, with a stop at the local winery. Rent bicycles to pedal around the easily accessible island.

If you have time for a longer island-hop, start with Lopez Island (p195), the closest and most agricultural, full of pastoral charm. Then press on toward Shaw Island (p196), where the traffic-free roads are a bicyclist's paradise. And don't miss San Juan Island (p194) itself. Its fetching Friday Harbor (p194) is hard not to love; this is a fairly substantial town, so there are plenty of options for dining and sleeping. The picturesque farmlands just outside the town are close enough to reach on foot.

Windy Ridge

NATURE

Seattle has the advantage of being one of the few major cities with easy access to wilderness right outside its backdoor. Nature is as close as Discovery Park (p89) and Seward Park (p94), and there's plenty more where that came from.

You can get utterly lost on the Olympic Peninsula by delving into the Hoh River Rain Forest (p202), where misty trails meander through regal forests. At the end of your hike, play on the rugged beach and sleep in a working farmhouse (p202).

To see what happens when nature has a bad day, visit the Mt St Helens Visitor Center (p200). The site does an amazing job of displaying the terrifying power of a volcano. Dramatically situated observation points put you practically inside the crater that was blown out of the side of the mountain more than 20 years ago. The adventurous (and fit) can hike up to the crater's edge, though you'll need to book in advance.

OUTDOOR ACTIVITIES

It's hard to resist a visit to majestic Mt Rainier; after all, you've probably been gazing wistfully at it through restaurant and hotel windows throughout your stay in Seattle. Tackle the summit (p198) and linger in Paradise (p196) to mingle with the wildlife.

There's also great hiking around the infamously volcanic Mt St Helens (p200). For adventures on a flatter scale, the islands of Puget Sound (p192), as well as the San Juans (p193) have leisurely but spectacular cycling routes. The islands are also great for water sports such as canoeing and sea kayaking. For downhill skiing and snowboarding, haul your gear over to Snoqualmie Valley (p199). See more on outdoor activities on p153.

TIME TRAVEL

The well-preserved historic buildings lining the streets of Port Townsend (p200), many of them housing shops filled with antiques and Victorian knickknacks, make it easy to believe you've taken the ferry to another era. Fort Warden State Park (p200), where *An Officer and a Gentleman* was partly filmed, enhances the illusion.

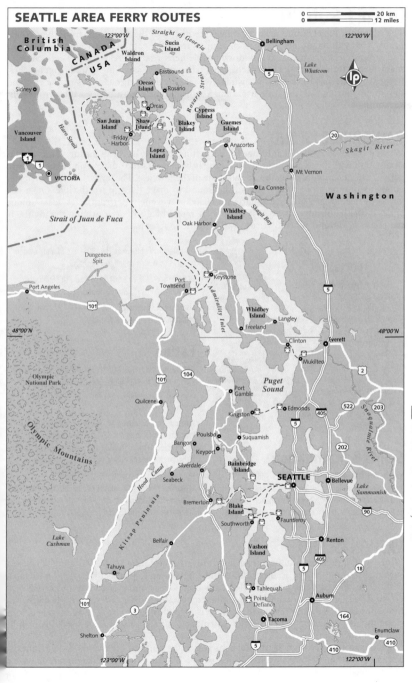

SEATTLE AREA FERRY ROUTES

PUGET SOUND

The islands of Puget Sound make a fantastic escape from the city. Aside from their scenic beauty – very different, despite their proximity, from the natural landscapes you'll find in and around Seattle – two activities draw people here: rest and relaxation. These come in many forms, from berry picking to leisurely cycling to wine sampling to lolling on beaches. Reset your internal clock to 'slow' while you take in the gorgeous views of the city and mountains during the ferry ride over, and you'll make the most of a vacation from your vacation.

BAINBRIDGE ISLAND

When it comes to visiting Bainbridge Island, getting there really is half the fun. It's a popular destination with locals and visitors alike, largely because it's the quickest and easiest way to get out on the water from Seattle. It's also one of the loveliest. The ferry ride alone provides enough stunning views of Seattle and the Sound to make the trip worthwhile. Once you get to the island, prepare to stroll around lazily, tour some waterfront cafés, taste unique wines at the Bainbridge Island Winery, maybe rent a bike and cycle around the invitingly flat countryside, and generally relax until it's time to ferry back.

Transportation

Distance from Seattle 9 miles
Direction West
Travel time 35 minutes
Ferry Washington State Ferries (☎ 206-464-6400, 800-843-3779; www.wsdot.wa.gov/ferries; main office Pier 52, Alaskan Way at Marion St) Vehicle ferries to Bainbridge Island board at the Washington State Ferries main terminal at Pier 52. Ferries run hourly in summer and several times a day in winter. Roundtrip fares for an adult/child during peak hours cost $5.70/4.60 and $5.40/4.40 at other times. A car and driver costs $9.50/12.50 and cyclists pay an extra $1.

Sights & Information

Bainbridge Island Winery (☎ 206-842-9463; ☷ tastings noon-5pm Wed-Sun summer, call in winter) This winery near Winslow is a good destination for cyclists, or for wine-lovers who don't mind a short walk (it's just 0.5 mile north of town on Hwy 305). It's a family-owned winery and is surrounded by vineyards.

BI Cycle (☎ 206-842-6413; 162 Bjune Dr SE; bicycle rental hr/day $5/25, 2hr minimum)

Chamber of Commerce (☎ 206-842-3700; www.bainbridgechamber.com; 590 Winslow Way E)

Eating

Café Nola (☎ 206-842-3822; 101 Winslow Way; mains $8-12) A visit to Bainbridge must include a meal at this popular café, serving a classy blend of Mediterranean and Northwest cooking.

Harbour Public House (☎ 206-842-0969; 231 Parfitt Way; starters $6-8, mains $8-12) After your bike ride, sit back and quaff microbrews at this public house. Seafood dishes, including the grilled salmon ($10.95) and a calamari appetizer ($7.95), are recommended.

Steamliner Diner (☎ 206-842-8595; 397 Winslow Way E; mains $6-8) Offering great home-style cooking, the Steamliner is especially good for breakfast.

VASHON ISLAND

More rural and countercultural than Bainbridge Island to the north, Vashon has resisted suburbanization – a rare accomplishment in Puget Sound. Much of the island is covered with farms and gardens, and its little towns double as commercial hubs and artists' enclaves. The island also provides unencumbered vistas of the Cascades, from Mt Rainier in the south to Mt Baker in the north. Vashon is a good island to explore by bicycle or car, stopping here and there to pick berries or fruit at a 'u-pick' garden or orchard. Plan a hike in one of the county parks.

Note that the ferry from Seattle deposits you in the north of the island, distant from the centers of Vashon commerce and culture, so you'll need to bring a bike or car, or have a lift arranged.

Transportation

Distance from Seattle About 10 miles
Direction Southwest
Travel time 25 minutes
Ferry Commuter-oriented passenger-only ferries to Vashon Island leave Pier 50, just south of the main ferry terminal, eight times a day on weekdays only. Fares cost $7.40/6.40 an adult/child for walk-on passengers. Car ferries also traverse the sound from the Fauntleroy Dock in West Seattle to Vashon Island. Fares are $12.25/15.50 off-peak/peak hours for car and driver, $3.50 passenger only from Fauntleroy.
Car Turn a visit to Vashon into a loop trip by taking the Tahlequah ferry from the southern end of the island to Tacoma, returning to Seattle via the mainland's I-5.

Eating & Sleeping

Back Bay Inn (☎ 206-463-5355; www.thebackbay inn.com; 24007 Vashon Hwy SW; dinner Wed-Sat from $12; r $110-115) Local home-style cuisine with an elegant touch is served a few nights a week, during summer only, in this delightful inn. For guests of the four rooms, the daily breakfast is a treat.

Emily's Café and Juice Bar (☎ 206-463-6404; Vashon Hwy SW at Bank Rd SW; mains $8-10) Light vegetarian fare.

HI Seattle/Vashon AYH Ranch (☎ 206-463-2592; www.vashonhostel.com; 12119 SW Cove St; dm $13-16, r $70-80) Budget travelers will be glad for this great hostel with bunk beds, teepee camping and rooms available in the summer; during the winter it operates as a lodge with private rooms.

BLAKE ISLAND

Blake Island is a state park and can only be approached by boat. This made it a safe place to host the 1993 APEC conference, where President Clinton met with 14 Asian Pacific leaders. Most people, however, go to the island to visit **Tillicum Village** (see below), which features the Northwest Coast Indian Cultural Center & Restaurant.

Sights & Information

Tillicum Village (☎ 206-443-1244; Pier 55 in Seattle; tours adult/child/senior $65/25/59) Tour package includes a traditional Indian salmon bake, dancing and a film about Northwest Native Americans. After the meal, there's time for a short hike or a bit of shopping.

Transportation

Distance from Seattle About 8 miles
Direction Southwest
Travel time Four hours (entire tour)
Ferry Daily departures from Pier 55 in Seattle from May to mid-October; weekends only the rest of the year.

SAN JUAN ISLANDS

The San Juan archipelago contains 457 islands sprawled across 750 sq miles of Pacific waters in the area where Puget Sound and the straits of Juan de Fuca and Georgia meet. About 200 of the islands are named and only a handful are inhabited. Washington State Ferries provides service to the four largest islands – San Juan, Orcas, Shaw and Lopez – while others are accessible only by private boat or plane.

Until about 25 years ago the islands were considered inaccessible and backward. Their patchwork fields, forests, lakes, sheep pastures and fishing boats setting sail from tiny rock-lined harbors were ignored by all but the fishers and farmers inhabiting them. Today, however, tourism is the mainstay of local economies: the islands are a major holiday destination without enough lodging to handle the crowds during the summer high season. And yet, despite the inevitable adulteration that 'discovery' brings, the islands retain their bucolic charm and make for a restful retreat.

Although many people come to the San Juan Islands for rest and recuperation, the outdoor activities are another reason to visit. The islands are small, largely flat and laced with deserted roads, making this a great getaway for cyclists. Sea kayaking is another favorite sport – the rocky coast and relatively protected waters make for a perfect environment to explore by kayak. Wildlife along the coastline – seabirds, seals and sea lions, otters and even orcas – is also abundant. Most marinas have sailboats for rent. Whale-watching trips are also popular excursions.

Keep in mind that many of the islands' beaches are privately owned, so your best bet for lying on the beach might be at a resort that owns some sandy oceanfront.

Lodging frequently fills up during the summer; don't even think about heading out without reservations during July and August or you may end up having to take the last ferry back to the mainland. Most reservations are made months ahead, and the most attractive places to stay are often booked even further in advance – but if your heart's set on a place, it's worth calling to ask if there have been cancellations. Accommodations are not inexpensive: you'll be pressed to find rooms for less than $100 a night during the summer.

Transportation

Distance from Seattle About 80 miles
Direction Northwest
Ferry Washington State Ferries goes between Seattle and the San Juan Islands; see each island's listing for details. Between the islands, transport is by inter-island ferries, which travel a circular route exclusively between the four main islands. Inter-island travel is $14 for car and driver.
Bicycle Bike-rental shops are almost as common as cafés in the islands' towns.
Car Rental cars are available in Friday Harbor.
Public transport There is no public transport on the San Juans, but most hotels and inns will pick up registered guests at the ferry if they are notified in advance.
Taxi Lopez and San Juan Islands have a taxi service.

Sights & Information

All Island Reservations (☎ 360-378-6977)

Harbor Air Lines (☎ 800-359-3220) Flights from Seattle-Tacoma International Airport to Friday Harbor Municipal Airport on San Juan Island.

Kenmore Air (☎ 360-486-1257, 800-543-9595) Flies to Lopez and San Juan Islands on seaplanes from Lake Union.

San Juan Islands Visitor Information Center (☎ 360-468-3663; www.guidetosanjuans.com; PO Box 65, Lopez, WA 98261) Great website with all sorts of useful info.

Victoria Clipper (☎ 360-448-5000, 800-888-2535) Ferry to San Juan.

Washington State Ferries (☎ 206-464-6400, in Washington ☎ 800-808-7977, automated information ☎ 800-843-3779; www.wsdot.wa.gov/ferries) From the mainland, car ferries leave from Anacortes and depart for the four busiest islands; not all ferries go to all islands, so read the ferry schedule carefully.

SAN JUAN ISLAND

Most visitors find that San Juan, of all the islands, offers the most hospitable blend of sophisticated amenities, rural landscapes and bustling harbors. A large part of the island's draw is **Friday Harbor** – with a population of about 2,000, it's the only real town in all the San Juan Islands. Even so, it's small enough to navigate on foot.

Most of the hotels and restaurants are either on or just off the main drag, Spring St, which runs uphill half a block over from the ferry landing. But follow any of the streets out of Friday Harbor and you're soon on a central plateau where small farms, dairies and lakes fill the verdant landscape.

The only other community of any size is **Roche Harbor**, on a beautiful bay to the northwest. The imposing complex included lime kilns, a grand hotel, a private estate, workers' cottages, a small railway, a company store, a chapel and a shipping wharf. The lime factory closed in the 1950s and the extensive buildings are now part of the Roche Harbor Resort.

Eating

Friday Harbor House (☎ 360-378-8455; 130 West St; mains $15-20) The intimate dining room has a fireplace and great views. The menu is small but tempting, with seasonal Northwest cuisine.

Front St Ale House & San Juan Brewing Company (☎ 360-378-2337; 1 Front St; mains $5-12) The island's only brewery serves up British-style beers in a real pub atmosphere. The food's good, too. Traditional British favorites like steak-and-kidney pie and bangers and mash keep good company with standbys such as chili, chowder and hamburgers.

Springtree Café (☎ 360-378-4848; 310 Spring St; meals $15-24) Casual bistro-style dining in a spare but comfortable café. The menu tends toward seafood and vegetarian dishes.

Sleeping

Blair House B&B (☎ 360-378-5907; www.slowseason.com/blair; 345 Blair Ave; r with breakfast $155-195, cottage $195) This woodsy, 1909 home has four rooms and a cottage.

Friday Harbor House (☎ 360-378-8455; www.fridayharborhouse.com; 130 West St; r with breakfast $225-325)

Transportation

Travel time 70 minutes
Ferry Anacortes to San Juan Island (Friday Harbor) during off-peak/peak hours costs $8.80/10.60 for passengers and $29.25/39.50 for car and driver. In summer the passenger-only Victoria Clipper travels twice daily from Seattle to Friday Harbor. In winter a weekend-only service goes from Seattle to the San Juans.

The most exclusive and whimsically elegant lodging in Friday Harbor. It's a modern boutique hotel with great views over the harbor; all rooms have a fireplace, Jacuzzi tub and other upscale niceties.

Inns at Friday Harbor (☎ 360-378-4000, 800-752-5752; www.friday-harbor.com; 410 Spring St & 680 Spring St) Two different lodgings separated by two blocks; the first is an older, well-maintained motel with a pool (rooms $130-170), while the second is a more modern complex with suite-style rooms ($140-290).

Lakedale Campground (☎ 360-378-2350; 2627 Roche Harbor Rd; camp sites $9, with car parking $26, cabins $45)

There are 73 tent sites, 10 sites reserved for cyclists and 19 RV sites, plus three tent cabins. This enormous campground is tucked into 50 acres of wilderness dotted with trout-stocked lakes (no license is required to fish, you just pay a fee at the campground). Canoe, paddle boat and kayak rentals are available.

Roche Harbor Resort (☎ 360-378-2155, 800-451-8910; www.rocheharbor.com; r from $85, ste from $160, cottages $229) Just about the nicest place to stay in all the San Juans. You can still spend the night at the imposing old Hotel de Haro on the resort's grounds, which has wide, ivy-covered verandas, and formal gardens. Refurbished workers' cottages, just a few yards from the swimming pool and playground, fill a grassy meadow above the harbor. Modern condominiums are discreetly tucked behind a stand of trees. In addition to the lodgings, there's a marina with boat rentals, restaurant, lounge and – on the dock – an old general store. You can even land your private jet on the airstrip.

San Juan Inn (☎ 360-378-2070, 800-742-8210; www.sanjuaninn.com; 50 Spring St; r/ste from $75/175) Another historic hotel that has been updated with modern conveniences without losing its Victorian charm, the San Juan Inn has several cozy, individually decorated rooms and suites.

LOPEZ ISLAND

Lopez is the most agricultural of the San Juan Islands and the closest to the mainland and has resisted the commercialization of its farmland better than the other islands. Here, pastures are for grazing sheep or hay-making – not merely the aesthetic backdrop for quaint country inns and B&Bs. If you want quiet, pastoral charm and don't need organized fun, Lopez is hard to beat.

Fields and pastures stretch across the island's central plateau, and the island gets rockier toward the south; near MacKaye Harbor, the stony fields and cliff-lined bay look for all the world like the Hebrides.

Eating

Nearly all the places to eat on Lopez are in Lopez Village; in fact, they practically constitute the village.

Bay Café (☎ 360-468-3700; mains from $12) The most noted restaurant on Lopez occupies an old storefront. Inventive ethnic seafood dishes headline the menu.

Love Dog Café (☎ 360-468-2150; meals from $5; ⏲ 8am-8pm Mon-Fri, 8am-9pm Sat & Sun) Sit on the veranda below the grape arbor and watch the boats in the harbor while munching on a hot deli sandwich.

Sleeping

Edenwild Inn (☎ 360-468-3238; www.edenwildinn.com; r with breakfast $135-175) Built to resemble a Victorian mansion, this eight-room inn is the most eye-catching building on the island, with lovely formal gardens, a wide porch and gables.

Inn at Swifts Bay (☎ 360-468-3636; www.swiftsbay .com; east on Port Stanley Rd; r with breakfast $95-185) This graceful inn offers a hot tub in addition to easy beach access and 3 acres of surrounding woods for solitude. To get here, look for mailbox No 856 and the banners hanging from the decks.

Transportation

Travel time 40 minutes
Ferry Anacortes to Lopez Island during off-peak/peak hours costs $8.80/10.60 for passengers and $22/29.75 for car and driver. Between the islands, transport is by inter-island ferries, which travel a circular route exclusively between the four main islands. Inter-island travel is $14 for car and driver.
Car Get to Anacortes by following I-5 north of Seattle for about 65 miles to exit 230. Take the exit and drive 20 miles west on Hwy 20 to the Anacortes Ferry Terminal.

Lopez Islander Resort (☎ 360-468-2233, 800-736-3434; www.lopezislander.com; 2864 Fisherman Bay Rd; r $80-260) South of Lopez Village, this is as close to a bona fide motel as you'll find in the San Juans. Across from the units is a bar and restaurant that gives onto a marina. All rooms have a deck.

MacKaye Harbor Inn (☎ 360-468-2253; www.mackaye harborinn.com; 949 MacKaye Harbor Rd; r $109-179)

Standing stalwart and white at the edge of a shallow bay near the south end of the island, this inn, a sea captain's home in the 1920s, provides bicycles, rowboats and kayaks for guests.

Spencer Spit State Park (☎ 360-468-2251, Reservations Northwest ☎ 800-452-5687; www.stateparks.com/spen cer_spit.html; camp sites $16-22) Five miles southeast of the ferry landing on Baker View Rd.

SHAW ISLAND

Shaw Island is the smallest of the San Juan Islands with a ferry service, and it has the fewest facilities for travelers. However, there is a good reason to disembark at Shaw, especially if you're on two wheels. The lack of an organized tourist industry means the island's roads are mostly free of traffic. The rolling hills are covered with sheep, whose wool plays a large part in Shaw's cottage industries – spinning and knitting.

The one thing that nearly everyone notes about the ferry landing at Shaw is that it is operated by Franciscan nuns. The nuns also operate the small general store and sell gas at the tiny marina near the ferry landing.

Sleeping

South Beach Park (☎ 360-378-1842; camp sites Apr-Oct $23, Nov-Mar $9-11) Run by San Juan County, this is basically the only place to stay on the island, with a dozen primitive campsites.

Transportation

Travel time 70 minutes
Ferry Anacortes to Shaw Island during off-peak/peak hours costs $8/80/10.60 for walk-on passengers and $26/35.25 for car and driver.

MT RAINIER NATIONAL PARK

At 14,410ft, Mt Rainier is the highest peak in the Cascades. The main entrance road, Hwy 706 (also known as the Nisqually–Longmire Rd), comes in through the town of Ashford, near the park's southwest corner, and follows the Nisqually River into the park. This route leads up to the **Paradise Viewpoint** and to the Paradise Inn (see Sleeping, later). Paradise is especially known for its alpine wildflower meadows, which are laced with hiking trails. Follow the Skyline Trail on foot for a good view of the **Nisqually Glacier**. All other roads to the park close down in the

Mt Rainier

winter, but this route is plowed as far as Paradise, which then becomes the setting-off point for cross-country skiers and snowshoers.

Some of the best views of Mt Rainier – with **Emmons Glacier** sliding down its face, **Little Tahoma Peak** in the foreground and the craggy **Goat Rocks Wilderness Area** off to the southeast – are from Sunrise. Sunrise's open meadows are scattered with trees and linked by hiking trails. Since it's on the mountain's east side, the Sunrise area benefits from Mt Rainier's rain shadow and receives less precipitation than the damp west side. It doesn't take long for hikers to become enraptured with Sunrise, which usually means you have to deal with crowds. Try to hike on a weekday and hit the trail early in the morning. Park naturalists lead a 1.5-mile hike each Sunday afternoon on a **Sunrise Goat Watch** from the Sourdough Ridge to explore the mountain goat's habitat. Get to Sunrise by following Hwy 410 east from Enumclaw.

For overnight trips, get a wilderness camping permit (free) from ranger stations or visitor centers. The six campgrounds in the park have running water and toilets, but no RV hookups.

Sights & Information

Bearfoot Backpacker (☎ 206-356-3347; 2115 E Mercer St; per person $95) Barefoot Backpacker runs an overnight camping trip to both Mt Rainier and Mt St Helens. The price includes all meals, park fees and camping gear. Trips leave from the HI Seattle hostel and from the Green Tortoise hostel.

Carbon River Ranger Station (☎ 360-829-9639)

Gray Line (☎ 206-624-5077; www.graylineseattle.com) Runs tours from Seattle at $54 per 10 hours.

Jackson Visitor Center (☎ 360-569-2211 ext 2328; ☺ May-Oct)

Longmire Hiker Information Center (☎ 360-569-2211 ext 3317; ☺ summer) Trail information and backcountry permits.

Packwood Ranger Station (☎ 360-494-0600)

Rainier Mountaineering (☎ 253-627-6242, in summer ☎ 360-569-2227; www.rmiguides.com; 3-day climb $770) Guided summit climbs.

Rainier Shuttle (☎ 360-569-2331) Runs between Sea-Tac airport and Ashford ($37, three daily) or Paradise ($46, once daily).

Road Conditions (☎ 800-695-7623)

Superintendent's Office (☎ 360-569-2211 ext 3314; www.nps.gov/mora; park admission per car/pedestrian/ pedestrian under 17 $10/5/free)

Sleeping

Plenty of accommodations can be found at Ashford, Packwood and Enumclaw. There are also two campgrounds near Longmire and one near Sunrise; for information on all thes campgrounds, call ☎ 360-569-2211 ext 2304. **Reservations** (☎ 800-365-2267; www .reservations.nps.gov; reserved sites on-/ off-season $15/12, unreserved sites $10) are strongly advised during summer months and can be made up to two months in advance by phone or online.

Hotel Packwood (☎ 360-494-5431; 104 Main St; s/d $29/39) This has clean, charming rooms and a mountain-view veranda.

Paradise Inn (☎ 360-569-2275; www.guestservices.com /rainier; r from $82; ☺ May-Oct) The grand Paradise Inn is a fantastic old log lodge on the mountain's south flank. Huge fireplaces anchor each end of the lobby, massive timbers hold up the ceiling and comfortable leather sofas and chairs face onto windows with views of the peak. **Longmire National Park Inn** (same contact information) is open year-round.

Mt Rainier Journal *by Rebecca Agiewich*

10am to 3pm

Hard to believe, but after a summer of preparation and years of procrastination, I'm actually climbing the second-highest mountain in the lower 48 states. Twenty of us, split into four teams, follow our **Rainier Mountaineering Inc** (RMI; ☎ 888-89-CLIMB) guides up the sunny Muir snowfield towards 10,000ft Camp Muir – our base camp for the night.

During breaks, we gulp air and admire Mt St Helens, Mt Adams, and Mt Hood sparkling to the south. None of them as majestic or dangerous as the big R, though. Tomorrow we'll see what Rainier is really made of when we rope up to cross three glaciers and hundreds of crevasses in a bid for the summit.

Did I mention I have a fear of heights?

Midnight

'All right everyone, let's go! It's a beautiful night out there!' The voice of Brent, our guide, shatters my restless dreams. It's a miracle I slept at all, stuffed into this creaky wood cabin filled with nervous climbers, forced into bed by our strict guides at 6:30pm. We're up instantly, and the cabin fills with the roar of rustling Gore-Tex.

1am

Five of us are roped up and ready to start. The night is calm, the sky a black velvet canvas splashed with glittering stars. The mountain looms above us, ghostly and ominous.

Headlamps, helmets, avalanche transceivers, crampons, ice axes, check.

'Ready?' says Brent. 'Let's climb!'

5:30am

13,000ft. Sunrise floods the mountain with pink and purple light. Behind me, an endless string of headlamps turn Mt Rainier into a twinkling Christmas tree.

From here, the best scenery is on the mountain itself. It's a wonderland of ice, snow and rock, with giant crevasses glinting cerulean blue, and seracs (box-car shaped blocks of ice) protruding from the Ingraham glacier.

Now that the rocky, treacherous Disappointment Cleaver – the 'crux' of the climb – is behind us, I can enjoy the view.

As long as I don't look down.

7:30am

14, 411ft. Planted on the summit of Rainier, looking down at western Washington, I'm so elated I can barely feel my heart racing from exertion and altitude.

I've gazed at this mountain with fear and longing for 12 years now. Circled it on foot, waved at it from my car. *And I'm finally on top of it!*

From here, it's all air and blue sky, with Liberty Cap, Rainier's northern summit, the only mountain nearby. The team poses for pictures, laughing and smiling, and I think, 'This is one of the best days of my life.'

9:30am

Or it will be, anyway, when I get across this freaking ledge. Vertical cliff on one side, crevasse on the other. Somehow this didn't seem as bad when we came up it, but everything is scarier on the descent. There's nowhere to look *but* down.

2:30pm

Back in wildflower-washed Paradise, we cruise towards the cars. Looking at our gear, tourists ask, with a hint of awe, 'Did you go all the way to the top?'

'Yeah,' we say, smiling modestly. As if to imply, '*It was nothing, really.*'

Seattle-based travel writer Rebecca Agiewich exaggerates her own bravery just slightly when writing about her outdoor adventures in the northwest and elsewhere.

SNOQUALMIE VALLEY

East of Seattle's Eastside, the Snoqualmie Valley has long been a quiet backwater of dairy farms, orchards and produce gardens. Although suburbs are quickly taking over the valley, there's still enough of a rural, small-town ambience to make for a pleasant drive or bike ride. Snoqualmie is also a popular ski and snowboard resort (p161).

Up the road, the little town of **Snoqualmie** has a number of antique stores and shops, including a store devoted to Northwest wines. The Snoqualmie and Tolt Rivers meet at John McDonald Park in **Carnation**, a great place for a picnic, a swim or a hike along the rivers. Carnation was once the center of the valley's dairy industry, and there are still a number of farms here. Stop by roadside stands for a basket of fruit or vegetables.

Further north, **Duvall** is far enough from Seattle to retain its rural small-town atmosphere. Wander Main St and check out the small shops and nurseries.

North Bend is *Twin Peaks* country, if you recall David Lynch's creepy hit TV series from the early 1990s. The former **Mar T's Café** in North Bend, now called Twede's, was the diner with the famous cherry pie and cups of joe; a fire gutted it in 2000, but it has been rebuilt and is still a good place for lunch or a slice of pie.

Salish Lodge and Spa (☎ 425-888-2556, 800-826-6124; r from $329) is a beautiful resort that sits atop 268ft Snoqualmie Falls. Many of the scenes in *Twin Peaks* were filmed in the lodge. Visitors can look at the falls from the lodge's dining room, or be more athletic and hike to the base along a winding trail.

Transportation

Distance from Seattle 31 miles
Direction East
Travel time 30 to 40 minutes
Car Follow I-90 east from Seattle. Exit at North Bend (31 miles), and get onto Hwy 202, which follows the Snoqualmie River north.

Salmon fishing, Snoqualmie Falls

MT ST HELENS NATIONAL VOLCANIC MONUMENT

On May 18, 1980, Mt St Helens erupted with the force of a 24-megaton blast, leveling hundreds of square miles of forest and blowing 1300ft off its peak. Slowly recovering from the devastation, the 171 sq miles of volcano-wracked wilderness can be visited as a day trip. Although driving from Seattle makes for a long day, the sights here are absolutely unique. For anyone interested in geology and natural history, this trip is well worth the expenditure of time. The whole experience even more dramatic for the contrast between the scarred mountainside and the gorgeous, shimmering Coldwater Lake at its feet – an ideal place to picnic.

If you're looking to hike Mt St Helens, you'll need to get a $15 permit ahead of time from the monument headquarters. The climb takes about four hours up and two hours down, though the difficulty changes depending on the weather. Be sure to check on conditions before heading up.

Sights & Information

Coldwater Ridge Visitor Center (☎ 360-274-2131; ⏰ 9am-5pm summer, 9am-4pm winter)

Johnston Ridge Visitors Center (☎ 360-274-2131; ⏰ 10am-6pm; adult single-/multiple-site pass $3/6, child $1/2) At the end of State Hwy 504, in the heart of the blast zone, this center provides views directly into the mouth of Mt St Helens' north-facing crater.

Monument Headquarters (☎ 360-247-3900) Issues hiking permits.

Mt St Helens Visitor Center (☎ 360-274-2100; just off I-5 exit 49 near Castle Rock; ⏰ 9am-5pm) Presents an overview of the site's history and geology.

Transportation

Distance from Seattle 120 miles (to Castle Rock visitor center)
Direction South
Travel time Three hours
Car Take I-5 South to Castle Rock; the Mt St Helens visitor center is east along Hwy 504.

OLYMPIC PENINSULA

The Olympic Peninsula is a rugged, remote area characterized by wild coastlines, deep old-growth forests and craggy mountains. Seafaring Native Americans have lived here for thousands of years. Only one road, US 101, rings the Peninsula. Although the highway is in excellent condition, distances are great, and visitors often find it takes a lot longer than expected to get where they're going. From Seattle, the fastest access to the peninsula is by ferry and bus via Bainbridge Island or on Washington State Ferries from Keystone, Whidbey Island.

Transportation

Distance from Seattle 56 miles
Direction Northwest
Travel time Two hours
Ferry To reach Port Townsend, take the ferry from downtown Seattle to Bainbridge Island ($5.10). At the ferry dock catch bus No 90 to Poulsbo ($1, 20 minutes), then pick up bus No 7 to Port Townsend ($1, 1 hour).

PORT TOWNSEND

Ferrying in to Port Townsend, one of the best-preserved Victorian-era seaports in the USA, is like sailing into a sepia-toned old photograph. The city experienced a building boom in 1890 followed by an immediate bust, leaving its architectural splendor largely intact.

Bonsai tree on a rocky outcrop, Olympic National Park

Beyond just strolling the main street and admiring the handsome town, one highlight is historic **Fort Worden State Park**, two miles north of the ferry landing.

Sights & Information

Coast Artillery Museum (admission $2; ☺ 11am-4pm daily Jun-Aug, Sat & Sun Mar-May & Sep-Oct)

Commanding Officer's Quarters (admission $1; ☺ 10am-5pm daily Jun-Aug, 1-4pm Sat & Sun Mar-May & Sep-Oct)

Fort Worden (☎ 360-385-4730) To reach Fort Worden State Park, which contains the Coast Artillery Museum and the Commanding Officer's Quarters (see above), go west from the ferry dock until you reach Walker St, take a right, and head north as Walker St becomes Cherry St, which takes you into the park.

Peninsula Taxi (☎ 360-385-1872)

Transportation

Distance from Seattle 140 miles (to Forks)
Direction West
Travel time About four hours (to Forks)
Car Hwy 101 circles the peninsula.

Port Townsend visitor center (☎ 360-385-2722; 2437 E Sims Way; ☺ 9am-5pm Mon-Fri, 9am-4pm Sat & Sun)

Washington State Ferries (☎ 206-464-6400; car & driver $8.75, passenger $2) It's 35 minutes one way to and from Keystone on Whidbey Island.

Eating

Landfall Restaurant (☎ 360-385-5814; 412 Water St; breakfast $5-8) This no-nonsense breakfast café, just inches from the Port Townsend marina, is full of locals starting their morning with one of the delicious scrambles ($5-7).

Sirens (☎ 360-379-1100; 832 Water St; mains $6-8) A dimly lit, romantic upstairs bar with a balcony overlooking the port, this is the perfect spot to have a burger and a beer and to wait for your ship.

Sleeping

HI Olympic Hostel (☎ 360-385-0655; olyhost@olympus .net; 272 Battery Way; dm $14-17) Within Fort Worden State Park in Port Townsend, this hostel has impeccable if spartan quarters in a former barracks; it's up the hill behind the Park Office.

Manresa Castle (☎ 360-385-5750, 800-732-1281; www
.manresacastle.com; 7th & Sheridan Sts; r/ste from $85/
105) The turreted, Prussian-style Manresa Castle, built in
1892, was later expanded to house Jesuit priests. The small-
ish rooms are decorated in a pretty, old-fashioned style that
suits the town. Even if you don't stay here, it's worth taking

a self-guided tour; check out the former chapel, truncated
to form a breakfast room and a banquet room.

Waterstreet Hotel (☎ 360-385-5467, 800-735-9810;
www.waterstreethotelporttownsend.com; 635 Water St;
r with/without bathroom from $75/55, ste $145) This
hotel in the center of town has loads of old-world charm at
reasonable rates. The suite has a deck over the water and a
kitchen. There's a brewpub on the first floor.

HOH RIVER RAIN FOREST

Isolated by distance and inclement weather, and facing the Olympic Coast National Marine Sanctuary, the Pacific side of the Olympics remains its wildest. Only US 101 offers access to its noted temperate rain forests and wild coastline. The Hoh River Rain Forest can get 12ft to 14ft of annual precipitation. Trails from the visitor center and campground, at the end of 19-mile Hoh River Rd, plunge into thick clusters of old-growth trees wearing furry green sweaters of moss. If you want to reenact *Lord of the Rings*, this is the place.

Transportation

Distance from Seattle 140 miles (to Forks)
Direction West
Travel time About four hours (to Forks)
Car Hwy 101 circles the peninsula.

Sights & Information

Forks Visitor Information Center (☎ 360-374-2531,
800-443-6757; 1411 S Forks Ave; ☺ 10am-4pm)
Suggested itineraries and seasonal information.

Hoh Forest Visitor Center (☎ 360-374-6925;
☺ 9am-4:30pm Sep-Jun, 9am-6pm Jul & Aug)

Sleeping

Hoh Humm Ranch (☎ 360-374-5337; www.olypen.com
/hohhumm; 171763 Hwy 101 near mile marker 172; r from
$35) Stay at the Waltons-esque Hoh Humm Ranch about 20
miles south of Forks, 57 miles from Neah Bay and convenient to the Hoh River Rain Forest and the Olympic coastline.
It's a B&B in a working farmhouse where balconies allow
you to gaze over riverside herds of sheep, cattle and llamas.
It's great for families. Cash only, shared bathrooms.

Directory

Directory

TRANSPORTATION

AIR

The quickest and most convenient way to reach Seattle is by air. Flights go into and out of Seattle-Tacoma International Airport daily (see below).

Airlines

Most major international and domestic carriers have a presence in Seattle. The following major airlines serve Seattle and offer toll-free telephone numbers:

Aeroflot (☎ 888-340-6400; www.aeroflot.org)

Air Canada (☎ 888-247-2262; www.aircanada.ca)

Alaska Airlines (☎ 800-252-7522; www.alaskair.com)

American Airlines (☎ 800-433-7300; www.aa.com)

British Airways (☎ 800-247-9297; www.britishairways.com)

Continental Airlines (☎ 800-523-3273; www.continental.com)

Delta Airlines (☎ 800-221-1212; www.delta.com)

EVA Air (☎ 800-695-1188; www.evaair.com)

Hawaiian Airlines (☎ 800-367-5320; www.hawaiianair.com)

Japan Airlines (☎ 800-525-3663; www.jal.com)

Northwest Airlines/KLM (☎ 800-225-2525; www.nwa.com)

Scandinavian Airlines (☎ 800-221-2350; www.sas.se)

Southwest Airlines (☎ 800-435-9792; www.iflyswa.com)

United Airlines (☎ 800-241-6522; www.ual.com)

US Airways (☎ 800-428-4322; www.usair.com)

FLIGHTS

In addition to the airline companies' own sites, which often offer Internet-only deals, a number of third-party websites can be helpful in finding you discounts on flights.

www.cheaptickets.com
www.expedia.com
www.go-today.com
www.hotwire.com
www.orbitz.com
www.priceline.com
www.site59.com
www.smarterliving.com
www.travelocity.com
www.travelzoo.com

Airport

Known simply as Sea-Tac, **Seattle-Tacoma International Airport** (Map p232–3; ☎ 206-431-4444) is the largest in the Pacific Northwest. It is located 13 miles south of Seattle on I-5. It has a daily service to Europe, Asia, Mexico and points throughout the USA and Canada, with frequent inexpensive flights to/from Portland and Vancouver, British Columbia. Small commuter airlines link Seattle to the San Juan Islands, Bellingham, Wenatchee, Yakima and Spokane.

Seattle-King County Visitors Bureau maintains an information booth in the center of the baggage claim level near baggage carousels eight and nine. There's a separate Japanese-language information booth near baggage carousel one. **Traveler's Aid** (⏱ 9:30am-9:30pm Mon-Fri, 10am-6pm Sat & Sun), on the ticketing level of the main terminal, provides assistance for children and elderly or disabled passengers.

Gray Line-Airport Express (☎ 206-626-6088; one-way/round-trip $8.50/14) runs every 15 minutes 5am to 11pm between Sea-Tac and downtown Seattle's major hotels. Shuttles leave from the north and south ends of the baggage claim area.

By far the cheapest way to get to downtown from the airport is by taking a **Metro Transit** (☎ 206-553-3060; one-way $2) public bus. Pick up bus No 174 or 194 (express) on the lower roadway outside the baggage claim area, near the taxi stand.

Shuttle Express (☎ 206-622-1424, 800-487-7433; downtown $18, neighborhoods $26) runs a one-way, door-to-door service 24 hours a day. Call at least a day in advance to ensure availability. No reservations are necessary from the airport; simply stop by the service desk at the south end of baggage claim.

Two **Thomas Cook** (☎ 206-248-6960) currency exchange booths operate in the main terminal. The one behind the Delta Airlines booth is open 6am to 8pm; the one behind Alaska Airlines is open 6am to 6pm. Another branch in the South Satellite is open 8am to 6pm. If your flight arrives after hours, you can get cash from the ATMs found throughout the airport.

To reach the airport Lost and Found, call ☎ 206-433-5312. For ground transportation information, call ☎ 206-431-5906.

BICYCLE

Despite its hilly terrain, a surprising number of people get around Seattle on bicycle, including a division of the Seattle Police Department. Motorists are generally not courteous to cyclists, so cycling through the city takes a certain amount of bravado. For both recreationists and commuters, the popular Burke-Gilman Trail (p102) provides the safest, most scenic and efficient artery through the city. This fabulous, mostly flat path follows an old railway bed from Kenmore's Log Boom Park on the Eastside to Ballard. The route skirts the University of Washington and travels through Gas Works Park. Cyclists jump off the trail and take either the Fremont or Ballard Bridges to get to downtown. Helmets are not required in Seattle, but it's highly advisable to wear one anyway. The quiet back roads of Bainbridge, Vashon and Mercer Islands are also popular places for bicycle outings. The **City of Seattle Transportation, Bicycle and Pedestrian Program** (☎ 206-684-7583) publishes an excellent map of Seattle's bike routes on paths and city streets. For more information on bike routes and rentals, see p158.

Bicycles on Public Transport

Metro buses are equipped with free bike racks; you just load your bike on before you get on the bus. Contact **Metro Transit** (☎ 206-553-3000) for instructions and bike-rack etiquette. Bicycles are also permitted on public ferries, although the number of bikes allowed per sailing is limited on passenger-only boats. Cyclists are usually loaded first and should wait for the ferry near the front of the loading area.

BOAT

Washington State has the largest ferry system in the US. The weekday commuter routes are usually busy, especially between downtown and Bainbridge Island. In summer, tourists pack the Edmonds–Kingston ferry. If you're driving, expect to wait up to three hours in line for peak routes (such as Anacortes to Victoria, BC) in summer. Walk-ons tend to have a much shorter wait. The price of tickets depends on distance traveled; most people buy a round-trip ticket up front. It's advisable to bring your own snacks, as ferry offerings are limited and expensive.

Clipper Navigation (☎ 206-448-5000; one way/round-trip $66/109) runs the passenger-only *Victoria Clipper*, which departs Pier 69 for Victoria four times daily in summer and takes three hours; the first departure stops at San Juan Island.

Washington State Ferries (☎ 206-464-6400, Washington ☎ 888-808-7977; www.wsdot.wa.gov/ferries) runs daily boats from Seattle to Bremerton (adult/child/car and driver $6.10/4.60/11.25, one hour); to Bainbridge Island ($5.10/3.60/11.25, 35 minutes); and to Vashon Island (adult/child $7.10/5.60, 25 minutes).

BUS

Seattle's bus system is thorough and efficient. Travel within the downtown core (bounded by I-5, 6th Ave, Elliot Bay, Jackson, Pine and Battery Sts) is free from 6am to 7pm. Otherwise, tickets are $1.25 ($1.50 during peak times of 6am to 9am and 3pm to 6pm Monday to Friday); pay when you board. You'll get a transfer stub, which is good for two hours. Be aware that drivers don't carry change, so have the exact amount ready. The bus stops are marked by yellow-and-white signs. Most buses run between 5am and 12:30am or 1:30am, but check schedules (at transit.metrokc.gov) to be sure.

Greyhound (Map pp234–5; ☎ 206-628-5526; 8th Ave & Stewart St)

Metro Transit (☎ 206-553-3060)

Quick Shuttle (☎ 800-665-2122; www.quickcoach.com) Quick Shuttle runs five daily express buses between Seattle and Vancouver, BC. Pickup is at Sea-Tac airport ($41) or the downtown Travelodge at 2213 8th Ave ($33).

CAR & MOTORCYCLE

Seattle is the hub of two major freeways. Interstate 5 (I-5) runs through the center of Seattle and links it with major cities south along the Pacific Coast, including Portland, San Francisco and Los Angeles. Northward I-5 goes to the Canadian border at Blaine (and continues into

Canada as 99). I-90 joins I-5 just south of downtown, providing the main link to the Eastside and to eastern Washington as it cuts across the center of the state to Spokane.

Hwy 520 links downtown with Kirkland and Bellevue via the 2-mile-long Evergreen Point Floating Bridge. I-405, known as the Eastside Fwy, cuts north–south through the suburbs east of Lake Washington.

Below are sample driving distances and approximate times for car travel between Seattle and nearby cities:

Destination	Distance	Duration
Olympia, WA	60 miles	1½hr
Portland, OR	172 miles	3hr
Spokane, WA	276 miles	5hr
San Francisco, CA	840 miles	15hr
Vancouver, BC	42 miles	3hr

Driving

No discussion of driving around Seattle can avoid mention of Seattle's sluggish traffic. In fact, studies show Seattle traffic is only marginally better than traffic in Los Angeles, which has the most hellish traffic in the nation. The bottleneck on I-5 rarely ceases and no amount of jaw clenching or dashboard hammering will help; you simply have to wait your turn. The backup is due in part to traffic heading over the two bridges to the Eastside and to the Boeing workers' shift-changes, which begin at 2:30pm. The average commuting speed in Seattle is 22mph and even when traffic is moving, heavy rains can make driving conditions nightmarish.

A few helpful phone numbers include:

Local traffic report (☎ 206-368-4499)

Seattle weather report (☎ 206-442-2800)

Washington state highway conditions (☎ 425-455-7700)

Parking

Parking is scarce and expensive in Seattle. Aside from availability, where you park also depends on how much you're willing to pay; $1 an hour for metered street parking or up to $20 a day for private-lot parking. Street parking or lots on the edge of downtown – especially in the International District or south of S Jackson St under the Alaskan Way Viaduct – are often cheaper, and public transportation can easily take you into the heart of the city. Unfortunately, these areas also have a bad reputation for car theft.

Metered street parking, available throughout most of downtown and surrounding neighborhoods, is the cheapest way to go, though meters are geared toward short-term parking needs and have designated time limits ranging from 10 minutes to three hours. Metered parking spaces are free on Sunday and public holidays and after business hours (7pm to 8am) Monday to Saturday. If you see a space but don't see a meter, look for 'no parking' signs or a colored curb. Red, yellow, white and blue paint on curbs indicates various parking restrictions. If there are no signs, and the curb is not painted, congratulations! You've just found a free parking spot. Parking fines range from $25 for an expired meter to $200 for parking in a zone designated for the disabled.

Attended parking garages are the most secure places to park but also the most expensive. City-owned public parking garages, such as the one beneath Pike Place Market, offer reasonable rates.

Many hotels charge $12 to $20 for parking in addition to the nightly room rate. Be sure to inquire about parking charges when making a reservation.

Rental

Typically, a small car will cost you around $40 a day or $200 a week. Be sure to ask if the rate includes unlimited mileage; if a rate looks like a real bargain, there is likely a per-mile charge after a certain distance. To rent a car, you must have a valid driver's license (even if you also have an International Driving Permit), be at least 25 years of age and have a major credit card. Return the car with a full tank of fuel; if you let the operator fill it up, the gas price will be much higher, unless you negotiate otherwise.

Most national rental car firms have booths at the airport. The following also maintain offices in the downtown area:

Avis (Map pp234-5; ☎ 206-448-1700, 800-831-2847; www.avis.com; 1919 5th Ave)

Budget (Map pp234-5; ☎ 206-448-1940, 800-527-0700; www.budget.com; 2001 Westlake Ave N)

Dollar (Map pp234-5; ☎ 206-682-1316, 800-800-4000; www.dollar.com; 710 Stewart St)

Enterprise (Map pp234-5; ☎ 206-382-1051, 800-736-8222; www.enterprise.com; 2116 Westlake Ave N)

Hertz (Map pp234-5; ☎ 206-903-6260, 800-654-3131; www.hertz.com; 720 Olive Way)

Rent-A-Wreck (Map pp234-5; ☎ 800-876-4670; www.rent-a-wreck.com; 2701 4th Ave S)

Thrifty (Map pp234-5; ☎ 206-625-1133, 800-847-4389; www.thrifty.com; 801 Virginia St)

TAXI

Probably due to the excellent transit system, Seattle's not the kind of city where you hop in a cab to get from A to B. Taxis aren't always easy to find in Seattle since they don't cruise the streets in the same way they do in New York. People in Seattle typically don't hail a taxi; when they want one they phone a cab company. It takes a while for a cab to show up, so be sure to order one at least 10 minutes before you want to leave. Taxis also wait for passengers outside large hotels, around Westlake Center (4th and 5th Aves at Pine St) and at the airport. Cab fare from the airport to downtown costs around $35. Drivers often expect a tip of about 10% of the fare.

Call one of the following:

Farwest Taxi (☎ 206-622-1717)

Graytop Cabs (☎ 206-282-8222)

Stita Taxi (☎ 206-246-9980)

Yellow Cabs (☎ 206-622-6500)

TRAIN

Amtrak (☎ 800-872-7245; 303 S Jackson St) provides long-distance service to the Seattle area. Trains depart and arrive daily from **King Street Station** (303 S Jackson St), where there are coin-operated left-luggage facilities and the Amtrak ticket counter. The most common routes and their frequency are listed below.

Destination	Cost	Duration	Frequency
Chicago	$217	2 days	1 daily
Portland	$23	3½hr	4 daily
San Francisco	$94	23hr	1 daily
Vancouver	$23	4hr	1 daily

Monorail

This 1½-mile experiment in mass transit was a signature piece at the 1962 World's Fair. The once-futuristic **Monorail** (☎ 206-441-6038; 🕑 7:30am-11pm Mon-Fri, 9am-11pm Sat & Sun; one-way $1.50) provides frequent transport between downtown's Westlake Center, Pine St at 4th Ave, and the Seattle Center. It runs through a purple slab of the Experience Music Project and stops at the Seattle Center

depot near the base of the Space Needle. Children love this two-minute trip. Cars run about every 10 minutes.

WATERFRONT STREETCAR

Seattle's old trolley system was dismantled in the 1940s, but one section has been kept alive. It is especially handy for visitors, as it links the area near Seattle Center (from the base of Broad St) to the Waterfront and Pike Place Market, and on to Pioneer Square and the International District. The vintage trolley cars, imports from Australia, stop at nine stations; the most northerly is at the foot of Broad St at Alaskan Way, about a 10-minute walk from the Seattle Center. The system ends in the International District, across from Union Station. Fares and transfers are the same as the city buses, but note that the streetcar is not included in the Ride Free Area. Tickets are good for 1½ hours after they're issued. Buy tickets as you board.

PRACTICALITIES
ACCOMMODATIONS

Hotel listings in this book are arranged by neighborhood, with 'cheap sleeps' listed at the end of each neighborhood section. The 'cheap sleeps' designation ranges from $18 for a dorm bed up to $80 for a hotel room. The rates listed are what you can expect to pay in peak season, though be aware they can vary wildly depending on demand and whether there are festivals or events going on in town. Seattle hotel rooms are also subject to a variable room tax of at least 14%. Hotels that include free parking are marked with a Ⓟ icon; if parking is available for a fee, the fee follows the icon. For detailed listings, see p177.

Seattle B&B Association

Seattle B&B Association (☎ 206-547-1020; PO Box 31772, Seattle, WA 98103-1772) offers a brochure listing the association's member B&Bs.

Seattle Super Saver Packages

From mid-November through March 31, most downtown hotels offer Seattle Super Saver Packages. These rates are generally 50% off the rack rates, and they come with a coupon book, which is good for savings on dining, shopping and attractions. To obtain the Super Saver Packages, or to get help finding a hotel when

Seattle is all booked up, call the **Seattle Hotel Hotline** (☎ 206-461-5882, 800-535-7071). You can also get information or make reservations on the website at www.seattlesupersaver.com.

BUSINESS HOURS

Businesses generally stay open 9am to 5pm, but there are no hard and fast rules. A few supermarkets and restaurants are open 24 hours, as are some gas stations and convenience stores like 7-Eleven. Shops are usually open 9am or 10am to 5pm or 6pm (often until 9pm in shopping malls), except Sunday when hours are noon to 5pm (often later in malls). Post offices are open 8am to 4pm or 5:30pm weekdays, and some are open 8am to 3pm Saturday. Banks are usually open 9am or 10am to 5pm or 6pm weekdays. A few banks are open until 2pm or 4pm Saturday. Hours are decided by individual branches so if you need specifics, give the branch a call. Many art galleries are closed Monday, as are most finer restaurants.

CHILDREN

Children get a lot of mileage out of **Seattle Center** (p61), home to the Seattle Children's Theatre, the Children's Museum, the Space Needle, the Monorail, an amusement park and the Pacific Science Center. The Seattle Children's Theatre presents six mainstage productions a year between June and September. Kids also enjoy the **Woodland Park Zoo** (p86), where animals roam free in large enclosures that simulate their natural environments. Ferry rides to and from Puget Sound islands are also a big hit with children.

Children less than five years old ride free on any Metro Transit bus. When making hotel reservations, inquire if there are special family discounts. Often hotels and motels let young children stay free.

A good addition to this general guidebook is the *Lobster Kids' Guide to Exploring Seattle* by Shelley Arenas and Cheryl Murfin Bond. For general information on enjoying travel with young ones, read Lonely Planet's *Travel with Children* by Cathy Lanigan.

CLIMATE

Yes, it does rain a lot in Seattle, but the temperature stays mild most of the year. Most travelers choose to visit in the summer and fall, when the weather is pleasant and the

rainfall less frequent – the city gets 65% of its precipitation from November to March. September and October often see gorgeous Indian summer weather. December, January and February can be miserable – though they're ideal for winter sports like skiing and snowboarding (p160).

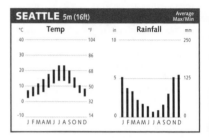

CUSTOMS

US customs allows each person over the age of 21 to bring one liter of liquor and 200 cigarettes duty free into the USA. Non-US citizens are allowed to bring in $100 worth of gifts from abroad; US citizens are allowed $400 worth. US law permits you to bring in, or take out, as much as $10,000 in US or foreign cash, traveler's checks or money orders without formality. Larger amounts of any or all of the above – there are no limits – must be declared to customs. For more information visit the website www.customs.gov/travel/travel.htm.

DISABLED TRAVELERS

All public buildings (including hotels, restaurants, theaters and museums) are required by law to provide wheelchair access and to have available restroom facilities. Telephone companies provide relay operators for the hearing impaired. Many banks provide ATM instructions in Braille. Dropped curbs are standard at intersections throughout the city.

Around 80% of Metro's buses are equipped with wheelchair lifts. Timetables marked with an 'L' indicate wheelchair accessibility. Be sure to let the driver know if you need your stop to be called and, if possible, pull the cord when you hear the call. Seeing-eye dogs are allowed on Metro buses. Disabled passengers qualify for a reduced fare but need to first contact **Metro** (☎ 206-553-3060, 684-2029 TTY) for a permit. See the Metro Transit map (p250) for wheelchair-accessible stops and stations.

Larger private and chain hotels have suites for disabled guests. Many car-rental agencies offer hand-controlled models at no extra charge; just make sure you give at least two days' notice. All major airlines, Greyhound buses and Amtrak trains allow seeing-eye dogs to accompany passengers and often sell two-for-one packages when attendants of seriously disabled passengers are required. Airlines will also provide assistance for connecting, boarding and disembarking the flight – just ask for assistance when making your reservation.

The following organizations and tour providers specialize in the needs of disabled travelers:

Access-Able Travel Service (www.access-able.com) Packed full of information, with tips on scooter rental, wheelchair travel, accessible transportation and more.

Easter Seal Society of Washington (☎ 206-281-5700; 521 2nd Ave W) Publishes the *Accessibility Handbook*, a very thorough guide to accessible businesses and programs; it costs $50.

Mobility International USA (☎ 541-343-1284, fax 541-343-6812; PO Box 10767, Eugene, OR 97440)

Moss Rehabilitation Hospital's Travel Information Service (☎ 215-456-9600, TTY 215-456-9602; 1200 W Tabor Rd, Philadelphia, PA 19141-3099)

Society for the Advancement of Travel for the Handicapped (☎ 212-447-7284; 347 Fifth Ave No 610, New York, NY 10016)

Twin Peaks Press (☎ 360-694-2462, 800-637-2256; PO Box 129, Vancouver, WA, 98666) Publishes a quarterly newsletter, directories and access guides.

DISCOUNT CARDS

If you're going to be in Seattle for a while and plan on seeing its premiere attractions, you might want to consider buying a CityPass. Good for nine days, the pass gets you entry into the Space Needle, Pacific Science Center, Seattle Aquarium, Argosy Cruises' Seattle Harbor Tour, the Museum of Flight and the Woodland Park Zoo. You wind up saving 50% of admission costs and you never have to stand in line. A CityPass costs $42/29 for an adult/child aged four to 13. You can buy one at whichever of the six venues you visit first or online at www.citypass.net.

ELECTRICITY

In the USA and Canada, voltage is 110V and the plugs have two (flat) or three (two flat, one round) pins. Plugs with three pins don't fit into a two-hole socket, but inexpensive adapters are widely available at drugstores, hardware stores and consumer electronics stores like Radio Shack.

EMBASSIES & CONSULATES

To find US embassies in other countries, visit the website usembassy.state.gov. Check the Yellow Pages under 'Consulates' for diplomatic representation in Seattle. For directory assistance with embassies and consulates outside Seattle, call ☎ 202-555-1212. Consulates include:

Austria (Map pp234-5; ☎ 206-624-9887; 1111 3rd Ave, Suite 2626)

Belgium (Map pp234-5; ☎ 206-728-5145; 2200 Alaskan Way)

Canada (Map pp234-5; ☎ 206-443-1372; Plaza 600, 600 Stewart St)

Denmark (Map pp232-3; ☎ 206-230-0888; 6204 E Mercer Way, Mercer Island)

Estonia (Map pp234-5; ☎ 206-467-6314; 500 Union St, Suite 930)

France (Map pp234-5; ☎ 206-256-6184; 2200 Alaskan Way, Suite 490)

Germany (Map pp234-5; ☎ 206-682-4312; 600 University St, Suite 2500)

Guatemala (Map pp234-5; ☎ 206-728-5920; 2001 6th Ave, Suite 3300)

Italy (Map pp232-3; ☎ 425-485-8626; 23732 Bothell-Everett Hwy, Bothell)

Japan (Map pp234-5; ☎ 206-682-9107; 601 Union St)

Korea (Map pp234-5; ☎ 206-441-1011; 2033 6th Ave)

Mexico (Map pp234-5; ☎ 206-448-3526; 2132 3rd Ave)

New Zealand (Map pp244-5; ☎ 206-525-9881; 6810 51st Ave NE)

Russia (Map pp234-5; ☎ 206-728-1910; 2001 6th Ave, Westin Bldg, Suite 2323)

Sweden (Map pp234-5; ☎ 206-622-5640; 1215 4th Ave)

UK (Map pp234-5; ☎ 206-622-9255; 900 4th Ave)

EMERGENCY

For all emergencies (police, ambulance, fire), call ☎ 911. Other useful numbers include:

Community Info Line (☎ 206-461-3200) Information on emergency services, housing and legal advice etc.

Seattle Police (☎ 206-625-5011)

Seattle Rape Relief (☎ 206-632-7273)

Washington State Patrol (☎ 425-649-4370)

GAY & LESBIAN TRAVELERS

Although Seattle is liberal-minded and accepting of alternative lifestyles, much of the rural Northwest is far more conservative. Travelers should be aware of this if they're planning excursions to outlying areas.

Capitol Hill (p75), with its unmatched vitality and creativity, is Seattle's principal gay and lesbian neighborhood. Nightclubs and bars are found along Pine and Pike Sts and along Broadway.

Useful resources include the following:

Bailey/Coy Books (Map pp242-3; ☎ 206-323-8842; 414 Broadway Ave E)

Beyond the Closet Bookstore (Map pp242-3; ☎ 206-322-4609; 518 E Pike St at Belmont Ave)

Gay/Lesbian Business Association (☎ 206-363-9188)

GSBA Guide & Directory You can pick up the directory at any of the participating gay-friendly businesses; for a list of participating businesses, contact the Gay/Lesbian Business Association.

Lambda Legal Defense Fund (New York City ☎ 212-995-8585, Los Angeles ☎ 213-937-2728) The number to call if you need legal counsel on an issue relating to your sexual orientation, or if you've been the victim of a hate crime.

Lesbian & Gay Pink Pages This listing of gay-friendly businesses can be picked up free at any of the listed businesses or by contacting the Business Association (☎ 206-363-9188).

Lesbian Resource Center (Map p249; ☎ 206-322-3953; 2214 S Jackson St) Provides social, housing, employment and other support services.

National Gay/Lesbian Task Force (☎ 202-332-6483; 1700 Kalorama Rd NW, Washington DC) A political organization that pushes for same-sex marriage and other gay-rights issues.

Seattle Counseling Service for Sexual Minorities (☎ 206-323-1768)

Seattle Gay News (☎ 206-324-4297) You can pick it up at most Capitol Hill bars and restaurants.

GUIDEBOOKS

The *Seattle Survival Guide* by Theresa Morrow is full of insider information about local services, businesses, schools, housing, cultural organizations and clubs, and it is a good resource for anyone putting roots down in Seattle. Another good relocation guide is *Newcomer's Handbook for Seattle*. Morton Beebe captures the spirit and history of two of the Pacific Northwest's most fascinating cities in *Cascadia: A Tale of Seattle and Vancouver, BC*.

If you're planning to explore beyond Seattle itself, grab a copy of Lonely Planet's *Pacific Northwest*, which covers Oregon, Washington, Vancouver and Vancouver Island. If you're heading north from Seattle, Lonely Planet's *British Columbia* covers the entire province and the Alberta Rockies.

Outdoorsy types should look for Stephen Whitney's *Nature Walks in and Around Seattle*, and visitors to the San Juan Islands should check out Marge and Ted Mueller's *The San Juan Islands Afoot and Afloat* for camping, trails and water activities on the San Juans. Travelers on bikes will want to pick up Lonely Planet's *Cycling West Coast USA*, and anyone trekking into the mountains should check out Lonely Planet's *Hiking USA*.

HOLIDAYS

For a calendar of Seattle events and holidays, see p8.

INTERNET ACCESS

Seattle's a high-tech town. Email and Internet access is as important to Seattleites as a good pair of shoes. As such, most business and top-end hotels offer high-speed modem connections, usually dataports on telephones. Be aware that your modem may not work once you leave your home country. For more information on traveling with a portable computer, see www.teleadapt.com.

For those traveling without hardware, stop by one of Seattle's public libraries, all of which are equipped to allow web-browsing and access to chat groups. Coffee houses throughout town also have Internet terminals for public use, including:

CapitolHill.net (Map pp242-3; ☎ 206-860-6858; 219 Broadway E; ⏱ 8am-midnight; per hr $6)

Online Coffee Company (Map pp242-3; ☎ 206-328-3713; 1720 Olive Way; ⏱ 8am-midnight; per hr $6)

LEGAL MATTERS

For the most part, police in Seattle are friendly and helpful, and you shouldn't expect a run-in during your visit. Drinking outdoors is prohibited, though drinking beer or wine is often permissible at street fairs or other events where vendors have obtained permits. Police in Seattle are surprisingly strict about jaywalking. Bumbling around drunk in the street is another way to attract police attention, and if you're drunk and obnoxious you could find yourself 'sleeping it off' in jail.

If you are stopped by the police for any reason, bear in mind that under no circumstances do you need to pay fines on the spot. If you are arrested for serious offenses, it is your right to remain silent until you've obtained legal advice. You are not legally bound to speak to a police officer, but never walk away from an officer until given permission, or they'll assume you're looking for trouble. Anyone who gets arrested gets the right to make one phone call. If you don't have a lawyer or family member to help you, call your embassy (p209); the police will give you the number upon request.

The drinking age is 21 in the US, and you need identification (ID) with your photograph on it to prove your age. Don't get caught driving under the influence of alcohol, or you'll get slammed with a Driving Under the Influence (DUI), which can result in stiff fines and jail time. A blood-alcohol reading of 0.08% or above is illegal, which loosely translates to about two drinks maximum in an average person. During festive holidays and special events, roadblocks are sometimes set up to deter drunk drivers.

MAPS

Seattle is a potentially challenging place to get around in, so it's a good idea to invest in a detailed map and to spend some time getting familiar with how the city is laid out before setting out, especially in a car. If you're not driving and only in town for a couple of days, the free maps given out by the tourist office will help you enough to get around downtown. There is a Downtown Metro Transit map on p250. You can also get transit information at the **main public library** (4th Ave at Madison St).

Streetwise Seattle is a handy laminated map that's easy to use while driving. Other good maps include *Thomas Brothers Atlas of King County* and *Rand McNally's Seattle City Map*. You can buy them and other maps at the following locations:

American Automobile Association (Map pp234-5; ☎ 206-448-5353; 330 6th Ave N)

King County Metro Transit Maps (Map pp236-7; ☎ 206-553-3000; 201 S Jackson St)

Metsker Maps (Map pp236-7; ☎ 206-623-8747; 702 1st Ave)

REI (Map pp240-1; ☎ 206-223-1944; 222 Yale Ave N)

MEDICAL SERVICES

Hospitals and medical centers, walk-in clinics and referral services are easily found throughout the area, especially around First Hill, where the mass of hospitals has earned it the name 'Pill Hill.' In a serious emergency, call ☎ 911 for an ambulance to take you to the nearest hospital's emergency room.

45th St Community Clinic (Map pp246-7; ☎ 206-633-3350; 1629 N 45th St, Wallingford) Medical and dental service.

Harborview Medical Center (Map pp236-7; ☎ 206-731-3000; 325 9th Ave) Full medical care, with emergency room.

Health South (Map pp234-5; ☎ 206-682-7418; 1151 Denny Way) A walk-in clinic for nonemergencies.

MONEY

The US dollar is divided into 100 cents (¢). Coins come in denominations of 1¢ (penny), 5¢ (nickel), 10¢ (dime), 25¢ (quarter) and the seldom seen 50¢ (half-dollar). Quarters are the most commonly used coins in vending machines and parking meters, so it's handy to have a stash of them. US dollar notes, usually called bills, can be confusing in that they are all the same color and size, so get used to checking the amounts. Dollar bills come in $1, $2, $5, $10, $20, $50 and $100 denominations – $2 bills are rare but perfectly legal. The government continually tries to bring $1 coins into mass circulation, but they have never proliferated in everyday commerce. You may get them as change from ticket and stamp machines. Beware that they look similar to quarters.

ATMs

Automated Teller Machines (ATMs) are easy to find in Seattle. Contact your bank if you lose your ATM card.

Credit Cards

Major credit cards are accepted at hotels, restaurants, gas stations, shops and car-rental agencies throughout the USA. In fact, you'll find it hard to perform certain transactions, such as renting a car or purchasing tickets to performances, without one.

Even if you loathe credit cards and prefer to rely on traveler's checks and ATMs, it's a good idea to carry one for emergencies. If you're planning to rely primarily upon credit cards, it would be wise to have a Visa or MasterCard in your wallet, since other cards aren't as widely accepted.

Places that accept Visa and MasterCard are also likely to accept debit cards. Unlike a credit card, a debit card deducts payment directly from the user's checking account. Instead of an interest rate, users are charged a minimal fee for the transaction. Debit cards from large commercial banks can often be used worldwide – be sure to check with your bank to confirm that your debit card will be accepted in other states or countries.

Carry copies of your credit card numbers separately from the cards. If you lose your credit cards or they get stolen, contact the company immediately. Following are toll-free numbers for the main credit card companies.

American Express (☎ 800-528-4800)

Diners Club (☎ 800-234-6377)

Discover (☎ 800-347-2683)

MasterCard (☎ 800-826-2181)

Visa (☎ 800-336-8472)

Currency & Exchange Rates

Banks usually offer the best rates when it comes to changing money. You can also change foreign currency at the following places:

American Express (Map pp234-5; ☎ 206-441-8622; 600 Stewart St; ☺ 8:30am-5:30pm Mon-Fri)

Thomas Cook Foreign Exchange (Map pp232-3; ☎ 206-248-6960; Sea-Tac airport; ☺ 6am-8pm)

Thomas Cook Foreign Exchange (Map pp234-5; ☎ 206-682-4525; 400 Pine St, Westlake Center; ☺ 9:30am-6pm Mon-Sat, 11am-5pm Sun)

Traveler's Checks

Traveler's checks offer good protection from theft or loss and are as good as cash in the USA; you do not have to go to a bank to cash traveler's checks, as most restaurants, hotels and stores will accept them just like cash. Only purchase traveler's checks in US dollars, as the savings you *might* make on exchange rates by carrying traveler's checks in a foreign currency don't make up for the hassle of exchanging them at banks. Don't bother getting traveler's checks in denominations less than US$100. Having to change smaller bills is inconvenient, and you may be nailed with service charges if you wind up having to cash them at banks.

Keeping a record of the check numbers and the checks you have used is vital when it comes to replacing lost checks. Keep this record separate from the checks themselves. For refunds or lost or stolen traveler's checks (not credit cards), you can make a call to **American Express** (☎ 800-221-7282), **MasterCard** (☎ 800-223-9920), **Thomas Cook** (☎ 800-223-7373) or **Visa** (☎ 800-227-6811).

If you plan on heading out into rural areas in the Northwest, you may want to exchange your money in Seattle first.

NEWSPAPERS & MAGAZINES

For specifics on Seattle's newspapers and magazines, see p17.

Seattle papers include:

Seattle Post-Intelligencer (www.seattlepi.com) The morning daily.

Seattle Times (www.seattletimes.com) The state's largest daily paper.

Seattle Weekly (www.seattleweekly.com) Free weekly with news and entertainment listings.

Stranger (www.thestranger.com) Free weekly with the best alternative news and entertainment listings; home of 'Savage Love.'

POST

Excepting those letters to Canada and Mexico, international airmail rates for letters under 1oz are 80¢; 2oz letters $1.60. International postcards cost 70¢. Letters to Canada are 60¢; 50¢ for a postcard. Letters to Mexico are 85¢; 50¢ for a postcard. Aerogrammes cost 70¢.

If you have the correct postage, you can drop your mail into any blue mailbox. To send a package 16oz or larger, you must take it to a post office. If you need to buy stamps or weigh your mail, go to the nearest post office. For the address of the nearest one, call ☎ 800-275-8777 or visit the main post office (see below).

You can have mail sent to you c/o General Delivery (poste restante) at any post office that has its own zip code. Mail is usually held for 10 days before it's returned to sender; you might ask your correspondents to write 'hold for arrival' on their letters. Alternatively, have mail sent to the local representative of American Express or Thomas Cook; both provide mail service for their customers.

Main Post Office (Map pp234-5; ☎ 206-748-5417; 301 Union St)

Broadway Station Post Office (Map pp242-3; ☎ 206-324-5474; 101 Broadway E)

University Station Post Office (Map pp244-5; ☎ 206-675-8114 ; 4244 NE University Way)

RADIO

The best source of new and underground music is University of Washington's KEXP (90.3 FM), formerly known as KCMU. Other Seattle stations include:

KBSG (97.3 FM) Oldies.

KIRO (710/1090 AM) News and talk.

KJR (950 AM) Sports.

KMTT (103.7 FM) Adult contemporary.

KNDD (107.7 FM) Alternative rock.

KUBE (93.3 FM) Hip-hop, top 40, R&B.

KZOK (102.5 FM) Classic rock.

SENIOR TRAVELERS

Travelers from 50 years and up can expect to receive cut rates and benefits. Be sure to inquire about special seniors' rates at hotels, museums and restaurants across Seattle.

Outside the city, costs can be cut greatly by using the Golden Age Passport, a card that allows US citizens aged 62 and over (and those traveling in the same car) free admission to national parks and a 50% reduction at National Park Service (NPS) campgrounds. You can apply in person for the Passport at any national park or regional office of the United States Forest Service (USFS) or NPS, or call **Destinet** (☎ 800-365-2267) for information and ordering.

Other resources for senior travelers:

American Association of Retired Persons (☎ 800-424-3410; 601 E St NW, Washington, DC 20049)

Elderhostel (☎ 877-426-8056; 75 Federal St, Boston, MA 02110-1941)

Grand Circle Travel (☎ 617-350-7500; fax 350-6206; 347 Congress St, Boston, MA 02210)

TAXES & REFUNDS

Washington's base state sales tax is 6.5%, but the rate of tax varies from community to community due to the fact that counties and cities can assess an additional few percent on top of this. Seattle's sales tax is 8.8%. This tax is not levied on food in grocery stores, but it does apply to food served in restaurants.

In fact, Seattle's tax on restaurant food is now 9.3%.

When inquiring about hotel or motel rates, you should be sure to ask whether taxes are included or not. The so-called 'bed tax' is added to the cost of accommodations in hotels, motels, lodges and B&Bs (the tax, variable but sitting at 14% – at least – is usually levied on all charges, including phone calls, parking fees and room service).

TELEPHONE

All phone numbers within the USA and Canada consist of a three-digit area code (Seattle's is ☎ 206) followed by a seven-digit local number. If you are calling long distance elsewhere in the USA or Canada, dial 1 + the three-digit area code + the seven-digit number. Within Seattle, even for local calls, you need to dial the full 10-digit number (without a ☎ 1).

The ☎ 800, ☎ 888, ☎ 877 and ☎ 866 area codes are designated toll-free numbers within the USA and, sometimes, Canada. If you are dialing locally, the toll-free number is not available; you have to use the regular local number (also free). Some ☎ 800 numbers are limited to specific regions; the number may work in Washington but not in Oregon. The ☎ 900 area code is designated for calls paid at a premium rate – phone sex, horoscopes, jokes and so on.

Due to a skyrocketing demand for phone numbers (for faxes, cellular phones and modems), the Puget Sound region now has multiple area codes.

Bainbridge and Vashon Islands ☎ 206

Eastern Washington ☎ 509

Eastside (Bellevue, Kirkland, Redmond) ☎ 425

Seattle proper ☎ 206

South of Seattle (Kent, Federal Way, Tacoma) ☎ 253

Western Washington ☎ 360 and ☎ 564

Calls to the Eastside and areas south of Seattle (excluding Tacoma, which is long-distance) remain local calls. For example, don't use ☎ 1 + 425 to call Bellevue from Seattle, just dial ☎ 425 plus the number.

If you're calling from abroad, the international country code for the USA and Canada is ☎ 1; follow this with the three-digit area code and then the seven-digit number.

To make an international call direct from Seattle, dial ☎ 011, then the country code, followed by the area code (city code) and the phone number. You may need to wait as long as 45 seconds for the ringing to start. Country and some city codes are listed in the front of the White Pages.

Local calls usually cost 50¢ at pay phones. Long-distance rates vary, depending on the destination, the time you call and which telephone company you use – call the operator (☎ 0) for rate information. Don't ask the operator to put your call through, however, because operator-assisted calls are much more expensive than direct-dial calls. Nights (11pm to 8am), all day Saturday and 8am to 5pm Sunday are generally the cheapest times to call. Evenings (5pm to 11pm Sunday to Friday) are mid-priced and daytime calls (8am to 5pm weekdays) are full-price calls within the USA.

Many hotels, especially the more expensive ones, add a service charge to each local call made from your room, and they have hefty surcharges for long-distance calls. When you check in ask whether local calls are free. If not, the public pay phones found in most lobbies are always cheaper.

For local directory assistance, dial ☎ 411. For directory assistance to places that are further afield, dial ☎ 1 + the three-digit area code of the place you want to call + 555-1212. For example, to obtain directory assistance for a toll-free number, dial ☎ 1-800-555-1212. The cost for directory assistance is 80¢ to $2, and there's an additional charge if the call is put through by the operator. For operator assistance dial ☎ 0. For international operator assistance dial ☎ 00. Area codes and country codes are listed in telephone directories.

Phone debit cards allow you to pay in advance for long-distance calls. Usually in amounts of $10, $20 and $50, phone cards are sold throughout the city at Western Union, corner stores, supermarkets and machines.

TIME

Seattle is in the Pacific Standard Time zone, eight hours behind Greenwich Mean Time (GMT/UTC). It is three hours behind New York City and 17 hours ahead of Tokyo. Washington observes the switch to daylight saving time: clocks go forward one hour on the first Sunday in April and back one hour on the last Sunday in October.

In the USA, dates are usually written with the month first, then the day, then the year.

TIPPING

Tipping is expected in restaurants, bars and better hotels, and by taxi drivers, hairdressers and baggage carriers. In restaurants, waiters are paid minimal wages and rely on tips for their livelihoods. Tip 15% unless the service is terrible (in which case a complaint to the manager is warranted) or up to 20% if the service is great. No need to tip in fast-food, take-out or buffet-style restaurants where you serve yourself. Tip bartenders around 10% to 15%.

Taxi drivers expect 10% and hairdressers get 15% if their service is satisfactory. Baggage carriers (skycaps in airports, attendants in hotels) get $1 per bag and 50¢ for each additional bag. In budget hotels (where there aren't attendants anyway), tips are not expected. It is courteous and common to leave $1 to $2 per day for the housekeepers at your hotel when you check out.

TOURIST INFORMATION

You can enter the **Seattle/King County Convention & Visitors Bureau** (Map pp234–5; ☎ 206-461-5840; 800 Convention Pl, Washington State Convention & Trade Center, 520 Pike St at 7th Ave, Suite 1300, Seattle, WA 98101), built directly above I-5, from either Pike St or the Union St underpass. Here you can get everything from glossy brochures to maps and practical information from the knowledgeable staff. A market **information booth** (Map pp238–9; 1st Ave at Pike St), just outside the Pike Place Market, also dispenses maps and brochures. At Sea-Tac airport, the **information center** (☎ 206-433-5288) is on the baggage-claim level and will help you with everything from booking hotels to getting transportation from the airport into the city.

For information about the rest of Washington State, contact the **Washington State Department Of Travel Counseling** (☎ 360-586-2088).

Internet Resources

A few Seattle-specific sites you might find helpful:

www.cityofseattle.net – official site of the City of Seattle.

www.nwsource.com – features excellent local information.

www.seattle.sidewalk.com – joint effort of *Seattle Weekly* and Microsoft.

www.seeseattle.org – official site of the Seattle/King County Convention & Visitors Bureau.

VISAS

The USA is in the middle of overhauling its entry requirements as it establishes new national security guidelines post-9/11. It is imperative that travelers double- and triple-check current regulations before coming to the USA, as changes will continue for several years.

To enter the US, Canadians need only proper proof of Canadian citizenship, such as a birth certificate and a photo ID or a passport. All other foreign visitors must have a valid passport and, unless they qualify under the reciprocal visa-waiver program, a US visa.

The reciprocal visa-waiver program allows citizens of certain countries to enter the USA (for stays of 90 days or less) without first obtaining a US visa. At the time of research these countries are: Andorra, Australia, Austria, Belgium, Brunei, Denmark, Finland, France, Germany, Iceland, Ireland, Italy, Japan, Liechtenstein, Luxembourg, Monaco, the Netherlands, New Zealand, Norway, Portugal, San Marino, Singapore, Slovenia, Spain, Sweden, Switzerland and the UK. Under this program you must have a round-trip ticket that is nonrefundable in the USA and proof of financial solvency, such as credit cards, a bank account with evidence of sufficient funds or employment in your home country. You will not be allowed to extend your stay beyond 90 days.

Other travelers will need to obtain a visa from a US consulate or embassy. In most countries the process can be done by mail or through a travel agent.

Your passport should be valid for at least six months longer than your intended stay in the USA, and you'll need to submit a recent photo 1.5 inches square (37mm x 37mm) with the application. Documents of financial stability and/or guarantees from a US resident are sometimes required, particularly for those from developing countries.

Visa applicants may be required to 'demonstrate binding obligations' that will ensure their return back home. Because of this requirement, those planning to travel through other countries before arriving in the USA are generally better off applying for their US visa while they are still in their home country, rather than while on the road.

The most common visa is a nonimmigrant visitor's visa: B1 for business purposes, B2 for tourism or visiting friends and relatives. A visitor's visa is good for one or five years with multiple entries, and it specifically prohibits the visitor from taking paid employment in the USA. The validity period depends on what country you're from. The length of time you'll be allowed to stay in the USA is ultimately determined by US immigration authorities at the port of entry.

Visa Extensions & Re-Entry

Tourists without visa waivers are usually granted a six-month stay on first arrival. If you extend that time, the first assumption will be that you are working illegally, so come prepared with concrete evidence that you've been traveling extensively and will continue to be a model tourist. A wad of traveler's checks looks much better than a solid and unmoving bank account. If you want, need or hope to stay in the USA longer than the date stamped on your passport, visit or call the local office of the **Immigration and Naturalization Service** (☎ 800-755-0777) or look in the local white pages telephone directory under US Government, *before* the stamped date.

Alternatively, cross the border into Mexico or Canada and apply for another period of entry when you come back. US officials don't usually collect the Departure Record cards from your passport when you leave at a land border, so they may not notice if you've overstayed by a couple of days. Returning to the USA, you go through the same procedure as when you entered the USA for the first time, so be ready with your proposed itinerary and evidence of sufficient funds. If you try this border hopping more than once, to get a third six-month period of entry, you may find the INS is very strict. Generally, it seems that they are reluctant to let you stay more than a year.

WOMEN TRAVELERS

Seattle is generally pretty safe, although, as in any large city, women should avoid walking alone in quiet areas after dark. Public drunkenness in the Pioneer Square area can be annoying but isn't usually dangerous. It's best to avoid late-night strolls in the Central District or through the outdoor parking area under the Alaskan Way viaduct. In case you run into trouble, the following are resources that might be useful for female travelers. If you need the police, call ☎ 911.

Abortion-Birth Control Referral Service (☎ 206-522-0973)

Aradia Women's Health Center (Map pp234–5; ☎ 206-323-9388; 1300 Spring St)

Community Info Line (☎ 206-461-3200)

Domestic Violence Hotline (☎ 800-562-6025)

Evening Referral Center (☎ 206-770-0156)

National Organization for Women (NOW; Map pp246-7; ☎ 206-632-8547; 4649 Sunnyside Ave N)

Noel House (☎ 206-441-3210) Referrals to safe houses.

Planned Parenthood of Seattle/King County (Map p249; ☎ 206-328-7700; 2211 E Madison)

Seattle Rape Relief (☎ 206-632-7273)

YWCA of Seattle (☎ 206-461-4888; 1118 5th Ave)

WORK

Foreign visitors are not legally allowed to work in the USA without an appropriate working visa. Recent legislation was enacted to cut down on illegal immigrants, which is what you'll be if you work while on a tourist visa.

If you're not a US citizen, you need to apply for a work visa from the US embassy in your home country before you leave. The type of visa varies depending on how long you're staying and the kind of work you plan to do. Generally, you need either a J-1 visa, which you can obtain by joining a visitor-exchange program, or a H-2B visa, which you get when sponsored by a US employer. The former is issued mostly to students for work in summer camps; the latter is not easy to obtain, because the employer has to prove that no US citizen or permanent resident is available to do the job.

Behind the Scenes

THE LONELY PLANET STORY

The story begins with a classic travel adventure: Tony and Maureen Wheeler's 1972 journey across Europe and Asia to Australia. There was no useful information about the overland trail then, so Tony and Maureen published the first Lonely Planet guidebook to meet a growing need.

From a kitchen table, Lonely Planet has grown to become the largest independent travel publisher in the world, with offices in Melbourne (Australia), Oakland (USA), London (UK) and Paris (France).

Today Lonely Planet guidebooks cover the globe. There is an ever-growing list of books and information in a variety of media. Some things haven't changed. The main aim is still to make it possible for adventurous travellers to get out there – to explore and better understand the world.

At Lonely Planet we believe travellers can make a positive contribution to the countries they visit – if they respect their host communities and spend their money wisely.

THIS BOOK

The 1st edition of Seattle was written by Bill McRae. The 2nd edition was written by Debra Miller. This, the 3rd edition, was written by Becky Ohlsen. Regional publishing manager Maria Donohoe guided the development of this title. This edition was commissioned in Lonely Planet's Oakland office and produced in Melbourne. The project team included:

Commissioning Editors Erin Corrigan, Sam Benson
Coordinating Editors Anastasia Safioleas, Nancy Ianni, Meg Worby
Coordinating Cartographers Anneka Imkamp, Chris Tsismetzis
Editor Pete Cruttenden
Layout Designers John Shippick, Michael Ruff, Katherine Marsh
Layout Managers Sally Darmody, Kate McDonald
Managing Editors Carolyn Boicos, Kerryn Burgess, Darren O'Connell
Proofreader Lara Morcombe
Index Evan Jones, Gabbi Wilson, Meg Worby
Cover Designer Yuki Kamimura
Series Designer Nic Lehman
Managing Cartographer Alison Lyall
Series Design Concept Andrew Weatherill, Nic Lehman
Mapping Development Paul Piaia
Regional Publishing Manager David Zingarelli
Series Publishing Manager Gabrielle Green
Project Manager Eoin Dunlevy

Thanks to Piotr Czajkowski, Melanie Dankel, Sally Darmody, Bruce Evans, Ryan Evans, James Hardy, Laura Jane, Adriana Mammarella, Kate McDonald, Laurie Mikkelsen, Tegan Murray, Andrew Weatherill, Tamsin Wilson, GIS Unit, Production Services

Cover photographs Pike Place Market, Terry W. Eggers, APL/corbis (top); Seattle skyline, Jorg Greuel, Getty/Image Bank (bottom); View of the skyline from Alki Beach, Lawrence Worcester/LPI (back).

Internal photographs by Lonely Planet Images and Lawrence Worcester except for the following: p146 (#3), p196 Tom Boyden; p145 (#2) Ann Cecil; p67 (#2), p146 (#1), p199 Richard Cummins; p144 (#2), p145 (#3), p146 (#2), p190 John Elk III; p145 (#1) Lee Foster; p201 Aaron McCoy; p144 (#3) Debra Miller. All images are the copyright of the photographers unless otherwise indicated. Many of the images in this guide are available for licensing from Lonely Planet Images: www.lonelyplanetimages.com.

ACKNOWLEDGMENTS

Many thanks to King County Metro Transit for the Seattle Transit map.

THANKS
BECK OHLSEN

Becky Ohlsen would like to thank the commissioning editor Erin Corrigan for her help and boundless patience; second-edition author Deb Miller for her excellent work, which made the job of updating this guide infinitely easier; Felix for its scapegoat value; Audrey Van Buskirk for advice and gossip; Josh Feit, Bob Young and Maureen O'Hagan for background information and insider tips; John Graham for moral support and the flask; Rory from Kells and Patrick from Gregg's Greenlake Cycle; Shorty's for tension relief and reality checks; Tom H. for sneaking me onto the rooftops above Pike Place Market; the 1991 Toyota Camry for performance above and beyond the call of duty; Tom Waits for eternity; and the Sang-Froid Riding Club for constantly replenished inspiration.

OUR READERS

Many thanks to the following travellers who used the last edition and wrote to us with helpful hints, useful advice and interesting anecdotes. Your names follow:

Shona Addison, Mark Bartlett, Lisa Bias, Kirsten Brandin, Alex Buchanan, Charles Citroen, Gee Gee Clemency, Mandy Comish, Chris DiPalma, Christopher Edwards, Dayna Gorman, Ronalie Green, Martin Hall, Mike Hawley, Jeff Howlett, Shamin Islam, Brandon Johnson, Don McManman, Carrie Mogged, Shannon O'Loughlin, Chad Perry, Edward Roberts, Jean Robinson, Ann Robinson, Susan Scott, David Simmonds, Madelyn Smallberg, Christine Wegener, Debbie Weijers, Chris Wills, Ben Wimmer, Albert Wong, Andrew Young

Notes

Notes

Index

000 map pages
000 photographs

EATING

000 map pages
000 photographs

SLEEPING

Index

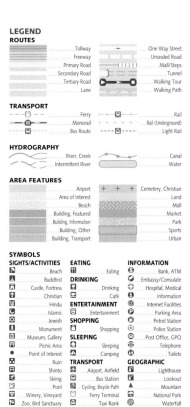

Map Section

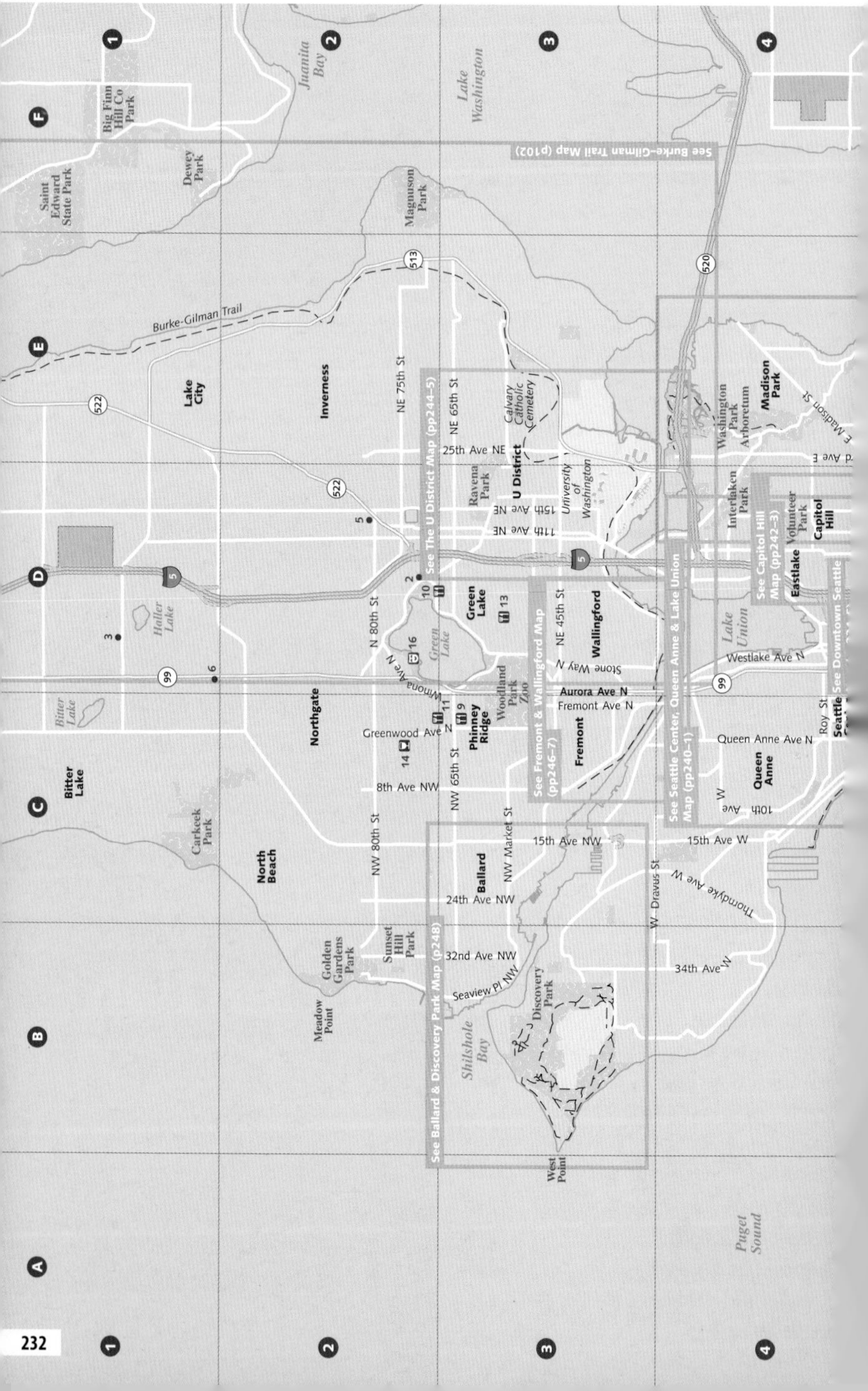

Juanita Bay

Lake Washington

Big Finn Hill Co Park

Dewey Park

Saint Edward State Park

See Burke-Gilman Trail Map (p102)

Burke-Gilman Trail

520

513

522

Lake City

Inverness

NE 75th St

NE 65th St

Calvary Catholic Cemetery

Washington Park Arboretum

Madison Park

E Madison St

25th Ave NE

Ravenna Park

U District

University of Washington

Interlaken Park

Volunteer Park

Capitol Hill

See The U District Map (pp244-5)

15th Ave NE

11th Ave NE

See Capitol Hill Map (pp242-3)

Eastlake

99

522

Haller Lake

Green Lake

NE 45th St

Stone Way N

Wallingford

Lake Union

Westlake Ave N

See Downtown Seattle

Seattle

Bitter Lake

Northgate

Green Lake

Woodland Park

Aurora Ave N

Fremont Ave N

Fremont

See Fremont & Wallingford Map (pp246-7)

See Seattle Center, Queen Anne & Lake Union Map (pp240-1)

Queen Anne Ave N

10th Ave

Roy St

Carkeek Park

North Beach

Greenwood Ave N

Phinney Ridge

8th Ave NW

NW 65th St

NW 80th St

Ballard

NW Market St

15th Ave NW

15th Ave W

W Dravus St

Queen Anne

Thorndike Ave W

Meadow Point

Golden Gardens Park

Sunset Hill Park

24th Ave NW

32nd Ave NW

Seaview Pl NW

See Ballard & Discovery Park Map (p248)

Discovery Park

Shilshole Bay

34th Ave W

West Point

Puget Sound

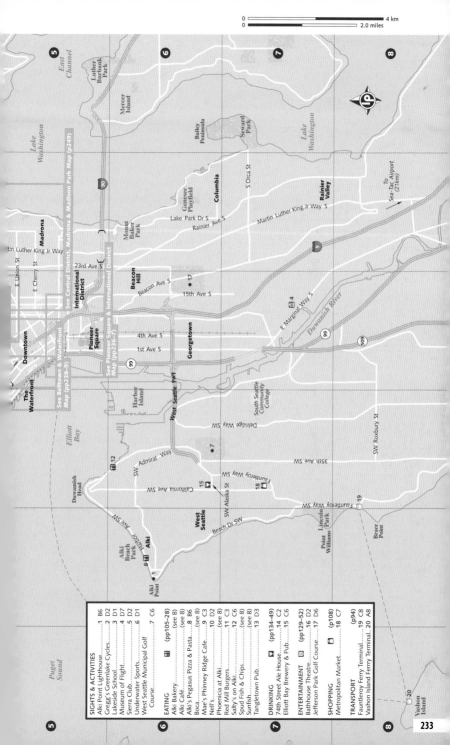

233

SIGHTS & ACTIVITIES (pp45–8)
Columbia Seafirst Center.....1 D7
Frye Art Museum.....2 F6
Hammering Man.....3 C6
Seattle Art Museum.....(see 3)
Seattle Trolley Tours Information
Center.....4 D5
See Seattle Walking Tour.....(see 34)
Stimson-Green Mansion.....5 F5
Thomas Cook Exchange.....(see 34)
Three Piece Sculpture: Vertebrae.....6 D7

EATING (pp108–10)
Dahlia Lounge.....7 B4
Georgian Room.....8 D6
Hunt Club.....(see 51)
icon Grill.....9 C4
Mae Pim Thai Restaurant.....10 C8
McCormick's Fish House & Bar.....11 D7
Metropolitan Grill.....12 B4
Nikko.....(see 34)
Palace Kitchen.....
Wild Ginger.....13 C6

DRINKING (pp134–49)
Bookstore Bar & Cafe.....14 C7
Dragonfish Asian Café.....(see 46)
Five Point Cafe.....15 A3
Noc Noc.....16 C6
Paramount.....17 D4
Rock Bottom Brewery.....18 D6

ENTERTAINMENT (pp129–52)
5th Ave Musical Theater Co......19 D6
A Contemporary Theatre
(ACT).....20 D5
Borders Books and Music.....21 C5
Dimitriou's Jazz Alley.....22 C4
Re-Bar.....23 D3
TicketMaster.....(see 34)

SHOPPING (pp167–8)
Bon-Macy's.....24 C5
Cameras West.....25 C4
City Centre Mall.....26 D5
Kits Cameras.....27 D7
Made in Washington.....(see 31)

Nordstrom.....28 C5
Nordstrom Rack.....29 B5
Pacific Place.....30 D5
Post Alley Market.....31 B6
Rainier Square.....32 D6
University Bookstore.....33 D6
Westlake Center.....34 C5

SLEEPING (pp178–81)
Alexis Hotel.....35 C7
Claremont Hotel.....36 B4
Days Inn Town Center.....37 B3
Green Tortoise Backpackers'
Guesthouse.....38 C6
Hotel Monaco Seattle.....39 D5
Hotel Vintage Park.....40 D6
Inn at Virginia Mason.....41 E6
King's Inn.....42 B4
Loyal Inn Best Western.....43 B3
Mayflower Park Hotel.....44 C5
Paramount Hotel.....45 D5
Ramada Inn Downtown.....46 B4
Renaissance Madison Hotel.....48 E6

Sheraton Seattle Hotel & Towers.....49 D5
Sixth Avenue Inn.....50 C4
Sorrento Hotel.....51 E6
Travelodge Seattle City Center.....52 B3
WestCoast Vance Hotel.....53 C4
Westin Seattle.....54 C4
YWCA of Seattle.....55 D6

TRANSPORT (p205)
Greyhound.....56 D4

INFORMATION
American Express.....57 C4
Arcadia Womens Health Center.....58 F5
Health South.....59 D3
Main Post Office.....60 C6
Post Office.....61 C7
Seattle/King County Convention & Visitors
Bureau.....62 D5
Swedish Medical Center.....63 F6
Virginia Mason Hospital.....64 E6

OTHER
24-Hour Fitness.....65 E3

Pier 56

A **B** **99** Spring St **C** **D**

Bank of America Building

1 Pier 55

Madison St

Washington St Station

Pier 54

Arctic Building

3rd Ave

4th Ave

5th Ave

Marion St
2nd Ave
Columbia St
1st Ave
Cherry St

Ferries to Bainbridge Island

Pier 53

38

Post Alley
Western Ave

10

Alaska Building

26
48
51
53

James St

Pier 52

Pioneer Square Park

29
5
4

2 Pier 51

25
50

6

Yesler Way

Ferries to Bremerton

55
27

Pioneer Square

3rd Ave S

Dilling Way

Pier 50

37

Ferries to Vashon Island

42
33

S Washington St

2nd Ave Extended S

36

See Belltown & Waterfront Map (pp238-9)

Occidental Park

34
30
2
35

Firefighters' Memorial

8
28

18

Pier 48

40
44

Occidental Park Station

Alaskan Way Viaduct

Occidental Square

46

3 Elliott Bay

39

52
24

S Jackson St

47
43
41
32

57

King Street Station (Amtrak)

15
13

1st Ave S

S King St

99

P

31

Occidental Ave S

S Railway Way

Seahawks Stadium

S Railroad Way

Washington State Exhibition Center

S Brougham Way

3rd Ave S

Safeco Field

S Atlantic St

Utah Ave S

1st Ave S

To Studio Seven (0.5mi)

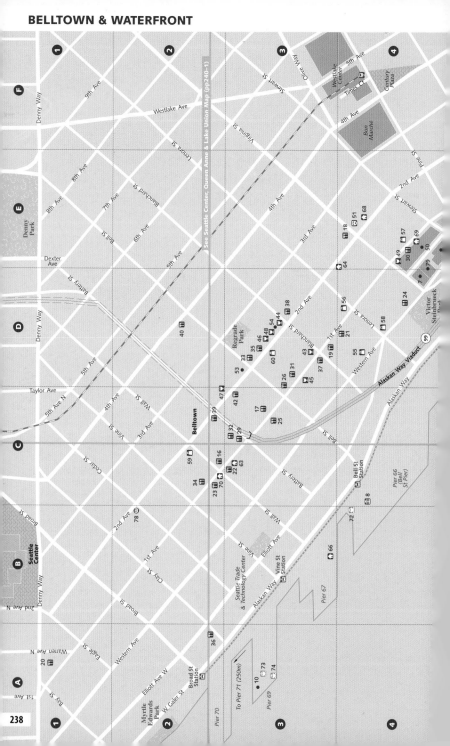

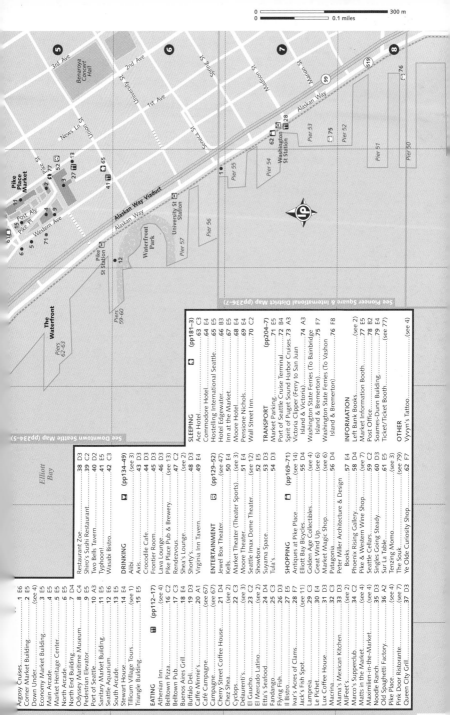

Argosy Cruises.............................1 E6
Corner Market Building.....................2 E5
Down Under.............................(see 4)
Economy Market Building....................3 E5
Main Arcade................................4 E5
Market Heritage Center.....................5 E5
North Arcade...............................6 E5
North End Building.........................7 D4
Odyssey Maritime Museum....................8 C4
Pedestrian Elevator........................9 E5
Port of Seattle...........................10 A3
Sanitary Market Building..................11 E5
Seattle Aquarium..........................12 E6
South Arcade..............................13 E5
Stewart House.............................14 E4
Tillicum Village Tours....................15 E5
Triangle Building.....................(see 1)

EATING 🍴 (pp112–17)
Athenian Inn..........................(see 4)
Belltown Pizza............................16 C2
Belltown Pub..............................17 C2
Buenos Aires Grill........................18 E4
Buffalo Deli..............................19 D3
Caffe Minnie's............................20 A1
Café Campagne........................(see 67)
Campagne.............................(see 67)
Cherry Street Coffee House................21 D4
Chez Shea.............................(see 2)
Cyclops...................................22 C3
Delaurenti's..........................(see 3)
El Gaucho.................................23 C2
El Mercado Latino.....................(see 2)
Etta's Seafood............................24 D4
Fandango..................................25 C3
Flying Fish...............................26 D3
Il Bistro.................................27 E4
Ivar's Acres of Clams.....................28 F7
Jack's Fish Spot.....................(see 11)
Lampreia..................................29 C3
Le Pichet.................................30 E4
Lux Coffee House..........................31 D3
Macrina...................................32 C3
Mama's Mexican Kitchen....................33 D3
Marco's Supperclub........................34 C2
Matts in the Market...................(see 2)
Maximillien-in-the-Market.............(see 4)
Noodle Ranch..............................35 D3
Old Spaghetti Factory.....................36 A2
Pike Place............................(see 4)
Pink Door Ristorante..................(see 7)
Queen City Grill..........................37 D3

Restaurant Zoe............................38 D3
Shiro's Sushi Restaurant..................39 C2
Two Bells Tavern..........................40 D2
Typhoon!..................................41 E5
Wasabi Bistro.............................42 C3

DRINKING 🍷 (pp134–49)
Alibi.................................(see 3)
Axis......................................43 D3
Crocodile Cafe............................44 D3
Frontier Room.............................45 D3
Lava Lounge...............................46 D3
Pike Place Pub & Brewery.............(see 13)
Rendezvous................................47 C2
Shea's Lounge.........................(see 2)
Shorty's..................................48 D3
Virginia Inn Tavern.......................49 E4

ENTERTAINMENT 🎭 (pp129–52)
Jewel Box Theater.........................50 E4
Kells.................................(see 3)
Market Theater (Theater Sports)...........51 E4
Moore Theater........................(see 12)
Seattle Imax Dome Theater............(see 12)
Showbox...................................52 E5
Suyama Space..............................53 D3
Tula's....................................54 D3

SHOPPING 🛍 (pp169–71)
Antiques at Pike Place...............(see 14)
Elliott Bay Bicycles......................55 D4
Golden Age Collectibles...............(see 4)
Great Wind Up.........................(see 6)
Market Magic Shop.....................(see 6)
Patagonia.................................56 D4
Peter Miller Architecture & Design
  Books...................................57 E4
Phoenix Rising Gallery....................58 D4
Pike & Western Wine Shop..............(see 7)
Seattle Cellars...........................59 C2
Singles Going Steady......................60 D3
Sur La Table..............................61 E5
Tenzing Momo..........................(see 3)
The Souk.............................(see 79)
Ye Olde Curiosity Shop....................62 F7

SLEEPING 🛏 (pp181–3)
Ace Hotel.................................63 C3
Commodore Hotel...........................64 E4
Hostelling International Seattle..........65 E5
Hotel Edgewater...........................66 B3
Inn at the Market.........................67 E4
Moore Hotel...............................68 E4
Pensione Nichols..........................69 E4
Wall Street Inn...........................70 C2

TRANSPORT (pp204–7)
Market Parking............................71 E5
Port of Puget Sound Harbor Cruises........72 B4
Spirit of Puget Sound Harbor Cruises......73 A3
Victoria Clipper (Ferry to San Juan
  Island & Victoria)......................74 A3
Washington State Ferries (To Bainbridge
  Island & Bremerton).....................75 F7
Washington State Ferries (To Vashon
  Island & Bremerton).....................76 F8

INFORMATION
Left Bank Books.......................(see 2)
Market Information Booth..................77 E5
Post Office...............................78 B2
Soames-Dunn Building......................79 E4
Ticket/Ticket Booth..................(see 77)

OTHER
Vyvyn's Tattoo........................(see 4)

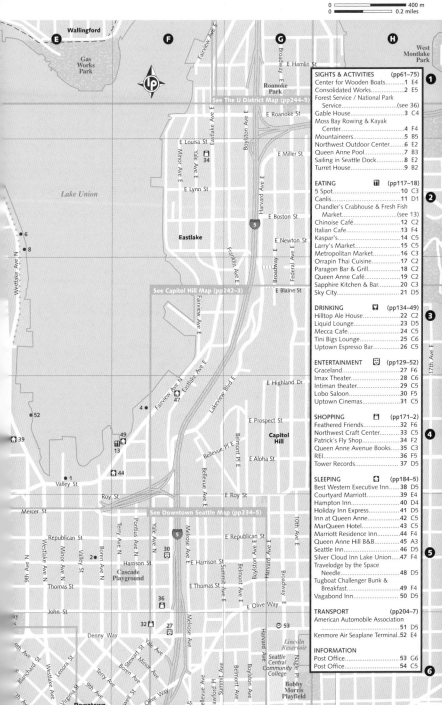

SIGHTS & ACTIVITIES (pp61–75)
Center for Wooden Boats...............1 E4
Consolidated Works........................2 E5
Forest Service / National Park
 Service.....................................(see 36)
Gable House....................................3 C4
Moss Bay Rowing & Kayak
 Center..4 F4
Mountaineers...................................5 B5
Northwest Outdoor Center............6 E2
Queen Anne Pool............................7 B3
Sailing in Seattle Dock...................8 E2
Turret House....................................9 B2

EATING (pp117–18)
5 Spot...10 C3
Canlis...11 D1
Chandler's Crabhouse & Fresh Fish
 Market....................................(see 13)
Chinoise Café.................................12 C2
Italian Cafe....................................13 F4
Kaspar's...14 C5
Larry's Market................................15 C5
Metropolitan Market......................16 C3
Orrapin Thai Cuisine......................17 C2
Paragon Bar & Grill........................18 C2
Queen Anne Café...........................19 C2
Sapphire Kitchen & Bar..................20 C3
Sky City..21 D5

DRINKING (pp134–49)
Hilltop Ale House............................22 C2
Liquid Lounge.................................23 D5
Mecca Cafe....................................24 C5
Tini Bigs Lounge............................25 C6
Uptown Espresso Bar......................26 C5

ENTERTAINMENT (pp129–52)
Graceland.......................................27 F6
Imax Theater..................................28 C6
Intiman theater...............................29 C5
Lobo Saloon...................................30 F5
Uptown Cinemas.............................31 C5

SHOPPING (pp171–2)
Feathered Friends...........................32 F6
Northwest Craft Center...................33 C5
Patrick's Fly Shop...........................34 F2
Queen Anne Avenue Books.............35 C3
REI..36 F5
Tower Records................................37 D5

SLEEPING (pp184–5)
Best Western Executive Inn.............38 D5
Courtyard Marriott..........................39 E4
Hampton Inn..................................40 D4
Holiday Inn Express.........................41 D5
Inn at Queen Anne.........................42 C5
MarQueen Hotel.............................43 C5
Marriott Residence Inn...................44 F4
Queen Anne Hill B&B.....................45 A3
Seattle Inn......................................46 D5
Silver Cloud Inn Lake Union...........47 F4
Travelodge by the Space
 Needle..48 D5
Tugboat Challenger Bunk &
 Breakfast...................................49 F4
Vagabond Inn.................................50 D5

TRANSPORT (pp204–7)
American Automobile Association...51 D5
Kenmore Air Seaplane Terminal....52 E4

INFORMATION
Post Office......................................53 G6
Post Office......................................54 C5

241

SIGHTS & ACTIVITIES (pp75–8)
Center of Contemporary Art........1 D8
Cornish College of the Arts........2 B4
Seattle Asian Art Museum..........3 D2
St Mark's Cathedral..................4 C2
Volunteer Park Conservatory......5 D2
Water Tower Observation Deck....6 D2

EATING (pp119–20)
Bimbo's Bitchin' Burrito Kitchen...7 B7
Caffe Minnie's.......................8 C4
Café Septieme........................9 C6
Capitol Club..........................10 B7
Coastal Kitchen......................11 E5
Gravity Bar...........................(see 59)
Green Cat Cafe.......................12 B6
Honeyhole............................13 B8
Kingfish Cafe.........................14 F4
La Cocina & Cantina Mexican
  Restaurant.........................15 C5
Madison Market.....................16 E7
Rainbow Natural Grocery..........17 E5
Ristorante Machiavelli..............18 A7
Satellite Lounge.....................19 D8

DRINKING (pp134–49)
Bad Juju lounge.....................20 D7
Barça..................................21 D8
Bauhaus..............................22 A7
Caffè Vita............................23 C8
Canterbury Ale & Eats.............24 E4
CapitolHill.net......................25 C6
CC Attle's............................26 E8
Coffee Messiah.....................27 B7
Comet................................28 C8
Elite..................................29 C4
Elysian Brewing Company.........30 D8
Hopscotch...........................31 E5
Linda's...............................32 B7
Online Coffee Company...........33 C6
R Place..............................34 B7
Six Arms Pub & Brewery..........35 A8
Vivace...............................36 C5
Wildrose.............................37 D8

ENTERTAINMENT (pp129–52)
B&O Espresso........................38 B6
Baltic Room..........................39 A8
Chop Suey............................40 D8
Egyptian..............................41 C7
Globe Cafe...........................42 D7
Harvard Exit..........................43 C4
Neighbours...........................44 C8
Richard Hugo House.................45 D7
Vogue.................................46 D8

SHOPPING (pp172–3)
Bailey/Coy Books....................47 C5
Beyond the Closet Bookstore......48 B8
Crossroads Trading Co.............49 C5
Dilettante Chocolates..............50 C5
Marco Polo............................51 C4
Multilingual Books & Software.....52 D8
Orpheum.............................53 C4
Platinum Records....................54 C8
Red Light.............................55 E5
Sonic Boom...........................56 E5
Toys In Babeland....................57 C8
Twice Sold Tales.....................58 C6
Urban Outfitters.....................59 C5
Velo Stores...........................60 C7
Wall of Sound........................61 A7

SLEEPING (pp185–6)
Bacon Mansion B&B................62 C3
Capitol Hill Inn B&B................63 B7
Gaslight Inn B&B...................64 E7
Hill House B&B......................65 D6
Mildred's B&B.......................66 E2
Salisbury House B&B...............67 E3
Shafer Baillie Mansion............68 D3

INFORMATION
Post Office...........................69 C6
Ticket/Ticket........................(see 59)

OTHER
Rudy's Barbershop.................70 B7

To Cassis (1km)

E Blaine St
E Garfield St
Franklin Ave E
Eastlake
E Galer St
E Blaine St
10th Ave E
Federal Ave E
E Galer St
Grandview Pl E
E Olin Pl
Interlaken Park
20th Ave E
16th Ave E
E Prospect St
E Galer St
E Highland Dr
15th Ave E
E Ward St
E Aloha St
Malden Ave E
14th Ave E
E Mercer St
E Roy St
E Mercer St
E Prospect St
Lakeview Blvd E
Belmont Pl E
Bellevue Pl E
Belmont Ave E
Broadway E
Harvard Ave E
E Roy St
Tashkent Park
Federal Ave E
11th Ave E
12th Ave E
13th Ave E
E Mercer St
Lakeview Cemetery
Volunteer Park
Reservoir
Volunteer Park Rd
E Highland Dr

See Central District, Madrona & Madison Park Map (p249)
See Downtown Seattle Map (pp234–5)

SIGHTS & ACTIVITIES	(pp81–5)
Bungalow Wine Bar & Cafe	(see 37)
Fremont Rocket	1 D5
Fremont Troll	2 D4
History House	3 D5
Lake Union Center	4 D5
Statue of Lenin	5 D4
Sunday Ice Cream Cruise	(see 4)
Waiting for the Interurban	6 D5

EATING	🍴	(pp122–5)
Asteroid Cafe	7 F2
Beso del Sol	8 E2
Bizzarro	9 E2
Boulangerie	10 G2
Caffé Ladro	11 C4
Chile Pepper	12 F2
Erotic Bakery	13 H2
Jitterbug Cafe	14 G2
Julia's of Wallingford	15 F2

Kabul	16 H2
Mandalay Café	17 F2
Mushushi's	18 F2
Patty's Eggnest	19 G2
Still Life in Fremont	20 D5
Swingside Cafe	21 D3
Teahouse Kuan Yin	22 G2
Triangle Lounge	23 D4

DRINKING	🍷	(pp134–49)
Dad Watson's Restaurant & Brewery	24 D4
Hale's Brewery & Pub	25 A2
Murphy's Pub	26 G2
Old Red Hook Brewery	(see 28)
Tost	27 D4

ENTERTAINMENT	🎭	(pp129–52)
Fremont Outdoor Movies	28 C5
Guild 45th St Theater	29 G2

SHOPPING	🛍	(pp174–5)
Astrology et al	30 F2
Bottleworks Inc	31 F2
City Cellars	32 F2
Deluxe Junk	33 D4
Frank and Dunya	34 D5
Fremont Antique Mall	35 D5
Fremont Place Book Co	36 D5
Open Books	37 H2
Wallingford Center	38 G2
Wide World Books & Maps	39 F2

INFORMATION	
45th St Community Clinic	40 F2

BALLARD & DISCOVERY PARK

0 ——————— 500 m
0 ——————— 0.3 miles

CENTRAL DISTRICT, MADRONA & MADISON PARK

0 ———— 500 m
0 ———— 0.3 miles

A **B** **C** **D**

Union Bay

1

Evergreen Point
Floating Bridge
(Governor Albert
D Rosellini Bridge)

West
Montlake
Park

E Shelby St
E Hamlin St

Marsh
Island

Foster Island Wetlands Trail

Foster
Island

520

520

Portage
Bay

See The U District Map (pp244–5)

E McGilvra St

Montlake
Park

E Roanoke St
E Louisa St
E Miller St

Broadmoor
Golf Club

40th Ave E

E Lynn St

2

E Calhoun St

E McGraw St

E Howe St
E Blaine St
Fuhrman Ave E

E Lynn St

E Shore Dr

16

42nd Ave E
43rd Ave E

E Newton St

23rd Ave E

Washington
Park
Arboretum

Arboretum Dr E

E Blaine St

6
12

5

Madison
Park

24th Ave E
25th Ave E
26th Ave E

Parkside Dr E
Shenandoah Dr E

Madison
Park

E Blaine St
38th Ave E
E Garfield St

Interlaken
Dr

Interlaken Pl E

Interlaken
Park

Boyer Ave E
E Interlaken Blvd

Lake Washington Blvd E

Benham Pl E

3

Lakeview
Cemetery

E Cres Dr

E Galer St

E Galer St
41st Ave E

Volunteer
Park

E Highland Dr

E Lee St

Parkside Dr E

E Lee St
McGilvra Blvd E

Seattle
Tennis
Club

Reservoir

E Prospect St

E Prospect St

E Helen St

Lake
Washington

E Madison St

E Ward St

E Helen St
E Ward St

28th Ave E

33rd Ave E
34th Ave E
E Ward St

E Aloha St

14th Ave E
15th Ave E
16th Ave E
18th Ave E
19th Ave E
20th Ave E
21st Ave E
22nd Ave E

E Valley St
E Roy St
E Mercer St

Madison
Valley

E Ford Pl

E Mercer St

12th Ave E

E Republican St

15

7

Dewey Pl E
31st Ave E
32nd Ave E

McGilvra Blvd E
39th Ave E

40th Ave E

Lakeview
Park

Denny
Blaine
Park

4

Capitol
Hill

E Thomas St

E Arthur Pl

E Harrison St

Harrison St

E Thomas St
E John St

26th Ave E
27th Ave E

Maiden Ln E

Viretta
Park

Thomas St
John St

13th Ave E

E John St

E Denny Way

E Howell St

Martin Luther King Jr Way

E Howell St

35th Ave E

37th Ave E
Maiden Ln

Madrona Pl E

E Olive St

Howell
Park

E Howell St

E Olive St

23rd Ave E

E Olive St

Evergreen Pl

Madrona
Park

E Pine St

See Seattle Center, Queen Anne & Lake Union Map (pp236–7)

3

37th Ave E

E Pine St
E Pike St

SIGHTS & ACTIVITIES (pp90–3)
Japanese Garden..................1 B3
Medger Evers Aquatic Center....2 B5
Mount Zion Baptist Church.......3 A4
Museum of History & Industry
  (MOHAI)......................4 B1

E Pike St

E Pine St

24th Ave
25th Ave
26th Ave

E Pike St

11
8

E Union St

13

See Capitol Hill Map (pp242–3)

E Spring St

Central
District

29th Ave
30th Ave
31st Ave

E Spring St

5

E Marion St

E Columbia St

Madrona

32nd Ave
33rd Ave
34th Ave
35th Ave
36th Ave

EATING (pp126–7)
Attic Alehouse & Eatery.........5 D2
Cactus..........................6 D2
Cafe Flora......................7 B4
Cafe Soleil.....................8 C5
Catfish Corner..................9 B5
Ezell's Fried Chicken..........10 B6
Hi Spot Cafe...................11 C5
Madison Park Cafe..............12 D2
Ms Helen's Soul Food...........13 B5
R&L Home of Good
  Bar-B-Que....................14 A6
Rover's........................15 B4

14th Ave
15th Ave
16th Ave
18th Ave

20th Ave
21st Ave
22nd Ave
23rd Ave

E Cherry St

9

2

Seattle
University

10

E Jefferson St

Martin Luther King Jr Way

E Jefferson St

E James St

E Jefferson St

E Terrace St

E Terrace St

E Alder St

17th Ave

E Spruce St
E Fir St

Spruce
Park

24th Ave S
25th Ave S

27th Ave

28th Ave

6

See Pioneer Square & International District Map (pp236–7)

14

E Yesler Way

Edwin
T Pratt
Park

Lavizzo
Park

23rd Ave S
24th Ave S
25th Ave S
26th Ave S

S Washington St

E Huron St

Frink
Park

Leschi
Park

INFORMATION
Graham Visitors Center & Gift
  Shop..........................16 C2

249

SEATTLE TRANSIT MAP

LEGEND

Routes shown provide service every 10-20 minutes; every 15-30 minutes evenings, Sunday and holidays. Metro routes with less frequent service through downtown are not shown.

1	Routes 1, 2, 13
3	Routes 3, 4
7	Routes 7, 11, 14, 36, 43
10	Routes 10, 12
15	Routes 15, 18, 21, 22, 56
16	Route 16
26	Routes 26, 28, 39, 42

Metro Tunnel (5 a.m. - 7 p.m. M-F, 10 a.m. - 6 p.m. Sat)

Tunnel Stations

▷ Tunnel Entrance

Accessible Entrance

? Metro Customer Service

Ride Free Area (6 a.m. to 7 p.m.)

George Benson Waterfront Streetcar

Seattle Center Monorail

Accessible Route

Footpath from Ferry to Tunnel

Stair Access

Parks

King County **METRO**

250

Washington State Exhibition Center